New Approaches to
Popular Romance Fiction

New Approaches to Popular Romance Fiction

Critical Essays

Edited by
Sarah S.G. Frantz
and
Eric Murphy Selinger

McFarland & Company, Inc., Publishers
Jefferson, North Carolina, and London

LIBRARY OF CONGRESS CATALOGUING-IN-PUBLICATION DATA

New approaches to popular romance fiction : critical essays
/ edited by Sarah S.G. Frantz and Eric Murphy Selinger.
p.   cm.

ISBN 978-0-7864-4190-7
softcover : acid free paper ∞

1. Love stories, American — History and criticism.
I. Frantz, Sarah S.G.   II. Selinger, Eric Murphy.
PS374.L6N49 2012   813'.08509 — dc23   2012004555

BRITISH LIBRARY CATALOGUING DATA ARE AVAILABLE

Front cover image: Pablo Picasso, *Tete d'une Femme Lisant*, 1906,
© 2012 Estate of Pablo Picasso / Artist Rights Society (ARS), New York

Manufactured in the United States of America

McFarland & Company, Inc., Publishers
Box 611, Jefferson, North Carolina 28640
www.mcfarlandpub.com

To my mother, Jas Kendall, who introduced me to romance novels, and to my husband, Jonathan, who introduced me to romance.

—SARAH S.G. FRANTZ

To my son —
Devil's Cub;
To my daughter —
Duchess Inside;
And to Rosalie Selinger Murphy —
No Rule but Love.

—ERIC MURPHY SELINGER

Acknowledgments

A volume of this scope does not happen through the efforts of its editors alone. We are grateful to Kat Schroeder, Dayna Harrett, and Angela Toscano for their work preparing the manuscript, and to our contributors, whose patience and enthusiasm buoyed us through many difficult passages.

When we began work on this collection, there was no organized community of popular romance scholars. As the volume has grown, so has the field, and we are grateful to our many colleagues in the International Association for the Study of Popular Romance, whose insights and suggestions — gratefully received at IASPR's conferences in Brisbane and Brussels, at the Princeton conference on "Romance Fiction and American Culture," at the annual gatherings of the Romance Area of the Popular Culture Association, and through comments on the Teach Me Tonight blog and the RomanceScholar listserv — have contributed to the essays gathered here.

Since the fall of 2005, DePaul University has invited Eric to teach nearly thirty courses on popular romance fiction, including undergraduate surveys, upper-division special topics courses, and graduate seminars. He is grateful for this ongoing — and, as far as he can tell, unprecedented — opportunity to explore romance fiction in an academic context, and to the many students in these courses, especially those in his senior interdisciplinary seminar on Laura Kinsale's *Flowers from the Storm*.

Both Eric and Sarah have been honored as recipients of the Academic Research Grant from the Romance Writers of North America. While the grant didn't specifically contribute to this volume, the monetary support is a pale shadow of the intellectual encouragement we have received from the full-time personnel, elected officials, and membership of RWA.

Excerpts from *Holding the Cards*, by Joey Hill, © 2002 by Joey W. Hill, are reprinted by permission of the author and Ellora's Cave Publishing, Inc.

Table of Contents

Introduction: New Approaches to Popular Romance Fiction

Eric Murphy Selinger and Sarah S.G. Frantz

In a memorable scene from _Lord of Scoundrels_, a deftly metatextual historical romance by the American author Loretta Chase, our hero and heroine, Sebastian Ballister, Marquess of Dain, and his new wife, Jessica Trent, sit in the library of Athcourt, Dain's estate, and read aloud together. The year is 1828; the marriage, unconsummated; the book, Lord Byron's _Don Juan_. "I can't believe you bought it and never read it," Jessica laughs at her husband as they pause in Canto Two. "You had no idea what you were missing, did you?" Dain masks his attraction, to her and the book, with a shrug.

> "I'm sure it was more amusing hearing it read in a ladylike voice," he said. "Certainly it's less work."
> "Then I'll read to you regularly," she said. "I shall make a romantic of you yet."
> He drew back, and his inert hand slid to the sofa. "You call that _romantic_? Byron's a complete cynic."
> "In my dictionary, romance is not maudlin, treacly sentiment," she said. "It is a curry, spiced with excitement and humor and a healthy dollop of cynicism." She lowered her lashes. "I think you will eventually make a fine curry, Dain — with a few minor seasoning adjustments."[1]

As you might expect, he bristles, they quarrel, and passion flares with their anger. As you might _not_ expect, especially if you've never read much popular romance, that passion plays out with Jessica first dominating, then seducing her husband, after which — eight pages later, when he's brought her to orgasm with the "big hands" that she loves — our heroine promptly falls asleep. ("That was what _he_ was supposed to do," Dain seethes as he carries her to bed.[2])

To the experienced romance reader, this scene offers a remarkable range of pleasures. In it, we savor an emotional "curry," just as Jessica promised, "spiced with excitement and humor and a healthy dollop of cynicism" — and, if we turn the page, a dash of tenderness as well.[3] (Dain does not carry his wife off to ravish or punish her, even with kisses, but simply to tuck her in.) Simultaneously, on an intellectual level, we may connect this work of popular romance fiction, still the most despised and rejected of genres, with several canonical precursors: obviously Byron's _Don Juan_, but also the well-known Paolo and Francesca passage from Dante's _Inferno_, where reading a romance about Lancelot and Guinevere stirs the adulterous lovers to sin. (Might _Lord of Scoundrels_ now act as the "go-between" between

1

its readers and their own lovers?[4] So be it, the novel smiles; today you'll read no further.) From a narrative perspective, there's the structural pleasure of finally reaching the couple's long-promised love scene; the sensual extravagance of that encounter; and the shiver of sur- prise we get from how the scene concludes. In terms of character, we get the delight of watching the novel's alpha male hero meet his match in its confident, feminist heroine, each of them, by turns, vowing to make the other one "beg." This final pleasure seems at once ideological, erotic, and, again, profoundly intertextual, part of the novel's dialogue with the conventions of its genre.

Listing these pleasures, the scholar of popular romance fiction may well hear a second voice, the novelist's, in Jessica's quip to her husband, "You had no idea what you were miss- ing, did you?" This is not to say that romance novels have not been studied. Far from it: critical work on popular romance fiction — the books, the readers, and the romance pub- lishing industry — has been going on for decades. A sociological study of reader preferences, commissioned by Mills & Boon, opened the field in 1969.[5] The following year, Germaine Greer cheerfully excoriated "the titillating mush of Cartland and her ilk": the first of many feminist inquiries, some critical, some celebratory, into the sexual politics of the genre.[6] Since the 1980s, scholars have investigated the impact of reading romance fiction on women's sexual behavior, religious lives, and expectations about love and marriage in the United States, India, and the United Kingdom.[7] Literary historians have traced the development of romance publishing and weighed the impact of international distribution on local production of romance in Australia, France, and Hong Kong.[8] The list goes on. Critics have attended to the racial, ethnic, and colonial discourse in romance, as well as to the ways that authors, whether white or of color, have braved the taboo of interracial desire.[9] They have anatomized the genre's narrative elements, teased out its covert homoeroticism and obsession with social class, and meditated on the enduring appeal of cross-dressing and dominant/submissive sexual motifs.[10] With counter-intuitive gusto, they have proposed that the romance hero embodies everything from "allegories of ontology"[11] to repressed memories of the reader's pre–Oedipal mother.[12]

What, then, could they possibly be "missing"? How can it be that, forty years on, a scholar like Mary Bly — a professor of Renaissance literature at Fordham University and also, as "Eloisa James," a bestselling author of historical romance novels — should claim in her essay for this volume that the "academic study of popular romance fiction is clearly in its infancy"? Could it be (one is tempted to ask, a little wickedly) that this middle-aged academic field, like Sebastian Ballister, Marquess of Dain, hero of *Lord of Scoundrels,* has spent those decades in the grips of childhood rejection and trauma, unable to see the value in its subject, or itself?

To answer this as a serious question, all wickedness and metaphor aside, let's take a second look at that forty-year scholarly record. If the academic study of popular romance fiction has matured unusually slowly, this is because it has had to clear several distinctive hurdles. First among these is the reputation of the genre itself. As the British popular culture scholar Joanne Hollows explains, "It has become part of contemporary 'common sense' that romantic fiction is a 'formulaic,' 'trivial' and 'escapist' form read by 'addicted' women," each of these charges dating back at least to the middle of the nineteenth century, each of them part of a profoundly gendered anxiety over mass culture more generally.[13] In a context where "feminine qualities — emotion, sentiment, passivity — are used to signify the worthlessness of mass culture,"[14] popular romance fiction has been triply shameful: it is, after all, a form overwhelmingly written and read by women, at least since the last century; a form dedicated to the exploration of emotion, including sentiment; and a form whose publishers and authors have embraced the mass-culture marketplace, eschewing literary difficulty and the aesthetics of estrangement even as modernism made these terms of unqualified praise. (Andreas Huyssen's famous thumbnail definition of modernism springs to mind: "an aesthetic based on the uncompromising repudiation of what Emma Bovary loved to read."[15])

If we turn from the broad British term used by Hollows, "romantic fiction," to the term preferred by American authors and scholars, the "romance novel," two more potential sources of embarrassment comes into focus. As the term is used in the United Kingdom, a work of "romantic fiction" must be, in some large part, a love story — but a tale of tragic love will serve as well as any romantic comedy. The website of the Romantic Novelists Association, a British professional organization, thus hints that *Dr. Zhivago* and *Anna Karenina* could fit the bill, perhaps to allay the concerns of writers who do not wish to be associated with a disparaged or unliterary genre. ("Many writers — even those who have just won an award for Romantic writing — deny that they write romantic fiction," the RNA website observes.[16]) The "romance novel," by contrast, is a "subset of both comedy and romance," defined as much by its upbeat ending as by its investment in romantic love.[17] "Romance novels end happily. Readers insist on it," the American critic Pamela Regis explains,[18] and the Romance Writers of America, unlike their British counterparts, freely espouse this structural constraint. "Two basic elements comprise every romance novel," the RWA explains: "a central love story" *and* "an emotionally-satisfying and optimistic ending" in which "the lovers who risk and struggle for each other and their relationship are rewarded with emotional justice and unconditional love."[19] Such uplift and encouragement was once an acceptable goal for high-art literature; to the young Keats, for example, the chief end of poetry was "to soothe the cares, and lift the thoughts of man" ("Sleep and Poetry"). Since the end of the 19th century, however, this comforting aspiration has struck critics and self-consciously sophisticated readers as "the essence of philistinism."[20] To offer encouragement and optimism in the name of love — and to do so *predictably*, novel after novel, with the lovers' Happily Ever After (HEA) never ultimately in doubt — makes the popular romance novel a disreputable form indeed.

Given its distinctive status as the despised and rejected "other" of modern literary writing, it should come as no surprise that popular romance has been treated very differently, by scholars and critics, from other forms of genre fiction. Mystery and detective novels, science fiction, fantasy, horror: all found critics to praise them as vigorous upstarts, evolving (at least at their best) into literature worthy of the name. The foundational studies of popular romance fiction make no such claims. Readily conceding the genre's lack of aesthetic interest — "the ridicule is certainly to some extent justified," Tania Modleski is quick to note[21] — books such as Modleski's *Loving with a Vengeance: Mass Produced Fantasies for Women*, Janice Radway's *Reading the Romance: Women, Patriarchy, and Popular Literature*, and Kay Mussell's *Fantasy and Reconciliation: Contemporary Formulas of Women's Romance Fiction* argued instead for the *ideological* complexity to be found in popular romance fiction and in the act of reading it. No longer were these novels "'formulaic,' 'trivial' and 'escapist.'"[22] Quite the contrary. What seemed like formulas were, in fact, a ritual struggle with "very real problems and tensions in women's lives"; beneath the trivial exterior lay "elements of protest and resistance," a "hidden plot" of "buried anger or hostility"; far from an escape, these novels encoded "anxieties, desires and wishes which if openly expressed would challenge the psychological and social order of things."[23] As for the emotionally-satisfying optimism of the genre, its offer to hearten and console, this first generation of critics saw right through that as well. Just as a "duality" lurked at the "very core of romances," reading these books will "inevitably increase the reader's own psychic conflicts," asserts Modleski; an opinion soon echoed in Janice Radway's much-repeated dictum that romance reading is "a profoundly conflicted activity centered on a profoundly conflicted form."[24]

Duality, conflict, ambivalence: the first generation of popular romance scholars made ready use of such tropes, not least as a way to project their own mixed feelings onto the genre they studied. Some of these feelings were personal. Years later, for example, Modleski would explain that she grew up as a reader of Harlequin category romances, drawn to the genre as a pre-teen by the way the heroes of these books helped her make sense of her father's "bouts of ridicule" and "black moods," her mother's "abject" appeasement of him, and her own sexual anxieties.[25] As British scholar jay Dixon has shown, the "brutal" hero that fascinated Modleski was hard to find in category romances before the late 1950s, and was later rejoined by other, contrasting figures, but the American critic's account of "the Harlequin novel" in *Loving with a Vengeance* was meant to "exorcise" the power these books had over her, collectively, not to distinguish one from another or explore their development over time.[26] When Modleski says that "guilt feelings" drive romance readers, again and again, to read the genre, it's a self-diagnosis, not a transferable insight.[27]

Professional concerns, too, shaped these studies. As Kay Mussell reflected in her introduction to a special issue of the journal *Paradoxa*, "Where's Love Gone? Transformations in Romance Fiction and Scholarship," "In the early 1980s, popular culture had not yet evolved into cultural studies, and women's entertainment forms were still marginalized in the academy."[28] In order to prove their worth to a skeptical, even scornful academic audience, scholars hedged their bets, striking condescending notes of their own. ("Romances are adolescent dramas that mirror the infantilism of women in a patriarchal culture," Mussell's early study thus avers.[29]) To bolster her experiment in literary ethnography, Janice Radway, neither a trained ethnographer nor a romance reader, embeds her interview and survey results in an elaborate, academically respectable matrix of post–Freudian theory. A generation later, the reader-based material remains fascinating, but the moves of psychoanalytical jujitsu look more awkward and self-conscious. (Radway says that the heroine's "terror and feeling of emptiness *most likely* evokes for the reader distant memories of her own initial separation from her mother," for example, but no woman she interviews mentions this "likely" reaction, or anything like it.[30])

To be fair, each of these foundational critics knew quite well that she was offering, in Modleski's words, an "early contribution"[31] to the study of popular romance. What sound like "conclusions" were in fact, as the critics themselves confess, provisional and unscientific "propositions," yet to be tested in any rigorous, systematic way.[32] Still, just as these scholars outlined "both what is laudable and what is deplorable in the appeal of such fiction,"[33] subsequent waves of romance scholars, readers, and authors have tried to distinguish what is laudable and what deplorable, or at least unfortunate, in their precursors' work.

In the "laudable" column, one would certainly list, first and foremost, the critics' core instinct to take popular romance fiction seriously, which means (in an academic context) to read the novels themselves in search of subtexts, self-contradictions, and other complexities, just as one reads any other text. Their attention to subtexts of *power*, in particular, has proved useful both for scholars and for romance authors; indeed, this subtext is an explicit concern of many of the novelists whose essays appear in *Dangerous Men and Adventurous Women*, the anthology edited by Jayne Anne Krantz which introduced the notion that romance authors could serve, like literary authors, as critics and theorists of their chosen genre.[34] (Laura Kinsale's expert rebuttal, in this book, of the critical bromide that female readers "identify" with the romance heroine has proven particularly valuable.[35]) Laudable, too, was the attention to the lived experience of "reading the romance," whether alone or as part of a community, in that first wave of romance scholarship. Without Radway's example, religious studies scholar Lynn S. Neal could never have written the sympathetic and insightful *Romancing God: Evangelical Women and Inspirational Fiction*; indeed, even Radway's falls from ethnographic grace prove useful to Neal, if only as a model to avoid. ("Rather than lament how these women's lives would be better if only they would read and believe differently, I analyze how my consultants maintain their religious commitments through evangelical romance reading," Neal coolly explains in her prologue.[36])

This laudable heritage, alas, arrives alongside other, less helpful legacies. The ideological focus of that first generation of scholars, for example, had its uses — but it also implicitly framed their work as an updated, feminist version of a very old, patently moralizing question: "Are these books good or bad for their readers?" The query has a noble pedigree. It goes back at least to Plato's *Republic*, and has since been raised about Elizabethan drama, the popular novel in all its many incarnations, movies, comics, hip hop, computer games, and most other forms of popular culture. Only with popular romance fiction, however, do otherwise sophisticated academics continue to treat this question seriously, whether raising it in the context of political debates or fretting over the practical, empiricist exigencies of how "to measure and understand the actual consequences of romance reading."[37] Even the "twenty-first century views" featured in Sally Goade's anthology, *Empowerment Versus Oppression*, often peer at the genre through this quizzing glass, darkly or lightly as the case may be.

As scholars debate the effects of "romance reading," they often perpetuate a second tic of early scholarship: the impulse to frame their discussion in terms of the genre as a whole. Kay Mussell's retrospective observation that the foundational works of popular romance criticism "were usually based on readings of very few texts," mostly chosen from "a narrow chronological range," rings sadly true for later scholarship as well.[38] When Juliet Flesch surveys the field in the opening chapter of *From Australia with Love*, an expansive, incisive history of Australian popular romance novels, she has seven more years of work to consider, including studies from the United States, Canada, the United Kingdom, India, and France. What does she find? Even ostensibly serious work continues to hold forth about "the romance," Flesch writes, as though there were "no distinction to be made between the books of several hundred writers of romance in English," as though individual writers wrote the same novel again and again over the course of their careers, and as though the genre itself were fixed and immutable, with "the romance novel of today [...] indistinguishable from titles published thirty, forty or fifty years ago."[39]

Why have scholars proceeded in this unscholarly fashion? Given the vast number of romance novels published year after year, in both single title and series formats (e.g., Harlequin's Blaze or Mills & Boon Medical romances), one practical reason springs immediately, if a bit cynically, to mind. Working on "the romance" or adopting some earlier scholar's generalization gives one an excuse for *not doing all of that reading*. Even the scrupulous Australian theorist and critic Lisa Fletcher succumbs, however briefly, to this temptation: "This massive genre is categorically unwieldy," she sighs in a footnote to *Historical Romance Fiction: Heterosexuality and Performativity*.

> These novels are too numerous and too fast-moving for scholarly researchers who are not themselves fans. Each title — and there are millions of them — only kisses the retail shelf for a brief moment before being kept, loaned, swapped, sold and resold in an informal network of friends, second-hand bookstores, op shops, school fetes and garage sales. Public libraries provide only fragmented collections as they regularly turn over their titles in order to keep up with both the volume of new releases and their apparently insatiable readers.[40]

It's a dirty job, keeping up with romance, and the ones who have to do it are not scholars, but those bibliographic Bacchae, the "fans," whose insatiability Fletcher describes with an old-school flicker of distaste. (What genre, one wonders, has *satiable* readers?)

Writing about "the romance," or even "the historical romance," then, also lets the scholar continue to keep her distance from it, whether in order to exorcise the fascination it has held over her own imagination (thus Greer and Modleski, in the early years) or to debunk and break its hold over others (thus Radway, and more recently Jeanne Dubino, and Fletcher herself).[41] Such antagonistic agendas can, to be sure, spur interesting scholarship — but the scholar in question must then be doubly careful to keep her argument free of selection bias, or simply of ignorance born of aversion. The lack of careful peer review in popular romance fiction studies, from the 1980s to the present, has allowed many a gaffe and stereotype to slip through. One recent meditation on the appeal of the romance hero, published by a respectable university press, uses Georgette Heyer's *These Old Shades* as its example of the "regency" romance, displacing the novel by fifty years or more — it's set no later than 1760, in a painstakingly-detailed Georgian context — and in subgenre.[42] A minor flaw? Perhaps — but try to imagine the author, her peer reviewers, and the editors at the press all giving the nod to a comparably sophisticated discussion of Agatha Christie's "hard-boiled" detective, Miss Marple, William Gibson's "space opera," *Neuromancer*, or that "fin-de-siècle" classic, *The Grapes of Wrath*.

Given this heritage of generalization, it should come as no surprise that popular romance scholarship has rarely attended in any detail to individual novelists, let alone individual novels. One sees in this gap the lingering effects of that early concession, by most of the first-wave critics, that romance novels were not of much interest, aesthetically speaking; one sees in it, as well, the legacy of that early psychoanalytic approach to the genre, in which everything really interesting about the romance novel was repressed or unconscious or latent, needing the critic-analyst to bring it to light. These were not the only approaches available, even in the early 1980s; John Cawelti's *Adventure, Mystery, and Romance: Formula Stories as Art and Popular Culture*, published in the mid–1970s, offered a sharply contrasting model of treating "formula literature [as], first of all, a kind of literary art": one which centers on "the artistic principle of variations on a theme."[43] Had Cawelti dwelt for more than two pages on popular romance fiction, we might now have a decades-long record of work on the interplay between convention and innovation in specific romance novels and across the careers of particularly accomplished novelists in the genre. We might also know a bit more about the experience of readers — not as they wrestle with patriarchy, but as they enjoy the aesthetic experience of reading these texts. As Thomas J. Roberts' *An Aesthetics of Junk Fiction* points out, "genre reading is system reading," and whether the genre is romance, science fiction, or mystery/detective fiction, competent readers (what Fletcher calls "fans") take their pleasure in individual texts by reading them at once within and against the traditions and possibilities of that system.[44] Take their pleasure—and their *dis*pleasure as well. The "insatiable readers" of popular romance fiction, in Fletcher's phrase, are hardly indiscriminate consumers. Indeed, they may grade harder than most literature professors and reviewers of literary fiction, handing "D" and "F" and "Epic Fail" to many a novel on websites like Dear Author and Smart Bitches, Trashy Books, on both artistic and political grounds.

New Approaches?

If the first wave of popular romance criticism crested in the 1980s, followed in the early 1990s by a second wave—essays by authors, notably those gathered in *Dangerous Men and Adventurous Women*—when did the current, third wave of scholarship begin? How are these "new approaches" different from the work that came before?

The first, chronological question turns out to be tricky to answer. In principle, one might date the current wave of scholarship to that 1997 special issue of the journal *Paradoxa*, where romance scholars, authors, and readers first met on a more-or-less equal footing. Mussell's introduction certainly trumpets the gathering as a new start for the field: in it, she writes, we finally find "single-author studies," work that "decisively refutes the 'romances are all alike' argument" by attending to the contrasts between subgenres, essays that "mount a challenge to dominant critical practices, including the hegemony of simplified feminist criticism," and a sizable bibliography.[45] Her paragraph on "what is left to be done" lays out an ambitious agenda:

> We need to come to a better, more nuanced understanding of the various segments of the romance audience. Who reads what? When? Why? How? (It is still all too common to find casual references to lower-class women or housewives as the readers of romances.) We need to incorporate analysis of lesbian and gay romances into our mostly heterosexual models. We need more careful follow-up or longitudinal studies based on readers and novels since the early 1980s; these would include more sophisticated readership studies, more single-author or even single-novel studies. We need to examine how romances (both translated and original) are read in other countries and how romance conventions appear in non–English-language works by American ethnic authors. We need to incorporate a better understanding of business and publishing practices. [...] We need more textual readings of individual authors. We need solid histories of the genre which directly address issues of change over time. [...] Finally, together we need to continue to struggle toward a reading of romances that takes into account the critical practices of feminists and other scholars as well as the creativity of writers and the experience of readers.[46]

The oddly anxious tone of that final sentence—"together we need to continue to *struggle toward* a reading"—hints at how long it would take, and hard it would prove, for this agenda to be realized. Within a year, after all, *Paradoxa* would publish a tart rejoinder from Modleski, who disdained what struck her as the amateurish and upbeat tone of some work in the previous issue, and also of the author-centered conference on "Re-Reading the Romance" hosted in 1997 by Bowling Green University. Modleski has not published on the genre since.

In retrospect, the *Paradoxa* gathering was more a harbinger than a transformative event. The issue did not circulate widely enough to displace those early, foundational studies in classrooms or graduate research carrels, nor did *Romantic Conventions*, an uneven, often unsophisticated collection of essays that followed two years later.[47] Some of that naiveté may be deliberate: while the first-wave critics made impressive use of cutting-edge literary and cultural theory, aiming at an audience of fellow academics, the introduction to *Romantic Conventions* stops to explain that "critics do more than criticize" and reassures readers that "our arguments are simple."[48] Why, though, should Dawn Heinecken's 1998 essay on "changing ideologies in romance fiction" make no reference to Carol Thurston's *The Romance Revolution: Erotic Novels and the Quest for a New Sexual Identity,* a book-length, impressively-researched study of these changes from ten years before?[49] That's not simple — it's just sloppy. Across the late 1990s and early 2000s, American scholars worked without reference to first-rate British work on both "romantic fiction" and on category romance.[50] The British, in turn, paid little attention to developments in the United States, including the remarkable artistic evolution of the genre in the hands of, among others, Nora Roberts, Laura Kinsale, Susan Elizabeth Phillips, Loretta Chase, and Jennifer Crusie. (Crusie was a contributor to both the *Paradoxa* issue and the *Romantic Conventions* anthology, but most of her provocative, critically-adept reflections on the genre were published in reader/author venues like *Romance Writer's Report, Inside Borders, Writer's Market, Springs Literary Supplement,* essentially invisible to academia.) Doctoral theses on popular romance were written, but never published; important new work on the genre in Europe, Asia, Australia, and Francophone Canada, though published, went largely unnoticed; anthology pieces by promising young scholars appeared, but made little impact on one another.[51] By and large, scholars of popular romance fiction worked in isolation, divided by both national and disciplinary boundaries.

When, then, did this archipelago of scholarship begin to coalesce into a recognizable academic "field"? Looking back from 2012, two transitions seem of crucial importance. The first came in 2003–4, when innovative book-length studies of romance fiction offered new critical models that could, at last, compete with those offered by first-wave feminist scholars. We have already mentioned Juliet Flesch's *From Australia with Love,* a book whose exploration of national, regional, and historical difference within popular romance fiction — both in English and in translation — made good on a fistful of wishes from Kay Mussell's *Paradoxa* list. Flesch was not the first to observe "the contempt scholars and critics reveal for [romance] readers and authors,"[52] but no one had followed such a bracing, comprehensive review and rebuttal of those charges, point by point, with such an impressive, persuasive new path into the genre. No one, that is, except perhaps Flesch's American contemporary, Pamela Regis. A contributor to the 1997 Paradoxa issue, Regis opens *A Natural History of the Romance Novel* with an equally adroit riposte to earlier accounts of popular romance fiction, but her study went on to advance a more purely literary, less historical agenda. Doubling back to the work of Northrop Frye, the great early theorist of "Romance" in the broadest sense, Regis offered a new definition of "the romance novel" that bridged the enduring critical divide between "popular" and "literary" instances of it. To frame her history of the romance novel from Samuel Richardson's *Pamela* to the works of Nora Roberts, Regis anatomizes "eight essential elements" that define the form: "a *definition of society,* always corrupt, that the romance novel will reform; the *meeting* between the heroine and hero; an account of their *attraction* for each other; the *barrier* between them; the *point of ritual death*; the *recognition* that fells the barrier; the *declaration* of heroine and hero that they love each other; and their *betrothal.*"[53] These elements can occur in any order, on-stage or off, and can each happen multiple times, giving a distinctive shape and rhythm to the novel as a whole. "Looking at the embodiment of any given element in any given romance novel," Regis observes, can be the critic's "key to understanding what is at stake in that novel."[54] That novel, and *not* some other one — which is to say that from Regis, a student or aspiring romance scholar can learn to read the genre book by book, with an eye to the variations and particularities that distinguish one text from another.

Even as Flesch and Regis offered new, disaggregating approaches to popular romance scholarship, a new infrastructure for popular romance fiction studies began to emerge. On the one hand, there was a financial infrastructure. In 2005, the Romance Writers of America inaugurated a competitive Academic Research Grant program, its grant review committee composed of academically-credentialed authors in the genre, many with doctorate degrees and some of them professors in their own right. Within two years the first grant recipient, Jayashree Kamble, had used the support to research and publish a fresh, insightful piece on reading popular romance in India, while the second, Eric Murphy Selinger, had set up a listserv network of international romance scholars that soon collaboratively produced an on-line Wiki bibliography of interdisciplinary scholarship (about five hundred entries are currently listed, and the number continues to grow) and the collaborative academic romance blog, Teach Me Tonight, now mostly written by British scholar Laura Vivanco. (The RomanceScholar listserv has since proved invaluable in spreading the word about new scholarship, conferences, and calls for papers, including the one for this volume.) The fourth recipient, Sarah S.G. Frantz, transformed Selinger's ad-hoc, on-line network into the first professional organization for scholars in the field, the International Association for the Study of Popular Romance (IASPR). With approximately two hundred members around the world (as of this writing) IASPR sponsors an annual international, interdisciplinary conference on romantic love in global popular media, and the on-line, peer-reviewed *Journal of Popular Romance Studies*. The RWA grant program is ongoing.

We do not mean to suggest that the RWA is solely responsible for this sudden explosion in popular romance scholarship. As we have shown, exciting new work was underway in many quarters, and local connections and communities had been forged through, for example, the Southwest Texas Popular Culture Association/American Culture Association (source of many of the essays in Sally Goade's *Empowerment Versus Oppression* anthology). Still, the arrival of popular romance studies as a self-conscious and on-going academic field owes a great deal to the RWA program, a remarkably successful example of the working "together" of scholars, writers, and readers that Mussell envisioned back in 1997.

The RWA's investment in romance scholarship would not have paid off so richly, however, were it not for another piece of collaborative infrastructure: the emergence of critically-sophisticated, exuberantly literate on-line romance communities in which scholars, authors, and fans interact publicly, in real time, more or less as equals. The roots of these communities date back to the 1990s, and RRA-L, the now-closed Romance Readers Anonymous listserv, was an early help to scholars. (In her *Paradoxa* introduction, Mussell credits RRA-L with reviving her interest in the genre, and Fletcher thanks the listserv for helping her select some popular historical romances to study.) With the emergence of romance reader websites, however — both collaboratively-written review websites and the blogs of individual readers — the insight and expertise to be found in the genre's audience became visible in a way that no listserv could match. The romance community's debates over individual novels and the progress of series, its lively mockery of incompetent writing, genre clichés, and painfully bad cover art, and its explicit, thoroughly conscious engagement with political issues and changes in the publishing industry: all of these give the lie to enduring stereotypes about the inanity of romance readers, some of them perpetuated in the first wave of romance scholarship. Indeed, not only do romance readers know the history and variety of the genre better, even now, than most academics who study it; many of them know the scholarship, as well. In *Beyond Heaving Bosoms: The Smart Bitches' Guide to Romance Novels*, for example, Sarah Wendell and Candy Tan, co-authors of the Smart Bitches, Trashy Books blog, deploy ideas from first wave, second wave, and third wave work on romance, citing by name Radway, Mussell, Regis, Vivanco, and several essayists from the *Dangerous Men and Adventurous Women* and *Romance Conventions* anthologies.[55] Several of the best new romance scholars have returned the compliment, joining existing reader websites as reviewers and publishing blogs of their own.

Clearly, then, the kind of romance criticism that Mussell called for in 1997 — the kind that "takes into account the critical practices of feminists and other scholars as well as the creativity of writers and the experience of readers"[56] — has not only emerged; it bids fair, at last, to become the normative model for how such reading is done. Academics of many disciplines take part in this field, as do authors, expert fans, and editors, in an ongoing, increasingly audible dialogue. (We list them separately — in fact, the romance scholar will often wear two or three of these hats, either at once or by turns.) Published alongside the first issues of the *Journal of Popular Romance Studies* and a string of new conferences on the genre at Princeton University, Brussels' Paleis der Academiën, and Brisbane, Australia's University of Queensland and Queensland University of Technology, this gathering of *New Approaches to Popular Romance Fiction* hopes to make the "fine curry" that is contemporary popular romance scholarship available to our fellow scholars, to students, and to general readers as well.

Structure of the Volume

New Approaches to Popular Romance Fiction is divided into four broad sections: "Close Reading the Romance," "Convention and Originality," "Love and Strife," and "Readers, Authors, Communities."

The essays in Part One, "Close Reading the Romance," challenge the continuing assumption that popular romance novels neither invite nor repay the kind of focused, individual inquiry that academics bring to other texts. Arranged in historical sequence, these pieces focus by turns on an individually interesting romance novel drawn from the romance boom of the late 1970s and early 1980s (Bertrice Small's *The Kadin*, from 1978), from the transformative decade of the 1990s (*Flowers from the Storm*, by Laura Kinsale, published in 1992), from the burgeoning world of romance e-publishing at the start of the new century (the 2002 BDSM erotic romance *Holding the Cards*, by Joey W. Hill), and from the recent proliferation of paranormal and vampire romance (the first of J.R. Ward's Black Dagger Brotherhood novels, *Dark Lover*, from 2005).

In "'Bertrice teaches you about history, and you don't even mind!': History and Revisionist Historiography in Bertrice Small's *The Kadin*," Australian novelist and historian Hsu-Ming Teo looks at the historical research and revisionist historiography that shape Bertrice Small's Orientalist historical romance, and argues that it serves as a harbinger of the radical feminist turn in historiography fifteen years later: a turn which placed women's domestic, familial, romantic, and sexual experiences, actions, and relationships at the center of historical narratives of power, statehood and empire. Whether or not every novel from the despised subgenre of the "bodice-ripper" will reward detailed, text-specific analysis, Teo shows this one certainly does. "How to Read a Romance Novel (and Fall in Love with Popular Romance)," by Eric Murphy Selinger, likewise rejects the assumption that popular romance criticism should address the genre as a whole. In his detailed exploration of Kinsale's *Flowers from the Storm*, Selinger traces the literary allusions, geometrical patterns, and theological surprises that make up the novel's intricate, aesthetically satisfying design — and, in the process, disproves a notion advanced by both skeptics and apologists for the popular romance genre: the notion that these novels appeal exclusively to the heart, and not also to the mind.

The final pieces in this section take contrasting approaches to close reading the romance. In "'How we love *is* our soul': Joey W. Hill's BDSM Romance *Holding the Cards*," Sarah S.G. Frantz situates Hill's groundbreaking novel — the first of her Nature of Desire series — in the transformations of romance publishing, particularly erotic romance publishing, that followed the arrival of e-publication. Drawing on the work of queer theorist and activist Ivo Dominguez, Jr., Frantz distinguishes between the "polysexual continua" that structure sexual identity in Hill's work (heterosexual/homosexual, monogamous/polyamorous, top/bottom, sadist/masochist, and dominant/submissive) and the more simplistic representations of BDSM in earlier romance fiction. This *particular* novel, she shows, uses BDSM to explore not simply the characters' sexual identities, but their relationships to previous characters and tropes in the genre, leaving polysexuality and metatextuality subtly and satisfyingly intertwined. Mary Bly's essay "On Popular Romance, J.R. Ward, and the Limits of Genre Study" likewise contrasts the modernist vision of artistic originality that has overshadowed popular romance criticism with an older, pre–Romantic vision of innovation within received genres, but this accomplished scholar of Renaissance literature (and, as Eloisa James, an accomplished author of historical romance novels) takes an overtly historicist approach to her chosen novel, J.R. Ward's *Dark Lover*. As she demonstrates, this bestselling paranormal romance novel bears a complex, previously unobserved relationship to American political discourse and social anxieties after 9/11: a relationship that cannot simply be mapped onto romance more generally or onto other bestsellers of the time, paranormal or otherwise.

The essays in our second section, "Convention and Originality," consider the ways that popular romance fiction negotiates the claims of generic convention and of artistic innovation. As the essays in this group demonstrate, the borders and definitions of popular romance fiction have grown fluid, even porous, as authors explore the complexities, self-contradictions, and polymorphic variety available within and around the genre.

We open this section with "Loving by the Book: Voice and Romance Authorship," by Belgian romance scholar An Goris. Goris considers the interaction between familiarity and novelty that constitutes "successful" romance writing — success here defined from within the romance industry by handbooks for would-be authors. In handbooks from the United States, Great Britain, Australia, and New Zealand, Goris finds a shared, paradoxical set of assumptions. To succeed, the romance author must supply both comfort and surprise; indeed, she must achieve "authenticity" of voice precisely by giving the reader what she wants and expects — but *differently*. The vision of aesthetic success within the romance community, Goris demonstrates, turns out to be more rhetorically complex and more self-consciously articulated than is traditionally assumed.

In "The 'Managing Female' in the Novels of Georgette Heyer," K. Elizabeth Spillman examines the novels of one particularly celebrated romance author, Georgette Heyer, whose publishing career spanned fifty years between 1921 and 1972. In the romance plot, already ubiquitous, the founder and Grande Dame of Regency romance found a fertile area for genre-and gender-bending literary play, manipulating and subverting genre stereotypes to construct heroines who simultaneously conform to the traditional model of a heroine, are contrasted to it, and challenge it through their assumption of masculine traits, their consciousness of their social roles, and their reflexivity. The heroines' conscious construction of themselves as both romance heroines and anti-heroines allows them to assert their agency throughout the novels, and has made them appealing models for subsequent developments in the genre.

Focusing closely on one enduring motif in popular romance fiction, "One Ring to Bind Them: Ring Symbolism in Popular Romance Fiction," by British scholar Laura Vivanco, begins to illuminate the complexities that can be found within a single convention in the genre. The essay takes its cue from a lively piece of mock-pedantry featured on the website of romance author Jennifer Crusie: a satirical theory (or satire *of* theory) that focuses on the romance heroine's uniquely empowering sexuality, her "glittery hoo-hah." Vivanco lays out the serious antecedents of this theory in the work of Shulamith Firestone, among others, and uses it to perform a close textual analysis of the symbolism of rings in a wide range of popular romance novels. As the essay shows, not only do romance authors use the giving of an engagement ring to represent the intersubjective, sexual love between the hero and heroine, but the actual kisses and sex scenes are often replete with references to jewels and rings, calling attention to their own symbolic function within the text.

While Vivanco approaches romance fiction synchronically, Carole Veldman-Genz brings her doctoral research and professional experience as a romance editor to bear on the evolution of a topos in the genre: a convention which has also been central, according to René Girard and Elaine Showalter, to canonical fiction about desire. In "The More the Merrier? Transformations of the Love Triangle Across the Romance," she shows that the love triangle is a dynamic structure, capable of producing radically disparate textual effects as authors appropriate it in pursuit of contrasting ideological ends. Rather than set forth a singular or monolithic meta-text of *the* romance, her essay attends to the heterogeneous uses of male/female/male and female/male/female triangles, highlighting the feminocentric potential these triangles harbor when employed in contemporary romances. In recent erotic romance, this essay shows, the triangle sometimes ceases to be an obstacle to romantic closure and instead replaces the dyadic pairing as romantic ideal.

"'Why would any woman want to read such stories?': The Distinctions Between Genre Romance and Slash Fiction" by Deborah Kaplan also explores the shifting boundaries and definitions of popular romance. Approaching the genre comparatively, Kaplan reads it alongside "slash" fiction: that is, fan fiction about amatory, often sexual relationships between same-sex characters. (The term "slash" derives from the punctuation mark in the original slash fiction, Kirk/Spock, rather than from characters being slashed or cut.) Reading slash stories deliberately written in the style of Harlequin or Mills & Boon romances and a same-sex love story by romance author Suzanne Brockman — the latter published in her line of mainstream romantic suspense novels — Kaplan illuminates the generic markers that must be transformed, removed, or replaced to bring the two genres into close contact, and their evident resistance to such change.

Our third section, "Love and Strife," takes its title from the classical pun that has linked *Eros* (love) and *Eris* (strife), since the days of Hesiod and Sappho. The essays in this section address the enduring themes of power, conflict, trauma, and healing through love in popular romance fiction. Such themes shape the enduringly popular, ideologically vexing genre of captivity romance, so we open with "Borderlands of Desire: Captivity, Romance, and the Revolutionary Power of Love." In this essay, Robin Harders contrasts the original seventeenth-century genre of captivity narrative with its modern descendants in popular romance. In the earlier genre, Harders argues, the female captive exemplifies the sexual purity, gender integrity, and cultural homogeneity of the Anglo-American domestic ideal, freed from her Indian captivity only to be re-enslaved by her role as a cultural symbol of the supremacy of civilized womanhood. Modern captivity romance, too, plays out a narrative of liberation and containment — and often, the liberation explored is not simply sexual, but cultural, a xenophilic fantasy of cultural hybridity that recent captivity novels explore in the distant past (Louise Allen's *Virgin Slave, Barbarian King*) and on other worlds (Elizabeth Vaughan's *Warprize*).

Like the subgenre she studies, Harders focuses primarily on the way love and strife affect the romance heroine. In "Patriotism, Passion, and PTSD: The Critique of War in Popular Romance Fiction," Jayashree Kamble turns our attention to the many warrior and soldier heroes who populate the genre, and to the cultural tensions that novels about them can illuminate. Looking at novels from the 1980s onward, Kamble shows how American romance authors have aligned the soldier hero with the capitalist, democratic nation, so that his devotion to his country (or some symbol of it) becomes the marker of his moral strength. As the novel's courtship or marriage plot conflicts with patriotic duty, the conflicts in these texts — historically-set, contemporary, and paranormal as well — bear witness to an ongoing conversation in the United States about war and its consequences.

War and captivity may be among the most dramatic sorts of conflict described in popular romance fiction, but they are hardly the only ones. As Kathleen Therrien demonstrates in "Straight to the Edges: Gay and Lesbian Characters and Cultural Conflict in Popular Romance Fiction," by tracking the deployment of gay and lesbian characters in heterosexual romances, we can see where these novels set the boundaries of cultural conflict and acceptable behavior: in effect, of the ideological territory that may or may not be acceptably contested within the text. Some romances, Therrien shows, use despicable gay and lesbian characters to limit the heroine's resistance to patriarchy, while others use sympathetic gay and lesbian characters as signposts to mark how much change must occur and how far it must extend. Culturally-sanctioned homophobia exemplifies, in these latter texts, the ideologies of gender and power that cause problems for the heterosexual hero and heroine as well: a progressive, reformist political construction, but one in which heteronormative monogamy may remain an unspoken cultural norm.

The final essay in this section looks at the love and strife that mark conversations among romance readers and authors on the influential romance website, Smart Bitches, Trashy Books (SBTB, for short). In "'You call me a bitch like that's a bad thing': Romance Criticism and Redefining the Word 'Bitch,'" "Smart Bitch" Sarah Wendell, the site's co-founder, reflects on the unspoken code of behavior that governs contributions to, and comments on, the site. In the world of romance reviews, where the pressure to "be nice" is tangible, the brash, sardonic style of argument treasured by the "Bitchery" has created a counter-community of writers, readers, editors, reviewers, scholars, and publishing professionals who (in the author's words) "celebrate the right to read and enjoy romance while still Being a Bitch."

Our final section, "Readers, Authors, Communities," sustains this focus on popular romance fiction as a community of readers, offering a range of new approaches to the intricately networked creative industries that links readers, authors, and texts. In "The Interactive Romance Community: The Case of 'Covers Gone Wild,'" Miriam Greenfeld-Benovitz uses ethnographic communications analysis to consider "Cover Snark," a regular feature on the Smart Bitches' website. Through interviews, archival investigation, and participant observation, Greenfeld-Benovitz documents this collective mocking of romance novel covers, and she explores how this ritual both constitutes and illuminates the values of the Smart Bitches, Trashy Books community.

As Wendell and Greenfeld-Benovitz demonstrate, romance readers in fact constitute a lively, reflective, highly-engaged community. Why, then, do the stereotypes persist of these readers as passive (or, worse, insatiably addicted) consumers? In "Happy Readers or Sad Ones? Romance Fiction and the Problems of the Media Effects Model," Australian scholar Glen Thomas recalls the history of this construction of the romance audience, and offers an alternative critical model by which to understand popular romance fiction as a "creative industry." Tracing the feedback loops through which reader preferences, authorial innovation, critical consideration, and market research by publishers continually interact, Thomas shows how we can use these loops to understand the creation, reception, and aftermath of one particularly controversial recent romance novel, *Claiming the Courtesan,* by his compatriot, Anna Campbell.

Although scholars of popular romance fiction have sometimes underestimated the intelligence and education of the genre's audience, popular romance authors have, as a rule, treated their readers with far more respect. In "'A consummation devoutly to be wished': Shakespeare in Popular Historical Romance Fiction," Tamara Whyte explores the ways that authors of historical romance fiction construct an implied readership for their work through the deployment of Shakespeare, an author who is at once supremely canonical and enduringly popular. Analyzing the various purposes to which historical romances apply references to Shakespeare's plays, either in quotes by the characters or in larger borrowings of theme or plot, Whyte argues that these references are not simply decorative or aspirational touches. Rather, in a typically postmodern blurring of high and low culture, they mark the author's trust in the sophistication of romance readers, even as they act as indicators of characterization, demonstrating the heroine's intelligence and the hero's suitability. In the hands of some authors, they even serve as metatextual points of reflection, used to situate the novel in question in a lively, revisionist dialogue with literary traditions of tragedy, comedy, and popular melodrama.

By any measure, Nora Roberts is the single most successful and most prominent romance author writing today. To bring this collection to a close, in "The Power of Three: Nora Roberts and Serial Magic," Christina A. Valeo investigates the astonishing market success of Roberts' romance trilogies. In the simplest of terms the trilogies multiply the pleasures available to readers: more meetings, more obstacles, more declarations, more happy endings. But a Roberts series quickly becomes more than the sum of its parts, interweaving genres and using the structure of the trilogy, Valeo speculates, to evoke the ancient significance of the number three: a set of associations which her novels bring to readers' attention, inviting them to enjoy the series' sophisticated play with generic convention.

Given the genre's current diversity and on-going evolution, this volume does not claim to give a detailed account of popular romance fiction as a whole. Indeed, a turn *away* from accounts of the genre "as a whole" seems a defining characteristic of the many "new approaches" featured here. In them, instead, a new generation of scholars — and bloggers, and editors, and romance authors themselves — take visible pleasure in teasing out for separate consideration the multiple, even self-contradictory values, conventions, themes, and audiences of the genre, often as these are inscribed within specific, surprisingly individual texts. Many more such texts deserve, but have yet to receive, attention from academics; in the world of popular romance fiction, especially considered as a *world* phenomenon, there are many issues, conventions, subgenres, and audiences that scholars have yet to explore. Rather than aspiring to offer the last word on our subject, we hope that the seventeen new essays collected in this volume will provoke our readers with thoughtful questions, fresh insights, and new twists in enduring debates, inspiring others to join the emerging field of popular romance studies.

NOTES

1. Loretta Chase, *Lord of Scoundrels* (New York: Avon, 1995), 205.

2. *Ibid.*, 214.

3. One notes, as well, a spark of pleasure of diction in that unexpected reference to "curry." Jessica might know the term; in 1810, eighteen years before the time-frame of the novel, an Indian immigrant named Sake Dean Mahomed opened the first Indian restaurant in England, "the Hindoostane Coffee House in George Street, central London" ("Curry House Founder Is Honoured," *BBC News*, September 29, 2005, http://news.bbc.co.uk/2/hi/uk_news/england/london/4290124.stm). Jessica's use of "curry" as a description of the aesthetics of romance, however, also calls to mind the use of the term "masala" to describe Indian films that mix elements of comedy, melodrama, action, romance, and more. With its mix of comedy, melodrama, and the like, *Lord of Scoundrels* is quite vividly a "masala" or "curry" of a romance novel.

4. In the first canto of *Don Juan*, we may recall, Byron tweaks Plato, the philosopher of erotic love, as "no better than a go-between" — the stanza is not quoted by Chase, but the lines just before it are — while in Canto V of Dante's *Inferno*, a chivalric romance and its author are the go-between, turning desire to action.

5. See Peter H. Mann, *The Romance Novel: A Survey of Reading Habits* (London: Mills & Boon, 1969). The study was commissioned to celebrate the publisher's 60th anniversary. Mann was an established sociologist who continued to investigate popular fiction in such works as *From Author to Reader: A Social Study of Books* (London: Routledge, 1982).

6. Germaine Greer, *The Female Eunuch* (London: Paladin, 1971), 185. For accounts of the sexual politics of romance fiction, see Rachel Anderson, *The Purple Heart Throbs: The Sub-literature of Love* (London: Hodder and Stoughton, 1974); Jennifer Anderson, *Mills & Boon: Love and Oppression* (Broadway: New South Wales Institute of Technology, 1981); Stephanie Burley, "What's a Nice Girl Like You Doing in a Book Like This? Homoerotic Reading and Popular Romance," in *Doubled Plots: Romance and History*, ed. Susan Strehle and Mary Paniccia Carden (Jackson: University Press of Mississippi, 2003): 127–46; Jan Cohn, *Romance and the Erotics of Property: Mass-Market Fiction for Women* (Durham: Duke University Press, 1988); Ann Douglas, "Soft-Porn Culture: Punishing the Liberated Woman," *The New Republic* 183, no. 9 (August 30, 1980): 25–29; Jeanne Dubino, "The Cinderella Complex: Romance Fiction, Patriarchy, and Capitalism," *Journal of Popular Culture* 27, no. 3 (1993): 103–118; Lisa Fletcher, *Historical Romance Fiction: Heterosexuality and Performativity* (Aldershot: Ashgate, 2008); Bridget Fowler, *The Alienated Reader: Women and Popular Romantic Literature in the Twentieth Century* (Brighton: Harvester Wheatsheaf, 1991); Mariam Darce Frenier, *Good-bye Heathcliff: Changing Heroes, Heroines, Roles, and Values in Women's Category Romances*, Contributions in Women's Studies, no. 94 (New York: Greenwood Press, 1988); Ann Rosalind Jones, "Mills & Boon Meets Feminism," in *The Progress of Romance: The Politics of Popular Fiction*, ed. Jean Radford (London: Routledge & Kegan Paul, 1986): 195–218; Tania Modleski, *Loving with a Vengeance: Mass-Produced Fantasies for Women* (New York: Routledge, 1982) and "My Life as a Romance Writer," *Paradoxa: Studies in World Literary Genres* 4, no. 9 (1998): 134–144; Kay Mussell, *Fantasy and Reconciliation: Contemporary Formulas of Women's Romance Fiction* (Westport, CT: Greenwood Press, 1984); Ann Barr Snitow, "Mass Market Romance: Pornography for Women Is Different," *Radical History Review* 20 (Spring/Summer 1979): 141–61, repub. *Women and Romance: A Reader*, ed. Susan Ostrov Weisser (New York: New York University Press, 2001): 307–22; Janice Radway, *Reading the Romance: Women, Patriarchy, and Popular*

Literature (1984; rpt. with new Introduction, Chapel Hill: University of North Carolina Press, 1991); Carol Thurston, *The Romance Revolution: Erotic Novels for Women and the Quest for a New Sexual Identity* (Urbana: University of Illinois Press, 1987); Stephanie Wardrop, "The Heroine Is Being Beaten: Freud, Sado-masochism, and Reading the Romance," *Style* 29 (1995): 459–73; Susan Ostrov Weisser, "The Wonderful-Terrible Bitch Figure in Harlequin Novels," in *Feminist Nightmares: Women at Odds: Feminism and the Problem of Sisterhood*, ed. Susan Ostrov Weisser and Jennifer Fleischner (New York: New York University Press, 1994): 269–82.

7. Studies of the appeal of romance and its effects on readers include J.K. Alberts, "The Role of Couples' Conversations in Relationship Development: A Content Analysis of Courtship Talk in Harlequin Romance Novels," *Communication Quarterly* 34 (1986): 127–142; Claire D. Coles and M. Johnna Shamp, "Some Sexual, Personality, and Demographic Characteristics of Women Readers of Erotic Romances," *Archives of Sexual Behavior* 13, no. 3 (1984): 187–209; Lynda L. Crane, "Romance Novel Readers: In Search of Feminist Change?" *Women's Studies* 23, no. 3 (1994): 257–69; Helen Hazen, *Endless Rapture: Rape, Romance, and the Female Imagination* (New York: Scribner's, 1983); Rita C. Hubbard, "The Changing-Unchanging Heroines and Heroes of Harlequin Romances, 1950–1979," in *The Hero in Transition*, ed. Ray B. Browne and Marshall W. Fishwick (Bowling Green, OH: Popular Press, 1983): 171–179; Margaret Ann Jensen, *Love's $weet Return: The Harlequin Story* (Toronto: Women's Educational Press, 1984); Jayashree Kamble, "Female Enfranchise-ment and the Popular Romance: Employing an Indian Perspective," in *Empowerment Versus Oppression: Twenty First Century Views of Popular Romance Novels*, ed. Sally Goade (Newcastle: Cambridge Scholars, 2007): 148–173; Daniela Kramer and Michael Moore, "Gender Roles, Romantic Fiction and Family Ther-apy," *Psycoloquy* 12, no. 24 (2001); Lynn S. Neal, *Romancing God: Evangelical Women and Inspirational Fiction* (Chapel Hill: University of North Carolina Press, 2006); Mairead Owen, "Re-inventing romance: Reading Popular Romantic Fiction," *Women's Studies International Forum* 20 no. 4 (1997): 537–46; Radhika Parameswaran, "Western Romance Fiction as English-Language Media in Postcolonial India," *Journal of Communication* 49, no. 3 (1999): 84–105 and "Reading Fictions of Romance: Gender, Sexuality, and Nationalism in Postcolonial India," *Journal of Communication* 52, no. 4 (2002): 832–851; Lynne Pearce and Jackie Stacey, eds., *Romance Revisited* (New York: New York University Press, 1995); Jyoti Puri, "Reading Romance Novels in Postcolonial India," *Gender & Society* 11, no. 4 (1997): 434–452; Radway's *Reading the Romance*; and Huei-Hsia Wu, "Gender, Romance Novels and Plastic Sexuality in the United States: A Focus on Female College Students," *Journal of International Women's Studies* 8, no. 1 (2006): 125–34.

8. For histories of romance publishing in Britain and the United States, see Jennifer Anderson, *Mills & Boon*; jay Dixon, *The Romance Fiction of Mills & Boon, 1909–1990s* (Philadelphia: UCL Press, 1999); Paul Grescoe, *The Merchants of Venus: Inside Harlequin and the Empire of Romance* (Vancouver: Raincoast, 1996); Joseph McAleer, *Passion's Fortune: The Story of Mills & Boon* (Oxford: Oxford University Press, 1999); and Carol Thurston, *Romance Revolution*. For studies of romance publishing in Europe, Australia, and China, and for attention to romance in translation, as export, and as local tradition, see Annick Capelle, "Harlequin Romances in Western Europe: The Cultural Interactions of Romantic Literature," in *European Readings of American Popular Culture*, ed. John Dean and Jean-Paul Gabilliet (Westport, CT: Greenwood Press, 1996): 91–100; Juliet Flesch, *From Australia with Love: A History of Modern Australian Popular Romance Novels* (Fremantle, Australia: Curtin University Books, 2004); Diana Holmes, *Romance and Readership in Twentieth-Century France: Love Stories* (Oxford: Oxford University Press, 2006); Amy Lee, "Forming a Local Identity: Romance Novels in Hong Kong," in *Empowerment Versus Oppression: Twenty First Century Views of Popular Romance Novels*, ed. Sally Goade (Newcastle: Cambridge Scholars, 2007): 174–197; Thomas J. Roberts, *An Aesthetics of Junk Fiction* (Athens: University of Georgia Press, 1990); and Eva Hemmungs Wirtén, "Harlequin Romances in Swedish: A Case Study in Globalized Publishing," *Logos* 11, no. 4 (2000): 203–7.

9. Significant scholars of colonialism, Orientalism, and white supremacy in romance include Evelyn Bach, "Sheik Fantasies: Orientalism and Feminine Desire in the Desert Romance," *Hecate* 23, no. 1 (1997): 9–40; Emily A. Haddad, "Bound to Love: Captivity in Harlequin Sheikh Novels," in *Empowerment Versus Oppression: Twenty First Century Views of Popular Romance Novels*, ed. Sally Goade (Newcastle: Cambridge Scholars, 2007), 42–64; Patricia Raub, "Issues of Passion and Power in E.M. Hull's *The Sheik*," *Women's Studies* 21 (1992): 119–128; and Hsu-Ming Teo, "The Romance of White Nations: Imperialism, Popular Culture and National Histories," in *After the Imperial Turn: Thinking with and Through the Nation*, ed. Antoinette Burton (Durham: Duke University Press, 2003): 279–292, "Romancing the Raj: Interracial Relations in Anglo-Indian Romance Novels," *History of Intellectual Culture* 4, no. 1 (2004), http://www.ucalgary.ca/hic/issues/vol4/3, and "Orientalism and Mass Market Romance Novels in the Twentieth Cen-tury," in *Edward Said: The Legacy of a Public Intellectual*, ed. Ned Curthoys and Debjani Ganguly (Mel-bourne: Melbourne University Press, 2007): 241–262. New scholarly work on race is currently underway by Jayashree Kamble. For studies of history and desire in African American romance see Rita B. Dandridge,

Black Women's Activism: Reading African American Women's Historical Romances, African-American Literature and Culture, no. 5 (New York: Peter Lang, 2004); and Guy Mark Foster, "How Dare a Black Woman Make Love to a White Man! Black Women Romance Novelists and the Taboo of Interracial Desire," in *Empowerment Versus Oppression: Twenty First Century Views of Popular Romance Novels*, ed. Sally Goade (Newcastle: Cambridge Scholars, 2007), 103–128.

10. For narrative elements, see John G. Cawelti, *Adventure, Mystery, and Romance: Formula Stories as Art and Popular Culture* (Chicago: University of Chicago Press, 1976); and Pamela Regis, *A Natural History of the Romance Novel* (Philadelphia: University of Pennsylvania Press, 2003). For homoeroticism and class see Stephanie Burley, "What's a Nice Girl," and George Paizis, "Category Romance in the Era of Globalization: The Story of Harlequin," in *The Global Literary Field*, ed. Anna Guttman, Michel Hockx, and George Paizis (Newcastle upon Tyne: Cambridge Scholars, 2006): 126–151. Scholarship on cross-dressing and dominant/submissive plots includes major work by Lisa Fletcher, *Historical Romance Fiction*; and Sarah S.G. Frantz, "'Expressing' Herself: The Romance Novel and the Feminine Will to Power," in *Scorned Literature: Essays on the History and Criticism of Popular Mass-Produced Fiction in America*, ed. Lydia Cushman Schurman and Deidre Johnson (Westport, CT: Greenwood Press, 2002): 17–36.

11. Deborah Lutz, *The Dangerous Lover: Gothic Villains, Byronism, and the Nineteenth-Century Seduction Narrative* (Columbus: Ohio State University Press, 2006), 87.

12. See Lutz, *Dangerous Lover*; Jan Cohn, *Erotics of Property*; Sarah S.G. Frantz, "Darcy's Vampiric Descendants: Austen's Perfect Romance Hero and J.R. Ward's Black Dagger Brotherhood," *Persuasions On-line* 30, no. 1 (2009), http://www.jasna.org/persuasions/on-line/vol30no1/frantz.html; and Janice Radway, *Reading the Romance*.

13. Joanne Hollows, *Feminism, Femininity, and Popular Culture* (Manchester: Manchester University Press, 2000), 70.

14. *Ibid.*, 71.

15. Andreas Huyssen, *After the Great Divide: Modernism, Mass Culture, Postmodernism* (Bloomington: Indiana University Press, 1986), 45.

16. "What is Romantic Fiction," Romantic Novelists' Association, http://www.romanticnovelistsasso ciation.org/index.php/about/what_is_romantic_fiction.

17. Regis, *A Natural History*, 28.

18. *Ibid.*, 10.

19. "About the Romance Genre," Romance Writers of America, http://www.rwanational.org/cs/the_ romance_genre.

20. Lionel Trilling, "The Fate of Pleasure," in *The Moral Obligation to Be Intelligent: Selected Essays by Lionel Trilling*, ed. Leon Wieseltier (New York: Farrar, Straus and Giroux, 2000), 435.

21. Modleski, *Loving with a Vengeance*, 14.

22. Hollows, *Feminism, Femininity, and Popular Culture*, 70.

23. Modleski, *Loving with a Vengeance*, 14, 25, 25, 25, 25, 30.

24. *Ibid.*, 32, 75; Radway, *Reading the Romance*, 14.

25. Modleski, "My Life as a Romance Reader," *Paradoxa: Studies in World Literary Genres* 3, nos. 1–2 (1997): 17. This implicit agenda gives a polemical force to her work in *Loving with a Vengeance*, but it also leads her to dismiss, disdain, or dream of revising romance novels that do not fit her expectations (see her "My Life as a Romance Writer," and the citations of her correspondence in Mary Beth Tegan's essay, "Becoming Both Poet and Poem: Feminists Repossess the Romance," in *Empowerment Versus Oppression: Twenty First Century Views of Popular Romance Novels*, ed. Sally Goade (Newcastle: Cambridge Scholars, 2007), 244–278.

26. Dixon, *Romance Fiction*, 71–73. For Modleski's reflection on her own earlier work as an attempt at exorcism, see "My Life as a Romance Reader."

27. Modleski, *Loving with a Vengeance*, 52.

28. Mussell, "Where's Love Gone? Transformations in Romance Fiction and Scholarship," *Paradoxa* 3, nos. 1–2 (1997): 8.

29. Mussell, *Fantasy and Reconciliation*, 184.

30. Radway, *Reading the Romance*, 138. Emphasis added.

31. Modleski, *Loving with a Vengeance*, 31.

32. Radway, *Reading the Romance*, 48–49. "It is clear that the Smithton group cannot be thought of as a scientifically designed random sample," Radway notes quite explicitly near the start of her much-reprinted chapter on "The Readers and Their Romances," adding that "the conclusions drawn from the study, therefore, should be extrapolated only with great caution to apply to other romance readers" (48). Her warning has not, alas, been taken to heart.

33. Modleski, *Loving with a Vengeance*, 36.

34. Jayne Ann Krentz, ed., *Dangerous Men and Adventurous Women: Romance Writers on the Appeal of the Romance* (1992; rpt., New York: HarperPaperbacks, 1996).

35. Laura Kinsale, "The Androgynous Reader: Point of View in the Romance," in *Dangerous Men and Adventurous Women: Romance Writers on the Appeal of the Romance*, ed. Jayne Ann Krentz (1992; rpt., New York: HarperPaperbacks, 1996), 37–54.

36. Neal, *Romancing God*, 10.

37. Mussell, "Where's Love Gone?" 12. Much of this work focuses on the impact of romance reading on the sexual lives of readers. An early study by Coles and Shamp (conducted in 1978, published in 1984) reported that "older readers reported having sexual intercourse twice as much as did nonreaders and, indeed, more frequently than the national average for all women" ("Some Sexual," 206). In a follow-up study of college students from 2006, sociologist Huei-Hsia Wu reported that "female readers of romance novels self-reported greater sex drive, and greater number or orgasms required for sexual satisfaction than male readers and female non-readers. However, female readers had fewer sex partners, and were older when they first thought about sex and had their first sexual intercourse" ("Gender, Romance," 125). Whether these effects are empowering or oppressive, we will leave to our readers to decide.

38. Mussell, "Where's Love Gone?" 10.

39. Flesch, *From Australia*, 11.

40. Fletcher, *Historical Romance Fiction*, n. 1, p. 73.

41. Fletcher's book thus sets out "to interrogate the terms and discourses of heterosexual hegemony" (7) by reading romance novels, which she calls — after excluding all gay, lesbian, and bisexual romances from consideration —"some of our culture's most sexist and homophobic texts" (8).

42. See Lutz, *Dangerous Lover*, 18–20, and footnotes 19 and 21 on page 97.

43. Cawelti, *Adventure, Mystery, and Romance*, 10.

44. Roberts, *Aesthetics*, 151.

45. Mussell, "Where's Love Gone?" 10, 11, 12.

46. *Ibid.*, 12.

47. Anne K. Kaler and Rosemary E. Johnson-Kurek, ed., *Romantic Conventions* (Bowling Green, OH: Bowling Green State University Popular Press, 1999).

48. Anne K. Kaler, "Introduction: Conventions of the Romance Genre," in *Romantic Conventions*, ed. Anne K. Kaler and Rosemary E. Johnson-Kurek (Bowling Green, OH: Bowling Green State University Popular Press, 1999), 2.

49. Dawn Heinecken, "Changing Ideologies in Romance Fiction," in *Romantic Conventions*, ed. Anne K. Kaler and Rosemary E. Johnson-Kurek (Bowling Green, OH: Bowling Green State University Popular Press, 1999), 149–172.

50. For work on "romantic fiction," see Pearce and Stacey's *Romance Revisited*. For work on category romance, see George Paizis's "Category Romance in the Era of Globalization" and Catherine Belsey's subtly-theorized *Desire: Love Stories in Western Culture*, especially chapter 2, "Reading Love Stories," 21–41 (Oxford: Wiley-Blackwell, 1994), and the histories of Mills & Boon by Joseph McAleer and jay Dixon.

51. For doctoral dissertations, see Deborah Kaye Chappel, "American Romances: Narratives of Culture and Identity" (PhD diss., Duke University, 1992); Lynn Coddington, "Romance and Power: Writing Romance Novels as a Practice of Critical Literacy" (PhD diss., University of California, Berkeley, 1997); Frances Kay Hurley, "In the Words of Girls: The Reading of Adolescent Romance Fiction" (PhD diss., Harvard University, 1999); Amanda Marette Kinard, "Forbidden Pleasures: The Romance and Its Readers" (PhD diss., Vanderbilt University, 1999); Radhika Parameswaran, "Public Images, Private Pleasures: Romance Reading at the Intersection of Gender, Class, and National Identities in Urban India" (PhD diss., University of Iowa, 1998); Evelyn Angelina Uddin-Khan, "Gender, Ethnicity and the Romance Novel" (PhD diss., Columbia University, 1995); Eva Hemmungs Wirtén, "Global Infatuation: Explorations in Transnational Publishing and Texts: The Case of Harlequin Enterprises and Sweden" (PhD diss., Uppsala University, 1998); Beth Rapp Young, "But Are They Any Good? Women Readers, Formula Fiction, and the Sacralization of the Literary Canon" (PhD diss., University of Southern California, 1995). For non–U.S.-based publications, see from the United Kingdom, Capelle's "Harlequin Romances"; Peter Darbyshire's "Romancing the World: Harlequin Romances, the Capitalist Dream, and the Conquest of Europe and Asia," *Studies in Popular Culture* 23, no. 1 (2000): 1–10; from India, Puri's "Reading Romance Novels in Postcolonial India"; Parameswaran's "Western Romance Fiction" and "Reading Fictions of Romance"; from Australia, Teo's "The Romance of White Nations" and "Romancing the Raj"; and from Francophone Canada, Annik Houel's *Le roman d'amour et sa letrice: une si longue passion, l'example Harlequin* (Paris: L'Harmattan, 1997). For observations about French romance and romance in translation, see George Paizis' "Category Romances: Translation, Realism, and Myth," *Translator* 4, no. 1 (1988): 1–24. For articles in disparate anthologies, see Susan L. Blake, "What 'Race' Is the Sheik?: Rereading a Desert Romance," in *Doubled*

Plots: Romance and History, ed. Susan Strehle and Mary Paniccia Carden (Jackson: University Press of Mississippi, 2003): 67–85; Burley, "What's a Nice Girl," and Frantz, "'Expressing' Herself" and "'I've tried my entire life to be a good man': Suzanne Brockmann's Sam Starrett, Ideal Romance Hero," in *Women Constructing Men: Female Novelists and their Male Characters, 1750–2000*, ed. Sarah S.G. Frantz and Katharina Rennhak (Lanham, MD: Lexington, 2009), 227–247.

    52. Flesch, *From Australia*, 16.

    53. Regis, *A Natural History*, 14.

    54. *Ibid.*, 31.

    55. Sarah Wendell and Candy Tan, *Beyond Heaving Bosoms: The Smart Bitches' Guide to Romance Novels* (New York: Fireside, 2009).

    56. Mussell, "Where's Love Gone?" 12.

1

"Bertrice teaches you about history, and you don't even mind!": History and Revisionist Historiography in Bertrice Small's *The Kadin*

Hsu-Ming Teo

In 1998 the president of the Middle East Studies Association commented that "1978 was a very good year for landmark books on the Middle East; Edward Said's *Orientalism* also appeared that year. I wonder if there's been a better year since?"[1] Philip Khoury's remark was more apt than he could possibly have realized, for coeval with the publication of Said's *Orientalism* came the birth of a cultural phenomenon centering on the Middle East that would have horrified the erudite author of *Orientalism*—a well-read, multilingual scholar who was also an accomplished classical pianist, and who disdained the "low-brow" tastes of mass-market popular culture. In 1977, the year that Said began writing *Orientalism*, historical romance novelist Johanna Lindsey published her first novel, *Captive Bride*, part of which was loosely based on the plot of E.M. Hull's 1919 novel *The Sheik*. The year 1978 saw the publication of Julia Fitzgerald's *Royal Slave*, Bertrice Small's *The Kadin* and *Love Wild and Fair*, Christina Nicholson's *The Savage Sands*, Julia Herbert's *Prisoner of the Harem* and Janette Seymour's *Purity's Ecstasy*.

American popular culture was suddenly awash with aristocratic blonde or red-headed heroines being abducted by swarthy Barbary corsairs, stripped naked in slave markets and sold as concubines into the oppressive harems of Oriental potentates where they tasted the erotic delights of sex and the exotic indulgence of the senses. At the very moment when Said began denouncing Western understandings and representations of the Middle East as an imperialist attempt to fix the Orient as its inferior "Other," reserving his cannon-fire for the Western literary canon, railing against all Western authors, artists, and academics who had attempted to study or portray the Middle East in the last two centuries as "racist, [...] imperialist, and almost totally ethnocentric,"[2] a new subgenre of popular literature began perpetuating the very stereotypes of the Middle East that he so passionately decried. From 1976 to 2007, there were only two years in which no historical harem romance was produced.

If, as Alison Light, Cleo McNelly Kearns, Helen Hughes, and Diana Wallace have argued, women's historical fiction has been poorly regarded throughout the twentieth century, prevailing opinion about the late–twentieth-century mass-market historical romance novel — often derisively known as the "bodice ripper"— is that it is beneath contempt.[3] Despite its phenomenal sales from the 1970s onwards, the bodice ripper has warranted scant attention from academics. Carol Thurston's *The Romance Revolution* was the first work to take seriously the historical romance novel, but Thurston's work focused on the bodice ripper as a revolutionary form of women's fiction expressing and exploring female desire and sexuality.[4] More recently, Lisa Fletcher's *Historical Romance Fiction* examined bodice rippers in conjunction with popular historical romance fiction from Georgette Heyer's novels to A.S. Byatt's *Possession*, but Fletcher was interested in representations of heterosexuality and cross-dressing.[5] The issues of history and historiography are never properly explored in the historical romance novel because it is simply assumed that these novels are fantasies rather than earnest engagements of fiction — let alone literature — with history.

This chapter explores the uses of history and the challenge to historiography latent in a particular bodice ripper: Bertrice Small's *The Kadin*.[6] Among the nine Orientalist historical romances published in 1978, Bertrice Small's *The Kadin* stands out for its meticulous historical research into the reigns of the Ottoman sultans Bajazet II (1481–1512), Selim I (1512–20), and Suleiman I (the Magnificent, 1520–1566). *The Kadin* blends historical fact with invention to achieve a romance. The narrative serves as an example of a feminist revisionist historiography of the Ottoman empire (albeit one that is still essentially Orientalist) which places women's domestic, familial, romantic, and sexual experiences, actions, and relationships at the centre of historical narratives of power, statehood, and empire. As the final section of this chapter will demonstrate, such revisionist historiography was — and remains — of considerable interest to general readers, and not simply to historians.

In the mid–1970s a budding author of erotic historical romance novels, Bertrice Small, began work on a novel set in the late-fifteenth and early–sixteenth-century Ottoman empire. Small's interest in Ottoman history stemmed from the mid–1950s when she attended university with Mihri-jahn Ozdemir, a young Turkish woman whose grandmother had lived in the harem of the last Ottoman sultan, Mehmed VI (r.1918–22). When Mehmed was deposed by the Ataturk revolution in 1923, the Topkapi palace was seized by revolutionaries and the harem system dismantled. Mihri's grandmother was "sent home with a respectable dower and married well as young ladies released from the Imperial harem were considered excellent choices for a well-to-do man."[7] Small began to read Turkish history and she was particularly intrigued by "a simple sentence in some long forgotten history book" which briefly described the mother of the sultan Suleiman the Magnificent as "a Western European by birth, and in her old age was known as Hafise, the Wise One."[8] Armed with this bit of knowledge, Small began to research Ottoman history and harem life, utilizing two works in particular: N.M. Penzer's *The Harem* (1936) and Fanny Davis's *The Palace of Topkapi in Istanbul* (1970). The result was her bestselling novel, *The Kadin*, first published in 1978, translated into several languages, and still in print today.

The Kadin tells the story of Janet Leslie, the daughter of a Scottish earl who is sent by James IV of Scotland as an ambassador to a mythical duchy in Italy in order to secure better Mediterranean trade relations with Venice and the East. In the tried and true traditions of Orientalist romance, Janet is kidnapped by pirates and sold as a slave, "Cyra," to the Ottoman Sultan. However, she refuses to be a victim of her fate and, together with two other newcomers to the harem, vows to become the most powerful woman in the Ottoman empire. "If we must be slaves," Janet/Cyra declares, "let us be powerful ones" that "we may someday rule not only the harem but the sultan as well" (53–54). Trained in the harem of sultan Bajazet II, Janet rises to become the favorite *kadin*— a favorite concubine who has born the sultan a son — and true love of the sultan Selim I, with whom she shares a romantic, companionate relationship despite the claims of his other concubines. Upon his death and the accession of her son Suleiman the Magnificent to the throne, she becomes the *valide sultan* "Hafise" — the queen mother who is the most powerful woman throughout the Ottoman empire. However, her unrivaled rule of the harem and, consequently, her influence over Ottoman imperial politics begins to be challenged by Suleiman's new favorite concubine: a Russian slave girl, Roxelana, who is renamed Khurrem. Out of love for her son Suleiman, Janet decides to bow out of Ottoman life after Khurrem attempts to poison her. However, before she stages her own death and returns to Scotland, she reminds her son Suleiman of the great debt that he owes to her and her sister-*kadins*:

> From the moment you were born, I have guided your destiny. Others have helped me. Without Firousi, Zuleika, and Sarina, would your childhood have been safe? They, too, bore your father sons. [...] Yet always our efforts were for you, and you alone. [...] When the Persian campaign was won, I was responsible for seeing that you were sent to Magnesia to learn how to govern. Who warned you not to follow your father into Syria and Egypt? I did! When my beloved Selim died, who held Constantinople in check until you had safely arrived? I did! Without my help you would have faltered a thousand times. [...] I solved your problems [357–358].

In other words, this Scottish-born harem concubine has ushered in the greatest age the Ottomans have known under the reign of Suleiman the Magnificent; an age when the empire was at its zenith as he built on Selim's conquests, and when the classical culture and architecture of the Ottomans flourished under the patronage of the court.

In the final, rather disjointed section of this novel, Janet establishes her own landed property back in Scotland, is raped by a neighboring aristocrat who had an eye on her when she was a young girl, and ends up taking him as her lover although she refuses to give up her independence to marry him. She is also raped by King James V of Scotland when he stays overnight at her castle. In return for sexual services rendered, the king makes her Scottish son an earl. Janet's brother, son, and many other men are eventually killed fighting for the king of Scotland against England, and so instead of the quiet, peaceful old age she had imagined, she spends her last days raising up her brother's and son's offspring to continue their Scottish dynasty. Janet thus generates two dynasties: the imperial Turkish dynasty through Suleiman the Magnificent, and a Scottish aristocratic dynasty whose exploits are recounted in Small's other novels. *The Kadin* ends with her grandson visiting Janet's grave: "In the years to come, those who read her epitaph, 'Born a Scot, she died a Scot,' would think her a poor, sad, spinster. They could never even begin to imagine those fantastic years between her birth and her death" (441).

Well, what are we to make of all this? First, we need to sort out the known historical facts from fiction or speculation. Three sultans are portrayed in *The Kadin*: Bajazet II, Selim I, and Suleiman I. Of the three, Bajazet is portrayed fairly accurately, but the known characters of Selim and Suleiman are deliberately distorted to fit the conventions of romance fiction. The following table sets out the historical facts as they are understood today, and the fictional elements in *The Kadin*.

Fact	Fiction
Hafsa Sultan (Hafise in the novel) was one of Selim's many concubines and the mother of Suleiman the Magnificent. We don't know whether she was Selim's favorite *kadin*.	Scottish Janet Leslie becomes Cyra/Hafise, Selim's favorite *kadin* and the mother of Suleiman.
Hafsa, like Selim's other concubines, was only permitted to bear one son, thus following the Ottoman reproductive principle of one son per mother.	Selim's four principal concubines — his *kadins* — bear him many sons.
Complying with Ottoman tradition, Hafsa was sent away from court with Suleiman when he came of age (i.e., fourteen years old).	Selim keeps Janet/Cyra/Hafise at court because he has a romantic, companionate relationship with her and she is his trusted adviser.
Selim I seizes Ottoman throne, deposing own father Bajazet II and possibly poisoning him, then killing his two brothers Ahmed and Korkut in civil war over the succession.	Bajazet II renounces his fat, dissolute, and pedophilic elder son Ahmed in favor of Selim. Korkut commits suicide because he is a scholar and doesn't want to be a focus of rebellion against Selim.
Selim comes to be known as "Selim the Grim" or *Yavuz* — "Selim the Terrible."	Selim is initially called "Selim the Just" by his people. Stomach cancer causes him to become "grim" later in life.
Selim probably murdered all his sons except Suleiman to give Suleiman clear accession to the throne.	Suleiman's brothers and half-brothers conveniently die in battle or by disease and are mourned by Selim.
Suleiman the Magnificent was a warrior sultan who, building on Selim's conquests, expanded the Ottoman empire and ushered in its greatest age. He was known by his people as "Suleiman the Just" or "Suleiman the Lawgiver" because he rectified many of his father's unjust laws.	Suleiman is a weak, easily influenced, and uxorious man who is ruled by his mother, then his favorite concubines, and has to be almost bullied into going to war.
Suleiman became monogamous and broke important Ottoman traditions for Khurrem. He: • married off other concubines in the harem; • allowed Khurrem to bear more than one child; • manumitted Khurrem; • and married Khurrem in a wedding marked with lavish public celebrations.	Suleiman's furtive, secret marriage to Khurrem is at her instigation. Janet causes Suleiman to divorce Khurrem. It is Selim who enjoys a companionate relationship with Janet/Cyra/Hafise, and Selim's concubines who are allowed to bear more than one son.
In 1651 Turhan, the favorite concubine of Sultan Ibrahim (r.1640–48), successfully poisoned his mother, the *valide sultan*, Kösem Mahpeyker.	In *The Kadin*, a scheming, ambitious and vengeful Khurrem tries to poison Suleiman's mother, Janet/Hafise.

The main point is that in order to fashion Selim the Terrible into an acceptable (if not ideal) romantic mate for Hafsa Sultan — the concubine upon whom Janet Leslie is based — aspects of Bajazet's and Suleiman's character and rule are attributed to Selim, while the deaths of all his sons apart from Suleiman are explained away through an improbable series of accidents and deadly disease. The unique conjugal, companionate relationship that actually existed between the historical Suleiman and Khurrem Sultan is attributed instead to Selim and Hafsa Sultan in order to enhance the romantic aspects of their story.

The Kadin also contains a number of inaccuracies based on the flaws of its historical sources, particularly N.M. Penzer's *The Harem*. The late sixteenth and seventeenth-century structure of the imperial harem and the power struggles of the harem between *valide sultan* (the queen mother) and *haseki* (favorite concubine) during the "sultanate of women" — a period when women were prominent in Ottoman politics — are anachronistically transposed to the late fifteenth- and early–sixteenth-century Ottoman harem. This confusion over the complexity of changing harem politics over the centuries is entirely understandable, for it was not until Leslie Peirce's *The Imperial Harem* was published in 1993 that the historical nature of the harem and Ottoman reproductive politics were closely analyzed in the English language.[9]

In obvious ways, then, *The Kadin* represents what many historians have always found objectionable in historical fiction: primarily, the foregrounding of historical personages over processes, and the bending of historical fact to suit romantic fantasy. Nevertheless, *The Kadin* raises significant questions about traditional western historiography. Women's historical novels may often play fast and loose with the known facts of history — the primary felony that outrages historians, linked to the slightly lesser of misdemeanors of being romantic and escapist. However, they present an unsettling view of the past which forces the reader to think about past gender and social orders which limited women's lives and condemned them to silence, preventing their stories from appearing in the historical record. According to Diana Wallace, the very excesses of historical fancy — the highlighting of sentiment and the concerns of the domestic sphere with its different rhythms and cycles that contrast with the received chronology of political history — "all work to disturb accepted accounts of 'history' and suggest that what it offers as 'truth' is in fact equally fictional, and damaging to women."[10] It is in this light that Bertrice Small's *The Kadin* challenges existing historiographies.

First, *The Kadin* presents an early, mid–1970s challenge to traditional Turkish understandings of the Ottoman imperial harem that was not explored by women historians until ten to fifteen years after the novel was first published. As mentioned before, it was not until the early 1990s that Leslie Peirce's pioneering work on women in the imperial harem transformed earlier understandings of the "sultanate of women" and the perceived connection of this period to imperial decline in the post–Suleiman period. Peirce notes that "modern historical accounts of this period have tended to represent the influence of the harem as an illegitimate usurpation of power that resulted from a weakening of the moral fiber and institutional integrity of Ottoman society and that in turn contributed to problems plaguing the empire toward the end of the sixteenth century."[11] By contrast, Peirce argues, far from being illegitimate, royal women's sources of power were based, like the men of the dynasty's, on family relationships and dynamics — something that was already recognized and carefully explored in *The Kadin*. Moreover, Peirce's *The Imperial Harem* challenged the idea that "gender segregation, so widely accepted as one of the hallmarks of traditional Islamic society, precluded women from playing anything more than a subordinate role within the household," demonstrating instead the myriad ways in which various women in the harem acquired or exerted power.[12] These ideas are already evident in *The Kadin* in 1978 even though, as mentioned above, the structure and dynamics of harem politics are anachronistic in the novel.

The Kadin also presents a challenge to European historical understanding of the harem as a place of bored and oppressed women, degraded sexual slavery, vicious jealousy, and pointless lives.[13] In *The Kadin*, the imperial harem is a complex, hierarchical place of ritual and relationship where women have agency and can accrue power. The novel demonstrates that the crucial relationship in the harem is not simply between sultan and slave, but that a woman's power is forged through her relationships with family, friends, associates, and those like the black eunuchs or the Jewish kiras — agents of the *valide sultan*— who mediate between the inner sanctum of the harem and the world outside. Janet has power in the novel because she is Selim's favorite, but also because she is Suleiman's mother and she enjoys the advantages of seniority in the harem after Selim's death. Her exercise of power is demonstrated through her firm rule over Selim's harem, and also in the way she builds factional power with other senior harem women and the Chief Black Eunuch. Yet another basis of power is her wealth, accumulated through her position as *haseki*— favorite concubine — as well as *valide sultan*. Historically, the wealth of high-ranking Ottoman women far outstripped that of women in Europe during the early modern period, and in this novel Janet's wealth accrued through her career in the harem later becomes the basis for building landed power in Scotland. *The Kadin* is therefore a novel which demonstrates women's agency rather than simply focusing on women's oppression, as Mary Ritter Beard had accused first-wave feminists of doing, and which radical feminists were still doing in their accounts of "victim" history in the 1970s.[14]

Small's novel is thus also part of the feminist challenge to extant historiographical practices up to the 1970s. Mary Spongberg has argued that "at the heart of feminist criticism of masculinist historiography was concern about its overt focus on the public sphere."[15] Feminist historians presented a revisionist challenge to such historiographical practice by turning the focus of research onto the cultural history of women and the domestic sphere from the late 1970s onwards. This focus on "women's private experience of marriage, religion, romantic friendships and family life" was done in order to "delineate the distinctive nature of women's rituals, values and beliefs."[16] It was an insistence that "the domestic realm and other women's spaces were just as important historically as the public realms of men."[17] In particular, Carroll Smith-Rosenberg's article "The Female World of Love and Ritual" (1975) generated what Spongberg has called a "paradigm shift in women's history."[18] Smith-Rosenberg re-articulated historical relationships between women to argue for the possibilities of companionship, support, and deep and intimate love between women whose lives were largely confined to the domestic sphere in the nineteenth century. In *The Kadin*, love is indeed possible in the harem: not merely between sultan and slave, but among women who support and are loyal to each other. This is a break with the British tradition of romance novels whereby the pre–1970s bifurcation of women into the pure and passive heroine, and the sexually aggressive "Other Woman" often precluded depictions of strong female friendship or sisterly solidarity.[19] Instead, in *The Kadin* the bonds of sisterhood — especially among Janet, Firousi, and Zuleika — are the basis of their power and advancement in the harem. That such an interpretation should have come from an American novelist is unsurprising, for as Spongberg commented, "The idea that the private sphere nurtured a sense of sisterhood" was particularly marked in American women's history: "in other countries the emphasis on women's culture was less pronounced," particularly in Britain where "the emphasis on class within women's history meant that 'the notion of universal sisterhood' was only rarely broached."[20]

By focusing on the "domestic sphere" of the harem, *The Kadin* teases out how Ottoman imperial relationships and dynastic ambitions were based on familial as well as sexual relationships. The novel shows that these relationships form an important basis of the sultans' and princes' power — something which Peirce affirmed in her 1993 work. The public sphere is thus intimately imbricated with the world of the harem and men's relationships with women. This is demonstrated in Janet's claims that she and other harem women have helped Suleiman attain the throne even though they do not appear in the historical record. Indeed, the closing lines of *The Kadin*— the simple epitaph on Janet Leslie's tomb that reads, "Born a Scot, she died a Scot" which hides "those fantastic years between her birth and her death"— emphasize how many women's lives have been omitted from the historical record or glossed over as insignificant, without posterity realizing the enormous impact these women must have had on their worlds through their relationships. The epitaph, moreover, obscures the transnational nature of Janet Leslie's life and identity, and this presents the final revisionist challenge that *The Kadin* posed to historiography of the 1970s.

The vast body of feminist historical work that appeared from the mid–1980s onwards in what has become known as the "New Imperial" history analyzing the dynamics of gender, race, and culture in European imperialism has led to substantial biographies on European and colonial women's lives. These biographical works have highlighted the inadequacy of the nation-state as a framework for understanding many people's lives, especially in the context of the international mobility that followed European colonial expansion. As the editors of *Transnational Lives* argue:

> Lives elude national boundaries; yet biography, the telling of life stories, has often been pressed into the service of nation, downplaying its fleeting acknowledgements of lives lived in motion. Dictionaries of national biography, in particular, reify and defend national boundaries by constructing individual significance and achievement within them. Overwhelmingly they have documented the lives of elite men who served their countries in war, politics, business, science or the arts. Although in recent years such projects have sought to rectify previous exclusions of race and sex [...] it remains the case that many individuals whose lives slipped between national borders have been lost to view.[21]

The Kadin demonstrates that the nation is an inadequate prism through which to understand women's lives and loyalties. Janet Leslie is undoubtedly a pawn in patriarchal political alliances in Europe and the Ottoman empire even though she discovers ways of overcoming her circumstances. The intertwining of domestic and public spheres, the life of the emotions and the politics of the wider world, are revealed in Janet's loyalty and forty-year service to the Ottoman empire arising not only from a strong sense of survival, but also her love for Selim and her son Suleiman, and her friendship and loyalty towards others in the harem. Her return to Scotland, however, shows that it is not the nation which determines her allegiance, but her ambitions for her family. To understand this character primarily as a Scots woman or thoroughly Turkish concubine (as many in the novel say she has become) is to misinterpret who she is, for the nation or empire is always subordinate to the claims of family and dynasty. Bertrice Small was therefore remarkable in penning this novel which encompassed such a varied transnational, cross-cultural life at a time when women historians were still inserting women into a national framework of historiography, and cultural historians were busy constructing an edifice of national identity.

All this is interesting to historians, of course, but how much do ordinary readers care about the historical content of these novels? How do readers understand "history" and the romance novel? What do they look for in these novels? The final section of this chapter looks at readers' responses to *The Kadin* as a historical romance novel. The development and growth of the internet has seen significant changes to the ways in which readers interact. Innumerable niche websites have mushroomed catering to the specific hobbies and interests of web users, including romance reader websites and blogs dedicated to Orientalist romance novels.[22] These sites have permitted romance readers to become far more assertive in voicing their likes and dislikes, and to pass on tips about good reads, thus creating online communities of readers who share an interest in Orientalist romance novels. What these websites demonstrate, however, is the utter impossibility, even futility, of talking about the generic "romance reader" because there isn't one. These readers vary in every conceivable way, and the only thing that is certain is that a novel that appeals to some groups will not appeal to others.

For my purposes here, I have found it illuminating to read the Amazon.com reader reviews of *The Kadin*. The Amazon.com site permits readers to post their own views on particular books so that, unlike many of the blogs where the discussion is more general — about the subgenre as a whole rather than about a specific novel — readers posting on the Amazon.com website are responding to a particular novel. This is helpful in ascertaining precisely what readers liked or disliked about a novel. Furthermore, blog discussions are often limited by time — the topic generates discussion only for a few weeks at most — before readers move on to something else more current. The Amazon.com site, on the other hand, shows all reviews from the first posting, hence some novels have discussions that span over a decade.

There are obviously limitations to this approach. First, authors have been accused of accessing the Amazon.com website to post positive reviews of their own novels or getting friends to do so in order to boost sales. On reading some of the excoriating (and sometimes excruciatingly funny) reviews given by readers, however, it is clear that this is not a huge problem where this subgenre is concerned. Second, the sample is self-selective and not representative of anything but romance readers — and almost overwhelmingly American romance readers at that — who feel strongly enough about a particular novel or about other people's reviews, and who are sufficiently motivated to post their responses on the Amazon.com site. In this respect, it is interesting that there are some novels — and *The Kadin* is one of them — that generate a lot more reader reviews than others, so much so that the discussion dates back to a decade ago when reader reviews first began appearing on the Amazon.com site around 1997. When this happens, these books appear to be considered important, landmark books even if they elicit negative reviews. Finally, the reviews only tell us what a small, self-selected group of readers think about the novel in recent years, not what the contemporary reception of a novel would have been when it was published in the 1970s and 1980s. With these limitations in mind, then, let us turn to what readers have made of *The Kadin*. I have used whatever names have been provided on the Amazon.com site; some of them are real names, some are monikers.

Of all the Orientalist historical romances available on the Amazon.com website, the three novels that generated the most heat and discussion among readers are Johanna Lindsey's *Captive Bride* (79 reviews as of July 2008), Bertrice Small's *The Kadin* (63 reviews) and Small's *Love Slave* (53 reviews).[23] Most other popular novels in this genre generate between a half-dozen to two dozen reviews. *The Kadin* was highly praised by readers for its historical content, although this was by no means unanimous. Most readers commented that the book was well-researched and gave them a fascinating insight into the Ottoman empire — something of which they had known very little when they first began reading the novel. All readers took for granted the accuracy of the historical information being offered in the novel. This is unsurprising because compared to other harem historical romances, Small's work is anchored in actual historical personages or events, meticulously detailed with extensive "costume" description and allusions to obscure, exotic customs and historical facts, thus creating the "reality effect" of a different historical and cultural world that Helen Hughes has referred to in her work on historical fiction.[24] An early 1997 review simply stated that "this book paints a very different picture of Sultan Selim I, usually called the Grim. It shows his love for his wives and children, his sense of fairness of the law, and the truth of his father's abdication of the throne. [...] A must read for anybody interested in Turkish history." Michelle Slaughter of Orlando agreed over a decade later that *The Kadin* provided "a fascinating glimpse into what the private lives and motivations of Selim I and Suleiman the Great might have been." Reading the novel prompted greater curiosity and interest in the Ottomans on the part of some readers. Terra Chadwick of Panama wrote, "The Kadin explained so much about the Sultan [*sic*] way of life, not known today. So much so, that I re-read certain parts of the novel today, and looked up on the internet all that I could find on Sultan Selim." Erika Overton of Poughkeepsie agreed that "it made me extremely interested in Turkish history and harem life in that time period." One reader who was not particularly enthused by history conceded that "Bertrice teaches you about history, and you don't even mind!"

Not all readers, however, were enamored with the historical aspects of the novel because they felt that it got in the way of a good romance novel. Hanna Bagai was disappointed that "it focused more on politics of Ottoman Empire, rather than on love or romance," and N. Pandit agreed that "the beginning was great [...] But I don't like politics at all. Just give me a good steamy novel while my husband is out of town. This book made me think about it and the characters so much when it was done that I had to remind myself that it was just a story. Gave me a heart-ache." A number of readers mentioned the emotional pain they felt reading this particular novel, much of it centering on the fact that Janet/Cyra has to deal with the polygamous nature of Ottoman culture. S. Fischel, for example, wrote, "If I had known this book centered around the theme of polygamy, I would never have started it. Having started it, I could not put it down however distasteful the theme was to me. A testament to what a great writer Small is. There is a tender and erotic beginning between Janet and the Sheik [*sic*], but it's all pain and heartbreak from there on. I could not finish the book, not because it was dull, but because it was too painful to continue it." Another anonymous reviewer warned readers, "I cannot really recommend this book unless you can stand the pain of the story. Some may see it as one woman's triumph over whatever life threw at her, but it was more than I could handle." The reviewer conceded that "Beatrice [*sic*] Small is a great writer and her sense of history is fantastic but I am a romance novel reader not a history buff." Thus in its achievement of historical verisimilitude, the novel failed its primary function as an escapist, feel-good romance novel, leaving these readers feeling pain and depression instead.

The novel covers most of the eight narrative events that Pamela Regis has identified as being essential to the definition of a romance novel, but the fact that both Selim and Janet have more than one sexual partner (although not more than one "true love") and the novel does not conclude with the betrothal of the couple and the union of the two raises questions about the status of *The Kadin* as a romance novel.[25] Certainly, readers heatedly discuss the acceptability of the polygamous plot and question the categorization of *The Kadin* as a romance novel. Many express disappointment that Janet/Cyra had to share Selim, not only with the other three *kadins*, but with the entire harem once he became sultan. For some readers this killed the romance even though "from a historical perspective it was very enlightening and interesting." An anonymous reviewer complained, "I'm sorry, but I just can't get past the idea of four women sharing one man — and then actually liking each other, too! Yes, I have a Western bias and I'm not ashamed to admit it. Slave auctions, spouse splitting, isolation, harem intrigue [...] Color me clueless, but how romantic is any of that? A 13-year-old girl sold naked on a slave auction block may have been in vogue for those times, but I think it should thoroughly repulse the modern reader." Interestingly enough, one reader acknowledged that the expectations of genre played a part in determining her response: "Had I set my expectations for a history lesson, my review may have been different." Generally, those who could accept the polygamous storyline and still view the relationship between Janet/Cyra and Selim as romantic excused it because it happened "in other cultures and other time periods." Similarly, Orientalist discourse shaped readers' acceptance of such practices, as in the following comment: "Wow. The historical detail in this novel was excellent, rivaled only by the love story between Cyra and Selim. For those who point out that they can't imagine sharing one man, please open your minds! This happened regularly during that time period, and it still goes on today in the Middle East." Thus for every reader who felt that *The Kadin* was not a romance novel, there were as many who claimed, "This is the greatest love story I have ever read," "This book is my first experience with romance novels, and I can say that I love it!" and "What makes this book a masterpiece is that it deviates from the typical romance novel where they live happily ever after." Small is nothing if not a polarizing author, even though there is unanimous agreement on her mastery of the historical novel.

Bertrice Small's *The Kadin* was among the first novels published in the mid– to late–1970s which laid the foundations for the development of the Orientalist historical romance novel. The events of September 11, 2001, made no dent on the steady output of this subgenre of historical romance, as the number of novels published in the years following the Al Qaeda attack on the United States show.[26] It appears that readers — especially American readers — *want* to know more about Middle Eastern cultures and history, and the harem historicals are an easy, enjoyable, and accessible way of learning about these things within an environment which is recognizably structured according to the conventions of Western Orientalist literature and romance novels. The importance of a well-researched historical background to the Oriental romance is demonstrated by the popularity of Bertrice Small's novels despite the strong reactions provoked among some readers. That the subgenre of harem historical novels are often "Orientalist" in Edward Said's pejorative redefinition of the term is undoubtedly true. The reiteration of Orientalist "facts" is certainly problematic and fails to add to a greater understanding of contemporary Middle Eastern politics. In the novels, the East is often depicted as sensual, violent, barbaric, despotic, debauched, and patriarchal to the point of misogyny. But then again, so was the historical West according to these novels, where the greatest villains are often not Muslims or Arabs or Ottomans but other European men. "History" was like that, as so many readers' reviews make clear. These readers have an instinctively progressive sense of their own history whereby the primitivisms of the past have evolved to the enlightened present of Western modernity, whereas the Middle East still seems to be snared in the Middle Ages—yet another Orientalist perception. But surely it is no small thing that readers of mass-market popular fiction continue to be interested in other cultures and other times in an age of Islamist terrorism and a global retreat from multiculturalism; that readers acknowledge their own history to be as "Orientalist" as the Middle East; and that the novels continue to affirm the possibilities of communication and relationship with the Oriental Other. In writing a novel that anticipated these needs, challenged existing historiographical assumptions of the 1970s, and humanized the Ottoman harem and its inhabitants, Small has earned her own special place in the history of the Orientalist historical romance novel.

NOTES

1. Philip S. Khoury, "Lessons from the Eastern Shore," *MESA Bulletin* 33, no. 1 (Summer 1999): 5.
2. Edward W. Said, *Orientalism* (New York: Pantheon, 1978), 204.
3. Alison Light, "'Young Bess': Historical Novels and Growing Up," *Feminist Review* 33 (Autumn 1989): 57–71; Cleo McNelly Kearns, "Dubious Pleasures: Dorothy Dunnett and the Historical Novel," *Critical Quarterly* 32, no. 1 (1990): 36–48; Helen Hughes, *The Historical Romance* (London and New York: Routledge, 1993); Diana Wallace, *The Woman's Historical Novel: British Women Writers, 1900–2000* (Houndsmill, Basingstoke: Palgrave Macmillan, 2005).
4. Carol Thurston, *The Romance Revolution: Erotic Novels for Women and the Quest for a New Sexual Identity* (Urbana: University of Illinois Press, 1987).
5. Lisa Fletcher, *Historical Romance Fiction: Heterosexuality and Performativity* (Aldershot: Ashgate, 2008).
6. Bertrice Small, *The Kadin* (New York: Avon, 1978). Further references will be included parenthetically.
7. Personal correspondence with Bertrice Small, June 22, 2008.
8. *Ibid.*
9. Leslie P. Peirce, *The Imperial Harem: Women and Sovereignty in the Ottoman Empire* (New York: Oxford University Press, 1993). There were earlier works published on women in the Ottoman empire, such as Fanny Davis's *The Ottoman Lady: A Social History from 1718 to 1918* (Westport, CT: Greenwood Press, 1986).
10. Wallace, *Woman's Historical Novel*, 17.
11. Peirce, *The Imperial Harem*, viii.
12. *Ibid.,* ix.
13. For discussions of western perceptions of the harem, see Ruth Bernard Yeazell, *Harems of the Mind: Passages of Western Art and Literature* (New Haven: Yale University Press, 2000).
14. See Mary Spongberg's discussion of Mary Ritter Beard's accusation and "victim" history in *Writing Women's History Since the Renaissance* (Houndsmill, Basingstoke: Palgrave Macmillan, 2002), 131 and 190–191.
15. *Ibid.,* 187.
16. *Ibid.,* 195.
17. *Ibid.,* 195.
18. Carroll Smith-Rosenberg, "The Female World of Love and Ritual: Relations Between Women in Nineteenth-Century America," *Signs* 1 (Autumn, 1975): 1–29; Spongberg, 197.
19. See Thurston's *Romance Revolution*, 36.
20. Spongberg, *Writing Women's History*, 199.
21. Desley Deacon, Penny Russell, and Angela Woollacott, introduction to *Transnational Lives: Biographies of Global Modernity, 1700–Present*, ed. Desley Deacon, Penny Russell, and Angela Woollacott (Houndsmill, Basingstoke: Palgrave Macmillan, 2010), 2.
22. See Sheikhs and Desert Love, http://sheikhs-and-desert-love.com; "Historical Romance Authors of Sheiks and the Exotic," Romance Reader at Heart: Your Romance Novel Resource ... From A to Z, http://romancereaderatheart.com/sheik/Authors.html; Romancing the Desert—Sheikh Books, http://romancing-the-desert—-sheikh-books.blogspot.com; and Shabby Sheikh: Romance Novels & Oriental Others, http://shabbysheikh.blogspot.com.

23. For reviews of *The Kadin*, see http://www.amazon.com/Kadin-Bertrice-Small/dp/0727817434/ref= sr_1_1?ie=UTF8&s=books&qid=1213856041&sr=1-1.

24. Hughes, *The Historical Romance*, 18–20.

25. Pamela Regis, *A Natural History of the Romance Novel* (Philadelphia: University of Pennsylvania Press, 2003), 30.

26. See the publication dates on the "Sheikhs and Desert Love" website, http://sheikhs-and-desert-love.com.

2

How to Read a Romance Novel
(and Fall in Love with Popular Romance)

Eric Murphy Selinger

They pack three shelves in my Chicago office. *Invitation to Poetry. The Art of Poetry. Reading Poetry. Sound and Sense.* Some strike a magisterial note: *Poems, Poets, Poetry,* for example, which hitches the stellar close-reading talents of Helen Vendler to the wagon of an undergraduate textbook.[1] Others buddy up to the audience, tugging at your sleeve: "What if I told you there was *all this stuff,* building up for thousands of years but readily available, that could truly make your life better?" asks Jack Timpane's *It Could Be Verse.* "Wouldn't you be curious? Just a little?"[2] Whether aimed at students or general readers, these volumes concur that poetry is a specialized discourse that demands a specialized, genre-specific approach. Whether your goal is to write critical essays that are attentive to "the *literariness* of the work," to discover that "you have a soul, and that other people do, too," or to have an "ecstatic response" to the "sometimes challenging devices and difficulties" that give the art its "aura of sacred practice," evidently it takes a how-to guide to read a poem.[3] Or, at least, to read one *properly.*

Is there a *proper* way to read a romance novel? When I took up the genre a decade ago, reading it strictly for pleasure, the question never crossed my mind. Had anyone asked, I would have joked that I was far more interested in reading such books *im*properly, precisely as an escape from the duty, propriety, and intellectual discipline of my life as an English professor. "Responsibility to pay attention and to appreciate makes us too anxious for pleasure, too bored for response," Pauline Kael observes in "Trash, Art, and the Movies," an essay that I first read, with a shock of self-recognition, as I set my sights on tenure:

> Far from supervision and official culture, in the darkness of the movies where nothing is asked of us and we are left alone, the liberation from duty and constraint allows us to develop our own aesthetic responses. Unsupervised enjoyment is probably not the only kind there is but it may feel like the only kind. Irresponsibility is part of the pleasure of all art; it is the part the schools cannot recognize.[4]

Like the young film critic — like my adolescent self, first falling in love with poetry — I craved the freedom to engage with a work of art impishly, glibly, however it happened, with nary a grade or a publication in sight. The more that poetry became my profession, the more I depended on my secret life as a romance reader for the opportunity to return, night after night, to some duty-free zone of the imagination, a place where books didn't have to hold up to close reading, let alone blossom to meet it.

Although I did not know it at the time, this reluctance to pay close, academic attention to popular romance novels placed me squarely in the mainstream of academic work on the genre. From Janice Radway's foundational decision to "give up [her] obsession with textual features and narrative details" and focus instead on "the significance of the *act of romance reading*" to Australian critic Glen Thomas's recent claim that "textual analysis of romance fiction" is a "dead end," scholars have routinely set aside the intensive study of individual romance novels in favor of extensive, even panoramic inquiries into the genre.[5] Even the romance authors gathered in *Dangerous Men and Adventurous Women* (1992), the landmark anthology of defenses of the genre, seem loath to ask for text-specific, aesthetically-focused attention. Kathleen Gilles Seidel may note, with justified annoyance, that scholars "seem unable to distinguish one book from another," but the central demand of her essay, announced in its title, is "Judge Me by the Joy I Bring," not "judge me by my mastery of language, dazzle of imagination, elegance of structure, deftness of allusion, strategic use of symbol, image, and ambiguity, fit between form and theme," and comparable criteria.[6]

Why are both scholars and authors of romance so wary of close reading? In the opening pages of *The Romance Fiction of Mills & Boon, 1909–1990s*, British scholar jay Dixon gives a revealing answer. Romance novels, her argument begins, are "straightforward stories," not "post-modern game-playing," but even these frankest of narratives "have to be read in a certain way in order for the reader to fully understand them."[7] This "way" bears little resemblance to the subtle, playful reading strategies that we may have acquired in order to understand poetry or literary fiction, postmodern or otherwise. Indeed, to read a romance properly, according to Dixon, means to read it quite *improperly*, at least by classroom standards: "The analytical part of the brain has to be switched off," she insists, so that we can "feel every emotion, see every setting, burn at every injustice, fall in love with the hero and become the heroine."[8] Rebutting a critic who suggests that "romance authors play games with their readers," and who justifies that claim by spotting a pattern of diction that has been deftly threaded from scene to scene across a Silhouette novel, Dixon insists that romance writing is "instinctive," not deliberate, and that such attention to textual details is fundamentally misguided.[9] "To enter the world of the romance," she insists, "the method of analyzing literature which is taught in schools and higher education must be abandoned."[10]

Dixon's rhetoric may seem hyperbolic, not least in its echo of the Gospel of Matthew ("unless you turn and become like children, you will never enter the kingdom of heaven"[11]). Her contrast between emotional and analytic approaches to literature, however, reminds us that the "method of reading which is [now] taught in schools" was developed, in no small part, as a way to resist and replace other, less rigorous ways of reading.[12] Consider, for example, the influential arguments of Q. D. Leavis. In *Fiction and the Reading Public* (1932), Leavis laments that most readers are willing, even eager, to lose themselves in novels where "sympathetic characters of a convincing verisimilitude touch off the warmer emotional responses."[13] To reach such readers, authors need only deploy "the key words of the emotional vocabulary which provoke the vague warm surges of feeling associated with religion and religion substitutes —*e.g.*, life, death, love, good, evil, sin, home, mother," and so on, and the audience will respond with "dangerous ease," willing to be manipulated in return for the temporary illusion of living an emotionally extravagant and satisfying life.[14] Only an "education specifically directed against such appeals" to stock responses and emotional identification, she warns, can shake the next generation of readers out of their torpor: no doubt something like the training in close reading espoused in her husband F. R. Leavis's *Practical Criticism: A Study in Judgment*, published the year before.[15]

Textbooks and teachers rose to the challenge. In British and American classrooms, close reading was soon preached as an essential element in "the training of taste."[16] Within a given genre, students were taught to distinguish "bad poetry and good" and "good poetry and great" (thus the two final chapters in Laurence Perrine's *Sound and Sense*[17]); more broadly, as John Guillory reminds us, students were taught to value literary language and the intellect needed to read it over the language and sensibility promoted within mass culture.[18] The texts and reading strategies to be avoided, Guillory notes, were often explicitly feminized.[19] When Cleanth Brooks, in *The Well-Wrought Urn*, wants to epitomize "desperately bad" literary taste, for example, he speaks of "the young lady who confesses to raptures over her confessions magazine," no doubt feeling every emotion, burning at every injustice, and so on, precisely as Dixon advises romance be read.[20] Far more than other forms of genre fiction — mysteries, spy thrillers, Westerns, science fiction — popular romance was then, and still remains, associated both with pre–New Critical reading strategies (emotionally sympathetic, even enraptured) and with what Andreas Huyssen famously described as "Mass Culture as Woman: Modernism's Other."[21] No wonder Dixon winces at the thought of scholars applying "the method of analyzing literature which is taught in schools and higher education" to popular romance fiction.[22] That "method" was designed, in no small part, to debunk, disarm, and dismiss precisely such texts, breaking the spell of sentiment to let us *think* again.

Is that, however, the only spell that a romance novel can cast? Must every romance novel "engage the emotion, not the intellect," as Dixon asserts, as though this distinction, this separation, were clear-cut and inevitable?[23] In *An Aesthetics of Junk Fiction*, Thomas J. Roberts argues that the experienced reader of any genre fiction reads, not just individual novels, but "the interplay among the texts": an "intensely self-conscious, self-referential, and aggressively literary" dialogue with earlier texts in the genre, with texts in other popular genres, and with canonical literature.[24] Surely this is an *intellectual* engagement with each new book, whatever emotions are also engaged. Likewise, in love poetry, my own primary field of expertise, extravagance of feeling has often gone hand in hand with a seductive subtlety of structure, thought, and expression. Sappho's "Hymn to Aphrodite," one of the foundational texts about love in Western culture, opens by praising the goddess's mind, not her visible beauty, and Sappho praises that mind as *poikilos*: "an adjective applicable to anything variegated, complex, or shifting," Anne Carson explains, "for example a 'dappled' fawn, a 'spangled' wing, an 'intricately wrought' metal, a 'complicated' labyrinth, an 'abstruse' mind, a 'subtle' lie, a 'devious' double-entendre."[25] When Eloisa James embeds a reflection on Aphrodite in *Duchess in Love*— our hero, Cam, a sculptor, is considering his next project — she calls this alluring intellectual complexity to mind:

> She would make a lovely Aphrodite. Unusual for an Aphrodite, of course. She was slimmer than the normal model, and her face was far more intelligent. The Aphrodites he could bring to mind had sensual, indolent faces, like that of Gina's statue. Whereas her face was thin with a look of curiosity. But why should Aphrodite, as the goddess of eros, of desire, be indolent? Why shouldn't she have precisely that innocent look combined with a gleam of erotic curiosity — the look in his wife's eyes?[26]

Why, after all, should *any* genre of eros be indolent? Why shouldn't a popular romance novel — not every novel, the "normal model," in Cam's phrase, but this or that particular book — have precisely the combination of "innocent look" and alluring "gleam" of intelligence that this imagined statue displays?[27] To read such a romance closely would not be to resist or dismiss it, but rather to let the mind of love we see at play in the text spark an answering excitement, an "erotic curiosity" of our own.

What would "close-reading a romance" (as opposed to "reading the romance") look like in practice? To illustrate, let me turn to what strikes me as one of the subtlest, most complex, and most aesthetically interesting of American romance novels, Laura Kinsale's 1992 bestseller, *Flowers from the Storm*, which I regularly teach in my courses on the genre.

Published by Avon Books, *Flowers from the Storm* stands most immediately in the tradition of long, erotically-charged historical romances from this publisher that began with Kathleen Woodiwiss's groundbreaking novel *The Flame and the Flower*, twenty years before. *The Flame and the Flower* remains quite readable, quite enjoyable, even, and its occasional aspirations to "art" are endearingly awkward, as when an early reference to *Hamlet* echoes in later soliloquies by our hero and heroine, Heather and Brandon, right nobly filled with "thees" and "thous" and poetical inversions. (The nods to Shakespeare in Victoria Holt's bestselling gothic romance, *Mistress of Mellyn*, look positively highbrow by comparison.) As a novel, the Woodiwiss is, for me, primarily of historical interest, both for its impact on romance publishing and for its ambivalent negotiations with Second Wave feminism, the sexual revolution, and the changing discourse of rape in the 1970s. It also, however, supplies much of the early pleasure of "interplay," in Roberts's terms, to be found in the later, far more accomplished novel by Kinsale.[28]

You don't have to read very far into *Flowers from the Storm* to note Kinsale's play with romance conventions made famous by *The Flame and the Flower*. Consider our hero, Christian Richard Nicholas Frances Langland, His Grace the Duke of Jervaulx. When we meet him first, he is a cynical, "dissolute" man marked by broad shoulders, long dark hair, Satanic bravado, and a "pirate mouth."[29] For comparison, here's our introduction to Brandon, the hero of *The Flame and the Flower*: "He had the look of a pirate about him, or even Satan himself, with his dark curly hair and long sideburns that accentuated the lean, handsome features of his face."[30] Kinsale's phrase "pirate mouth" may be inscrutable on its own (a mouth with an eye-patch? a mouth that says "arrrr"?), but it makes sense as stock-response shorthand, a way to trigger the sort of associations spelled out at greater length by Woodiwiss and intensify them through brevity and juxtaposition. We read "pirate," feel the appropriate *frisson*, and attribute it to our hero's mouth — the same way, to show my age for a moment, that we are meant to respond to Bob Dylan's reference to a "cowboy mouth" in "Sad Eyed Lady of the Lowlands."[31] Certainly the marketing department of Avon Books wanted to emphasize the familiarity of this hero: their original cover for the novel featured the well-known model Fabio, holding out a bouquet to the potential reader, in his windswept, shirtless glory.

To read the novel, of course, is quickly to realize that this cover image is quite incongruous. Jervaulx the virile, cynical rake, is also Jervaulx the mathematician, preparing as the novel opens to give a joint paper at the Analytical Society that demonstrates, for the first time, the possibility of a geometry in which Euclid's fifth postulate does not apply, such that *"through a point C lying outside a line AB there can be drawn in the plane more than one line not meeting AB"* (129).[32] A few pages after he presents this discovery, a cerebral aneurysm leaves Jervaulx unable to speak and struggling to understand others, with a loss of perception and motor control on his right side — so much for Fabio's strong right arm holding out those flowers. Believed mad, the Duke gets sent to Blythedale Hall, publically known as "the most lavish private lunatic asylum in the country" (45), but also, in the view of our prim, Quaker heroine, Archimedea "Maddy" Timms, "a very comfortable and ghastly sort of purgatory" (48).[33] The daughter of Jervaulx's mathematical collaborator, blind Mr. Timms, Maddy knows the Duke from his days of intellectual and sensual glory, days when "the bright, cool world of functions and hyperbolic distances" would fill his mind "like unfailing music" (9) and he could make elegant double-entendres about "the allure of certain irresistible curved surfaces" (27). At Blythedale, she finds him bestial, aphasic, incoherent, partly paralyzed, and tormented by his absolute interiority.

The opening chapters of *Flowers from the Storm* are as emotionally engaging as anything Dixon could ask for—indeed, as anything in popular romance. Individual scenes have become famous, and justly so: the pages before the Duke's stroke when Jervaulx describes Maddy's face to her blind father, simultaneously flirting with her and doing a deep, abiding kindness to Mr. Timms; the uncanny moment in the Seclusion Room of the madhouse when Maddy realizes, simply and ineluctably, that Jervaulx *"isn't mad; he is maddened"* (65) and that she has a Quaker Calling to help him; the wrenching doubleness of our response when Jervaulx, still in the madhouse, viciously embittered, decides to punish Maddy for raising and dashing his hopes for freedom:

> A thought came to him, a madman's thought, the kind of thought he would not ever in his real life have entertained. But here there was no such thing as honor. Here there was only brute force and feeling, and he was going to make her understand. He was going to make her know how it felt to be broken down to the last depth of disgrace, to lose every rag of self-respect. Lure her to her own shame, make her bring it upon herself, as she had seduced him so easily into hot humiliation.
>
> *Prim thee thou spinster puritan;* he knew exactly how he was going to do it [107].

Because Kinsale does not tell us immediately what that "madman's thought" is, we fear it. Does he plan to rape her? Given the genre, it's not impossible, and although rapist romance heroes were rare by the early 1990s, they hadn't disappeared entirely. (Patricia Gaffney's *To Have and to Hold*, published three years later, revisits the motif in a particularly harrowing way.) A page later, we learn that he plans to seduce and ruin her, not to use violence: a despicable decision, but also one which enables Jervaulx to view his disability, for the first time, simply as an obstacle to be overcome. Kinsale ensures that we admire this flash of the Duke's pre-stroke arrogance. "To lie chained in the dark and plan a seduction required a potent bend of reality," Kinsale's narrator observes: "A twist of ferocity and humor, to swallow his affliction whole, to face the truth of himself and then proceed as if it were merely an inconvenience: a husband or a lover, a perverse floorplan of widely separated bedrooms in a country house, an inquisitive aunt or cousin, something to be worked around in pursuit of the ultimate goal. A challenge" (108). Emotionally engaging, these passages are also quite emotionally complex. To borrow Sappho's adjective, they are *poikilos*, dappled, intricately wrought, sparking antithetical desires. We want, and do not want, Jervaulx to succeed.

The novel's invocation of non–Euclidean geometry also signals the *poikilos* quality of the text's appeal to the mind, as well as the heart. In my classes—I've had a double-major, English and math—I was thrilled to see that Kinsale "gets the math right"—but the author does more than check her equations. Rather, by introducing non–Euclidean geometry near the start of the book Kinsale invites us to keep the idea of parallelism in mind as we consider the relationships between the pure, self-evident truths of geometry and the self-evident Truth and Light announced by Quaker theology, or between the competing explanations for Maddy's behavior, one sacred, one secular, with no point of intersection. To Maddy, strength of character had nothing to do with her ability to brave a "madman's cell — head up [...] no fear"; rather, "it was an Opening" (523). Jervaulx will have none of it: "It was ... *you*," he insists. "Duchess. [...] A duchess inside" (523). In an elegant twist, Kinsale does not limit herself to the non–Euclidean geometry discovered by Jervaulx and Mr. Timms: a hyperbolic geometry, in which there can be multiple parallels drawn through point C to any given line AB. Rather, having opened the door to a "whole new universe" (29) in which Euclid's fifth postulate does not apply, she silently adopts a second, elliptical, non–Euclidean geometry for much of the novel. In elliptical geometry, there are *no* parallel lines, such that the parallel lives of Maddy and Jervaulx, separated by social class, and their parallel minds, separated by epistemology, by disability, and by temperament, can indeed meet. "It cannot be; we are impossible," Maddy thinks during their first love scene (346), but the geometry of the novel, as much as the conventions of the genre, refutes her.

Once you begin thinking about the novel geometrically, other patterns emerge. There's the chiasmus that links Maddy, who is a Christian, with Christian, who is mad; likewise, after his stroke Jervaulx is a soul trapped in a body, while Maddy's sexuality is hemmed in by her religious scruples, a body trapped in a soul. A brilliant set of parallels connects repeated scenes where knowledge is not accessible directly, but only through some circuit of publication and reflection. Jervaulx cannot see the errors in his handwriting when looking directly at them, but only when they are reproduced by a "Writing Machine" that copies his penmanship (401); likewise the truth or falsehood of Maddy's marriage to the Duke can only be determined by her public reading of a "paper of condemnation" and the Duke's public response, not through introspection or private reflection (519). The novel, we might say, has a horror of epistemological privacy; in it, nothing can truly be known until it has been represented to others. In one crucial instance, publication *creates* the fact that it asserts: the Duke's finances depend on "trust," on "the rock-solid confidence in him by the men who advanced their money with his" (380). To rebuild that confidence, he must be seen to live like a Duke, his actual power depending on the appearance of power, his wealth depending on the illusion of wealth, and so on, so that only through "false witness in appearances," as Maddy calls it, can the fact become, performatively, true (385).[34] Is there a parallel to this instance elsewhere in the text? The pattern says there must be at least one, and to find it, we need look no further than the central plot of the novel, the rushed, arguably fraudulent marriage between Jervaulx and Maddy, the fundamental truth or falsity of which spurs much debate, and drives much of the action, in the second half of the novel.

Such "forced marriage" and "marriage of convenience" plots abound in popular romance fiction. Not every novelist unfolds their implications, but they offer themselves to the author as a context in which to explore questions about the nature of marriage as both social institution and as a lived interpersonal enterprise. As Stanley Cavell reminds us in *Pursuits of Happiness*, his philosophical study of Hollywood comedies of remarriage from the 1930s, these questions look back to the English Renaissance, a time when debates about marriage, spurred by the Reformation, preoccupied preachers, dramatists, and poets. "These comedies illustrate, or materialize, the view of marriage formulated in John Milton's eloquent *Doctrine and Discipline of Divorce*," Cavell argues of *It Happened One Night*, *The Awful Truth*, *The Philadelphia Story*, and the other movies in the docket; in particular, these films put into vivid action the poet's insistence that the test of "what is marriage and what is not marriage" can be found in the ability of a couple to sustain a "meet and happy conversation."[35]

Cavell's treatment of romantic comedy films has long struck me as an appealing model for future scholarship on popular romance fiction: a model in which the critic can summon the highest of highbrow cultural icons (Milton, Emerson, Kant) in order to think through icons of popular culture (Cary Grant, Katharine Hepburn), not to demonstrate "our capacity for bringing our wild intelligence to bear on just about anything," but rather to enable us "to see [...] the intelligence that a film has *already* brought to bear in its making."[36] More romance novels than most readers expect — general readers *and* romance scholars, I believe — will reward such scrutiny, but few invite it quite as explicitly as *Flowers from the Storm.* The specific invitation comes not long after Maddy convinces her cousin, the director of Blythedale asylum, to allow Jervaulx to leave for London, under supervision, to face a competency hearing. Maddy, the Duke, Cousin Edward, and Mr. Timms set off by carriage, only to stop for tea "in a small and ancient village" where "half-timbered brick cottages with split slate roofs and garden walls seemed to warp themselves to the contour of the hill, a treacle flow of buildings instead of a neat, straight modern line" (148). What do they find, having left behind "modernity" (circa 1827)? Jervaulx tries to speak. "His jaw tightened with effort. 'Pah ...' he managed, and then, '*Lost*'" (148). Cousin Edward tut-tuts, trying to calm him down. "We know precisely where we are, I assure you. Chalfont St. Giles ... we're not lost. Not a bit." The Duke snorts in disgust: "*Lost*," he repeats, with increasing frustration, to the point where Edward fears he will have a violent, manic outbreak. Only Mr. Timms remains unworried. "He sounded to me quite rational," the blind man notes — asking, a few lines later, whether Maddy sees a cottage with a sign on it nearby.

> Maddy looked. "Milton's Cottage."
> Her father said nothing. She hesitated, gazing at the modest village home. Understanding dawned.
> She burst into a laugh. "Oh no — he is a blockhead! And so am I! We aren't lost at all, are we?" She made an imitation of Cousin Edward's soothing reassurance to the duke. "'Why, you mustn't worry, Master Christian. We know precisely where we are, Master Christian. Chalfont St. Giles.' *Paradise Lost*."
> "The very house where Milton wrote it. Thy mother and I stopped to visit among the Friends here when thou wast only a babe in arms" [150].

Unlike the movies that Cavell extols, this novel doesn't just "illustrate, or materialize" ideas from Milton. It invokes him by name, stops by his house, and vividly associates *Paradise Lost* with Maddy's parents and with Jervaulx's hidden intelligence. If we want to know "precisely where we are" as we read this novel, we will need to think about Milton — so, at least, I teach my students to read the scene.

The book moves on, and never turns back. But the minute we accept Kinsale's exegetical challenge, playing along with what we might either call (with Dixon) the novel's "postmodern game-playing"[37] or (with Roberts) its "interplay with the art of the past,"[38] we realize that Miltonic echoes are everywhere in the text. Three examples will suffice. First, the novel makes something of a fetish of Maddy's long hair: it was her "only worldly vanity," we're told, as it was her late mother's (21). Jervaulx tells his friend Durham that he wants to marry Maddy in order to see her "braid down" (251). In their second love scene, the Duke takes down her hair and draws it "forward in a curtain over her breasts" (362), leaving her simultaneously both "virginal [...] and seductive" (363, 364, 366). If you know Milton, you know that hairdo: it's Eve's, from our first glimpse of her in Book Four:

> She as a veil down to the slender waist
> Her unadorned golden tresses wore
> Disheveld, but in wanton ringlets wav'd
> As the Vine curles her tendrils, which impli'd
> Subjection, but requir'd with gentle sway,
> And by her yielded, by him best receivd,
> Yielded with coy submission, modest pride,
> And sweet reluctant amorous delay [394].

Other iconic women have worn their hair this way — Botticelli's Venus, for example. But Maddy's enduring "curiosity" (108), the fact that she is a gardener (196) who dreams of having a "working garden" of her own (258) and gets kissed the first time by Jervaulx in a garden (117–118), and the "full-length figure of Eve, the apple at her feet and only a coyly placed hand for covering" that hangs on the wall of Jervaulx's chamber (332), clinch the association.

If Maddy is an Eve, the Duke should by rights be an Adam. But aside from the early moment when Jervaulx stands naked before Maddy "the way God made him" (82) and the later, poignant turn, after they argue, when the Duke tells Maddy to "Go then!" (390) (an echo of Adam's repeated "Go" in Book 9, which sends Eve off to fall), the Duke does not seem terribly Adamic.[39] Rather, Kinsale associates him with that original bad-boy hero, Milton's Satan. He has a dog named Devil, who loves Maddy right from the start (5, 30). Maddy calls Jervaulx, repeatedly, "the Devil" (124, 137, 437, 447). Admittedly, you don't have to look very hard to find popular romance heroes associated with the Devil: E. M. Hull's Sheik Ahmed ben Hassan (*The Sheik*, 1919), Georgette Heyer's Duke of Avon (*These Old Shades*, 1926) and his son, Dominic (*Devil's Cub*, 1932) come immediately to mind, and I have already quoted the initial description of Brandon from *The Flame and the Flower* (1972), who looks like "Satan himself." But when Kinsale has Maddy muse that Jervaulx "chose to reign in Hell, like Satan *in the poem*" (391, my emphasis), she underscores that in her hands, the stock comparison has reverted to an actual allusion: a gesture we can think about, as well as react to emotionally.

As the novel ends, Maddy revisits and dwells on Jervaulx's resemblance to Satan. "Thou art the duke," she says, "a bad wicked man [...] A star that I could only look up and wonder at [...] I'm glad thou fell, and I can hold thee in my hands" (526). The religious myth implied is as remarkable as it is heretical. In Kinsale's revision of *Paradise Lost*, Satan and Eve, not Adam and Eve, become the original romantic couple. Jervaulx/Lucifer's "fall" into the hell of Blythedale is a *felix culpa*, since only in his fallen state can he tempt and seduce Maddy/Eve, thereby saving her from meekness and solitude. The "fall" of Maddy/Eve becomes a sensual incarnation, since only when her spirit is fully and erotically embodied can she save Jervaulx/Satan, her tempter. In popular romance fiction, terms like "temptation," "wickedness," and "falling" have long since been transvalued, but Kinsale deploys them simultaneously in their popular and theological senses, ordering the universe of the novel such that her characters' mutual human love is the site at once of the highest spiritual Callings and the most sensual, even "animal" sexual desires (437). It's no accident that the novel's most erotic scene, in which Maddy and her husband couple in full daylight, "like every wild creature that God had made of clay to walk the earth," takes place in Jervaulx's library (435–8). Body and soul, sex and text, salvation and the fall: Kinsale implicates each in the other, and, in the process, implicates the popular and the literary, too.

A few paragraphs ago I noted the emphasis on "conversation" as the test of marriage in Milton's *Doctrine and Discipline of Divorce*. In Milton's essay, the idea of conversation frequently appears in conjunction with a metaphor of fire, specifically the soul's aboriginal "burning" for an end to solitude. Glossing Paul's admission that it is better to marry than it is to burn, Milton wonders "who hath the power to struggle with an intelligible flame, not in paradise to be resisted?" (875). That flame can't be reduced to merely sexual desire, he insists; rather, it's the soul's "pure and more inbred desire of joining to it selfe in conjugall fellowship a fit conversing soul (which desire is properly call'd love)" (875). In such flaming "fellowship," sex, words, and mutual help will overlap and conspire. *Flowers from the Storm* takes this complex Miltonic figure to heart. Maddy is quite literally the only one who can, at first, "converse" with the stroke-aphasic Duke, and as they learn to converse with one another — through words, through looks, through humor, and through arguments about family budgets and home economics, as well as through the sexual "flame" between them — we see precisely the mix of literal and figurative "conversation" that Milton has in mind. In a remarkable turn, the novel then aligns this therapeutic process, a medical/marital healing, with a more modern version of this aboriginal love: that of parent and child. As the Duke looks down at his abandoned illegitimate daughter he sees a version of himself— baffled, unsure, unable to communicate — at which moment "her sudden smile broke out glowing, the way a lover would turn to discover him in a crowd. *You're here!* The silent message lit her up like a candle, caught him up instantly in it, too" (500). The "fire" of erotic desire, the light of spirit and intelligence in someone's eye, the candle of mutual recognition: each is an instance of that "intelligible flame" that Milton projects into Eden. Each of them assuages one's fear of being, in Jervaulx's words from the madhouse, "deserted, discarded, disowned" (93).

Why might the novel so insistently revisit these Miltonic precedents? One cynical answer comes immediately to mind: they allow the novel to flatter its less-educated readers that they, too, have access to an allusive, high-art text, even as they assuage the guilt that better-educated readers might feel for reading something as déclassé as a popular romance. The problem with this answer lies in the clumsiness of its cynicism, its inability to say anything different about this novel's use of Milton than it does about the highbrow allusions in Raymond Chandler's *Farewell, My Lovely* (with its noir temptress named Helen Grayle), the deployment of topoi from Spenser and Melville in *Nova*, by science fiction novelist Samuel R. Delany, or even the Shakespearean soliloquies in Kathleen Woodiwiss's *The Flame and the Flower*, mentioned some pages ago.

A second, better answer comes when we place this pattern of Miltonic allusions into the broader structural logic of the novel. Remember the context in which the poet is first mentioned: a moment when characters leave the "modern" world of the novel for an "ancient village," and when the past of Maddy's parents suddenly intersects her present. As a historical romance, this novel, too, is an "ancient village" to us modern readers; do we find in it, then, a glimpse of some relevant past? (To put the question geometrically, through this point M, does there exist either one or more timeline that is parallel to our own?) Maddy and Jervaulx are an early-nineteenth-century couple whose arguments over issues of authority and equality in marriage sound suspiciously like much later twentieth-century feminist debates — but as the novel reminds us, through this set of Miltonic allusions, those debates also raged during the "love revolution" that brought the ideal of companionate love into prominence in the seventeenth century, a good two hundred years before Maddy was born. It's Milton, after all, who insists that Adam was meant to rule over Eve even before the Fall of man — they were "not equal, as their sex not equal seemed" (296) — and it's the early Quakers, Maddy's spiritual parents, who held that male dominance and female subjection were a curse imposed by God *because* of the Fall, a curse from which the regenerate Christian couple had been redeemed. Quaker brides deliberately did not say that they would "obey" their husbands in their wedding declarations; to do so would be to insult the equality of the Christ in each of them.[40] Quaker husbands and wives, said the London Meeting, were to have "no rule but love" between them — the very words that Kinsale gives Maddy to say when she and Jervaulx are wed: "Thou art my husband, and I am thy wife, with no rule but love between us" (279).[41]

Does Kinsale's use of the past — not just as setting, but as a palimpsestic history of love — constitute an "act of nostalgia" or of "discovery"? I take the terms from essayist Vivian Gornick, whose mordant *The End of the Novel of Love* argues, as its title suggests, that in the 1990s, the days of the former are long over. "Put romantic love at the center of a novel today," she asks, "and who could be persuaded that in its pursuit the characters are going to get to something large?"[42] The answer strikes her as obvious: "No one" (165). Such a deployment of romantic love is now "an act of nostalgia, not of discovery" (165). Arguably, though, a good enough author can use "nostalgia" precisely in order to raise the sort of "large" questions that Gornick wants novels to explore: "how we got to be as we are, or how the time in which we live got to be as it is" (165). The author might use nostalgia in an investigatory way, mixing utopian critique, historical aura, and a dash of metaleptic reversal, that rhetorical move that takes contemporary ideas and reads them back into an earlier period or text. Indeed, just as *Paradise Lost* projects seventeenth-century ideals of love and marriage back onto the first days of Creation, *Flowers from the Storm* projects late-twentieth century ideas about women's sexuality and egalitarian marriage onto the screen of 1827. And just as Milton uses scriptural precedent to imply that these ideals are not in fact modern, but aboriginally true, Kinsale uses Milton to suggest that the leveling "love revolution" of Second-Wave feminism — the object of considerable "backlash" in the new decade, as Susan Faludi argued a year before Kinsale's novel appeared — is not in fact a recent phenomenon, but an enduring critique embedded deep within Anglo-American amatory and religious culture.[43]

To find out "how we got to be as we are, or how the time in which we live got to be as it is" (165), in Gornick's words, turns out, at least in this novel, to depend on acknowledging the knowledge we already have, rather than discovering something entirely new. That knowledge includes Milton and Quakers, to be sure, but also the modernist abjection of sentiment and the uplifting "novel of love" and the post–New Critical pedagogy of close reading that still pervades American schools, rendering all-but-invisible the craft, self-consciousness, and artistic achievement to be found in the best of popular romance fiction. "There have been hardly any great novelists of love for almost a century," philosopher Allan Bloom fretted a few months after *Flowers from the Storm* was published, blaming the "de-eroticization of the world" and consequent "disastrous decline in the rhetoric of love" on his usual suspects: feminists, sexologists, the ghost of Jean-Jacques Rousseau, and the intellectual laziness of American readers.[44] And yet, even as "reading classic books has become less and less of a taste among the educated," he observes, "cheap romantic novels, the kind that are sometimes stuck into boxes of household detergent, apparently flourish among housewives who haven't heard that Eros is dead."[45] Like pagans who never got the memo about Great Pan's demise, romance novels and the women who read them turn out to be the last refuge of that old-time religion of love, and Kinsale's novel seems to know this context, too.

To speak of a novel "knowing" anything, of course, is a rather weasily literary-critical metaphor — a way to dodge what remains, every quarter, my students' most stubborn objection, and the one expressed so vividly by Dixon: "the commentator claimed that the author had done this deliberately," but "this shows a fundamental misunderstanding of how this type of fiction is written."[46] To praise Kinsale's novel, I may well want to play the "games" I find in it, to use Dixon's term, just as I play the postmodern mind games of A. S. Byatt's bestselling *Possession: A Romance*, published just two years before *Flowers from the Storm*. But although we are, as literary scholars, quite comfortable in giving Byatt credit for her allusive clues and labyrinthine narrative structures, and still more in genuflecting to Milton, it sounds odd, *feels* odd, to praise a romance novelist this way. And where other recent romance authors have written at length, in essays and on websites, about the literary background or symbolic patterns that structure their work, often spotted and intensified during the process of editing and revision, Laura Kinsale herself has not drawn attention to such elements in her novels.[47] Quite the contrary: although she stresses the deliberate research behind this novel's description of Jervaulx's stroke and recovery, her interviews otherwise emphasize (in Dixon's term) the "instinctive" quality of her craft. "My books are totally character-driven," she tells *The Romance Reader* in an interview. "I do not write a synopsis, and sometimes you might even see the final book vaguely outlined in there, but that's only if I'm lucky! It is generally what I find most difficult about a book, keeping the story going in some rational direction."[48]

Might everything I have described as "artistry" here be simply an accident, not the result of some "rational" scheme? In the classroom, when this question comes up — and it *always* comes up — I like to remind my students that "the method of analyzing literature which is taught in schools" was supposed to free them from precisely this anxiety, whether that method was old-school New Criticism or an approach derived from contemporary literary theory. Helen Vendler's poetry textbook, *Poems, Poets, Poetry*, for example, teaches students to search out the "meaningful patterning" that gives a poem its "analytic shape," but she is quick to remind them that "such patterns occur in lightning-quick ways to the trained mind of the poet," just as decisions about melody, harmony, or rhythm occur to a composer.[49] "It is only later that analysts demonstrate the patterns that make the music seem intended, not chaotic," she admits, and she has no qualms about asserting that "the swift internal processes of composition organize the temporal, spatial, grammatical, and syntactic shapes of the poem more by instinct than by conscious plan."[50] Dixon's assumption that the "instinctive writing" to be found in romance novels differs categorically from the "deliberately" artful composition of literary fiction will not hold up to inspection, from either end. Students who learn this lesson are equipped to read high-art literature with a little less piety, and popular fiction with a little more respect — in both cases, I suspect, enjoying the works much more.

Flowers from the Storm ends on Christmas Eve, its epilogue set a year after the narrative proper. It's a comfortable, comforting gesture by Kinsale: a signal that the novel's geometrical and historical "games" have not taken it outside the boundaries of the genre at its most conventional. Maddy, Jervaulx, his friend Durham (the priest who presided at their true-false wedding) and his grandmother, the redoubtable Lady de Marly, dance a quadrille; Christian gives his wife a "long, hard, branding kiss" that would do a Kathleen Woodiwiss novel proud; as the couple make their way to the bedroom, the narrator revisits earlier thematic material and ethical debates, tying up loose threads, bringing the book to satisfying closure. In the final pages, as dawn breaks, one last thread gets accounted for: a ghost story, mentioned once, briefly, two hundred pages earlier. Evidently a staghound haunts Jervaulx Castle, occasionally appearing, as he does now, in order to announce that the "lady of the castle was soon to produce and safely raise another offspring" (341).

We expect the good to end happily and the bad unhappily in a romance novel. That is one of the things, as Miss Prism might say, that romance fiction means. But for a novel with this much intellectual appeal to close with a Christmas pregnancy and a canine herald angel might well seem a bit *de trop*, a lapse in its art, a break in its patterns, a fall from the grace of its gaming. Some of my best students have reacted this way — and, for a while, I joined them. Then I flipped back to the staghound's first mention, and found that the author was there before us. Jervaulx "thought the tale overly maudlin for any self-respecting apparition," we read, "but it was true" (341). Like the epilogue, and perhaps like the novel as a whole, this "tale" dares us to dismiss it as "overly maudlin," even as it invites us to place ourselves in the "buffle-headed" position of its hero, the "bad wicked man" who "could recognize a miracle when he saw one" (533). I'm tempted to say that the "miracle" in question must be *Flowers from the Storm* itself — but to say that is to pluck this novel far too dramatically out of its context, singling it out too separately for praise. As one of the handful of professors regularly to offer courses devoted entirely to popular romance fiction — well over twenty-five, as of this essay, for everyone from entering freshmen to graduate students in English — I'd rather say that the "miracle" is the appearance, on our intellectual horizon, of some as-yet-uncharted number of novels waiting to be read with the same demanding, passionate precision that we bring to any other text or genre. That may not be the only proper way to read a romance novel, even in the academy, but it's not a bad way to start.

NOTES

1. Helen Vendler, *Poems, Poets, Poetry: An Introduction and Anthology*, 3d ed. (New York: Bedford/St. Martin's, 2009).

2. Jack Timpane, *It Could Be Verse: Anybody's Guide to Poetry* (Albany, CA: BOAZ, 1995), 1.

3. Terry Eagleton, *How to Read a Poem* (Malden, MA: Blackwell, 2007), 3; Molly Peacock, *How to Read a Poem . . . and Start a Poetry Circle* (New York: Riverhead Books, 1999), 188; Edward Hirsch, *How to Read a Poem (and Fall in Love with Poetry)* (San Diego: Harcourt, 1999), xiii.

4. Pauline Kael, *For Keeps* (New York: Dutton, 1994), 211.

5. Janice Radway, *Reading the Romance: Women, Patriarchy, and Popular Literature* (1984; rpt. with new Introduction, Chapel Hill: University of North Carolina Press, 1991), 86; Glen Thomas, "Romance: The Perfect Creative Industry? A Case Study of Harlequin — Mills and Boon Australia," in *Empowerment Versus Oppression: Twenty-First Century Views of Popular Romance Novels*, ed. Sally Goade (Cambridge: Cambridge Scholars, 2007), 22. For a discussion of earlier, panoramic approaches to popular romance fiction, see the Introduction to this volume.

6. Katherine Gilles Seidel, "Judge Me By the Joy I Bring," in *Dangerous Men and Adventurous Women: Romance Writers on the Appeal of the Romance*, ed. Jayne Ann Krentz (New York: HarperPaperbacks, 1992), 212.

7. jay Dixon, *The Romance Fiction of Mills & Boon, 1909–1990s* (UCL Press, 1999; rpt. London and New York: Routledge, 2003), 5.

8. *Ibid.*, 5, 11.

9. *Ibid.*, 10.

10. *Ibid.*, 10.

11. Matthew 18:3.

12. Dixon, *Romance Fiction*, 10. For a history of close-reading pedagogy, and other methods of engaging with literature in schools, see Joan Shelley Rubin, *Songs of Ourselves: The Uses of Poetry in America* (Cambridge, MA: Belknap Press of Harvard University Press, 2007), 107–164.

13. Q. D. Leavis, *Fiction and the Reading Public* (1932; rpt. London: Chatto and Windus, 1939), 58.

14. *Ibid.*, 64, 65.

15. *Ibid.*, 271.

16. *Ibid.*, 271.

17. Laurence Perrine, *Sound and Sense* (New York: Harcourt Brace Jovanovich College, 1992).

18. John Guillory, *Cultural Capital: The Problem of Literary Canon Formation* (Chicago: University of Chicago Press, 1993), 172–3.

19. *Ibid.*, 173.

20. Cleanth Brooks, *The Well-Wrought Urn: Studies in the Structure of Poetry* (New York: Harcourt, Brace, and World, 1947), 233.

21. Andreas Huyssen, "Mass Culture as Woman: Modernism's Other," in *After the Great Divide: Modernism, Mass Culture, Postmodernism* (Bloomington: Indiana University Press, 1986), 44–64.

22. Dixon, *Romance Fiction*, 10.

23. *Ibid.*, 5.

24. Thomas J. Roberts, *An Aesthetics of Junk Fiction* (Athens: University of Georgia Press, 1990), 63, 17.

25. Anne Carson, *Eros the Bittersweet* (1996; rpt. Normal, IL: Dalkey Archive Press, 1998), 24.

26. Eloisa James, *Duchess in Love* (New York: Avon, 2002), 146.

27. John Irwin identifies a whole sub-genre of "'symbolist works' of 'textual self-inclusion' where 'the qualities the text attributes to the symbolic object are for the most part the attributes of the text itself" (qtd. in Mark McGurl, *The Novel Art: Elevations of American Fiction after Henry James* [Princeton: Princeton University Press, 2001], 32). Irwin's examples include "The Purloined Letter," *Moby Dick*, and *The Scarlet Letter*; to them, McGurl adds *The Golden Bowl* and *The Maltese Falcon*; I see no reason why James's *Duchess in Love* should not join them.

28. Roberts, *Aesthetics*, 19.

29. Laura Kinsale, *Flowers from the Storm* (New York: Avon, 1992), 34. Further references will be included parenthetically.

30. Kathleen Woodiwiss, *The Flame and the Flower* (New York: Avon, 1972), 26.

31. See (or, rather, hear) Bob Dylan, "Sad Eyed Lady of the Lowlands," on *Blonde on Blonde* (Columbia Records, 1966).

32. The novel begins, "Eleven years after the Beau [Brummell] had fled his creditors to France" (10), which places it in 1827; the non–Euclidean discoveries of Gauss, Lobachewski, and Bolyai date from the start of the 19th century, and were published in the late 1820s and early 1830s.

33. The name of Blythedale Hall is, perhaps, a nod to Nathaniel Hawthorne's *The Blithedale Romance*.

34. Australian critic Lisa Fletcher has written at theoretical length on the centrality of performative utterances to the historical romance novel, in both its literary and popular forms; in particular, she focuses on the citational quality of the declaration "I love you." See Lisa Fletcher, *Historical Romance Fiction: Heterosexuality and Performativity* (Aldershot, UK: Ashgate, 2008).

35. John Milton, "The Doctrine and Discipline of Divorce" (1644), qtd. in Stanley Cavell, *Pursuits of Happiness: The Hollywood Comedy of Remarriage* (Cambridge, MA: Harvard University Press, 1981), 87. We see in Milton, perhaps, a source for this novel's concern with epistemological privacy: "An Existentialist may regard hell as other people," Cavell notes, "but for a sensibility such as Milton's, myself am hell" (87). Only marriage to what Milton calls an "intimate and speaking help" allows us to escape the primordial "Loneliness of the soul" that God declares, in Genesis, not to be good (*The Complete Poetry and Essential Prose of John Milton*, ed. William Kerrigan and John Peter Rumrich [New York: Modern Library, 2007], 875). Further references to Milton will be from this edition, and included parenthetically.

36. Cavell, *Pursuits of Happiness*, 10.

37. Dixon, *Romance Fiction*, 5.

38. Roberts, *Aesthetics*, 19.

39. Indeed, the novel offers us an alternative figure for Adam: Richard Gill, the Duke's Quaker rival for Maddy. Gill is the male "gardener" (442) in the novel, an expert in "botanical science" (444).

40. See, for example, Jacques Tual, "Sexual Equality and Conjugal Harmony: The Way to Celestial Bliss. A View of Early Quaker Matrimony," *The Journal of the Friends' Historical Society* 55, no. 6 (1988): 161–174.

41. See Kristen Olsen, *Chronology of Women's History* (Westport, CT: Greenwood Press, 1994), 67.

42. Vivian Gornick, *The End of the Novel of Love* (Boston: Beacon Press, 1997), 165. Further references will be included parenthetically.

43. See Susan Faludi, *Backlash: The Undeclared War Against American Women* (1991; rpt. New York: Three Rivers Press, 2006).

44. Allan Bloom, *Love and Friendship* (New York: Simon & Schuster, 1993), 15; 25, 25.

45. Bloom, *Love and Friendship*, 25.

46. Dixon, *Romance Fiction*, 10.

47. See, for example, the website of romance author Lydia Joyce, whose "Behind the Scenes" pages detail the allusions and literary echoes the author had in mind. http://www.lydiajoyce.com.

48. Meredith Moore, "Meet Author Laura Kinsale," The Romance Reader, http://www.thero mancereader.com/kinsale.html.

49. Vendler, *Poems, Poets, Poetry*, 31.

50. *Ibid.*, 31.

3

"How we love *is* our soul": Joey W. Hill's BDSM Romance *Holding the Cards*

Sarah S.G. Frantz

In 2000, Joey W. Hill published her first book, *Make Her Dreams Come True*, an erotic, male-dominant/female-submissive BDSM romance, with Dreams Unlimited, an online publisher (or e-press) that quickly folded, both symptom and victim of the extreme volatility of the early digital publishing field. In 2001, *Make Her Dreams Come True* was briefly re-released by another e-press, LTD Books, a publisher that did not focus on romance (and that folded in 2005). Hill finally found a permanent digital publishing home when she released *Make Her Dreams Come True* for a third and last time with Ellora's Cave in 2002, followed by *Holding the Cards* later the same year.[1] Ellora's Cave was the first and most successful of the digital presses of the early 2000s dedicated to publishing erotic romance. Started in November 2000 by Tina Marie Engler because she was unable to sell her sexually explicit erotic romances to traditional print publishers, Ellora's Cave, with its digital-only business model, stable of authors with few other places to publish, and readers with few other places to buy what Ellora's Cave sold, quickly became a multi-million dollar-a-year company. The success of Ellora's Cave and of erotic romance as a niche digital market both reflected and contributed to the eroticization of the traditional print romance market in the late 1990s and early 2000s.[2]

According to Passionate Ink, the erotic romance special interest chapter of the Romance Writers of America, erotic romances are "stories written about the development of a romantic relationship through sexual interaction. The sex is an inherent part of the story, character growth, and relationship development, and couldn't be removed without damaging the storyline."[3] Similarly, Ellora's Cave defines "Romantica"—a term Ellora's Cave has copyrighted—as "both erotic and romantic": "The sexual relationship must be integral to and an important element of the storyline and the character development. Sex scenes should contribute to furthering the plot or affecting the development of the romantic relationship or the growth of the characters."[4] While most romance novels now include explicitly described sex, erotic romances rely on sexual interaction specifically to build the characters and their emotional arcs. In erotic romance, then, sexual interaction between the main characters supplies most of Pamela Regis' eight narrative elements of a romance: "a *definition of society*, always corrupt, that the romance novel will reform; the *meeting* between the [protagonists]; an account of their *attraction* for each other; the *barrier* between them; the *point of ritual death*; the *recognition* that fells the barrier; the *declaration* of the [protagonists] that they love each other; and their *betrothal*."[5] Joey W. Hill's career, then, with her success as a writer — she was one of Ellora's Cave's early authors, one of their most successful authors, and successfully moved to traditional print publishing in 2007 — and her novels' single-minded focus on sexual exploration as the core of the romance narrative, mirrors the trajectories of both digital publishing and erotic romance.

Hill's erotic romances are significant not only because they embody on a small scale the larger development and rise of electronic publishing and erotic romance over the last decade, but also because they almost singlehandedly established a new sub-genre of romance fiction, which opened up new ways for the romance genre to think about the relationships between sexuality and romantic love. The key component of Hill's career, of her explorations into the relationships between love and sexuality, and of her challenges to the conventions of the romance genre, is that almost all of her novels, digital or print, are not just erotic romances, but are BDSM erotic romances.

BDSM is a combination of the abbreviations of the main elements of a variety of non-standard sexual practices: Bondage/Discipline (BD), Domination/Submission (DS), and Sadism/Masochism (SM). Bondage can include any sexual restraint, from the most vanilla of sex play with scarves and blindfolds, all the way to elaborate rope bondage, rope suspension, and the Japanese erotic rope art, Shibari. Discipline ranges from the practice of "punishing" naughty submissives during encounters that often include role play, to specific fetishes like over the knee (OTK) spanking, and caning. Domination and submission refer to sexual identities and practices in which one partner is submissive to a dominant partner, doing what they are ordered to do, usually, but not always, in sexual situations. Sadism and masochism are much more specific sexual paraphilia: sadists receive pleasure and sexual arousal from inflicting pain on their partners, while masochists receive pleasure and sexual arousal from having pain inflicted on them.[6] A BDSM romance, therefore, must explore Regis's elements particularly through, by, and with one or more of the "kinky" sexual practices encompassed by the acronym. Rather than using a kinky activity merely as spice to sex, as a standard erotic romance might, in BDSM romance the kinky activity must be integral to the characters' emotional trajectory and to the relationship they build together. However, although the BDSM label encompasses a wide range of activities, in general, most BDSM erotic romances construct the relationship between the characters using the mutually-constitutive pairing of Domination/Submission (D/s). That is, two (or more) protagonists establish an emotional and physical relationship, overcome the emotional barriers between them, and achieve their happy ending, through exploration of the D/s dynamic in which one protagonist sexually dominates the other.[7]

But BDSM does not refer merely to sexual activities and practices; for some, BDSM goes much deeper than what they *do*. For them, BDSM is their primary sexual identity: it becomes who they *are*. In *Beneath the Skins*, a call for a BDSM community identity and activism similar to that in the GLBT community, Ivo Dominguez Jr. argues that while Kinsey's ground-breaking "concept of sexual orientation made it possible to see homosexuality as a deeply rooted part of self-identity rather than as a perverse choice," it inadvertently created a "myth of monosexuality" which envisions sexuality as a single "continuum with heterosexual and homosexual as its poles."[8] Monosexuality, then, precludes recognition and understanding of additional sexual orientation continua that are just as deeply rooted in the psyche as the traditional orientation of gender attraction; instead, other alternate sexualities besides homosexuality are seen as sexual *practices*, just as homosexuality itself was seen before the twentieth century. In opposition to the traditional doctrine of monosexuality, Dominguez posits instead a theory of polysexuality: "a complex pattern of many continuums, each describing an important part of the individual's sexuality."[9] As such, polysexuality includes at least the axes of heterosexual/homosexual, monogamous/polyamorous, top/bottom, butch/femme or masculine/effeminate, voyeur/exhibitionist, public/private, sadist/masochist, and dominant/submissive, with the additional complications of yes/no alignments for bondage, role play, and many more specific fetishes. For every individual, then, one or more axes eclipse the others, acting as the primary sexual orientation(s), with the others relegated either to secondary or to absent status. Therefore, rather than a single "choice" between gay, straight, and bi, with some kinky activities thrown in for fun, sexual identity examined from the perspective of polysexuality is instead a multi-dimensional, inter-woven combination of orientations. Hill's characters reflect this concept of polysexuality: their involvement in and use of BDSM is an incontrovertible part of their sexual and personal identity and their emotional and romantic journey, rather than something they merely play with during sex: "How we love *is* our soul," one of the heroes in *Rough Canvas* argues vehemently.[10]

Hill was one of the first and is certainly one of the most successful erotic romance authors to use BDSM to construct both the identities of her main characters and the trajectory of their romance narratives. Prior to Hill's groundbreaking Nature of Desire series, almost all erotic romance that depicted BDSM positively showed BDSM only as a series of sexual practices, not as an identity; indeed, prior to Hill's positive depiction of polysexuality, a happy ending and BDSM identity were rarely allowed to coexist.[11] As a necessary step to deserve their happy ending, characters were routinely obliged to renounce BDSM *as* an identity, relegating it instead to the level of mere practice, a "spice" to be added to their otherwise essentially "vanilla" sexual orientation, at most on an occasional basis. In 1999, for example, erotic romance author Emma Holly published two romances with Black Lace Books with characters who self-identified as kinky: *The Top of Her Game* follows a female dominant and *Velvet Glove* follows a male dominant/female submissive couple. At the end of both novels, the couples have "normalized" their relationship, eschewing their BDSM identities. While not necessarily "cured," they retreat from seeing BDSM as part of their identity or essential to their relationship and will admit only to perhaps using it to add flavor to their future sexual interactions. In 2002, the year Hill published her first two BDSM novels with Ellora's Cave, the epublisher released three other novels with BDSM themes: J.W. McKenna's *Trackers* and *Darkest Hour*, books about non-consensual sexual slavery in which the romance is either non-existent or an escape from the slavery, and McKenna's *Lord of Avalon*, a futuristic-set novel in which the whole society is based on female sexual slavery.[12] In these texts, BDSM is an enforced social practice signaling a hierarchal social code—one that has no intrinsic relationship with the sexual orientations or emotional desires of the protagonists. In Hill's novels, by contrast, the BDSM play is not simply consensual, but practiced by characters who are individually BDSM-identified, so much so that the barrier to the happy ending is often precisely that the characters need to recognize and accept how deeply rooted their BDSM identities are in their identities as a whole. That is, they cannot achieve their happy ending without integrating it with their continued BDSM identification.

Love and "the game we all hope isn't a game"

Joey W. Hills' *Holding the Cards*, the first book in her Nature of Desire series of BDSM romances, begins with the heroine, Lauren, talking with her friend, Lisette, a romance novelist successful enough to own a second home on a semi-private tropical island at which Lauren will be staying for the weekend.[13] While Lisette is a very minor character, mentioned only a few times, her professional description of the hero, Josh, introduces a meta-fictional thread into the novel: "'It's like he's so used to silence, he has to think about how to form words.'" Lauren jokes to her novelist friend, "'I sense a character about to be born,'" but Lisette tells her, "'Honey, that's a done deal. You remember *Gazing at Sirius*, Jeremy —.'"[14] Before we ever meet him, then, we know that Josh is romance-fantasy worthy. Lisette has already read him as an example of the genre-defining strong, silent, tormented hero and used that as inspiration for a character in one of her books. Although Lisette misreads Josh as gay — hardly romance hero material for a heterosexual romance — and does not explicitly say that she used him as her inspiration for a romance hero, Lauren and the narrative of *Holding the Cards* itself continue to employ the construction of Josh as a meta-fictional commentary on the generic romance hero.

In fact, every subsequent mention of romance novels in *Holding the Cards* codes Josh not only as the hero of this particular novel, but as the generic hero of popular romance fiction more generally. After she meets Josh, for example, Lauren thinks to herself:

> She had been sucked into some parallel dimension, where every tawdry cliché from a cheap romance novel was going to be played out. If everything went true to form, one of the men, probably the one she found most irritating yet mysteriously irresistible, would swing her easily up into his arms.
> "Okay, then," Josh nodded, hooked her arms around his neck, bent and scooped her up. "We'll take you back upstairs and get that wrapped." He lifted a brow at her snort of laughter. "What?"
> "Nothing," Lauren shook her head. "Nothing at all" [23].

Admittedly, Lauren has sprained her ankle, necessitating Josh's sweeping actions, but Lauren's humorous reflections overtly code Josh as the annoying Alpha Male romance hero, à la Rhett Butler in *Gone with the Wind*. Later in the novel, Lauren despairs of her feelings of instantaneous connection for romantic partners that have landed her in trouble in the past and that she's feeling for Josh now: "Nothing more pathetic than a woman trying to heal a brooding man. The cliché of practically every mainstream romance, and something every woman who reached thirty knew almost never happened. Still, those romances sold millions for a reason. There was a germ of hope in them, the hope that, if they did kiss the frog, he really would turn into a prince" (108). Here, Josh is not only the typical romance hero; according to the critics of modern popular romance fiction (and indeed critics of popular fiction for women for the last three hundred years[15]), he is the worst kind: the damaged hero with the "dark, brooding personality" (75) who must be reformed by the love of and his love for the heroine.

Despite the meta-fictional coding of him as the typical Alpha Male romance hero, Josh is never overtly presented as a sexual dominant in *Holding the Cards*. In fact, from his first appearance in the story, and certainly from the very start of his relationship with Lauren, he both acts and is described as a sexual submissive. Josh's submissiveness first manifests itself as he is rescuing Lauren from her own foolishness in locking herself out of her borrowed house. During the rescue, Josh kisses Lauren:

Something about her said the kiss would be welcome, that it was essential he communicate how much he wanted her, right from the beginning. If they were on the level ground, he might have displayed it in an altogether more reverent fashion. A gentle kiss laid on the knuckles of her bare toes. He would brush his hair against her calf, an intentional caress as he raised his head for a brief look into her blue eyes, showing her his desire to please, and protect, and cherish.

It was a strange thought, the type of thought he had never had before, but one that felt right as he thought of her again, sitting proudly in the tree gazing down at him, like a tribal goddess [20].

His protectiveness and care for Lauren code him as heroic — Lauren's knight in shining armor — but Josh's "reverence" reveals him to be Hill's first example of her "'palace guard' concept of a male submissive — an alpha male in service to a powerful female character, willing to do anything to protect her, yet often struggling with an unexpected need to surrender to her sexually."[16] Hill elaborates elsewhere: "He serves his lady, obeys her will, but protects her with his life and cherishes her completely."[17] Hill's palace guard submissive hero still displays the typical Alpha Male romance hero's protective jealousy and autocratic concern for the heroine's safety, but he tempers this with the instinctive desire to submit himself to her sexual will. The conscious understanding of this instinct is new to Josh, something he's only ever been aware of feeling with Lauren. And although he has always acted upon the unconscious instincts that reflect his sublimated identity, he has never and still does not recognize either his instincts or his identity for what they are; he therefore does not yet understand the implications — moral, ethical, interpersonal — of his resulting actions. This is the Barrier to his happiness and is what he must learn through the progress of the novel.

Lauren, on the other hand, is comfortable with herself and her sexuality. At the beginning of *Holding the Cards*, after she has left Lisette and is sailing by herself to the island retreat, Lauren muses about her sexual identity: "Lauren had been aware of being a Dom sexually since college, thanks to an adventurous first boyfriend. She used the shortened insider term often instead of Dominatrix. She liked the word, but knew it had become a caricature in people's minds; a woman with a God-complex dressed up in leather and thigh high boots, wielding a whip and a smirk" (8). Hill uses the innocuous but important verb "being" to designate Lauren's sexuality. Lauren just "is" a sexual dominant, at all times, and unashamedly so, without playacting or posturing, and her identity as a sexual dominant is just as important to her understanding of herself as her heterosexuality. The whys and wherefores of her orientation are as unknowable and unnecessary as asking why someone is gay. This depiction of BDSM as part of Lauren's identity, as part of the way she defines herself, is not only a choice of character portrayal but is a political and thematic statement on Hill's part. Lauren's sexual identity is immediately constructed in direct opposition to the stereotypes and caricatures of a Dominatrix that rely on appearances, rather than on a deeper understanding of what the identity entails in lived experience.

From her position of acceptance of and comfort with her own sexual identity, Lauren is immediately able to diagnose (she is, after all, a doctor) not only Josh's sublimated submissiveness, but also its wounded, almost mutilated, condition:

Just as homosexuals often knew another homosexual just from picking up vibes, so a Dominant could pick up the scent of a submissive. She felt it in Josh, but there was an oddness to it, almost as if it had been brought into consciousness and then buried again. He had powerful hands, but they were hesitant. Not hesitant as in awkward, but as if he paused at the door, waiting for the invitation because he couldn't enter without it. That was normal for a sub, but there was a wounded quality to it [20].

Indeed, Josh's sexuality and his personal identity have been so devastated by his past romantic relationship that his friend, Marcus, on the island visiting Josh, tells Lauren that Josh has "locked himself in a cage, as if he's afraid he's a danger to others" (74). Josh, in fact, considers himself a "monster" (133). The narrative arc of the novel itself becomes, as a result, the "catharsis, purging and release" (134) of Josh's pain, healing him enough to make him a suitable partner for his One True Love. And precisely because Josh is repeatedly cast as the generic romance hero, *Holding the Cards* argues more broadly that the purpose of the romance genre as a whole is to stage for the reader's pleasure and insight the sexual and emotional healing of the romance hero.

After Lauren's initial rescue, Marcus cons Josh and Lauren into playing a game of High Card Wins. This game not only titles the book — Lauren is "holding the cards" because she wins the card draw — but it also provides a major theme of the novel. Marcus asks Josh and Lauren, "'What if we let down our defenses, all those social walls we create to fence in acceptable behavior and fence out anything else, and found the children in ourselves again? That sense of wondrous, unselfconscious adventure, when games were fun and yet utterly serious, the fate of the universe hanging on our shoulders until Mother called us home to dinner'" (37). Marcus argues that this game would evoke "'[t]hat time when we openly embraced our need for someone to love us, care about us, believe that we were essentially good people, worthy of being loved'" (37). Or, as Lauren summarizes, they "'should play this game like children. The fate of the Universe in the balance, and absolute trust in our companions'" (46). With its connection to the innocence and sense of wonder of childhood, Marcus's game is, on the surface, utterly different from the "game" of sexual domination and submission with which both Lauren and Josh have struggled in the past. And yet, Lauren responds to Marcus's announcement of the prize — the right to ask anything of Josh and Marcus and they will obey — with weak knees and "a rush of liquid arousal between [her] thighs" (39). The card game, therefore, connects life and sex, all within a framework of vulnerability, trust, and the need to love and be loved. If BDSM is a game, as the novel claims, it also proclaims that life and love are the same game, with the same rules.

Lauren's first demand after winning the card draw is to feed Josh dinner by hand, her second for Marcus to tell them a wicked story from his childhood, the third to play Monopoly, and her fourth is for Josh and Marcus to spend the night with her, literally to sleep with her. The next morning, they tour the island together on the back of Josh's pet elephant and build sandcastles together on the beach. All of these commands and actions establish an innocent, even childlike, almost fantastical, intimacy between the characters, within the D/s context of the story. This intimacy demonstrates that the D/s connection is about more than just sex; it is about day-to-day care and comfort between lovers, about compatible personalities, about mutual support and goals — and about the imagination necessary to make that happen. Or, as Lauren thinks: "Translation: Do you understand me? Can I trust you? Will you play the game we all hope isn't a game? Can I believe, at least for tonight, that somewhere out there are people willing to comfort and nurture, love us and build us up instead of drain us, who won't rip our hearts from our chests and laugh at us?" (46). The games — the card game and the "game" of dominant/submissive interaction it echoes — are truly "games," fun, light-hearted, and diverting, played between intimate companions; but, at the same time, are also deadly serious commentary on the need for connection as the foundation of all relationships, but especially in BDSM relationships. Lauren's "demands," then, show Josh and her falling in love with, rather than just lusting for, each other, demonstrating that a successful BDSM relationship, just like any other romantic relationship, requires a fundamental bond between partners.

Lauren's relationship with her ex-lover Jonathan, from which she is attempting to heal with her trip to the island, failed precisely because of the lack of a deep connection. Lauren, momentarily buying into the belief that BDSM and romantic intimacy cannot coexist, has wondered whether BDSM was the reason for the failure of her relationship with Jonathan. At the very beginning of the novel, she feels a "familiar spiral of terror that she would always be like this, always destined to end up alone because of who she was" (10) and prior to her arrival on the island, she had wondered "[m]aybe this game is what's the matter with me" (11). She later tells the hero Josh and his friend Marcus, a sexual dominant, "'I almost went vanilla. I ran from the truth. I wrote off the whole D/s set-up as destructive. Kinky games had destroyed our relationship, destroyed me'" (105). But what Lauren realizes even before she arrives on the island is that her relationship with Jonathan did not fail because of her innate dominant nature or the "games" she and Jonathan played, but because Jonathan himself, although a sexual submissive, was emotionally "sadistic" (10), a "sick, sociopathic son of a bitch" (105), who used as a weapon Lauren's natural, affirming desire for a deep emotional connection with her submissive: "She had wanted love, and he had used her belief in that to almost destroy her. It was only when she realized love was not what drove him, and, more importantly, that she could not change that, that she had been able to break free" (36). The narrative, then, rejects, even demonizes, a relationship in which "all they had ever shared was sex and the game" (15).[18] But, importantly, it also refuses to lay the blame on "the game" itself; unlike those in other BDSM romances from the 1990s and early 2000s, that is, Hill's protagonists do not have to deny or be cured of their BDSM desires to deserve their happy ending.

The option left available to the characters, then, is to establish relationships in which "the game"—their undeniable BDSM identity—is joined with the love, trust, and commitment of a deeply emotional romantic connection. As Lauren muses:

> There was an intimacy to a relationship between a Dominant and submissive that pulled on the elemental need for unconditional love and trust. So while she did not share her preferences with those closest to her, Lauren desperately wanted to find someone to share them with, as well as a lifetime of love, marriage and all the rest. It was not just the submissive who had needs. The Dominant had vulnerabilities that were comforted and healed by the faith and pleasure of the submissive. They were two parts of a whole [8].

Lauren insists, even before she meets Josh, that the universal, natural desire for deep emotional connection in a loving, sexual relationship is as necessary to and as natural in power-exchange relationships as conventional relationships. But perhaps more importantly, she also rewrites the common perception of BDSM power dynamics, which assumes that the dominant is and should be in control not only of sexual encounters but of the emotional aspects of a power-exchange relationship. As a sexual dominant, Lauren lays claim to the right to be vulnerable. Intimacy and trust are both cause and effect of vulnerability and Lauren seems to be arguing that BDSM relationships are more susceptible to the breakdown and more open to the power, pleasure, and rewards of intimacy and trust. Conversely, then, BDSM relationships without intimacy and trust are and should be doomed.

Holding the Cards not only constructs love and BDSM identification as necessarily mutually constitutive; it also makes the more sweeping assertion that BDSM—more specifically, Domination/submission—is at the core of all romance fiction. Lauren reminds herself at the start of her relationship with Josh that "[t]wo committed people choosing to exercise their sexuality in a dominant and submissive fashion was not the problem. Everything in nature reflected the assertion of those characteristics. Every interaction between the beasts in the forest started with it, and animals were far more connected with what was 'natural' than humans" (61). BDSM identities, by this formulation, are natural, innate, a return to the safety and comfort of our primeval roots. During the denouement, Lauren expands her claim, telling Josh, "'Dominant and submissive exist in all relationships, whether they role play it or not. What protects people when they play is love, and the trust that comes with it, when it's real'" (145). BDSM, then, is *not* about power games, not about who is in control in a relationship, but is instead about the trust and vulnerability necessary to the success of any relationship that the power games both expose and nurture. Lauren knows that a "Dominant needed a sub's devotion as much as the sub desired the focused attention of her dominance over him. When it came down to it, they were willing captives of each other, the lines of control and possession ever shifting because of it" (68). As such, the power games that Lauren and Josh play, games that are fundamentally necessary for them to be able to heal each other and build their relationship, in fact establish their relationship as more natural, more authentic, and more profound than conventional non–BDSM relationships.

This construction of BDSM as essential not only to an individual's identity but also to romantic relationships as a whole becomes part of the meta-fictional assessment of the romance genre in *Holding the Cards*. Even though Lauren has never told her romance author friend Lisette about her sexuality, "[s]ubconsciously, Lisette did understand, Lauren knew. In the alpha-male heroes and submissive-yet-feisty heroines of her romance novels, Lisette instinctively created characters that danced around a fragile triangle of control, trust and sex, and a few million readers just as instinctively responded to it" (8). Hill explicitly connects the identity and practice of BDSM to the subtle negotiations of gendered power dynamics present in all romance novels, embodied in the battle of wills between alpha male heroes and submissive heroines. Tellingly, however, *Holding the Cards* is not about a male dominant and his female submissive, as a direct comparison with the "alpha-male heroes and submissive-yet-feisty heroines" would logically suggest. It is, of course, about a female dominant and a male submissive. In fact, the entire narrative crisis, the recognition that permits the happy ending, is the very fact that Josh — the romance-fantasy worthy hero — must understand and accept the fact that he is not, after all, a sexual dominant as he thought, but a natural, perfect submissive.

The message that relationships without intimacy, trust, and love are perversions of the values and aims of BDSM and of the romance narrative is reinforced by the emotional climax of the narrative during which Josh relates the story of the collapse of his disastrous marriage with Winona and the emotional devastation that it caused him. Just as Lauren is visiting the island to exorcize the final wisps of Jonathan's ghost from her psyche, Josh is on the island attempting to heal the psychological and emotional wounds left by his ruinous marriage with Winona. The difference is that Lauren's visit lasts two days; Josh has lived on the island for two years so far, unable to restore his self-worth and trust in himself. Throughout the novel, the reasons for the breakdown of Josh's marriage and the damage it caused him are presented as a mystery, as the key to Josh's recovery: "'Josh, what did she do to you?'" (49), Lauren asks more than once. Josh's extended confession serves, then, as the culmination of all narrative tension and suspense. That the novel's emotional climax centers on — indeed, is dependent on — the hero's confession and healing indicates the vital importance of the construction of the hero's submissive masculinity to the narrative's themes and message. That is, both the hero's masculinity and the hero's sexual submissiveness are of primary importance to the success of both the romantic relationship and the generic romance narrative itself.

The narrative significance of Josh's confession is indicated precisely by how necessary Lauren's dominance is to forcing his confession, how difficult it is to pry it out of him, and how cathartic it is for Josh to finally unburden himself. In *The History of Sexuality*, Michel Foucault describes the ritual of confession as

> a ritual that unfolds within a power relationship, for one does not confess without the presence (or virtual presence) of a partner who is not simply the interlocutor but the authority who requires the confession, prescribes and appreciates it, and intervenes in order to judge, punish, forgive, console and reconcile; a ritual in which the truth is corroborated by the obstacles and resistances it has had to surmount in order to be formulated; and finally, a ritual in which the expression alone, independently of its external consequences, produces intrinsic modifications in the person who articulated it: it exonerates, redeems, and purifies him; it unburdens him of his wrongs, liberates him, and promises him salvation.[19]

Lauren's natural dominance over Josh makes explicit and natural the power dynamic between confessor and confessed. She demands that Josh unburden himself, while also assuring him that the confession will be productive: "'I'm here, Josh, and I'm going to make it all right. You're going to give me everything, and I'm going to heal it, and put it back inside you. Okay?'" (128). Even so, Josh only confesses after being stripped naked and bound to a piece of BDSM furniture called a St. Andrew's Cross "at the ankle, calf and mid thigh for each leg, and the wrist, elbow and bicep for the arms" (126), and by the throat, forehead, and waist. In addition, he is blindfolded with a head-mask and his penis is restrained, displayed, "framed, mounted for [Lauren's] pleasure" (129) in a cock harness that is itself also chained to his ankle cuffs. The super-abundant imprisonment of body, sight, and phallus paradoxically allows Josh the freedom to confess by signifying the importance of his confession through the effort needed to obtain it.[20] The restraint and display of his penis specifically demonstrate that this narrative climax — pun intended — is indeed primarily and ultimately a meditation on and mediation in the construction of *masculinity* in particular.

Thus restrained, Josh confesses to a carnivalesque BDSM world turned upside down in which the axes of sexuality intersect in ways the novel portrays as aberrant. Josh begins the confession of his supposed wrongdoing by describing Winona — "'She was a sub. She liked me to really take control'" — but he contradicts himself when he elaborates, "'She wanted me to dress her sexy when we were out, make her expose herself. We'd go to a club and she'd beg me to make her lift her skirt when she was dancing, let other people see her bare ass. She'd usually have me spank it good before we went out, hard with a belt, so it would have red welts on it'" (135). Josh is describing here an extreme case of what is known as "topping from the bottom," in which the person ostensibly in the submissive position actually runs the scene. In real-life BDSM interactions, topping from the bottom is usually considered at the very least incredibly bad manners, if not outright dangerous, because it blurs the lines of control in potentially unsafe ways. Despite Lauren's claim to the right for sexual dominants to be emotionally vulnerable in a relationship, the narrative argues that, during a sexual scene in which the protagonists enact their dominant and submissive roles, the dominant should be in emotional as well as physical control of the submissive, because a scene of BDSM play can raise conflicting and conflicted feelings. If the dominant is not truly in control, these emotional responses could damage both submissive and dominant.

The narrative constructs the axes of polysexuality in such a way that a dominant character is normally and naturally also a sexual top and, if appropriate, a sadist, while a submissive character is normally and naturally a sexual bottom and a masochist. Hill is asserting in *Holding the Cards*— not unproblematically — that the polysexual axis of domination/submission must naturally align with the axes of top/bottom and sadist/masochist. As first depicted, Winona occupies the position of villain precisely because she breaks these natural connections: she is a dominant who prefers to be a sexual bottom and a masochist. In the situations Josh describes during his confession, Winona is actually acting as the dominant, in emotional control of the scene, even though Josh thinks she was his submissive. The narrative seems to argue that the "natural" result of Winona's unnatural merging of sexualities is that the combination of her dominance and her masochism produces a kind of emotional sadism that she inflicts on Josh, similar to but more extreme than the emotional sadism Jonathan inflicted on Lauren. In forcing Josh to hurt her physically, therefore, Winona delights in hurting him emotionally. She is not merely a rare and therefore confused dominant masochist; rather, the narrative claims that her confusing combination of polysexual axes into dominant masochism is unnatural, even evil, and therefore becomes overtly sadistic.

Winona's form of villainy is not without precedent. In the romance genre, villains often have a sadistic sexual identity. It used to be that homosexuality was the immediately identifiable mark of wickedness and evil in romance villains. In 2000, Candy Tan critiqued "The Completely Despicable Gay Über-Villain" at All About Romance's At the Back Fence blog, deploring "the constant and pretty much consistent association of homosexuality, bisexuality and almost anything other than regular heterosexual sex with everything evil," labeling it as "the lure of Instant Depravity—'For Immediate and Complete Evilness, Just Add Homosexuality!'"[21] I argue, however, that Gay Insta-Evil has almost always gone hand-in-hand with Insta-Evil Sadism. Separating these two sexual identities — and recognizing both *as* sexual identities, as is possible using polysexuality — reveals that sadism is actually a much more reliable indicator of über-villainy than homosexuality. For example, Mary Novak, concurring with Tan at AAR, argues that Jack Randall of Diana Gabaldon's time-travel romance *Outlander* "is a pretty extreme villain for any romance, but the fact that he's also bisexual doesn't offend me the way some less extreme gay villains have. Why?" Because "it's clear that sadism is Randall's main pathology, and his sexual inclination is relatively incidental."[22] Although Novak doesn't see sadism as a sexual "inclination," her conclusion demonstrates that it is both acceptable and expected to represent sadism as a pathology and therefore as a mark of villainy, because clearly, all sadists must be evil: why else would someone get off on inflicting pain? While the world has changed enough that it is mostly unacceptable to use homosexuality as a short-cut symbol of depravity in popular romance anymore, sadism is a natural, obvious, and logical replacement.

This "natural" merging of sadism and villainy is true even in BDSM romances, but there the romance villain's sadism is, above all else, non-consensual. The most important tenet of BDSM is embodied in the phrase "Safe, Sane, Consensual": all play, whether sexual or otherwise, should follow all three principles. It should be performed as safely as possible. It should only be attempted by people in their right minds: not under the influence of alcohol or drugs, for example. And it must be consensual: all participants in the activities must understand the risks involved and give their express permission and approval of everything that is happening. Sadistic romance villains rarely practice safe, sane, consensual kink, and Winona is no exception. And her non-consensual emotional sadism is even more damaging than non-consensual physical sadism because Josh ends up blaming himself for the pain that is inflicted on him. It is revealed that the damage he suffered is the result of a chain of cause and effect: most directly, he is emotionally shattered by Winona's corruption of the natural connections between the polysexual axes of BDSM; but this is, in turn, only possible because of Josh's own ignorance of his sexual identity, which is itself caused by Josh's blind acceptance of traditional but outdated, even dangerous, gender and genre roles.

Winona's final unforgiveable crime, the proof that she is not merely confused but villainous, is to plan and execute a scene in which three men attack her and Josh in an alley; Josh, who thinks this is a real attack, is pinned down by two of the men, while the third "rapes" Winona, forcing Josh to watch: "'It was a fucking game. A game she had engineered. She wanted to get off on me being helpless while she was raped, which of course wasn't rape'" (139). For Winona, the pleasure in the scene was not in the sex act itself, but in witnessing Josh's torment while she is raped — torment compounded by his unspoken and immediately despised relief that, after torturing him for so long, she was "finally getting what she deserves" (138). As Lauren explains to Josh, "She enjoyed the violence, but more than that, she enjoyed watching it make you think you were sick" (142). Winona misappropriates the worst sexual violence a woman can suffer, and inflicts on Josh the guilt of having articulated the worst expression of patriarchal victim-blaming and rape justification. As such, she perpetrates a devastating emotional violence against her male partner, without his consent, forcing him to label himself a monster. The damage that patriarchy does, the narrative argues, devastates more than just women. It is precisely the men worthy of being romance heroes, men committed to the health, safety, and physical and emotional comfort of women, who are also harmed by patriarchal structures of gender roles and violence against women.

None of this would have been possible, however, if Josh had understood his own sexual identity. He is devastated because he feels he has failed his patriarchally-prescribed role of male sexual dominance. Instead, Lauren explains to Josh: "'You're not a Dom, not a Master, Josh,' she said. 'You've never even been close. You're a submissive. A gorgeous, incredibly sensual submissive that any Mistress in her right mind would cherish forever. You were doing as your Mistress told you to do, and she used you cruelly'" (145). Josh's response to Lauren's revelation is fury and denial: "The rage swelled up, and the hurt, and he did manage to jerk from her grasp, causing her nails to slice across his skin. 'No,' he snarled, struggling so she saw red lines of welts just below the cuff lines on his wrists, proof of his strength. He could not get free, but he could destroy himself trying. 'No, no, no!'" (142). Josh's violence represents the shock, even horror, of a man losing the belief— reinforced by everything in society — that he is in charge. He denies it vehemently, unwilling to lose the illusion of power and control. But when Lauren releases him so that he might take her, force her, enact the patriarchal role of aggressive sexual consumer, Josh cannot deny his inherently submissive nature. Lauren taunts Josh, "'Come after me, Josh. You want to prove me wrong? Prove you'll take what you want, that you like hurting women, like watching them be raped. Big pussy'" (143). But even the threat of being labeled a woman — a "pussy" — for not enacting patriarchal violence against the heroine cannot change Josh's essential nature. Instead of attacking her, Josh protects her as they fall to the floor. Instead of having sex with her, his penis is poised at the entrance of her vagina, but he cannot bring himself to "push through that barrier, though the desire to do so would have been unbearable to resist to almost anyone" (144). "'You see?'" Lauren asks him. "'You can't do it, Josh. You can't take me against my will. Not just because you're a submissive at heart. Not just because I didn't tell you that you could. You're a decent human being. You're a good man'" (144–5).

The opposite of the aggressive sexual consumer, then, the "good man" who rejects the patriarchal imperative to dominate and subdue women, is the submissive romance hero. Josh is able to heal when he finally understands that he is not a sexual dominant. He realizes, in fact, that the gendered expectation that he *be* dominant is a perversion of his identity, of BDSM, and of love itself — or at least, of the successful romance narrative. Josh, the ultimate romance hero, is represented as a "natural" submissive who has to figure out — indeed, has to be told by his heroine — that he is not the sexual dominant and sadist he thought he was, that it is precisely his submissiveness, which manifests as protectiveness of his heroine, awareness of her needs, and willingness to do anything to see to her emotional comfort, that makes him the perfect hero, the perfect and good man.

In fact, it is precisely in Lauren's sexual and emotional healing of Josh that Hill interrogates and rewrites the romance genre's construction of ideal masculinity and, indeed, of the romance genre itself. In order to overcome the mental and emotional barriers both to his relationship with the heroine Lauren and to his own self-actualization, the hero Josh must recognize and accept his BDSM identity as a sexual submissive. Once he does, he is able to share with Lauren a heightened understanding of love and achieve an otherwise unattainably transcendent relationship with her. The narrative is structured in such a way that the hero's willing submission of his body, heart, soul, and, eventually, his very identity to the heroine is not simply an essential requirement for the successful relationship between the female dominant and male submissive BDSM couple; rather, such willing submission is framed by Hill as the essence of the romance genre *as such*, an essence that BDSM romance fiction can represent more vividly, and reflect on more honestly, than conventional, non–BDSM romance.

NOTES

I wish to thank the Romance Writers of America for awarding me the 2008–2009 Academic Research Grant, funding time free from other obligations to conceptualize this chapter. This chapter started life as presentations at the annual national conferences of the Popular Culture Association in 2008, 2009, and 2010, and at "Love as the Practice of Freedom? Romance Fiction and American Culture. A Two-Day Interdisciplinary Conference" at Princeton University in 2009. I thank my audiences for their questions and remarks, as they have helped me formulate my thoughts. Thanks also to the astute commentary of Eric Murphy Selinger and Jonathan A. Allan on the many drafts of this chapter. I extend my deepest gratitude to Joey W. Hill and Ellora's Cave Publishing, Inc., for their permission to use extensive quotations from Hill's *Holding the Cards*. Finally, my thanks and deepest love to Jonathan Frantz and Dayna Harrett for acting as sounding boards and for keeping me on task and sane.

1. Many thanks to Joey W. Hill for explaining to me in a personal email the mystery of the many copyright dates for *Make Her Dreams Come True*.

2. Many in the digital publishing world would claim that the rise and success of erotic romance in traditional publishing was due to the traditional authors and publishers jumping on the erotic bandwagon created by digital publishing. However, erotic historical romances by Susan Johnson and Robin Schone were bestsellers throughout the 1990s. Traditional print publishers like Black Lace in England, which opened in 1993, Red Sage in the U.S., which released its first erotic anthology in 1995, and Kensington, which began to release erotic anthologies starting in 1999, also contributed to the rise of erotic romance. In the new millennium, the digital publishers brought erotic romance to contemporary, paranormal, and futuristic settings, and, of course, to an online audience. Besides Ellora's Cave, the earliest digital publishers of romance still in business are: Mundania Press, which started in August 2002 and opened its erotic romance imprint Phaze in November 2004; Amber Quill Press, an invitation-only digital publisher that opened in October 2002; Torquere Books, started in 2003, which publishes exclusively GLBT romance; Loose Id,

started in February 2004; and Samhain Publishing, started in November 2005. (Thank you to Theresa Stevens for her help with this chronology.)

3. "FAQ," Passionate Ink, http://www.passionateink.org/faq. The definition finishes: "Happily Ever After is a REQUIREMENT to be an erotic romance."

4. "What is Romantica©?" Ellora's Cave, http://www.jasminejade.com/t-romantica.aspx. Ellora's Cave includes two more elements in their description of Romantica: first, the "story must include abundant and explicit sex and sexual tension, starting early and continuing throughout. Sex scenes must be described in graphic detail and explicit wording, not delicate euphemisms or purple prose," and second, it "must meet the definition of a romance novel: the primary focus must be on the development of a romantic relationship, and there must be an emotionally satisfying committed ending for the main characters."

5. Pamela Regis, *A Natural History of the Romance Novel* (Philadelphia: University of Pennsylvania Press, 2003), 14. In person, Regis has lamented the heteronormativity of her use of "hero and heroine" to designate the protagonists of romance novels. She believes her definition should now use "protagonists" instead, thereby including gay male romances, lesbian romances, and even ménage romances.

6. In real life practice, although rarely in the BDSM romance genre, the term BDSM as a whole also encompasses a wide variety of sexual fetishes like foot or rubber fetishes.

7. Very few BDSM erotic romances explore the romance between the characters through Sadism/Masochism instead of Domination/Submission. Some exceptions include Anah Crow's gay male romance, *Uneven* (Round Rock, TX: Torquere Press, 2007); A.M. Riley's gay male romantic suspense, *The Elegant Corpse* (San Francisco: Loose Id, 2008); Victoria Dahl's heterosexual, male-dominant novella, *The Wicked West* (Don Mills, Ontario: HQN, 2009); and Heidi Cullinan's gay male romance *Nowhere Ranch* (San Francisco: Loose Id, 2011).

8. Ivo Dominguez, Jr., *Beneath the Skins: The New Spirit and Politics of the Kink Community* (Los Angeles: Daedalus, 1994), 15, 16.

9. *Ibid.*, 16.

10. Joey W. Hill, *Rough Canvas* (Akron: Ellora's Cave, 2007), 197.

11. This holds true only for BDSM romance novels. BDSM novels *not* written or marketed as romance novels have a much longer history and their own generic conventions.

12. Many thanks to Raelene Gorlinski, publisher at Ellora's Cave, for her help with publication dates.

13. The Nature of Desire series currently encompasses seven books: *Holding the Cards* (2002), the subject of this chapter, follows a female dominant and a male submissive, as does Hill's most famous book, *Natural Law* (2004); *Ice Queen* (2006) and its sequel *Mirror of My Soul* (2006) follow Tyler and Marguerite, both sexual dominants, as they establish a male-dominant/female-submissive relationship; *Mistress of Redemption* (2006) is a paranormal female-dominant/male-submissive romance, although still set in the same universe as the otherwise mundane, non-paranormal series; *Rough Canvas* (2007) is a D/s romance between two gay men; finally *Branded Sanctuary* (2010) moves away from the BDSM aspect of the Nature of Desire series when a recurring male-submissive character falls in love with a "vanilla" woman.

14. Joey W. Hill, *Holding the Cards* (Hudson, OH: Ellora's Cave, 2002), 6–7. Further references will be included parenthetically.

15. See especially *Novel Definitions: An Anthology of Commentary on the Novel, 1688–1815*, ed. Cheryl L. Nixon (Peterborough: Broadview Press, 2008).

16. "Joey W. Hill Interview," Author Island, http://www.authorisland.com/index.php?option=com_content&task=view&id=4340&Itemid=602.

17. "Guest Opinion: The Power of the Male Submissive by Joey Hill," Dear Author, http://dearauthor.com/wordpress/2008/10/21/guest-opinion-the-power-of-the-male-submissive-by-joey-hill/.

18. Jonathan's loveless BDSM relationships are literally demonized in the fifth book of the series, *Mistress of Redemption*, in which Jonathan is sent to Purgatory to be shown by a demon the damage he caused throughout his life. At the end of the book, his sins are literally burned away in Hell before he is allowed to deserve his happy ending with the demon who has acted as his "Mistress of Redemption."

19. Michel Foucault, *The History of Sexuality. Volume I: An Introduction*, trans. Robert Hurley (New York: Vintage Books, 1990), 61–62.

20. For a much more detailed discussion of the power of masculine confession in popular romance fiction, see my "'Expressing' Herself: The Romance Novel and the Female Will to Power," in *Scorned Literature: Essays on the History and Criticism of Popular Mass-Produced Fiction in America*, ed. Lydia Cushman Schurman and Deidre Johnson (Westport, CT: Greenwood Press, 2002), 17–36.

21. Candy Tan, "The Completely Despicable Gay Über-Villain," At the Back Fence, Issue #106 (November 15, 2000), *All About Romance*, http://www.likesbooks.com/106.html.

22. Mary Novak, "The Multi-Pervert Gay Villain cliché," At the Back Fence, Issue #106 (November 15, 2000), *All About Romance*, http://www.likesbooks.com/106.html.

4

On Popular Romance, J.R. Ward, and the Limits of Genre Study

Mary Bly

Academic study of popular romance fiction is clearly in its infancy, given the paucity of published work. But, more importantly, much of the existing scholarship (with notable exceptions) is theoretically naïve, depending on essentialized versions of both gender and genre. The work is primarily feminist, tackling at once the theory and practice of both sexuality and literature.[1] A recurring problem is the treatment of culture not as multifarious in its practices, but as simplistic, as if the word were synonymous with "patriarchy." And "the patriarchy" is portrayed as a monolithic and inexorable opponent, dictating women's lives through reading practices. Rather than conceive of the patriarchy as protean and various in its tools, romance scholars bandy about the word as if the force, mechanisms, and effect of patriarchy in 1980s culture are precisely the same decades later. Some scholars denounce romance fiction as a patriarchal tool, and others celebrate it as a subversive adversary.[2] Either way, the novels in question, the patriarchy itself, and the readers of romance fiction are reduced to ciphers in an ideological argument whose wide parameters diminish its value. Analysis of romance novels would greatly benefit from more rigorous assessments of the complex and time-specific ways by which culture influences women's lives.

This chapter argues that literary engagements with culture and readers cannot be appraised by consideration of the genre as a whole. A scholar who moves from study of a few romance novels to wholesale claims about the genre, and from there to analysis of the personal conduct and erotic choices of all romance readers, impoverishes her own argument. The mistake is not necessarily in the assessment of the workings of patriarchy in the novels she studies, but in the leap to genre and then to readers as an undifferentiated whole. Whether mass market romance or literary fiction, a few examples drawn from any genre that spans decades' worth of novels and thousands of authors cannot support a thoughtful thesis about sexuality, let alone consideration of the workings of patriarchy in a given historical moment. While gender will always be the crucial analytic category for feminist readings of romance fiction, that work needs to be grounded in an inquiry that addresses the specific discourses and types of knowledge in play during a novel's creation. As a genre, romance is no more static than the signifiers of patriarchal order. While defense of the genre is tempting, what is needed at this point is a morally neutral approach that emphasizes fact over conviction.

I will begin by examining the rationale behind the domination of genre study in popular fiction, as opposed to its comparatively negligible influence in the study of literary fiction. I will then turn to a 2005 novel, *Dark Lover,* by J. R. Ward. *Dark Lover* reflects a complex relation between the ideology mobilized in support of patriarchal control between 2001 and 2005, and an eroticization of male homosocial culture that structures, and eventually disrupts, Ward's portrayal of normative heterosexual marriage.

The pattern of a duel between feminism and the patriarchy, applicable to each and every romance novel, was set in two seminal works on the genre: Tania Modleski's *Loving with a Vengeance: Mass-Produced Fantasies for Women* (1982) and Janice Radway's *Reading the Romance: Women, Patriarchy and Popular Culture* (1984). Radway's subdued Introduction to a 1991 reissue of *Reading the Romance* acknowledges numerous inadequacies in her sociological approach to her romance-reading subjects, not the least of which was disregard of variables such as age, race, and class. In addition, Radway's early work was exclusively preoccupied, in her own words, with "a fairly rigid notion of patriarchy."[3] Modleski's book was reissued in 2008; her new introduction is far more thoughtful and theoretically nuanced than Radway's, as was her earlier study. Modleski's new Introduction notes her former disregard for cross-gender and cross-sexuality identifications among readers. Yet both critics still insist on their original point about all romance novels, notwithstanding changes in the genre; Modleski, for example, sees the primary influence on readers as the eroticization of male domination and rape.[4]

Tellingly, both consider culture, rather than individual authors, as generative of romance fiction. Radway's new Introduction does gesture toward the authors, noting that "romance *is* being changed and struggled over by the women who write them" (16). But she is unwilling to give those authors agency, concluding that "it cannot be said with any certainty whether the writers who are trying to incorporate feminist demands into the genre have been moved to do so by their recognition of the contradictions within the genre itself or by the pressures exerted by developments in the larger culture" (17). Radway finishes her Introduction by merging writers and readers: "romance writers and readers are themselves struggling with gender definitions and sexual politics *on their own terms* and [...] what they may need most [...] is our support rather than our criticism or direction" (18). Unfortunately, she concludes that that support will be difficult to offer: "Our segregation by class, occupation, and race, once again, moves against us" (18).

While I am certainly not advocating biographical criticism, recognition that romance authors are likely to be as intelligent and as well-educated as scholars might blunt the impulse to condescend, and therefore to suggest a simple causal link between the genre and unfortunate aspects of hegemonic culture. At the same time, I want to clarify that this article will not argue that all romance novels are feminist, although many romance authors would not agree with me.[5] Probably the strongest voice characterizing the genre as inherently feminist is that of the writer Jennifer Crusie. Crusie left a doctoral program — after completing a master's degree in feminist criticism — to write women's fiction. Now a wildly popular author, she has spearheaded a fierce rebuttal to feminist attacks on romance, pointing to sloppy scholarship and lax, simplistic assumptions about both readers and writers.[6] However, in my view, Crusie's wide-ranging statements about the genre acquiesce with the common omission of the author in the study of popular genres. Her own novels are fiercely feminist; they are not unique in that respect, but they also are not representative. In fact, I would argue that there is no one representative romance novel. I might be able to identify a representative "2010 urban vampire romance," but no single novel represents the whole of the romance genre.

This article, then, is not a defense of the genre. Reading romance may well be a rebellious act, but equally well it may not be. A specific reader may engage in a subversive reading of a specific book, but neither books nor readers are interchangeable. Crucially, the machinations of hegemonic culture are far more complicated and time-responsive than can be described by wide-ranging statements about a genre's effect, apparently applicable to thousands of novels published over several centuries. For example, in considering a burst of paranormal romances featuring heroines able to control the weather followed Hurricane Katrina, which struck in 2005, a scholar might observe a deep strain of anxiety aroused by Katrina, but to claim that romance readers in general feel more powerful in the face of bad weather would be absurd.[7]

The wide focus on genre that ignores creative anomaly stems from the perception that romance novels are "mass produced," so that like automobiles, it doesn't really matter which factory (or author) produces the texts.[8] Novels that fall under the rubric "mass-market romance" are often studied together due to the perception that the conventions of the genre are more important — and more influential — than a specific author's effort. In *The Work of Art in the Age of Mechanical Reproduction* (1935), Walter Benjamin identifies the "technique of reproduction" as the key to popular art.[9] Mechanical reproduction, he says, separates popular art from "high" art. Benjamin is writing about photography; assessments of romance fiction have often viewed these novels as if they were reprints of one photograph. In other words, the books offer the same snapshot over and over: that of a smiling heterosexual couple, the subject and conclusion of the novels dictated by formula. This argument insists that the romance novel's resolution — a happy relationship between two people — in itself limits originality, and thus the value of the work.

Theodor Adorno's distinction between classical and popular music is also useful in understanding how romance became ensnared (and scorned) by its consignment to a genre. He argues that the fundamental characteristic of popular music is standardization. The established themes and subjects of hit songs — songs about mothers, songs about home, laments for a lost girl — reappear in untold numbers. Most important, "the harmonic cornerstones of each hit — the beginning and the end of each part — must beat out the standard scheme."[10] The parallel between romance and pop music, at least in Adorno's conception, is clear. The formula (the subject and happy ending) leads to standardization, and thus to lack of originality (standard harmonic cornerstones). "Complications," Adorno continues, "have no consequences [...] the hit will lead back to the same familiar experience, and nothing fundamentally novel will be introduced."[11] Radway would certainly agree with Adorno: she disdainfully reports that readers understand "themselves to be reading particular and individual authors, whose special marks of style they could recount in detail," as opposed to authors who, according to Radway (echoing Adorno), actually write "identical, factory-produced commodities" (11).

Modleski uses Adorno's work to argue that while details of romance novels may change after being given, in Adorno's words, a "veneer of individual 'effects,'" the iron-clad grip of genre trivializes such small alterations.[12] But I would disagree. I think the error here lies not so much in Adorno's hypotheses about listeners, but in the very idea that standardization itself is problematic — or, crucially, in the idea that it stifles originality. I do not believe that the parameters of a genre are, in themselves, limiting to an artist. Shakespeare's *Hamlet*, for example, falls precisely into the genre of revenge tragedy — and yet its originality is undisputed.[13]

Lawrence Danson opens a chapter of his *Shakespeare's Dramatic Genres* with a newspaper headline, "Boy Killed in Tragedy."[14] Obviously, our idea of a tragedy is very different from Aristotle's or Shakespeare's. Genres are mutable.[15] Yet Danson's most important observation is that we now distrust the very idea that a tragedy — or any work — written *in* a genre could be good. We eagerly read tragedies reported on the front page of the newspaper, but not between the covers of a work of fiction. A contemporary genre novel may be the best of its kind, he argues, but "the modern idea is that great works belong to no specific kind at all."[16]

Yet when Shakespeare decided to write about the death of a young boy, he chose a specific genre: the comedy. Because of *The Winter's Tale*'s similarity to medieval romance, literary scholars have now recategorized it as a "romance," but John Hemmings and Henry Condell, Shakespeare's first editors, placed it among his comedies in their 1623 edition of the plays. In Act II of *The Winter's Tale*, the queen bids her young son, Mamillius, to tell her a story, and he asks, "Merry, or sad, shall't be?"[17] His mother leaves the choice to him, and he announces, "A sad tale's best for winter. I have one / Of sprites and goblins."[18] After this point, Mamillius disappears from the play. In Act III, the queen's lady announces his death; Mamillius has died of a broken heart while separated from his imprisoned mother.[19] To modern readers, this is manifestly a tragedy. My students, for example, are rarely able to rejoice in the play's happy ending, when the king regains his wife and lost daughter. Rather, they return again and again to Mamillius, the child whose tale gives the play its title, the storyteller who died offstage.

But to an early modern audience *The Winter's Tale* was manifestly a comedy. The formula of the genre at the time dictated a happy ending, generally concluding with marriages for all unattached characters. *The Winter's Tale* conforms to that dictate. In the last speech of the play, the king abruptly turns to a spare lady, widowed in the course of the play, and says, "Come, Camillo, / And take her by the hand, whose worth and honesty / Is richly noted."[20] By then the lost daughter has fallen in love and been reunited with her parents. Her parents are together once again, and only Mamillius has no part in the happy ending. Danson's work forces attention to the inherent pleasures of fiction, as well as to the question of why we insist that truly original work cannot adhere to a traditional structure. The pleasures of fiction are now supposed to be genre-free.

My point is that an author needn't be an innovator in form to produce creative work. To reverse the paradigm, study of Shakespeare through the lens of genre may omit his most creative work, given that he clearly saw genres as opportunities for inventiveness. Adorno's theory about popular music identifies the relationship between the framework of a piece of art and its details as the crux of the problem. In classical music, he argues, every detail derives its musical sense from the totality of the whole. But in popular music, "[t]he primary effect of this relation between the framework and the detail is that the listener becomes prone to evince stronger reactions to the part than to the whole."[21] Even given that Adorno was disparaging work of this nature, he does suggest that originality can reside in "parts." Ophelia's eroticized mad scenes, for example, are "parts," unscripted within the revenge tragedy genre; feminist scholars have done excellent work pointing out how the romanticization of Ophelia's madness and death reflects fear of female sexuality, stemming in part from early modern inheritance law. Obviously, literature that falls into a specific genre, whether that genre is popular romance or early modern comedy, conforms to a given framework, to use Adorno's term.[22] In the early modern genre revenge tragedy, for example, the hero must revenge a familial death. Both Hamlet's delayed revenge and Ophelia's madness were deeply original, and have certainly evinced strong reactions, but in the end Hamlet does kill his father's murderer: the genre's framework, its concluding rule, is satisfied.

I argue that the key to understanding genre novels, then, is to be found in study of the parts, rather than the framework. Critics have made large claims based on romance's parameters, but I think it's quite possible that we run the risk of missing the boots carrying Birnam wood to Dunsinane. In short, we're ignoring the trees for the forest. The modernist longing for "original" work that falls into no genre is a product of anxiety, the result of being in an age in which mechanical reproduction is not only possible, but ubiquitous and inescapable.[23] I would suggest that scholars refocus their attention, looking to the originality, and in particular, to the engagements with ideology and history, that can be found in romance novels' "parts."

It follows that the remainder of this essay, which looks closely at J. R. Ward's *Dark Lover* (2005), argues that it is in the parts — rather than the framework dictating a happy ending — that one can observe social and material forces working in support of hegemonic, patriarchal order. Even so, a historically specific analysis of *Dark Lover* makes it clear that "patriarchal order" is a deeply fraught, strained term that, like "genre romance," is difficult to identify and analyze.

Dark Lover is Jessica Bird's first novel published under the pseudonym J. R. Ward. As of 2011, the series has grown to nine novels, including several #1 *New York Times* bestsellers. *Dark Lover* conjures a paranormal version of contemporary America in which the Black Dagger Brotherhood, an army of elite vampires, fight soul-less humans who seek to kill both vampires and humans. Crucially, in Ward's construction, vampires are a separate species, rather than human beings transformed by a vampire's bite, à la Bram Stoker's *Dracula*. Ward's hero, Wrath, is king of the vampires.

Dark Lover opens in a bar; Wrath is introduced when "a sea of humans split as they steered clear of an imposing, dark shadow that towered over them. The flight response was a good survival reflex."[24] Wrath is immediately established as a dominant, aggressive male. While this is not unusual for romance, the socioeconomic codes structuring Ward's description are interesting:

> Wrath was six feet, six inches of pure terror dressed in leather. His hair was long and black, falling straight from a widow's peak. Wraparound sunglasses hid eyes that no one had ever seen revealed. Shoulders were twice the size of most males'. With a face that was both aristocratic and brutal, he looked like the king he was by birthright and the soldier he'd become by destiny [3].

The fact that Wrath is referred to as "pure terror" and "brutal" emphasizes his physical strength. But I would also suggest that the description deliberately unbalances the idea of kingship by giving Wrath the clothing and accessories of two distinctly lower socioeconomic groups: the motorcycle club Hells Angels, and American hip-hop performers. The Hells Angels are well known for their black leather jackets, death's head insignia, and a penchant for addressing each other with one-word nicknames.[25] As one law enforcement official put it, "When you had that patch on your back, internationally, every criminal knew you were a righteous bad guy."[26] Hip-hop clothing, or "urban wear" as it's sometimes called, plays a similar role in announcing opposition to the legal system. Hip-hop artists, particularly those specializing in "gangsta" rap, have cultivated a media image reflecting the economically disenfranchised and frequently violent daily life of inner city black youth.[27]

Wrath is explicitly a "righteous bad guy" in dress and manner: "He was wearing a biker jacket in spite of the heat, and his long legs were covered in leather as well. He had steel-toed shitkicker boots on, and he moved like a predator" (62). The Brotherhood is depicted as a society of vampires who are secretive, dangerous, and loyal only to each other. They smoke a cannabis-like drug, "red smoke," and address each other by one-word labels (e.g., Wrath, Vishous, Zsadist). I argue that Judith Butler's ideas about the "performability" of gender are key to understanding these characters.[28] Wrath's sartorial choices result in what Butler has termed "stylization of the body," and his bodily gestures, movements, etc. accentuate his consciously cultivated performance of hyper-masculinity.[29] He jealously guards these performative attributes: when he dons a suit in an effort to woo Beth, the novel's heroine, he immediately recognizes the contingent nature of his identity: "He was changing himself for a female. For no other reason than to try to please her" (184).

Yet if Ward hedges her male characters' gender by insisting on a hyperbolic performance of masculinity, she somewhat nervously also establishes biology as the basis for her hero's worth as a male. Wrath's stature is repeatedly mentioned; the heroine distinguishes between his body and that of other males on that basis: "Good lord, he was huge. And stacked. His upper arms were the size of her thighs. His abdomen was ribbed as if he were smuggling paint rollers under his skin. His legs were thick and corded. And his sex was as big and magnificent as the rest of him" (77). Here Wrath's body transforms into a grotesque exaggeration of an adult human male which, because of his "othered" species, reads like a hyper-extended assortment of biological characteristics.

Oddly, Wrath only gained this body at the age of twenty-five. Ward portrays male vampires under twenty-five years old as effeminate and impotent boys, who acquire the adult vampire body only after a painful transformation. Wrath describes his earlier self as "scrawny and weak" (58), and unable to maintain an erection. At twenty-five he transitioned overnight to adult, waking with a new body, including thighs four times their previous size. Thus *Dark Lover* oscillates between viewing gender as a repetition of stylized acts, and presenting gender as destiny, the result of hormonal, physical changes in the body. Ward's construction of masculinity is both Butleresque and not. It both undermines and relies on ontological gender.

The story pairs Wrath with a human newspaper reporter, Beth Randall. We are introduced to the character when she is attacked by two men, who drag her into an alley in an unsuccessful rape attempt. One of them, Billy Riddle, is described in detail: "with his polo shirt and his khaki shorts, he was BMOC handsome. Real all-American material" (7). Later, Billy is linked to widely held theories about sexual psychopaths when he reveals that as a young boy he enjoyed killing small animals. The rapist Billy is set up as a counterpoint to Wrath: Wrath is the son of a king; Billy is the son of a senator. Wrath is a hyper-masculine, outlaw-styled soldier fighting soul-less criminals; Billy is boyish, clean-cut, and dangerous to the weak, taking out his aggression on vulnerable women.

The threat to Beth is doubled once Billy converts to the literally heartless society of "*lessers*" and she is kidnapped by the head *lesser*, who plans to torture and then kill her. Ward's *lessers* are a society of humans who have traded their souls for one hundred years of "sanctioned killing."[30] They live undetected in the general populace, led by a sadistic figure called the Omega who exists in a non-temporal realm. Thus Beth is portrayed as imperiled by attackers, human and *lesser*, none of whom appear malevolent at first glance. Billy, for instance, seems to be stylized along the lines of a "preppie murderer," a term stemming from media attention to the Robert Chambers murder trial in 1986. The *lessers*, on the other hand, evoke a far more present-day threat, that of the clandestine terrorist living on American soil.

I suggest that Ward uses Billy in the first chapter to instill an atmosphere of menace without overtly placing the book in a post 9/11 world. While 9/11 is never mentioned in the novel, that historical event and its aftermath in America are crucial to understanding Ward's novel. *Dark Lover*'s construction of masculinity springs explicitly from the American response to 9/11 during the years immediately following the terrorist attacks. America reacted to the terrorist attacks on September 11, 2001, with a mixture of grief and shock. When the U.S. suffered an incursion against civilian targets by assailants who could not be identified as representing any particular nation, the popular myth of national invincibility was abruptly shattered. As president, George W. Bush announced the beginning of a "different type of war," immediately signaling his intention to weave a sense of America's vulnerability to attack into the fabric of everyday culture.[31] A signal effect of the creation of the Department of Homeland Security (DHS) directly after the attacks in 2001 was the reinforcement of the atmosphere of threat that became a hallmark of the Bush administration. For example, Clark Kent Ervin, the first Inspector General of the Department of Homeland Security (2003–2004), wrote an op-ed piece for *The New York Times* in 2007 in which he stated that "the supply of young people who are willing and even eager to attack Americans seems limitless."[32] He finished his opinion piece by warning that "it is only a matter of time before another catastrophic attack is attempted."[33]

During Bush's second term, his administration repeatedly turned to such fear-producing language, announcing reports with such titles as "The Terrorist Threat to the U.S. Homeland." The word "homeland" itself carries great weight, implying that the U.S. is a domesticated, homogeneous population of vulnerable persons. According to *The Washington Post*, and as was revealed by several national polls, one effect of this tactic was to cause a large percentage of Americans to fear American Muslims, although they were generally middle class, moderate, and well assimilated.[34] Another was simply to raise citizens' anxiety levels. As Edward Luttwak wrote in Toronto's *The Globe and Mail* in 2004, the public threat warnings issued frequently by the DHS were "so vague as to time, place, objectives and methods that they [...] cannot help to intercept, prevent or avoid terrorist attacks."[35] Luttwak argued that the greatest cost was psychological, leading to "self-inflicted wounds in the struggle against terrorism." The Center for Defense Information pointed out in 2003 that psychological effects of a terrorist attack "outweigh any physical destruction it may cause"[36]; given the Bush administration's fear politics, those psychological effects were inevitable, even without a second domestic attack. My point is that an environment of insecurity is as damaging as an attack itself, and the discourse of fear vividly manifested itself in a craving for protection.

One of the striking aspects of the 9/11 attacks was that they were carried out not by another nation, but by people who had lived on U.S. soil and had obtained U.S. drivers' licenses. They came from Saudi Arabia, Egypt, and the United Arab Emirates. There was no clear way to distinguish them from naturalized American citizens who might have emigrated from any of those countries. Official anti-terror neighborhood programs, therefore, focused on training citizens to "Watch America," according to the motto of a widely used community antiterrorism curriculum. Training conducted under the aegis of the CAT (Community Anti-Terrorism Training Initiative) emphasized that terrorists blend in with the population: "A terrorist could be anybody, [Sgt. Charles Marsch] said, showing pictures of Timothy McVeigh, white supremacists, Osama bin Laden, and others. They might pose as clergy, utility workers, police [...] 'They'll blend in the best they can.'"[37] Ward's vampire world makes use of the fear behind initiatives such as the CAT program; *lessers*, like the seemingly all-American boys who try to rape Beth, pose a terrible risk because they blend into the normal human population. They can be detected only by the smell of baby powder — hardly a fail-safe warning sign. The connection to a "different" kind of war is made painfully clear in Wrath's assessment of *lessers*: "The bastards had no honor anymore. At least their precursors, going back for centuries, had fought like warriors. This new breed were cowards who hid behind technology" (24). In an eerie echo of Clark Kent Ervin's claims about the "limitless" supply of young terrorists, Wrath feels he is fighting a losing battle: "though his warriors were hitting the society's legions of slayers hard, there were so few of the brothers going against an inexhaustible, self-generating pool of *lessers*" (29).

The Bush administration was insistent that a "different" war was now taking place, in the homeland, on front doorsteps. Since that message accompanied calls for military action and suspension of civil liberties, it implied that law enforcement was not (currently) sufficient, that the populace needed protection. Accordingly, *Dark Lover* identifies Wrath primarily as a soldier: "I fight to protect, not because I've got a jones for murder. But I've killed thousands" (193). The "self-inflicted wounds" Luttwak identifies as a side-effect of DHS public security threat warnings are clearly visible in a world in which Wrath strolls down the street in his black leather, a "wave of menace rolling ahead of him" (3). The need for a personal soldier or, in Beth's phrase, a "beautiful warrior" (373), ties directly to the aftermath of the 9/11 attacks.

Along with apprehension about domestic insurgents, an explicitly female vulnerability is reflected in *Dark Lover*.[38] A side effect of the Bush's administration's emphasis on the threat of war inside the United States was a contingent emphasis on the need for protection — implicitly and explicitly characterized as masculine. The misogynistic tone of the discourse was particularly clear in the early days of the 2008 presidential race, when Hilary Clinton unsuccessfully tried to co-opt fear tactics in her now infamous "3 A.M." campaign advertisement, in which a (white) sleeping child became the metaphor for an America threatened by a horrific event being reported via a middle-of-the-night call to the presidential hotline. The advertisement suggested that women and children are especially vulnerable, even as a woman was trying to take on the male warrior role. The extraordinarily hostile response to Clinton's challenge to male control of the standard fear discourse signals the twinning of patriarchal control and domestic policy. Susan Faludi has argued that such gendered fear tactics connect directly back to tales of early American male defenders saving white women from jeopardy, restoring "the defense of helpless femininity."[39] She cites the Bush administration's much-trumpeted claims to be saving Afghan women, Iraqi women, and even Private Jessica Lynch, "rescued" from the hospital to which her caregivers had brought her. The discourses geared to exalt male aggression simultaneously naturalize a passive, weak female populace.

Ward delicately negotiates the gendered aspect of the "different" war. While Beth is portrayed as a strong and feminist woman — as when she thwarts Billy Riddle's rape attempt — Ward's emphasis on gender as rooted in anatomy results in an essential need for male protection.[40] As the target of first Riddle and then the *lessers*, Beth is portrayed as at risk. Wrath's response to Beth is a protective one: "Darius's daughter was never going to walk the night unprotected again" (41). Yet Ward's most interesting gender moves do not have to do with clichéd distinctions between manly men and vulnerable women. Her portrayal of the Brotherhood constantly emphasizes the fragile border between phallic heroism and its negative "other," the effeminized, impotent male.[41] From this perspective, *Dark Lover* reifies both ontological male sexual characteristics and acculturated masculine behavior. Yet confusingly, these conflicting modes of masculinity are seen as vulnerable to change. Even biological characteristics are not fixed.

The *lessers*, for example, slowly turn whiter and whiter, losing pigmentation in their hair, skin, and eyes. Their characteristic baby-powder smell is only the most obvious attribute of their de-sexualized state. The head *lesser* is described as "a 1950s milkman, with blond hair that had obviously been hit with some pomade and a bright, annoying smile that had missed its Pepsodent ad by nearly half a century" (177). This "safe," pre-9/11 masculinity links to the already established hierarchy between good and evil, Wrath's flaunting display of "brutal" masculinity versus Riddle's "all-American" masculinity.[42] Crucially, *lessers* become impotent on accepting that status. So just as Brothers gain potency after transitioning to adult male status, *lessers* lose their potency. In the case of both *lessers* and Brothers, biological characteristics are not crudely fixed, but detachable and tenuous, emphasized by the fact that *lessers* keep their hearts in ceramic jars. The functional phallus, then, becomes a linchpin in competing modes of masculinity, particularly in the battle between good and evil.[43]

As Ward engages in a complex and vitriolic construction of impotent masculinity, its opposite gains a feverish eroticism — one rooted in potency but also explicitly homosocial. The Brothers live together, and are presented as a band of homosocial warriors, brothers-in-love, if not brothers-in-blood. *Dark Lover* exemplifies why study of romance *as a genre* is unable to encompass all the novels grouped within it; as Ward's series continues, the male homosocial society presented in *Dark Lover* moves to the erotic center of the novels. The first novel in the series fiercely guards the boundary between homosocial and homoerotic. Butch, a human who later becomes a vampire, greets the Brothers in *Dark Lover* with characteristic homophobic language: "Do you wear that leather to turn each other on? I mean, is it a dick thing with you all?" (258). Later, when Butch wakes up in a twin bed next to Vishous, he responds to Vishous's praise by policing the same line: "don't get all mushy on me. We ain't dating" (307). Yet Butch's own name, often used in a homoerotic context, points to non-heterosexual eroticism.

Successive books in the series further breach the distinction between heterosexual and homoerotic. In *Lover Awakened* (2006), for example, three naked Brothers, including Butch and Vishous, end up sleeping in the same bed.[44] In *Lover Revealed*, Vishous and Butch embrace, only to find that they are "two halves making a whole"[45]; the language generally reserved for heterosexual union is now shifted to men. The language used when Vishous initiates Butch to the Brotherhood at the end of *Lover Revealed* is homoerotic (even given that the novel's frame is Butch's love for a woman): "the warmth of their bodies so close, the way V's hair felt soft on his jaw, the slide of a powerful male arm as it slipped around his waist."[46] In the next novel, *Lover Unbound* (2007), Vishous's feelings are clarified: "As Butch stretched out on Vishous's bed, V was ashamed to admit it, but he'd spent a lot of days wondering what this would be like. Feel like. Smell like."[47] In this book, Vishous's relationship with a human woman provides the ostensible frame, but his feelings are obviously conflicted: "with a stab of guilt, V recalled the times he'd imagined himself with Butch, imagined the two of them lying as they were now."[48] The novel's adulation of male bodies sidelines the heroine; by the end of the story, Vishous's wife Jane is transformed — literally — into a ghost. And in *Lover Enshrined* (2008), one young male vampire declares his love for another, who declines to sleep with him (while making it clear that he enjoys both men and women).

Clearly, the boundaries between the homosocial and the homoerotic have broken down by Ward's 2007 and 2008 novels, since the symbolic center of the Brotherhood series is not male-female relationships (as is commonly assumed with mass-market romance) but rather identification with male-male relationships. We are left with a world in which the most revered relationships are between two men, rather than between a man and a woman. Ward's emphasis on the functional phallus as the key to good and evil leads to a singular focus on the male body — and in return that admiration threatens to swamp the heteronormative drive of the frame, or male-female romance. Here the "parts," to return to Adorno's formulation, are quite likely to elicit a stronger response than the heterosexual relationship that structures the plot.

It can be argued that the move toward acceptance, if not idolization, of male homoerotic desire reflects shifts in American popular culture between the years 2005 and 2008. The Brotherhood series is not the only recent romance fiction that includes a testosterone-drenched story of male-male love; the cover and back copy of Suzanne Brockmann's *Force of Nature* (2007) signal a standard romance, akin to Brockmann's previous novels featuring Navy SEALs. However, the plot depicts a love affair between an FBI agent, Jules Cassidy, and a closeted male movie star with the androgynous name of Robin Chadwick. While the book's back cover conspicuously uses masculine pronouns (e.g. "Robin's in town promoting his latest film"), a reader skimming the back cover text might well mistake Robin for a woman and believe this novel to be in line with Brockmann's earlier, hetero-normative novels. In fact, this is essentially a homosexual romance novel, complete with male-male sex scenes, packaged as a standard heterosexual romance. Scholarship that bases its conclusions on romance fiction as a mass-market genre cannot account for novels such as *Force of Nature*, let alone Ward's Brotherhood series. While patriarchal discourse is certainly mobilized in them, at least in terms of women's subordinate status, these and other novels also force a reconsideration of the genre. It cannot be summarized as eroticizing male rape; the creative aspects of Ward's vampire world reformulate the formula.

We could simply note that the patriarchy is not uniform at the moment of production, and leave it there. Hegemonies negotiate and naturalize new ways of interpreting the world. They evolve. But perhaps a more interesting, if speculative, question is precisely what happened *to* the patriarchy by 2008 that encouraged novels of this nature? It's a subject beyond the scope of this paper, but I would suggest that 9/11 had a signal effect on female desire, and not just with respect to increased admiration of warrior males. These novels speak painfully to bewilderment about the nature of a "different" war, a war waged by men who look like neighbors.

Dark Lover presents a world in which the Pepsodent-smiling male idolized in 1950s television, not to mention 1950s romance novels, turns out to be impotent and (literally) heartless. At the same time, the dangerous men formerly "othered" with respect to Pepsodent males — Hells Angels, gangsta rappers — are presented as the good guys, based on their potency and their protectiveness. With these males, what you see is what you get; in fact, their exteriors supersize sexuality and violence, as though defanging them by literalizing and stylizing them.[49] One crucial fact about hip-hop and Hells Angels is that both groups tightly control their membership. If a prospective recruit doesn't have the credentials—which include the correct socio-economic background, language, and clothing—he cannot join.[50] Passing is neither acceptable nor likely. Therefore, these men are exactly what they appear to be. While Hell's Angels and hip-hop music began in America, they quickly became international phenomena. But there doesn't seem to be a *Confrérie Noir*. The American nature of the brothers runs in their blood along with their vampire genes. Their sartorial characteristics and normative behavior are intrinsically American, and thereby, reassuring.

What these books are not, of course, is reassuring to a feminist scholar. Anxiously shoring up male performability by deifying male biological characteristics—and then undermining the whole idea that biology fixes bodily parts, including the heart—J. R. Ward's novels perform a delicate, strange dance at the boundaries between homosocial, homoerotic, and heteronormative. The "patriarchy" is a queer thing in Ward's novels.

[handwritten margin note: She makes the patriarchy queer]

NOTES

This essay benefited greatly from conversations and detailed commentary by Anne Connell, Julie Crawford, Jennifer Crusie, Sarah S. G. Frantz, Tania Modleski, Sharon O'Dair, Eric Murphy Selinger, and J. R. Ward.

1. A standard question is as follows: "What might it mean for young women in the throes of negotiating their own social and sexual relationships to consume this genre in a culture in which social and sexual objectification and violence against women run rampant?" (Carol Ricker-Wilson, "Busting Textual Bodices: Gender, Reading, and the Popular Romance," *English Journal* 88, n0.3 [1999]: 57.)

2. Linda J. Lee comes to the same conclusion: "Most scholarship on romance novels falls into one of two polarized camps that view these novels as conservative forms that uphold the existing patriarchal structure, or as subversive, resistant forms that challenge the existing structure" ("Guilty Pleasures: Reading Romance Novels as Reworked Fairy Tales," *Marvels & Tales: Journal of Fairy-Tale Studies* 22, n0.1 [2008]: 54). One interesting piece that mediates between the two extremes is Alison Light's article on *Rebecca*, which argues that reading romances "is, I think, as much a measure of their deep dissatisfaction with heterosexual options as of any desire to be fully identified with the submissive versions of femininity the texts endorse" ("'Returning to Manderley': Romance Fiction, Female Sexuality and Class," *Feminist Review* 16, no. 2 [1984]: 22).

3. Janice Radway, "Introduction: *Writing* Reading the Romance," in *Reading the Romance: Women, Patriarchy, and Popular Literature* (Chapel Hill: University of North Carolina Press, 1991), 9. Further references will be provided parenthetically.

4. Tania Modleski, "Introduction to the Second Edition," in *Loving with a Vengeance: Mass-Produced Fantasies for Women* (New York; Routledge, 2008): xxvi. Modleski repeats this point in a different reassessment of *Loving with a Vengeance*: "One of the main points of my analysis of romances is that the novels take the actual situation of women in our society, a situation in which the rape of women is a distressingly common if not routine event, and put it into a context that is soothing and flattering to women, allowing female readers to interpret instances of male brutality, even rape, not as expressions of rape and hostility, but of overwhelming desire and love" (*Old Wives' Tales and Other Women's Stories* [New York: New York University Press, 1998], 49).

5. Many such articles were printed in Jayne Ann Krentz's edited anthology, *Dangerous Men and Adventurous Women: Romance Writers on the Appeal of Romance* (Philadelphia: University of Pennsylvania Press, 1992); Susan Elizabeth Phillips, for example, argued that romances offer "a fantasy of female empowerment" ("The Romance and the Empowerment of Women," 55). In 1997, the journal *ParaDoxa* published a volume devoted to the romance genre, which included a number of interviews with romance authors, as well as articles written by them. Jennifer Crusie Smith was the most forthright in her feminist argument that romance puts women at the center of their own sexuality ("Romancing Reality: The Power of Romance Fiction to Reinforce and Re-Vision the Real," *ParaDoxa* 3, nos. 1–2 [1997]: 81–93).

6. See, for example, Crusie's essay (as Jennifer Crusie Smith) "Romancing Reality."

7. After Hurricane Katrina struck in August 2005, the Weather Channel put out a press release announcing that it had become one of the top five cable channels in terms of viewership. Laura Anne Gilman's *Staying Dead* (New York: Luna), published June 2006, features a heroine who feeds her magical powers by tapping into lightning strikes. A popular series at the time was Rachel Caine's Weather Wardens. Her *Firestorm* (New York: ROC), published September 2006, features a heroine who's something of a weather cop, heading off natural disasters with paranormal powers.

8. Modleski offers the most sophisticated theorization of this assessment, arguing that "individual products do not escape the imprint of ideology" ("Introduction to the Second Edition," xxxii).

9. Walter Benjamin, "The Work of Art in the Age of Mechanical Reproduction," in *Illuminations*, ed. Hannah Arendt, trans. Harry Zohn (New York: Schocken Books, 1969), 221.

10. Theodor Adorno, "On Popular Music," *Cultural Theory and Popular Culture: A Reader*, 2d ed., ed. John Storey (Athens: University of Georgia Press, 1998), 198.

11. *Ibid.*, 198.

12. Modleski, *Old Wives' Tales*, 57.

13. Martin Wiggins approaches the same divide between modern and historical attitudes toward genre in his *Shakespeare and the Drama of his Time* (Oxford: Oxford University Press, 2000). He opens with the assertion that the conception of the dramatist's "absolute originality and effortless superiority ignores everything we know about the occupational circumstances of play-writing in his time" (4). Shakespeare's originality, Wiggins argues, was built on a foundation of other playwrights' brilliance and always played itself out within specific genres. Moving away from the early modern period, Fredric Jameson argued in 1977 that the "disappearance of genre" is merely a historical "feature" of contemporary modernism, rather than an "eternal characteristic" ("Ideology, Narrative Analysis, and Popular Culture," *Theory and Society* 4, no. 4 [1977]: 546).

14. Lawrence Danson, *Shakespeare's Dramatic Genres* (Oxford: Oxford University Press, 2000), 113.

15. An Goris made an interesting point about the instability of genre in a paper given at the Popular Culture Association conference in 2008. She concludes that genre theory does not, at present, offer a model that allows for conceptualization of pop culture, given its textual complexities. (As yet unpublished work; personal communication.)

16. Danson, *Shakespeare's Dramatic Genres*, 143.

17. William Shakespeare, *The Winter's Tale*, *The Riverside Shakespeare*, ed. G. Blakemore Evans (Boston: Houghton Mifflin, 1997), II.i.23.

18. *Ibid.*, II.i.25–6.

19. *Ibid.*, III.ii.194–5.

20. *Ibid.*, V.iii.143–5.

21. Adorno, "On Popular Music," 198.

22. An ancillary argument here is the point that our classical art was, in many cases, originally consumed as popular art. See Richard Shusterman, "Don't Believe the Hype: Animadversions of the Critique of Popular Art," *Poetics Today* 14, no. 1 (1993): 108.

23. I am writing here about attitudes toward genre as a category, but there is, of course, also a widespread and specific distaste for the genre of romance. While these critics do point to formulaic, mass production, much of their distaste stems, I would argue, from fear of female sexuality together with entrenched academic disdain for the market. Sharon O'Dair's brilliant observations about Shakespeareans' denigration of the market and the "people" applies in a wider sense to prevailing academic attitudes toward romance (*Class, Critics, and Shakespeare: Bottom Lines on the Culture Wars* [Ann Arbor: University of Michigan Press, 2000]).

24. J. R. Ward, *Dark Lover: A Novel of the Black Dagger Brotherhood* (New York: New American Library, 2005), 3. Further references will be provided parenthetically.

25. Andrew Malone, "Dark Heart of this Cult," *Daily Mail* (London), August 14, 2007, 11.

26. Tim Shufelt, "Police Finally Infiltrate Hells Angels," *National Post* (Canada), March 22, 2008, A15.

27. See Jeff Chang, *Can't Stop Won't Stop: A History of the Hip-Hop Generation* (New York: St. Martin's Press, 2005).

28. See Butler's *Gender Trouble: Feminism and the Subversion of Identity* (New York: Routledge, 1990), as well as her later work.

29. Judith Butler, "Performative Acts and Gender Constitution: An Essay in Phenomenology and Feminist Theory," *Theatre Journal* 40 (1988): 519.

30. See J. R. Ward, *The Black Dagger Brotherhood: An Insider's Guide* (New York: New American Library, 2008), 224.

31. An editorial in *The New York Times* in 2007 emphasized the systemic nature of Bush's use of fear: "This administration has never hesitated to play on fear for political gain" ("The Politics of Fear," July 18, 2007). Greg Schneiders argues in "PR shares in blame for climate of fear that is gripping America" that Bush's tactics have spawned a "homeland security" industry (*PR Week*, August 25, 2008, 9).

32. Clark Kent Ervin, "Answering Al Qaeda," *The New York Times*, May 8, 2007, 25.

33. In another flagrant example, Alexander Chancellor noted that Michael Chertoff, U.S. Secretary of Homeland Security in 2007, warned of heightened terrorist risks in the summer of 2007, basing that assessment on a "gut feeling." Alexander Chancellor asks, in his title, "What's the point of being told the terrorist

beast is on the prowl if we don't know when or where it will strike?" (*The Guardian* [London], July 13, 2007, 5).

34. Fareed Zakaria, "A Rhetoric of Danger," *The Washington Post*, June 4, 2007, A15; Rick Hampson cites a Gallup Poll citing 39 percent of U.S. citizens with some fear of Muslims, while about a third believe that American Muslims sympathize with al-Qaeda ("Fear 'as bad as after 9/11'; In Michigan and elsewhere, Muslims worry about hostile neighbors and surveillance," *USA Today*, December 13, 2006, 1A).

35. Edward Luttwak, "More harm than good," *The Globe and Mail* (Toronto), January 16, 2004, A17.

36. Qtd. in David Von Drehle, "Uncertain is Sea Where All Swim: Vague, Looming Threat Calls Citizens to Brace for the Worst — Whatever That Is," *Washington Post*, February 16, 2003, A15.

37. Lini S. Kadaba, "Anti-terror programs training neighbors to spy on each other," *Philadelphia Inquirer*, December 13, 2002, n.p.

38. Ellen Micheletti, "Interview with J.R. Ward," *All About Romance*, March 1, 2007, http://www.likesbooks.com/jrward2007.html. Ward sees the alpha male focus of the society she depicts to be a direct consequence of war. In an interview, she explained, "The society is very male-centric by tradition and that stems from the ongoing war with the *lessers* and survival issues within the species."

39. Susan Faludi, "America's Guardian Myths," *The New York Times*, September 7, 2007, 29. Of course similar rhetoric has been employed in other countries, as in Britain during World War II.

40. Beth is certainly portrayed as brave in her own right: she fights off rapists and saves Wrath from an attacking pit bull. But Ward insists that Beth needs Wrath's protection on a biological level: she literally cannot survive without him.

41. I borrow the term "phallic heroism" from Mary Beth Rose, *Gender and Heroism in Early Modern Literature* (Chicago: University of Chicago Press, 2001), 16.

42. See R. W. Connell's *Masculinities* (Berkeley: University of California Press, 1995) for discussion of hegemonic men contrasted with subordinate men.

43. Judith Lorber points out that most wars offer a "careful construction of two very different types of masculinity — the good-doers and the evil-doers" ("Heroes, Warriors, and Burqas: A Feminist Sociologist's Reflections on September 11," *Sociological Forum* 17, no. 3 [2002]: 383). She turns to a very interesting discussion of the multiplicity of gendering in U.S. post–9/11 rhetoric.

44. Butch begins the series as a human male, but undergoes an "ancestor regression" that brings out his vampire DNA, transitioning him to adult vampire. At the end, his shoulders are twice as big and he's much taller. His lover, Marissa, explicitly notes that it was "what males went through, particularly warriors" (*Lover Revealed* [New York: New American Library, 2007], 368).

45. Ward, *Lover Revealed*, 399.

46. *Ibid.*, 443.

47. J. R. Ward, *Lover Unbound* (New York: New American Library, 2007), 135.

48. *Ibid.*, 136

49. This comment was made by Eric Murphy Selinger (private communication).

50. The Hells Angels are notoriously difficult to join, and the police did not manage to infiltrate the group until 2008. See Shufelt, "Police Finally Infiltrate Hells Angels."

5

Loving by the Book:
Voice and Romance Authorship

An Goris

The romance novel's enduring appeal is often perceived as one of contemporary pop culture's most mystifying phenomena. Given the general puzzlement and even disdain over the genre's commercial triumphs, it is remarkable that the romance community's own take on its success — i.e. the appeal of the genre as a whole and the particular popularity of individual romance authors — is so often disregarded or overlooked. This chapter seeks to mend that error by focusing on the genre's self-perception. In an attempt to understand how the romance genre itself accounts for and envisions its (commercial) appeal, I explore how successful romance writing is defined and conceptualized from within the romance industry itself.

The romance industry's own opinion on what constitutes a successful romance novel is laid out in handbooks for writing romance novels. In such manuals experienced romance authors and/or editors explain the basics of writing and publishing a (category) romance novel. In this articulation of the aesthetically ideal romance, the roles of the genre's texts, users, and industry are taken into account, resulting in a consistent double focus: the manuals simultaneously encourage their pupils to express their individuality uninhibitedly and authentically in their writing while also directing the resulting texts towards the (commercial) demands of the genre's industry and readers. Guiding eager and aspirant writers towards creative self-confidence and commercial success, the handbooks mediate between the genre's authors, texts, users, and industry and offer a behind-the-scenes conceptualization of the ideal — i.e. commercially successful — romance novel.

The Corpus

Although creative writing manuals have, in recent years, steadily become a commercially prominent genre of their own, they have up till now been largely ignored in the field of literary studies.[1] The concrete corpus on which this study is based consists of six romance manuals selected as a representative sample of the multitude of handbooks available on the market today. In order to represent cultural, temporal, and institutional variations the corpus includes handbooks written by American, Australian, New Zealand, and British authors between 1997 and 2004, all published by different publishers, often in specific series such as the *Dummies* series or the *Writing Handbooks* series. An analysis of this corpus reveals that while there are many slight differences between the handbooks, their core advice regarding romance writing is overall remarkably similar. The main differences regard superficial elements such as the handbooks' scope (that is, the aspects of the writing and publishing processes on which the handbooks focus[2]) and the way in which they represent their advice (e.g. the books' layout, organization in chapters, the use of indices, etc.). But despite these surface differences, the handbooks concur on central elements of the genre such as the structure of the basic romance plot and the underlying aesthetic strategies that shape the texts.

The handbooks' didactic and commercial aims require them to approach their endeavor in a dual way. To the extent that they need to encourage their pupils to write, they adopt a descriptive approach and present creative writing as an easy, natural, and even self-evident act. To the extent that they need to ensure the resulting texts are commercially viable, they adopt a prescriptive approach and direct their pupils' efforts towards the demands of the genre's institutions and readers. The resulting alternations between a descriptive and a prescriptive approach to the writing of a romance novel engage with the handbooks' considerations of the romance genre's texts, users, and industry; the alternations moreover seem to be inherent in the genre of the creative writing manual itself.

As commercial publications, the handbooks' first goal is to encourage their readers to write. In order to do this they present creative writing as an easy activity, essentially based on readily available knowledge about the genre as well as natural, creative talent. The generic knowledge which must inform the pupils' writing is available to them as avid readers of the romance genre, and all the handbooks emphasize that being a sincere lover and reader of the genre is a *sine qua non* condition for becoming a successful romance author:

> And there is an important secret to this sort of writing that, while it can't guarantee any sort of success, will give you a far better chance of creating a romance that an editor will be interested in reading. [...] **[W]rite from the heart**. It's no coincidence that many of the most successful romance writers were also — and still are — ardent romance readers themselves. The people who love reading romance value it for the special sort of writing it is and they appreciate the stories as the emotional reads they are. As a result they can write successful novels because they write them from the heart.[3]

As appears from this quote, "successful" romance writing is considered to be based on a true "love" for "the special sort of writing it is." Thus the crossover between readership and authorship is generally accepted, even required, within the romance community. This quote equally hints at the widespread notion in the handbooks that successful romance writing is also based on the writer's own innate, natural talent. To "write from the heart" not only indicates the necessity of a sincere love for the genre, but also implies that the authentic and *natural* expression of the author's individuality and innate creative gift is of crucial importance.

Even in their self-positioning, the handbook authors' duality of approach is present. By consistently and explicitly framing the manuals as based on the authors' own extensive experience in the romance industry, the authors legitimize their own expert status while they narrow down the gap between themselves and their pupil-readers:

> When I started writing romances [...m]ost of my learning was of the "hands-on" variety and the most painful of all, trial and error. In an attempt to help other writers short-cut this stage, I wrote out in the form of a home study course everything I wish someone had told me when I started out.[4]

Each of us had our first romance released by Mills & Boon in 1977. Between us we have had over a hundred romantic novels published. This book is the result of all that experience.[5]

I've been in the romance biz for 25 years. [...] In this book, I distill everything that I've learned as a romance editor into a step-by-step, topic-based guide to help aspiring romance authors take an idea and grow it into a published novel.[6]

The handbooks are then presented as "an attempt to help" based on "all that experience" and are thus framed as reliable and accessible sources of advice. An added benefit of this strategy is its implicit support of the notion that this advice is based on the reality of the romance genre. It then sustains the implicit notion that the advice is in fact largely a reminder of a reality the reader is partly already familiar with.

Although the handbooks ostensibly reject a prescriptive or authoritarian approach to creative writing,[7] they still need to ensure the novels produced with their help are commercially viable by directing their pupils towards the latest demands of the romance industry and readers. To this extent, then, the handbooks do adopt a prescriptive attitude. While this approach is only very rarely manifested explicitly — for example, by the use of explicit prohibitions and obligations when discussing relatively recent generic changes pertaining to the portrayal of sexual violence[8] — it is nonetheless an integral part of the handbooks' overall makeup, as the way in which the handbooks are framed and marketed by their publishers indicates:

> Valerie Parv has written a comprehensive guide for new writers [Parv cover].
>
> If you want to write romance and be a professional writer then this book is a must for you. [... L]earn from what she tells you and you will be able to write and publish your novels [Walker cover].
>
> Get the inside track on creating and marketing your romance novel [Wainger cover].

On the paratextual level, then, the handbooks are presented as prescriptive "guide[s]" and directives aimed at "new" and "professional writer[s]" looking for commercial (publishing) success. Hence aspiring authors are encouraged to take the advice as normative rules rather than merely as descriptive suggestions.

Moreover, the romance genre's own commerce-driven nature tends to reinforce this apparently contradictory mechanism. From the commercial point of view inherent to the genre, the actual publication of a manuscript is an indispensable condition to consider it a romance novel.[9] Consequentially the factual criteria by which publishers select manuscripts tend to act as prescriptive norms for those aspirant authors who wish to be published. Since the handbook authors are successful — i.e. published — romance writers and/or editors themselves, the descriptions of their experiences thus seem to offer insight into the behind-the-scenes ("inside track") normative logic used by the publishers. As such the advice then operates on a prescriptive level.

This dual approach furthermore allows us to formulate some tentative suggestions regarding the handbooks' intended public. As didactic writings the manuals are directed at an intended reader — a theoretic construct itself — who is dynamic in nature; the reader theoretically changes from an unskilled, lay would-be writer to a professionally skilled and potentially published author. The handbooks' alternations between a descriptive and prescriptive tone then seem to accommodate this changing reader as the tone evolves from addressing a pupil to addressing an (almost) equal.

Finally, these alternations are indicative of the handbooks' relation to the reality of the genre. As the descriptive tone and approach suggest, to a great extent the handbooks describe the genre as it is; the handbooks' authors' extensive experience with the state of affairs in the romance genre serves as the basis of (most) of their formulated advice. The image of the romance novel formulated in these publications is then firmly rooted in the genre's reality. However, the manuals' prescriptive approach equally indicates that to a certain extent the handbooks formulate rules and norms which play a role in shaping this reality. Insofar as the handbooks display a directive approach towards the writing of romance novels, they might in fact be formulating a theoretic and ideal image of the genre. Overall, then, I consider the handbooks' conceptualization of the romance novel as both real and ideal; these two aspects interact to such an extent in the discourse analyzed here it seems impossible—and more importantly, superfluous—to distinguish between them.

Romance Poetics

Contrary to the widespread stereotypical image of the romance novel as repetitive and formulaic—and hence literarily worthless—the handbooks define and locate the genre's success precisely in its ability to integrate familiarity with innovation, thus offering its readers experiences of both comfort and surprise. The romance author must give the reader what she wants and expects, but differently. The seemingly paradoxical set of assumptions shared by all romance manuals in this study defines success in the romance genre as the occurrence of similarity as difference, of familiarity as novelty, of the constant interaction of comfort and surprise. To accomplish this, the handbooks suggest, the author must write with absolute sincerity and authenticity, while still complying with the genre's overall conventions. Aesthetically speaking, constant interaction between comfort and surprise in the reading experience translates into the simultaneous and interacting occurrence of familiar and new creative features in the romance's narrative as well as its rhetoric, thus profoundly influencing readers' entire textual experience.

As the handbooks construct the ideal romance reading experience as one in which comfort and familiarity play a major role, they extensively discuss the genre's elements that would be familiar to an experienced romance reader. The manuals construct the most important of these as having to do with the romance novel's basic plot and protagonists. The handbooks indicate romance protagonists are always morally good and physically appealing people, although importantly the heroine tends to be quite unaware of her own beauty. The romance plot, the handbooks further suggest, minimally consists of the following six plot phases: the protagonists' (first) meeting, their mutual attraction, the internal and external conflict between them, the crisis or outburst of the conflict, the black moment in which the relationship seems doomed and finally the happy ending.[10] In making up the generic framework these features play a major role in providing the reader with experiences of recognition, familiarity, and comfort.

While the romance genre has often been scathingly criticized for its reliance on familiarity and repetition—these characteristics indeed seem to form the basis of the widespread cultural disdain for the genre—the handbooks nevertheless suggest the experiences of comfort and recognition they provide are crucial to the genre's overall commercial functioning. As a commercial genre the romance novel aims to give the reader what she wants; that is, to fulfill the functions the reader ascribes to the reading act. These functions, Janice Radway's classic ethnographic study on the genre indicates, are to provide escape, relaxation, and happy, upbeat feelings.[11] To achieve this goal the romance reader uses an emotional reading strategy, identifying with the romance's protagonists, thus vicariously experiencing their adventures. Consequently, the ideal romance text facilitates readers' identification with the protagonists and offers its readers experiences of escape, relaxation, and positive emotions.

It is no coincidence that the genre's narrative framework tightly interacts with these complex requirements. For example, identification is facilitated by characters who share points of convergence with the reader, or more precisely with the reader's self-image. Moral goodness and a lack of vanity are presumably part of most women's self-image and thus indeed facilitate the process of identification.[12] At the same time the protagonists' invariable good looks play into the fantasy and escapist aspect of the romance reading experience. A similar process takes place with regard to the familiar elements in the romance's plot. These elements provide an emotional roller coaster in which the emotionally invested reader easily gets caught up, enabling her to fully relax and mentally escape her own day-to-day reality. The happy ending, finally, provides the readers with the positive, upbeat feelings she seeks in the reading act. All of this indicates the romance genre's narrative framework as presented in the handbooks is indeed very well adapted to the reader's expectations and treatment of the text and thus serves the genre's (commercial) purposes.

Moreover, the fact that this narrative framework is used in all novels belonging to the genre is in itself an important condition for the optimal functioning of the genre. The repetitive nature of the framework ensures the reader that the narrative features essential to the specific reading experience she seeks occur in all new, unread instances of the genre. This reassuring certainty is a necessary condition for the reader to be willing to employ the above discussed emotional reading strategy — which is in turn crucial to the overall functioning and thereby to the commercial appeal of the genre — as it limits the risks inherent to this strategy (e.g. emotional involvement in a story with an unhappy ending). Familiarity and repetition, then, play an important role in the romance genre on both the concrete and the abstract level.

The crucial role taken up by the concrete familiar features and by the abstract notions of familiarity, recognition, and repetition in the romance genre explains why the handbooks extensively focus on these elements, even though they are presumably already known to their pupils. The industry — the institutions surrounding the genre — translates reader expectations and preferences into concrete demands which published romance novels must live up to. As such, the handbooks must perform an extensive rearticulating of the genre's narrative conventions that the pupils are already familiar with as readers, transforming them into textual norms that the pupils need to implement as writers.

However, familiarity, repetition, and recognition alone are not enough to create a successful romance novel. The handbooks consistently suggest that romance readers seek surprise along with comfort in their reading experience. While the simultaneous experience of comfort and surprise might seem paradoxical, the handbooks indicate the very interaction of the two is a crucial aspect of the romance reading experience. Notwithstanding the importance of the generic narrative framework, the romance reader expects and demands a new, exciting, and surprising reading experience every time she picks up a romance novel. That is, she expects a unique new story which is still somehow familiar. In fact, some handbooks point out, precisely because the reader is thoroughly familiar with the generic framework, she is even more attentive to surprise *within* this framework. So in order to meet the reader's expectations a romance novel has to simultaneously be familiar and new.

All handbooks in this study indicate that the implementation of novelty in the romance genre is located on the level of the concrete, individual embodiment of the abstract generic conventions. The narrative and textual surface manifestations of the genre's underlying deep structure easily allow for variations and differentiations. The handbooks highlight the ensuing uniqueness of each romance novel in two complementary ways: by refuting the conceptualization of generic conventions as creatively stifling and by emphasizing the unique personal input of each individual author as she writes her romance novel.

The handbooks' attempt to bring the romance novel's uniqueness to the fore starts with explicitly refusing to associate the romance novel with the negatively connoted term "formula":

> The so called formula is merely a set of conventions ... Within the conventions you can write your own story [Parv, 1].
> This is not a formula; it's a guide. [... T]his information can be used any way you want, but it must be "added to" in order to make a good story. The kind of stuff you're cooking is up to you, and the choices are almost limitless.[13]
> The romance "formula" is only a framework in the same way that the poetic form of a sonnet is a framework, within which you can write anything you want and work in any way you want [Walker, 9].

As Kate Walker's remark implies, all genres provide "frameworks," but when these generic frameworks are discussed in the context of popular culture, they are often reconceptualized as "formula," triggering a set of negative connotations. Romance scholar Pamela Regis notes that the term formula "implies hack-work, subliterature, and imagination reduced to a mechanism for creating 'product.'"[14] The association with the term formula then implicitly conceptualizes the writing of a romance novel as a creatively passive, mindless, impersonal, and inherently unimaginative process, thus ignoring and even negating the role of the individual author. The handbooks therefore explicitly refute this term, instead using terms — "set of conventions," "a guide," or "a framework" — which recognize the importance of the individual author and her personal input of creativity, originality, novelty, and uniqueness.

While the handbooks thus explicitly reject the conceptualization of generic conventions as creatively stifling, they do point out that respecting the genre's framework while still maintaining one's individuality and creativity is difficult: "So the problem with writing a romance plot is not one of creating a totally new and different idea, but one of putting a new twist, a new spin on the old tried and tested stories that have been around for years" (Walker, 95). "[P]utting a new twist, a new spin on the old tried and tested stories" is, however, precisely what the romance genre is all about, as it is this mechanism which provides the paradoxical combination of comfort and surprise in the reading experience. Still, the handbooks emphasize the author's personal input, particularly with regard to the development of characters, which is considered to be the primary aspect of the story in which the individual author has most leeway. Valerie Parv urges her pupils, "Because of built-in restrictions of the genre it is a real art to create unique heroes and heroines who will live on in readers' minds. So much has already been done in romance fiction that you have to work hard at creating new and different heroes and heroines who still 'fit' the requirements of romance" (18). The "built-in restrictions of the genre" are subtly reconceptualized here as a challenge, rather than a "problem"; respecting the generic conventions while being "new and different" is presented as "a real art." The role played by the genre's basic conventions is then essentially redefined: the conventions are no longer considered creatively smothering but stimulating:

> Pondering one of the more common plot situations can provide you with an idea for a new story, provided you can come up with an original treatment of it [Parv, 77].
>
> [T]here are basic and classic situations that readers still like. A fresh, new approach to the Cinderella plot, for example, is going to excite both editors and readers [Clair and Donald, 94].

The individual author brings this "original treatment" or "fresh, new approach" to the genre's impersonal conventions, thus making every romance novel unique. In refuting the notion of formula, the handbooks strongly imply that generic conventions do not determine the romance novel in absolute terms; they complement this line of reasoning by further emphasizing the crucial role played by the individual author. All handbooks in this study extensively focus on the narrative and textual manifestation of the author's individuality, designated by the term "voice," and its far-reaching consequences for the entire romance genre.

Voice is an often-used concept in such disciplines as linguistics and rhetoric where it essentially refers to the expression of identity and the "individual or personal quality in writing."[15] Extensively influenced by Western ideologies of individualism, this notion of voice implies that to the extent texts are written by inherently unique individuals they are necessarily and inherently unique themselves because the individual inevitably marks his writing. The handbooks repeatedly use the notion of voice to signify the individual author's profound influence on the romance text ostensibly dominated by abstract, familiar conventions.

In the handbooks, voice is presented as one of the major strategies by which essential differentiation between romance texts is not only possible but becomes prominent as well: "With a limited pool of potential plots for your romance ... how do you manage to create anything that is original? You write using your own voice. [... A] narrator has their own particular *style* of telling that story. And that is what you can bring to the story you are writing — the touch of individuality that lifts your book ... even if you are telling the oldest story in the world" (Walker, 96). Some handbooks suggest voice makes the story and the text unique because it is essentially a reflection of the writer's unique conglomerate of experiences: "[P]ut an individual twist or flavor into the story you're writing. Again, don't try to copy what has gone before. Be yourself. We are all unique, with our own life histories and experiences, and so that is what we bring to writing" (Walker, 97–98). This somewhat naïve belief in "be[ing] yourself" is also apparent in the handbooks' respective conceptualizations of voice as having to do with authenticity and with the natural expression of the inner self. Although all handbooks' understandings of the concept of voice revolve around notions of individuality and uniqueness, their precise interpretations tend to differ slightly.[16] Kate Walker, for example, interprets the term as expressing notions of authenticity as well as/besides individuality:

> You need to have your own individual voice that marks your book out from all the others, not just turn in some pale copy of an author who has gone before [11].
>
> You should try your hardest to write *authentically*. To write as you, tell the story you want in the words you want to use. Then your writing will have the individuality that will lead people to recognize your voice out of the hundreds of romances published every year.[17]

The notion that voice is somehow related to authenticity is also present in other handbooks, which tend to relate voice to the (authentic) expression of the author's inner self. Handbook authors such as Daphne Clair, Robyn Donald, and Leslie Wainger then interpret voice as the expression of innate, natural talent: "Voice comes naturally from within the writer" (Clair and Donald, 8); "Finding your author voice involves recognizing and going with your natural bent [...] and the developing of an awareness of your own language, rhythms and vocabulary" (Wainger, 128). As such then, the handbooks depict voice as most manifestly expressed on the rhetorical level, in "language, rhythms and vocabulary."

As is apparent in many of these quotes, the handbooks tend to display a rather naïve faith in this seemingly unproblematic narrative and textual expression of individuality and authenticity. The notion that a story's "individual twist or flavour" is, at least in part, the result of the writer bringing her "own life histor[y] and experience [...] to writing" is indicative of the underlying assumption of the effortless, even natural transition of life experience into language and text. Language is essentially considered as an immediate, neutral, and transparent medium of expression and communication. The handbook authors, then, do not adhere to post-modernist and post-structuralist conceptions of language that severely critique this notion of neutrality and transparency. Indeed, the handbook authors do not recognize that language is instrumental in constructing the world; they simply present it as offering an open window on the world.[18]

As the textual manifestation of individuality, voice is also considered to be indicative of a particular writer, and as such commercially vital. Handbook author Rebecca Vinyard points out that "[b]estselling authors have very distinct voices. If someone handed me one of their books without their names on them, I could identify the writing of Nora Roberts, Julie Garwood, Linda Howard and others of their calibre."[19] This remark hints at the apparently crucial commercial function voice has within the romance genre. This is indeed confirmed by Vinyard's observation regarding the pervasive influence voice has on the communication between the reader and the writer taking place in the text: "An author's voice is not so much *what* you write as *how* you write and how it sounds to your reader. [...] Voice has a lot to do with whether or not your story *speaks* to your reader. [...] Voice is the personal connection between writer and reader. If the connection isn't there, then odds are the reader won't enjoy the story" (110). Not only is voice, then, one of the most important strategies of differentiation between individual romance novels, it apparently also vitally influences whether or not the reader likes the writing, making its commercial function obvious.[20] Representing individuality, difference, and reader appeal, voice is then indeed a central commercial parameter in a genre revolving around difference in sameness as surprise in comfort.

Voice's apparent importance in the romance genre indeed makes sense when considering the pervasive influence it has on the narrative and textual surface-manifestation of the genre's underlying structure. Its extensive influence on both the narrative and textual-linguistic dimension of the individual romance text is hinted at by the handbooks' diverse general descriptions of this phenomenon: "the words you want to use" (Walker, 97); "your own language, rhythms and vocabulary" (Wainger, 128); "your handling of an idea ... your way of telling a story, your own style" (Parv, 8); "how you write" (Vinyard, 110). Thus narrative elements, in particular character portrayal, seem to be influenced by voice. Furthermore, voice is manifested extensively on the textual level, influencing vocabulary, grammatical constructions and collocations, expressions, language rhythm, etc. (see Wainger, 127–138). These elements in turn affect the dialogues, style, tone, and mood of a story. Given this pervasive textual influence on the individual romance novel and its ensuing significance to the reader, it is no surprise then that voice is an important factor in the romance industry. Indeed, the handbooks point out that romance publishers and editors often set great store by an author's voice: "Editors and readers [...] want writers with their own fresh voices" (Clair and Donald, 8); "Voice is an elusive quality. But elusive or not, it's a quality that editors look for more than anything else" (Vinyard, 110). Voice is therefore perceived as an all-important criterion in the selection of manuscripts by romance editors and publishers. Avon editor Lucia Marco indeed confirms in Vinyard's *The Romance Writer's Handbook*: "We're just looking for authors who have a high level of creativity [and] have a wonderful voice and are able to tell their story in a vivid and fascinating and wonderful and romantic way" (258).

In fact, the handbooks are not the only sources in the romance industry that set so much store by an author's voice. As the entire genre revolves around the interaction of familiarity and novelty, romance publishers themselves explicitly state that the quality of one's voice can be decisive in this genre. For example, voice is an often-used concept in the writer's guidelines for new writers published by romance publishers,[21] and it is mentioned explicitly as one of three main evaluation and selection criteria in a Harlequin Presents' writing competition:

> Entries will be judged by a panel of members of the Harlequin Presents editorial staff, based on the following criteria:
> Voice
> Content
> Writing Skills
> in equal measure.[22]

It is remarkable that although Harlequin explicitly mentions voice as the first of their main evaluation criteria, they do not further qualify this notion. By distinguishing between voice, content, and writing skills, however, Harlequin does imply voice cannot be equalized to either one of the other concepts. While it is then indeed an elusive quality, it clearly plays a central role in the romance industry.

The central place the notion of voice thus takes up in the romance genre can be accounted for by the fact that it anticipates and accommodates the interaction and tension between familiarity and novelty around which the romance genre seems to revolve. As I have remarked earlier, romance readers seek surprise in comfort as difference in sameness. It is this paradoxical quality voice in fact seems to enable. Handbook author Valerie Parv remarks: "It is your handling of the idea, not the idea itself, which makes it unique. [...] You must work towards developing your own unique way of telling a story, your own style, adapted to the special demands of the romance genre" (8–9). To the extent that voice refers to the "unique handling" of an idea and "not the idea itself," it seems to enable familiar elements to appear — and to a certain extent in fact to *be*— new. Voice then embodies the very interaction between sameness and difference so very crucial to the popular romance genre.

Endings

Romance writing, then, triggered by the reader's paradoxical search for simultaneous experiences of comfort and surprise, continuously revolves around interweaving convention and originality, expressing authentic individuality in profoundly familiar structures, and is essentially paradoxical in nature. While it is ostensibly dominated by familiar and repetitive generic conventions, the handbooks strongly suggest it is the difference within the sameness which eventually matters most. This seemingly contradictory dynamic is exemplified by the role of the happy ending:

> Reader expectations must be met. At the same time the writer must feed the reader's desire to be delighted and satisfied by the eventual resolution of a seemingly insurmountable problem. The romance writer aims to keep the reader interested and excited about what will happen next, even though the reader knows what will happen in the end. It takes considerable skill [...] to keep the reader in suspense not about *who* or *what* but about *how* and *why* [Clair and Donald, 4].

Although absolutely crucial to the reader's overall experience of comfort, the actual happy ending itself is in fact not of paramount importance in the reading act because "the reader knows what will happen in the end." The romance genre's paradoxical aesthetics then eventually seem to partly disrupt and displace its ostensible focus on its (in)famous happy ending, and reveals an apparent lack of a teleological orientation

The process-oriented nature of romance reading directed at the experience of difference within uniformity might finally hint at a blurring of the firm distinction and hierarchy between high-brow and low-brow strands of our contemporary culture. The self-conception of the romance put forth in the handbooks ultimately suggests that this commercial, low-brow genre adopts in its own way some of high-brow culture's core values, such as creativity, authorship, originality, and authenticity. The invocation of traditionally high-brow values in the self-perception of an iconic low-brow genre might in the first place be a culturally effective strategy of self-legitimation; the readers of these handbooks find the cultural value of writing romance novels affirmed in language quite similar to the discourse used in manuals about writing more privileged, less commercial genres, such as poetry or literary fiction. But the invocation of these values seems, to me, equally based on the romance reader's concrete textual experience. The highly conventional nature of the romance genre paradoxically facilitates recognition of individuality, creativity, and authorship in the text, or at least it does to fluent, experienced readers. If previous romance scholarship has found these subtleties and criteria of aesthetic success hard to articulate, future work in the field will need to address them, whether or not it does so in the terms put forth by the handbooks themselves.

NOTES

I would like to thank Dirk De Geest, Elke D'Hoker, Theo D'Haen, and Hilde Heynen for reading drafts of this paper and discussing them with me. Their suggestions have proven to be invaluable.

1. For a more detailed exploration of (romance) handbooks as the formulation of narratological norms or constraints, see Dirk De Geest and An Goris, "Constrained Writing, Creative Writing. The Case of Handbooks for Writing Romances," *Poetics Today* 31, no. 1 (2010): 81–106.

2. In this regard a distinction needs to be made between the aesthetic and pragmatic aspects of writing and publishing a romance novel. Aesthetic aspects are the elements of the handbooks concerning the actual writing process, while pragmatic aspects refer to matters surrounding the submission and publishing process, such as selecting a suitable publisher, formatting a manuscript and sending it to a publisher, hiring an agent, etc. Although I do not focus on these pragmatic aspects of the handbooks' advice, it is important to realize a significant part of my corpus deals precisely with these matters. The extent to which the handbooks focus on either aspect of the writing and publishing process differs greatly within the corpus.

3. Kate Walker, *Kate Walker's 12-Point Guide to Writing Romance* (Somerset: Studymates Limited, 2004), 10. Emphasis in the original. Further references will be included parenthetically.

4. Valerie Parv, *The Art of Romance Writing* (St Leonards, Australia: Allen & Unwin, 1997), xi. Further references will be included parenthetically.

5. Daphne Clair and Robyn Donald, *Writing Romantic Fiction* (London: A & C Black, 1999), 1. Further references will be included parenthetically.

6. Leslie Wainger, *Writing a Romance Novel for Dummies* (Indianapolis: Wiley, 2004), 1–2. Further references will be included parenthetically.

7. Remarks such as "I'm not big on rules and regulations when it comes to writing a romance novel, because [...] too many do's and don'ts make a writer self-conscious and stifle her creativity" (Wainger 2) or "[a]ll advice on how to write — including ours — should be taken with a grain of salt, and there is no rule which cannot be broken in the interests of a better story" (Clair and Donald 2) indeed seem to indicate the handbooks do not wish to install strict rules or norms.

8. For more a more detailed discussion of this observation and concrete examples, see De Geest and Goris, "Constrained Writing."

9. Actual publication is not an indispensable condition in all genres. A poem, for example, belongs to the genre of poetry, whether it has been published or not.

10. Note the similarities with Pamela Regis' widely accepted definition of the genre: "the definition: the romance novel is a work of prose fiction that tells the story of the courtship and betrothal of one or more heroines. All romance novels contain eight narrative elements: a *definition of society*, always corrupt, that the romance novel will reform; the *meeting* between the heroine and hero; an account of their *attraction* for each other; the *barrier* between them; the *point of ritual death*; the *recognition* that fells the barrier; the *declaration* of heroine and hero that they love each other; and their *betrothal*" (*A Natural History of the Romance Novel* [Philadelphia: University of Pennsylvania Press, 2003], 14. Emphasis in the original).

11. Janice Radway, *Reading the Romance. Women, Patriarchy, and Popular Literature* (1984; rpt. with a new Introduction, Chapel Hill: University of North Carolina Press, 1991). Although I am aware of the profound criticism Radway's study has been subjected to ever since its first appearance, I believe there is presently no indication that these basic findings are in any way wrong or problematic.

12. While most handbooks indicate the identification between reader and heroine is primary, the majority also stress the importance of allowing identification with the hero by showing the hero's softer side and using double point of view.

13. Rita Clay Estrada and Rita Gallagher, *You Can Write a Romance* (Cincinnati: Writer's Digest Books, 1999), 99.

14. Regis, *Natural History*, 23.

15. Paul Kei Matsuda and Christine M. Tardy, "Voice in Academic Writing: The Rhetorical Construction of Author Identity in Blind Manuscript Review," *English for Specific Purposes* 26, no. 2 (2007): 236.

16. This is not unlike the academic world, where many subtly different definitions of the concept exist.

17. Walker, *Kate Walker's 12-Point Guide*, 97. Emphasis in the original.

18. Janice Radway remarked that romance readers as well as romance authors hold such a naive conceptualization of language (*Reading the Romance*, 189–191).

19. Rebecca Vinyard, *The Romance Writer's Handbook* (Waukesha, Canada: The Writer Books, 2004), 110. Further references will be included parenthetically.

20. This understanding of voice and the crucial role it plays in the reader's experience of the romance text seems to be confirmed by the habitual excerpt printed on the very first page of a category romance novel. The main function of this excerpt seems indeed to give the reader the opportunity of checking whether or not she likes the writing (= voice).

21. For example, Harlequin Romance: "What we want in a nutshell [...] Unique, fresh voices" ("How to Write the Perfect Romance!" *Harlequin Enterprises Limited*, http://www.eharlequin.com/articlepage. html?articleId=1425&chapter=0).

22. Tessa Shapcott, "Harlequin Presents Writing Competition: Official Rules at I (Heart) Presents," http://www.iheartpresents.com/?p=146. I would like to thank Sarah S. G. Frantz for bringing my attention to this competition and its use of voice.

6

The "Managing Female" in the Novels of Georgette Heyer

K. Elizabeth Spillman

Widely known for her mysteries and for her historical novels, Georgette Heyer wrote in several genres and historical periods before perfecting a comedy of manners set in the Regency period that owes much to Jane Austen's influence. The popularity of her work gave rise to a category romance genre, the Regency romance, popular in the 1980s and 1990s. While most imprints have dispensed with the Regency romance as a distinct category, the sustained enthusiasm for the period as a fictional setting is apparent in the proliferation of mysteries, films, and Austen homages set in that period, and also in the renewed interest in Heyer's romances. Since her death in 1974, successive mass-market paperback editions have kept her novels continuously in print, marketed to readers of the growing romance genre. More recently, Arrow Books and Sourcebooks have launched new trade paperback editions; with period paintings on their covers, these volumes visually echo modern editions of the works of nineteenth-century women novelists. Their literary value is further asserted by the stamp of Margaret Drabble's approval on their covers and by their shelving in the mainstream fiction sections of most bookstores. Visually and spatially, Georgette Heyer's works are now positioned closer to Jane Austen's than to Barbara Cartland's, although all three are indubitably writers of romances.

This positioning, and Heyer's sustained popularity even after the demise of the category she inspired, suggest that Heyer's authorial voice continues to resonate both within and beyond the romance genre. Over nearly a century, her romances have been popularly acclaimed but critically ignored, heralded but neglected, widely influential but overlooked by the literary establishment. The same claims could be made on behalf of many popular writers, but Heyer is of particular interest for the longevity of her work; for its survival of the publishing category to which it gave rise; and for her liminal position in literary history, spanning periods and genres, and confounding easy compartmentalization. To study Heyer's work and its influence is to look both backwards and forwards in the history of popular romance: in reacting against the conventions of the genre her novels helped shape its development, mostly notably through her creation of heroines whose agency and self-awareness challenged the traditional limitations of a romantic heroine.

Georgette Heyer published her first novel in 1921, when she was nineteen. *The Black Moth* is an improbable tale of disgraced nobility, duels, highway robbery, abduction, and rescue, set in Georgian England. A contemporary notice in *The Saturday Review* acknowledged the familiarity of the characters and situations: "The hero takes care to appear in appropriate costume on each occasion we meet him; his horse and his fencing are of the best. Seriously, the author has made quite a respectable story of these old properties, far more life-like than could have been expected."[1] Despite being heavily derivative, more Baroness Orczy than Jane Austen, the novel bears some of the hallmarks of Heyer's later, greater work: fluid action sequences; easy, natural discourse between the major male characters; and an emphasis on the importance of friendship. Mills & Boon, at that time a publisher of general fiction, released Heyer's second book in 1923 under the pseudonym Stella Martin.[2] Something of a misfit among her other romances, *The Transformation of Philip Jettan* concerns a hero's reassessment of his own identity to please a capricious heroine; ultimately, of course, she sees his true worth and it is she who is transformed, conveniently and unconvincingly. The heroine of *The Black Moth* is both utterly conventional and entirely unmemorable, but the heroine of *The Transformation* seems to be an early expression of Heyer's dissatisfaction with that stereotype; Cleone is almost a caricature of a traditional heroine, not just beautiful and willful, but spoilt, snobbish, demanding, and not entirely sympathetic, a type Heyer later relegated to the subsidiary romance plot.

At this stage Heyer began to experiment with other forms, writing four serious, unsuccessful contemporary novels in her twenties, as well as a string of well-researched historical romantic adventures and later a mystery series, but she returned frequently to the romance, gradually developing a distinct, light-hearted style. Her first decade as a novelist also saw the publication of *These Old Shades* (1926) and *The Masqueraders* (1928), both adventurous Georgian romances featuring cross-dressing and other forms of vexed identity; the sword-fighting heroines of these novels must still be rescued, in the usual fashion, by appropriate heroes. In the romances Heyer wrote during the following decade — the Georgian-set *Devil's Cub* (1932), *The Convenient Marriage* (1934), her first Regency-period novel, *Regency Buck* (1935), and *The Talisman Ring* (1936) — the sword-play and other violence were mostly played for laughs, but her early themes of identity and transformation remained central. Likewise, the heroines' problems continued to be resolved primarily through the hero's intervention, or by marriage to him. There followed the more serious *An Infamous Army* (1937), acclaimed for its lucid account of the complex events surrounding the Battle of Waterloo. But with *The Corinthian* (1940), Heyer perfected the formula for which she was afterwards famous: deft plotting coupled with a light comic touch, and a writing style that ably evoked the imagined elegance of the Regency period. It was the last novel in which she employed cross-dressing as a device, and here she used it for comic rather than dramatic effect, signaling a major shift in her writing from the adventurous romance to the comedy of manners. From 1940 on, she was principally a writer of Regency romances.

The development of her style is gradual, but as early as her fourth romance novel, *Devil's Cub* (1932), she had acquired an ironic consciousness of the conventions of the historical romance and a habit of mocking them, as in the following ballroom scene:

> Miss Marling, at the moment of the Marquis's entry, was going down the dance [...]. She caught sight of her cousin, gave an unmaidenly shriek, and seizing her partner by the hand, left the dance without ceremony, and rushed to greet him.
> "Vidal!" she exclaimed, and gave him both her hands.
> "Don't be a hoyden, Ju," said his lordship.
> Half the young ladies in the room regarded her enviously [...] .

"It is her cousin, the wicked Marquis," whispered a brunette to a languishing blonde.
"How she is fortunate!" sighed the blonde.[3]

The brunette and the blonde know that a wicked Marquis is a romantic hero indeed; for the passage to succeed as humor, the reader must recognize this too. A basic intertextuality exists in romance novels, in that every novel is to a certain extent dependent on the heroine's and the reader's recognition of its tropes. Because of the formulaic nature of the basic romance plot, and because of the great number of romance novels written throughout the past two centuries, many of them bear a close resemblance to one another; part of Heyer's appeal was and is the distinctness of her style, if not her plotting.

Heyer's Marquis has come to find Miss Marling, his cousin; she is able to recognize him as a hero but she knows that she is not the heroine of his story. Yet, she yearns to be a heroine; and since a heroine must have a hero — is in fact, defined by having a hero — she tries to create a romantic hero like her cousin in the exceedingly proper and unromantic person of her fiancé, Mr. Comyn:

> The Vicomte, who was well aware of Mr. Comyn's pretensions, was impelled by an innate love of mischief to flirt outrageously with Juliana [Marling] under the very nose of her stiff and disapproving lover. Juliana, anxious to awake a spark of jealousy in what at that moment seemed to her an unresponsive heart, encouraged him. All she wanted was to be treated to a display of ruthless and possessive manhood. If Mr. Comyn, later, had seized her in his arms in a decently romantic fashion there would have been an end to the Vicomte's flirtation. But Mr. Comyn was deeply hurt, and he did not recognize in these signs a perverted expression of his Juliana's love for him [161–62].

Propelled by her desire to be the heroine of her own imagining, Juliana Marling tries to manipulate her lover, quarrels with him, renounces him, pursues him and, of course, reunites with him — a drama of two, cynically observed by the other characters:

> "How," demanded Juliana tragically, "Can you suppose that I could think of food at such a time?"
> "Do you know," said the Marquis gently, "I find you excessively tedious, Juliana. You complain of the speed at which I choose to travel; you talk a deal of damned nonsense about my incivility and your sensibilities; you spurn dinner as though it were poisoned; you behave, in short, like a heroine out of a melodrama" [190–91].

Heyer revisited Juliana Marling's type often: young, beautiful, impetuous, tempestuous, the very image of a heroine of romance novels. She is not, however, the heroine of this novel. Her fortunes are intertwined with the primary romance plot, but her distorted or "perverted" desires and assumptions are used to gently mock the conventions of the genre.

The novel's heroine, Mary Challoner, has not needed to manufacture melodrama. Though creating circumstances that are more truly dramatic and also more dangerous, Heyer underplays both elements, and despite their adventures, the Marquis and Mary Challoner address their linked fates with humor, with common sense, and, when circumstances call for it, with aplomb. Neither Mary Challoner nor Juliana Marling fulfills the role of heroine in a predictable fashion: calm Mary cannot appreciate her good fortune in being cast as a persecuted heroine, while romantic Juliana yearns for an unfolding drama in which to star. In this and in Heyer's other novels, attention is deflected from dramatic or sexual tension and focused instead on the mundane, confounding readerly expectations: Miss Challoner suffers from seasickness; she strictly supervises the Marquis's convalescence after she has shot him; and she ends a fight by dousing the participants with water as if they were stray dogs. In *Friday's Child* (1944), young Viscount Sheringham is dismayed to discover that the object of his professed adoration has been afflicted with measles, a childish and indeed anti-romantic ailment. In *The Reluctant Widow* (1946), Elinor Rochdale copes with a decaying mansion by mending the linens. Heyer consistently redirects the reader's attention from the passionate to the pragmatic, presenting realism when romance is most expected, or at her best, deflating drama for comic effect. The reader's recognition of romantic conventions is essential and the reader is complicit in the joke. At the same time, the primary romance plot moves forward to fulfill the very expectations being confounded elsewhere, producing a sophisticated, reflexive text with a satisfying and familiar conclusion.

This play upon convention in a text from well before the era of the Harlequin novel not only asserts the long-standing importance of the romance plot as a literary device, but also suggests that its very ubiquity made it a fertile area for gender-bending literary play. The sphere of female action is necessarily limited, by the social conventions of the historical period, to the private, domestic territory of friends and family, with chaperoned forays to private ballrooms or the Pump Room in Bath. However, Heyer's heroines consistently demonstrate both independence and initiative within that realm, more often resembling an interfering Emma Woodhouse or a provocative Elizabeth Bennett than a docile Jane Bennett or a dutiful Fanny Price. Contemporary reviewers as well as recent critics, including Jane Aiken Hodge and Karin E. Westman, have noted how naturally and effectively Heyer portrays both the public, male world and the heroine's easy interactions with it.[4] Heyer's heroines consistently challenge the limits of agency accorded to a traditional romantic heroine, but her most successful heroines do not transgress them, maintaining a finely crafted equilibrium between expanding their traditional gendered and generic roles, and exceeding them. They engage confidently with males and with the public realm, but they do not become mannish in so doing; they do not act like men. Moreover, her most accomplished heroines achieve self-awareness within their own stories, recognizing themselves as distinct from the traditional romantic heroine and redefining that role.

The most problematic aspect of this analysis is the difficulty of distinguishing what is merely traditional in the romantic heroine and what is definitive: is she the heroine of eighteenth- or nineteenth-century novels? the ideal woman of her society and time period? of the period in which the novel was written? of the fiction of the period in which the novel was written? Heyer published her first romance in 1921 and her last in 1972, so her writing career spans the emergence of the romance as a publishing category and she was influential in shaping that genre. The traditional or typical romantic heroine must have been something of a moving target during that fifty-year period, and yet all authors of romances, and thus all heroines of romances, work in relationship to the generic conventions.

Heyer allowed the women in her novels, both the heroines and the supporting cast, to describe the romantic heroine to us, and it is to this person that they contrast themselves:

> Cecilia might read novels, but she knew that the spirited behavior of her favorite heroines was not for her to emulate.[5]
> "We used to talk of it, my cousin Henriette and I. We made up our minds we should be entirely brave, not crying, of course, but perhaps a little pale, in a proud way [...]. You would be very sorry for a young girl in a tumbril, dressed all in white, pale, but quite unafraid [...]. The people I have met in England," said Eustacie after a short silence, "consider it very romantic that I was rescued from the Terror."[6]
> A delicately nurtured female (unless all the books lied) would have swooned from the shock of being kissed by a strange man, or at the very least would have been cast into the greatest affliction, her peace cut up, her spirits wholly overpowered.[7]

Like Diana of *The Black Moth* and Cleone of *The Transformation of Philip Jettan* — and like Marianne Dashwood — the traditional romantic heroine is young, virtuous, feminine, emotional. The persecution by her relatives engages readerly sympathy. The harassment of unworthy suitors is her lot in life. Her powers are constrained by her own sensitivity. The story arc of the romance threatens her domestic happiness — either by an intrusion into the domestic sphere, or by her exclusion from it — and restores security and harmony through the creation of a new sanctuary in the form of her marriage at the close of the novel. The ideal young woman dutifully resists the call of adventure — by literally losing consciousness if necessary — while a traditional heroine has it thrust upon her by cruel circumstances, to which she rises with "spirited behavior." This portrait is admittedly a stereotype, but the idea, at least, of the traditional romantic heroine must exist for her to be subverted by Heyer or by other novelists.

Heyer's most important contribution to this project was in her exploration of female agency, demonstrating that the traditional romantic heroine is not the definitive romantic heroine. She portrayed an unironic traditional heroine only in her very first romance; even then, Diana Beauleigh remained in the background while the hero and the villain and their friends bantered and dueled, as if the author had little interest in her own heroine. Her discomfort with convention was evident by her second novel. Her early novels often contrasted a calm, capable heroine (a Mary Challoner) and an excitable, emotional one (a Juliana Marling), exploring the distinction between a heroine who acts decisively and one who is less effective in asserting agency; inevitably the former acted as mentor to the latter. In later novels such obvious comparisons retreated into the background, and as the style of Heyer's writing was increasingly anchored in a more realistic portrayal of society, the heroine's range of action was reduced to reflect a more plausible role.[8] There could be no more cross-dressing or sword-fighting, and there was no more need for heroic rescues. In a more realistic (if still patently fictitious) world, Heyer imagined a form of female agency that neither contravened social norms by mimicking male actions, nor violated the romance plot.

By the 1950s, midway through her career, Heyer had not only perfected the elegant and lively style of her Regency novels but had also developed a heroine reflective of this style — attractive, vigorous, witty — and three of the novels of this period, in particular, illustrate the possibilities and the potential pitfalls of such a heroine. The eponymous heroine of *The Grand Sophy* (1950) is the unquestionable star of this immensely successful comic novel, the overwhelming strength of her character casting her own romance plot into the shade. The less complex plot of *Bath Tangle* (1955) maintains a focus on the principal relationship but the heroine's very strength of character is not an asset to her, but a liability. Only with *Venetia* (1958) did Heyer perfect a heroine who exercises effective agency to assert her independence, triumphing without transgressing her gender role, aware of her own relationship to the traditional romantic heroine and rejecting that ideal. Sophy Stanton-Lacy and Lady Serena Carlow should be seen as generic, as well as chronological, predecessors of Venetia Lanyon.

The first of these heroines confounds the expectations of her unhappy London relatives from the moment of her descent upon their household: instead of a meek, motherless girl Sophy is a confident and even commanding figure who sets about solving everyone's problems, romantic and otherwise. Sometimes adroit, sometimes overbearing, her actions breach the boundaries of the traditionally feminine sphere but for the most part they excite admiration rather than rejection in her audience (both the familial audience and the readerly one); however, despite manipulating the romances of others Sophy fails to recognize herself as a participant in romance — as a heroine — until the very end of the novel.

Raised by an indulgent father, Sophy has been encouraged to act independently and assertively both in the domestic sphere and in her interactions with the male world, running her father's itinerant household, hosting his diplomatic parties, befriending officers, and evidently developing a propensity to extend her managerial skills quite boldly on behalf of others. A military friend recalls, "When last I saw you, you were engaged in arranging in the most ruthless fashion the affairs of the most bewildered family of Belgians I have yet encountered. They had all my sympathy, but there was nothing I could do to help them; I know my limitations."[9]

The most egregious example of Sophy's mastery is her brush with a moneylender who has made an illegal loan to her cousin Hubert, a minor. Recognizing Hubert's distress and coaxing him to confide in her, she enacts a sisterly or even maternal role; but in confronting the moneylender she penetrates into a male world — or underworld — of finance, violence, and action. When the usurer threatens her, she draws a pistol from her muff, responding to a physical threat by upping the ante with a more deadly weapon. In effect she overpowers him through her comprehension of the tools he will employ, defeating him through verbal intimidation and the threat of violence. Additionally, Sophy's sense of fair play is male: although the initial loan to a minor was illegal she adheres to a gentleman's code of honor, redeeming Hubert's bond by (in effect) exchanging her diamond earrings for it. At the end of their interview the moneylender has been "revolted by [her] unwomanly knowledge of the law" (207) and is relieved to recover even the principal of his loan.

Her identification with the male perspective does not stop at understanding it, but frequently extends to aligning herself with it. She partners with a male in his courtship of her cousin. Cecilia loves an ineligible poet; with a marked dismissal of the claims of sisterhood, Sophy decrees that she must be detached from him, promoting the attractions of an Earl instead. Her methods are pragmatic: she devises situations to showcase the poet's practical failings (such as his inability to procure a sedan chair in a rainstorm) and at the same time rehabilitates the Earl by casting him in a more heroic role (after shooting him in the shoulder she claims that his wound was sustained protecting her from highwaymen). She constructs him as an object of sympathy and admiration. In the end Cecilia's opinions are changed, her affections altered, but in manipulating her Sophy has removed her agency and made Cecilia's story a sort of anti-romance in which a girl who is too silly to recognize what she really needs must be tricked into acquiescence. A common plot resolution in the romance genre is the hero's trick or ploy to persuade a proud or recalcitrant heroine to accept him; here Sophy stands in for the supposed hero, who is too kind or too meek to do his own wooing.[10] In the final scene — a set-piece at an abandoned manor, starring a cast of Sophy's assembling — Cecilia succumbs to the approved suitor and is given into his possession in a passage that, removed from its comic context, almost chills:

> Between [Sophy's] efforts, and those of Lord Charlbury, she was presently escorted, resistless, out of the house, and handed up into the chaise. His lordship, pausing only to bestow upon his benefactress a hearty embrace, jumped up after her; the steps were let up, the door slammed upon the happy couple, and the equipage was driven away [339].

Sophy is intent on severing her eldest cousin Charles' engagement no less than Cecilia's. His worthy fiancée alienates the household by trying to guide them — a privilege reserved, it seems, for Sophy herself. Sophy's superior abilities challenge Miss Wraxton's chosen role just as Sophy's greater charms challenge Miss Wraxton's romance, and in Miss Wraxton's frustration Heyer demonstrates a keen insight into the psychology of female rivalry. Ostensibly the unlovable Miss Wraxton must be removed for the happiness of the family at large and especially for Charles' sake; Sophy seems unaware that she herself may be nursing an ulterior motive, although her own match with Charles is expected by other characters before the book's final scene, when his erstwhile fiancée and his ostensible rival both offer him their felicitations, with varying degrees of sincerity. Sophy's complete lack of awareness of the development of her own romance is in some degree belied by her complete lack of surprise at Charles' proposal, but this is the only indication in the text whether or not this outcome could be some deep-laid plan of her own.

In the terms of the romance genre, Sophy's manipulations are more successful than not: at the end of the novel everyone is appropriately paired, even Miss Wraxton having been provided with a consolation prize.[11] Sophy herself has performed as the ultimate self-actualizing heroine, bringing her desires into reality. An expert shot who carries a pistol, an expert rider with a restive mount, an expert driver even when she has stolen her cousin's prized horses, she consistently challenges the boundaries of her gender and is mostly admired for it. At only one point in the novel does she surpass the limits of what her family can accept: goaded by Miss Wraxton's patronizing, she drives the mortified young woman down forbidden St. James Street.[12] Yet, despite the indulgence of the other characters, the story itself staggers under Sophy's contravention of not only gender, but also genre.

A romance novel principally concerns the romance between hero and heroine; while other plots unfold, that relationship is the story's emotional core.[13] However, the emotional center of *The Grand Sophy* is simply, Sophy: her antics, her humor, and her outrageous manipulations take center stage. Somehow unaware of her own romance and thus unable to bring it to the fore, Sophy nonetheless demonstrates greater insight into everyone else, on short acquaintance, than Charles does as the head of the household. Her interpersonal scheming is generally more effective than his commands, and when it is not, she usurps his male role through decisively male action, stepping outside the privacy of the domestic sphere to confront a villain, embarrass a rival, shoot a friend. Charles' loud temper is an empty threat. Sophy's domineering ways emasculate her hero, whose dominance of his household she overthrows.

Sophy herself behaves like a hero. She does so with charm and grace, but the transgression lies not in her tone, or the few forbidden blocks she drives, or even in her marksmanship: it lies in her assumption of authority over the other characters of the story and her rejection (through disinclination or negligence) of the insight that would have given her a better understanding of her own happiness. By stepping too far across those gendered boundaries she compromises her role as heroine: in asserting her dominance over her family, she denies agency to others, especially other women. Meanwhile, Sophy herself needs nothing, neither a rescuer nor a friend; she is so masterful, so nearly invulnerable, that there is no particular role for a hero to play in her life. The peculiar result of this novel is to leave readers—like the characters!—with a lasting affection for Sophy and a certain sense of disquiet. One of Heyer's most popular novels, with one of her most beloved heroines, *The Grand Sophy* functions brilliantly as comedy but only imperfectly as a romance.

Oddly, the heroine most like Sophy is Heyer's least successful, Lady Serena Carlow of *Bath Tangle* (1955): like Sophy, Serena is sophisticated, assertive, and intelligent; unlike Sophy, she misunderstands every major character in the novel and is given to dramatic, sometimes public displays of ill temper. Only the hero can stand up to her temper (by matching it) and curb her violence (through force), creating a somewhat disturbing forecast of mutual abuse. Having once been engaged to him, quarreled, and broken it off, at the novel's opening Lady Serena is furious to find him re-entering her life as her Trustee:

> "He?" The word burst from Serena's lips. She swept round and bore down upon the Marquis, as lithe as a wild cat, and as dangerous [...] "I will never be so enforced!"
>
> [...] She flung away from him, and resumed her restless pacing, tears of rage running down her face. Fanny went to her, laying a hand on her arm and saying in a beseeching tone, "Serena! Dearest Serena!"
>
> She stood rigidly, her throat working. "Fanny, don't touch me! I am not safe!"[14]

The melodrama that Heyer usually eschewed is surprisingly employed here to give shape to Serena's character, capable of rage so strong that it extinguishes comedy. The hero ends this tantrum by imprisoning her wrists, to keep her from striking out, and sharply reminding her how inappropriate her behavior is; having transgressed her gender's ideal norms and been scolded for it, she retires from the room to regain control of her temper, leaving a group of male relatives and lawyers to finish discussing the terms of her future. Thus as the novel opens we see that whereas Sophy's mastery extended over all, Serena cannot even master herself, and thus cannot exert complete control over her circumstances.

She soon meets and becomes infatuated with another former suitor; at first his admiration for her is rekindled but over the novel's course he falls in love with her more acceptably feminine young stepmother Fanny. This goes unnoticed by Lady Serena, as does Fanny's reciprocation of his regard. Meanwhile, the hero contracts an engagement of his own in order to prick Lady Serena to the same jealousy he feels; later he tries to frighten his young fiancée into jilting him, overplays his hand, and frightens her into flight. Acting in the mode of hero/rescuer, Lady Serena pursues her, and restores her to him in the sincere belief that he wants her. Like Sophy, she aligns herself with the male against the female. It is left to the hero to cut the tangle created by her lack of insight, pairing up the lover and the stepmother, setting his own naive fiancée free, and concluding by forcing his way into Serena's house and crushing her in his embrace in a display of masculine force. Completing his conquest, he explains how she has been mistaken in every particular; he, of course, has been correct in his interpretations, more insightful than she. Thus the most masterful of Heyer's heroines is ultimately subdued by her hero, not just because he is physically stronger than she but also because he is more knowing, more the master of the situation. If effectiveness is the mark of success, Lady Serena is a failed heroine.[15]

It is important, then, to note that a self-willed heroine is not always a self-actuating heroine, that strength must be matched by insight in order for the heroine to navigate an effective course of action. It is largely this that distinguishes Sophy from Serena, for Sophy exhibits a far greater understanding of other people. Although Sophy may not be fully aware of her own feelings she is for the most part fully in control of their effect on her actions (unlike tempestuous Serena). Sophy's sovereignty derives from loving exploitation but Serena dominates with the power of her temper. Most importantly, Serena's impulsive action coupled with her lack of insight makes awkwardness and trouble for those she loves while Sophy's keen intuition and superior management improve the lives of her friends; in the end, their happiness is a form of acceptance, even approval of her tactics.

Unlike Sophy, the heroine of *Venetia* (1958) does not carry all before her, vanquishing her foes with a high hand; indeed, her inability to exert agency, to adequately manage others, precipitates the novel's crisis. Yet Venetia stands as the exemplar of Heyer's heroines: not only does she conform to the traditional model of the heroine, but she is simultaneously contrasted to it through her reflections upon her own role, and challenges it through her assumption of agency. Although unable to exert perfect control over her environment, she acts decisively to effect her own happiness.

Venetia Lanyon lives in remote Yorkshire, keeping house for a crippled younger brother and waiting for their elder brother to return from the wars; after an absence of years, the notorious rake Lord Damerel arrives in the neighborhood. He encounters Venetia picking blackberries at the edge of his usually unoccupied property, and mistaking her for a tenant, promptly molests her. Although he does no more than kiss her, the potential of a greater sexual threat is implied, and the action could be read as a symbolic rape if not for Venetia's response, which is hardly defeatist. Struggling free, she does not flee but rather confronts her attacker, disrupting the physical threat by transforming the encounter into a war of words.

> "And as for you, sir," said Venetia, meeting that searching stare with a flaming look, "your quo-
> tations don't make your advances a whit more acceptable to me — and they don't deceive me into
> thinking you anything but a pestilent, complete knave!"
> He burst out laughing. "Bravo! Where did you find that?"
> Venetia, who had suddenly remembered the rest of the quotation, replied, "If you don't know,
> I certainly shan't tell you. That phrase is apt enough, but the context won't do."
> "Oho! My curiosity is now thoroughly roused! I recognize my hand, and see that I must carefully
> study my Shakespeare!"
> "I should think you had seldom employed your time more worthily!"[16]

Later Damerel follows her quotation with another from *Othello*, showing that he has discovered her source; they move on to *Twelfth Night* and then cap one another with Thomas Campion, demonstrating that from the outset there is a bond of understanding between them, and leaving the readers — if not the characters — in little doubt that antagonism must give way to affection.

The intertextuality of this passage of arms is underscored by Venetia's consciousness that she has not behaved as a heroine, and although the reader has already identified her as such, she has not yet so identified herself:

> [A]fter dwelling on the impropriety of Damerel's conduct, and telling herself how fortunate she
> had been to have escaped a worse fate, it rather horrifyingly occurred to her that she had shown
> herself to be lacking in sensibility. A delicately nurtured female (unless all the books lied) would
> have swooned from the shock of being kissed by a strange man, or at the very least would have
> been cast into the greatest affliction, her peace cut up, her spirits wholly overpowered. What she
> would not have done was to have stayed to bandy words with her wolfish assailant. Nor would
> she have been conscious of a feeling of exhilaration [32].

At this moment she calls her own identity into question, recognizing her failure to conform to the ideal behavior of a "delicately nurtured female," yet failing to recognize herself as the heroine of her own story. She differs from a Juliana Marling or Austen's Catherine Morland, who believe in the reality of heroines and so believing, are eager to see romance and to cast themselves in the heroine's role; likewise she differs from a Serena Carlow or Austen's Emma Woodhouse, who lack the self-knowledge to read themselves or others accurately. Instead, Venetia knows herself all too well to embrace the unrealistic role of traditional heroine, or to imagine that romance lurks in every stranger. Her story will be her own to author, and it is clear to the careful reader that as an unconventional heroine, Venetia will revise her genre's conventions.

When her younger brother falls from his horse near Damerel's gates, Venetia comes to nurse him. It might be expected of a heroine — and Damerel does expect it — that she should betray some righteous indignation in meeting her molester again, especially in such awkward circumstances. However,

> Venetia had no guile, and no affectations; she knew the world only by the books she had read; experience had never taught her to doubt the sincerity of anyone who did her a kindness. So when Damerel, seeing the approach of a carriage round a bend in the avenue, strolled out to meet his guest it was neither a wrathful goddess nor a young lady on her dignity who sprang down from the vehicle and gave him both her hands, but a beautiful, ingenuous creature with no consciousness in her frank eyes, but only a warm glow of gratitude. She exclaimed, as he took her hands, "I am so much obliged to you!" [46].

Heyer's Regency novels unfold with a marked lack of the sensational elements present in her earlier novels, but just as the prosaic intruded to quench the melodrama in *Devil's Cub*, it is deployed in *Venetia* to dispel sexual tension. No menace is present in Damerel's compassion, no self-consciousness possible in Aubrey's sickroom; the sexual threat of their early encounter is negated.

The local community is ready to imagine impropriety in the friendship thus established, and their response takes form in the disapproval of friends and relatives, and the jealousy of Venetia's two suitors. The elder of these is her sole marital prospect, a foil for Damerel in every respect: sedate instead of wild, prosperous instead of ruined, respectable instead of rakish, tedious instead of companionable. He is the very parody of a false suitor, an empty threat to the hero's conquest. The younger suitor, however, casts himself in the role of hero (much as Juliana Marling perceived herself as a heroine) and recognizes Damerel as his real rival. Yearning to be the very figure of romance that Damerel (like the Marquis of Vidal) only appears to be, he attempts to perform the role of conquering hero, subjecting Venetia to the novel's second molestation: hurt and jealous, he attempts to kiss her and is ejected from the room by Damerel, conveniently at hand. Rather than a romantic duel, a vulgar fistfight is about to ensue when Venetia asserts herself. "You may leave this to me, Damerel! In fact, I order you to do so!" (119). She scolds Oswald for the mortification he will have brought upon his parents, if his persistence forces her to inform them of it. The terms of her rebuke reduce him to the stature of a little boy, and she negates his sexual threat by disallowing it, making it clear that she regards him as no threat at all. No harsher blow could be applied to youthful male vanity. Not only has Venetia again been threatened with the worst of fates (implied rape), but she has again proved capable of defending herself, and furthermore she has (again) done so in such as way as to demonstrate her effective engagement with male discourse: just as she was able to deflect Damerel's physical assault by turning it into a verbal contest, meeting him on his own intellectual terms, she responds to Oswald's physical assault by deflating his ego, selecting the particular reproach calculated to wither his infatuation. She does not need to act the part of a hero to assert agency; she just needs to prevent her opponent from acting like a villain.

Venetia's character is by now established, not as masculine, but as capable of mediation with the masculine: early responsibilities and the company of men have taught her to be capable and confident, not self-conscious, and she is able to assert herself effectively in managing not only the domestic (female) sphere but also in disarming external (male) threats. The opponent who finally presents a real obstacle to her happiness does it by intruding into Venetia's home, threatening her efficacy in the socially accepted, indeed, socially mandated role of chatelaine. Her elder brother has married on the Continent, and has sent his shy new wife and his shrewish mother-in-law home ahead of him.

Although the new Lady Lanyon is but a slight presence in the book, she does function as a foil for Venetia. Pretty, docile, and devoted, she is everything that a young woman is ideally supposed to be, and yet unlike Juliana Marling of *Devil's Cub*, she has no desire to be a heroine, no expectation of being at the center of attention, and no aptitude for it. She cannot assert herself in any way except, passively, by requiring help; the family's aged spaniel frightens her into a state of nervous prostration. Despite having been anointed as Venetia's successor, she is not Venetia's equal.[17]

Her mother sits at quite the opposite end of the spectrum: Mrs. Scorrier is too assertive, jealous of her position in the social hierarchy, and determined to assure it through constant criticism and agitation, and "an uncontrollable desire to show everyone, from Venetia down to the garden boy, a better way of performing any given task" (153). Hers is an ineffective form of self-assertion, as her life history proves: through both domestic and social quarreling, she has alienated in turn her husband's family and her daughters' husbands (155). Within hours of her arrival at Undershaw she offends the butler, housekeeper, and nurse. We may infer from the circumstances of the text that Mrs. Scorrier's bullying nature is to blame for her daughter's passivity and helplessness. She is a mis-manager, not socially adept, not domestically adept, not maternally adept, failing in every area of conventional female responsibility. It is precisely because of this comprehensive failure that she is a problem without a solution.

The text suggests that her brother may rely on Venetia to manage a problem he cannot — his mother-in-law — and he has certainly granted her complete authority over Undershaw in his absence, even providing her with a power of attorney; like Sophy, Venetia has an "unwomanly" knowledge of the law but Venetia cannot deploy it against an opponent who challenges the family from within without further denying her feminine role as preserver, not disturber, of domestic tranquility. Despite her many powers, she finds herself with little leverage over Mrs. Scorrier. Mrs. Scorrier comprehensively rejects Venetia because she wishes to elevate her own daughter to the position of authority that the new Lady Lanyon holds in name, but Venetia in fact, as chatelaine. Having rejected the traditionally female ideals of cooperative behavior and domestic harmony, Mrs. Scorrier is impervious to Venetia's verbal management. Only when Venetia also rejects those ideals can she gain ground against her opponent, in small victories dubious at best. Crossing swords with her over Damerel's visits to Undershaw, she wins the encounter but realizes that she must lose the war:

> She blamed herself for having allowed Mrs. Scorrier to goad her into retort, yet felt that sooner or later she must have been forced into taking a stand against a woman whose passion for mastery must, if unchecked, set the whole household by the ears. She entertained no hope that Mrs. Scorrier would not bear malice: she had seen implacable enmity in that lady's eyes, and knew that she would lose no opportunity now to hurt and to annoy. [...] It was a prelude to a week more nearly resembling a nightmare than any Venetia had ever endured [177].

In Heyer's hands the situation is sketched with humor, but it is nonetheless clear that the peace of the house is cut up and domestic life has become a misery. Displaced in her own home, subjected to the acid of Mrs. Scorrier's constant antagonism, and unable to mediate successfully between the indignant incumbents and the encroaching incomers, "the better part of [Venetia's] time was consequently spent either in endorsing Mrs. Scorrier's commands, or in the hopeless attempt to reconcile bitter opponents" (178). Venetia's adroit "management" is thus frustrated by Mrs. Scorrier's "mis-management," an unlovely quality that has never previously been checked or stifled by any male or female relative. The only relief to be obtained is in ejecting her from the residence, as her male relatives have done, but although Venetia has the legal and moral authority to act in this male realm and follow suit, to do so would be an unforgivable transgression of her female roles as gracious hostess and as guardian of domestic peace.

Venetia's period of tranquility with Damerel is thus broken not by male threats but by female ones, and her inability to surmount them is ultimately the result of her refusal to step outside the boundaries of the feminine ideal: she is unwilling to promote disharmony in her own house. Instead it is Venetia who is ejected. In order to restore some measure of domestic tranquility on behalf of her dependents, her staff, and her brother's helpless bride, she must leave — since it is she from whom Mrs. Scorrier is trying to wrest power. In retiring from the lists for the sake of the greater good of her household, Venetia proves herself essentially the bigger man.

At this point in the plot, an offer of marriage from Damerel would have solved Venetia's problems to her satisfaction, allowing her to remain in the neighborhood and providing a socially acceptable reason for her departure from home as well as, of course, uniting her with him. The hero could rescue the heroine who, at this point, needs a rescuer. However, no such offer is forthcoming; instead, Damerel declares that their relationship was too good to be true, that he is damaged goods and she too good for him. His chivalry in rejecting what he most desires in order to promote her best interests only denies her agency in deciding her own fate at a time when that fate is most uncertain. At his most traditionally heroic moment, masterful and self-abnegating, he attempts to save her and succeeds in belittling her.

At this moment of crisis in the novel, all seems lost: Venetia has restored the peace of her home only by leaving it, and since Damerel has declined to offer another option, she perforce retires to the London house of her relatives. She has not been able to create a new path for herself, a path either to happiness or to independence. However, with emotional recovery and self-examination, clarity and purpose are restored to her. Realizing that their mutual happiness lies together in spite of Damerel's better self, she decides to force him into marriage. This is an undeniably revolutionary course of action for a heroine, who is more often found responding to such force than exerting it; in her vigor, her exertion of agency, and her defiance of social convention, Venetia is challenging the boundaries of female power and revising and extending the traditional definition of a heroine. Moreover, she takes action by doing the unthinkable: courting her own social ruin (in order to use the prospect of her ruin as leverage). In the early nineteenth century, her good reputation (or rather, the perception of her virtue) was of inestimable value to an unmarried woman; in Jane Austen's *Pride and Prejudice*, all of the Bennet sisters will be tarnished by the ruin of one. The preservation of a woman's reputation or the threat of its destruction frequently features as a plot element in novels set in the Regency period; Heyer's deft comedies seldom address this issue as seriously as in *Venetia*, when her reputation becomes not just capital but power, not over the heroine, but for the heroine.

Having determined how she might best — most conveniently and most comfortably — ruin her own reputation by taking up with the most scandalous of her relations, Venetia returns to Damerel to turn the tables on him, taking any real choice out of his hands, for his own good, as he had previously done to her. Ultimately he acquiesces and will be the happier for it, much as a more traditional heroine ultimately gives in to the wishes of a male in the heroic mold. Because Venetia trades in the female currency of virtue, perception, reputation, and emotion rather than in the male currency of action, independence, or violence, this expansion of her role does nothing to disturb the novel's effect; rather, Venetia's self-empowerment adds an extra fillip of exultation to the conclusion. She wins, triumphing over circumstance, misfortune, and the well-meaning but misguided people who love her.

In exercising her wit and her options, in exerting control over her own fate, Venetia is the very epitome of a "managing female": without cross-dressing, sword-fighting, taking to the highway or entering the public arena, without legal recourse, without help from a man, without straying out of her gender-defined sphere or transgressing it, without Mrs. Scorrier's stridency, without Juliana Marling's dramatics, without Serena Carlow's appalling temper, without Sophy's useful pistol — but with her brazen self-confidence — Venetia changes the course of her own story, transforming star-crossed separation into something more satisfying. In expanding the heroine's role she procures her own chosen happy ending.

The heroine of this story is so capable that she leaves the hero nothing to do for her except to be her friend, providing her with the social and intellectual companionship she needs. This is the very core of the romantic attachment between Heyer's heroes and heroines, sometimes explicitly stated, sometimes merely implied by the narrative; the deep friendship they share is as important as passion to their relationship, and often only the hero's advent teaches the heroine how alone she has been, rendering his friendship as poignant as his love.

Venetia stands as the exemplar of the Heyer heroine. The typical Heyer heroine exists in contrast to other women in the text, who are shown to be more sensitive but less effective; her intelligence and her independence compel the reader's respect and the hero's; her good sense and good sense of humor arouse his affections; and her ability to take decisive action within the text establishes her authorship of her own romance. If few can rival Venetia's achievement in self-determination, all take an active role in propelling themselves forward to their chosen conclusion. In this, they have been placed by their author apart both from their gender and their genre. Although they find more in common with the hero than with any female friend, they are neither heroic themselves, nor unfeminine; Heyer abandoned the experimental cross-dressing of the early novels in favor of more subtle expansions of the heroine's sphere. No subsequent Heyer heroine so disregarded the appearance, at least, of upholding the conventions of her society.

Play upon convention and expectation remained a principal theme from early works such as *Devil's Cub,* through the development of the Regency romance and the evolution of the heroine, to Heyer's very last novel, *Lady of Quality* (1972). As she progressed from an author of adventurous historical romances to an author of mannered, comedic romances, Heyer refined her heroines, gradually paring away the eventfulness of the earlier novels in favor of somewhat more restricted and more realistic situations that emphasized strong character rather than significant action. The Grand Sophy carries and uses a gun, but Venetia's only weapon is words.

In Heyer's final novel, almost nothing happens. It is a novel of character, almost devoid of incident: independent Annis Wychwood foils a seeming elopement by chance, and after this false start — the promise of adventure, arrested — the novel follows her mentorship of the runaways in the face of familial disapproval. The girl's guardian uncle is the hero and his skepticism provides the necessary tension between them. In accordance with readerly expectation, Annis wins her point by making a success of her surrogacy and furthermore wins the heart of the gruff uncle; their identity as a couple is to take precedence over Annis' experiment of motherhood, and having proven herself, she relinquishes the role of mother for that of wife. Without drama or trauma, she compels male respect for her competence as a caretaker and as the head of her household, respect for her agency and for her independence. Indeed, although independence is of immeasurable importance to the majority of Heyer's heroines, to Annis Wychwood it is as important as love:

> "I refused them all, because I preferred my — my independence to marriage. I think I still do. Indeed, I am almost sure of it."
> "But not quite sure?"
> "No, not quite sure," she said, in a troubled tone. "And when I ask myself what you could give me in exchange for my liberty, which is very dear to me, I — oh, I don't know, I don't know! [...] It's true that I don't regard you with indifference, but this is such a big step to take — such an important step — that you must grant me a little time to think it over carefully before I answer you."[18]

Of course, in the end, she chooses marriage, but it is a carefully considered choice: not just the hero's character must pass under her review, but also her own. Her verdict is based on self-knowledge.

Heyer was certainly not the only pioneer shaping the romance genre, nor the only author who used her fiction to explore the limits of female agency within that genre — but her success during her lifetime and her enduring popularity since suggest that her romances have a resonance that transcends genre. Her most important contribution to the field of popular romance was in demonstrating, resoundingly, that the traditional romantic heroine is not the definitive romantic heroine: that the female sphere of power is more spacious than was once supposed, and that without violating social mores a heroine can effect and maintain agency in her own life, as real women have always done in theirs. Heyer's heroines understand that their romances do not exist in a vacuum, but are contextualized by the circumstances of their lives; indeed, no one understands this better than Sophy, who need only manipulate circumstances to direct the course of Cecilia's affections. Heyer's heroines do not choose a hero who appears in the role of rescuer, ready to resolve all problems; rather, they themselves address the problems and predicaments of their own lives, rising to their own challenges and proving their real power and independence — and perversely it is this very self-empowerment that makes them suitable mates for a powerful hero. If the promise of perfect union at the end of a romance novel is the heroine's reward, it is no less the hero's, for in her he finds an equal match.

By entering companionate partnerships, Heyer's heroines embrace an ideal of marriage that was still taking shape in the years of the Regency at the beginning of the nineteenth century. As the Enlightenment waned and the Industrial Revolution gained steam, women of the middle and upper classes were beginning to have more leisure than ever before and to be expected to fill it not just with practical tasks but with educational and artistic attainments; their husbands might hope to find not just social assets and domestic partners in their wives, but also knowledgeable companions. This tenuous idea, illustrated so well in Austen's novels, gradually grew into today's ideal of marriage. Heyer wrote throughout the twentieth century and now, in the early years of the twenty-first, her depiction of romantic happiness founded upon shared humor, intellectual parity, and equality of agency is not just recognizable, but the ideal many individuals seek in their own lives.

Legally, socially, and financially, women of the present have greater latitude than ever before in actively pursuing this ideal, and its importance to them is perhaps indicated by the very existence of the romance genre. The enduring popularity of Heyer's Regency romances, as well as the way they defy easy critical categorization, may lie not in lively dialogue and deft plotting alone, but in heroines who are more reflective of the condition of women of the twenty-first century than of the nineteenth: financially and emotionally independent, they prefer a solitary state to a subordinate position, and will consider only a marriage of equals. The Heyer heroine is, as Frederica self-deprecatingly describes herself, "a managing female"[19] but in Heyer's novels this is ultimately an accolade, for her heroines are all "managing" their own romances and, indeed, their own lives.

Notes

1. Anonymous, *The Saturday Review* (London) 132, 5 November 1921, p. 542. Reprinted in Mary Fahnestock-Thomas, *Georgette Heyer: A Critical Retrospective* (Saraland, AL: PrinnyWorld Press, 2001).

2. Only later did Mills & Boon come to specialize in romance, but Heyer never published with them again or re-used that pseudonym. In 1930 Heyer's long-time publisher Heinemann reprinted *Transformation* under Heyer's own name as *Powder and Patch*, omitting the final chapter.

3. Georgette Heyer, *The Devil's Cub* (1932; rpt., London: Heinemann, 1966), 122. Further references will be included parenthetically.

4. Perhaps in compensation, her heroes are exaggeratedly male: they tend to be autocratic, ill-tempered, bad-mannered, adventure-seeking alpha males, although exceptions exist, most notably in the gentle heroes of *The Foundling* (1948) and *Cotillion* (1953).

5. Georgette Heyer, *The Grand Sophy* (London: Heinemann, 1950), 26.

6. Georgette Heyer, *The Talisman Ring* (1936; rpt., London: Heinemann, 1970), 10–11.

7. Georgette Heyer, *Venetia* (London: Heinemann, 1958), 13.

8. A comedy of manners relies on the constraints imposed by society, but in addition to this, Heyer was a meticulous historical researcher. Anachronistic attitudes or behaviors would have marred the precision of her style.

9. Heyer, *The Grand Sophy*, 86. Further references will be included parenthetically.

10. Moreover, he is further emasculated by Sophy's bullet.

11. Sophy has decided to provide Miss Wraxton with a cast-off suitor of her own.

12. St. James Street was lined with private men's clubs, and respectable females did not set foot on its pavement — a social prohibition more meaningful to Sophy's family than to Sophy's readers.

13. Romance Writers of America, Inc., "About the Romance Genre," http://www.rwa.org/cs/the_romance_genre.

14. Georgette Heyer, *Bath Tangle* (London: Heinemann, 1955), 16–17.

15. Karin E. Westman presents a more positive interpretation of Lady Serena Carlow's abilities in her essay "A Story of Her Weaving: The Self-Authoring Heroines of Georgette Heyer's Regency Romance," in *Doubled Plots: Romance and History*, ed. Susan Strehle and Mary Paniccia Carden (Jackson: University Press of Mississippi, 2003), 165–184. Westman's work was crucial in shaping and clarifying my own contrasting ideas about *Bath Tangle*, in particular, and it remains of inarguable value to readers with an interest in the construction of gender in Heyer.

16. Heyer, *Venetia*, 28. Further references will be included parenthetically.

17. The new Lady Lanyon's lack of appeal suggests what Heyer may have thought of the feminine ideal, and why all her heroines after the first are revisions of it.

18. Georgette Heyer, *Lady of Quality* (London: Heinemann, 1972), 182–83.

19. Georgette Heyer, *Frederica* (London: Heinemann, 1965), 36.

7

One Ring to Bind Them:
Ring Symbolism in Popular Romance Fiction

Laura Vivanco

Every lover believes that his or her beloved is special: "Romantic love begins as an individual comes to regard another as special, even unique. The lover then intensely focuses his or her attention on this preferred individual, aggrandizing the beloved's better traits and over-looking or minimizing his or her flaws."[1] In addition, although "empirical evidence indicates that sexual desire is not a prerequisite for romantic love, even in its earliest, passionate stages," scientists have observed that "people who have fallen madly in love generally begin to find their beloved enormously sexually attractive."[2]

Outside observers of this phenomenon, whether it is enacted in real life or represented in fiction, are much more likely to be skeptical of the claim that the beloved possesses any special attractions. Shulamith Firestone, a radical Second Wave feminist, stated that "because the distinguishing characteristic of women's exploitation as a class is sexual, a special means must be found to make them unaware that they are considered all alike sexually," and this "special means" has been "so effective that most women have come to believe seriously that the world needs their particular sexual contributions to go on. ('She thinks her pussy is made of gold.')."[3] Firestone was, however, prepared to concede that the lovers of such women might also believe something of this sort: "Perhaps when a man marries he chooses from this undistinguishable lot with care, for [...] he holds a special high place in his mental reserve for 'The One,' by virtue of her close association with himself."[4]

A more recent variant of this theory emerged at the internet discussion board *Television Without Pity* where commentators

> gathered to discuss a particular type of character on soap operas. She was always blond, always beautiful, and always good-natured and kind, and always stupid beyond the telling of it. [...] And yet ... there is a man. We'll call him ... Hero. Hero is handsome, he is strong, and ... well, yes, okay, he's kinda dumb, too, but still he manages to rescue her every single time she's in trouble ... which is approximately twice a show. He stays by her side and loves her through thick and thin. [...] The Hero is loyal and loving and doesn't seem to mind the fact that she is so FREAKIN' stupid. How can this be??
>
> Well, my friends, it comes down to the power of the Glittery HooHa, or the GHH for short. A woman with an HH as G as this girl merely needs to walk around as glitter falls from her nether-parts, leaving a trail for Hero to follow. And once he finds her, it only takes one dip in the GHH to snare him forever, for yea, no matter how many HooHas he might see, never will there be one as Glittery as hers...[5]

The theories of the "pussy [...] made of gold" and the "Glittery HooHa" acknowledge the mystery of love, which can cause people to believe that their beloved is special and the only one with whom they wish to have a sexual relationship. The heroes of romance novels believe this about their heroines and in many romances a ring, given to the heroine by the hero and placed upon her finger, symbolizes the union between the heroine's Glittery HooHa and the hero's phallus.[6]

The ring itself is the shape of the entrance to the heroine's HooHa and the giving of her hand in marriage, or the promising of that hand in an engagement to marry, enables the heroine's finger to represent the hero's phallus:

> To define man and wife as one flesh can be taken to imply that in some sense each participates in the sexual identity of the other. This mingling of sexual identity is implied in the symbolism of the medieval and modern marriage ceremony in which the man places a ring upon the outstretched finger of the woman. The phallic gesture is offered by the woman and the vaginal symbol is given by the man.[7]

The vaginal symbolism of the wedding ring has long been acknowledged, as Bruno Bettelheim argues:

> The ring, a symbol for the vagina, is given by the groom to his bride; she offers him in return her outstretched finger, so that he may complete the ritual. [...] By having the ring put onto her finger, the bride acknowledges that from now on, her husband to some degree will have possession of her vagina, and she of his penis.[8]

This sexual symbolism of the wedding ring underlies some seventeenth-century cures for impotence:

> Astrologer-herbalist Nicholas Culpeper and midwife Jane Sharp recommended that a man, who due to magic could not give his wife "due benevolence," should piss through her wedding ring. In France the man was enjoined to piss or pour white wine either through the wedding ring or through the keyhole of the church in which he had been married.[9]

Although engagement and wedding rings may be considered to possess a similar sexual symbolism, wedding rings are much more closely associated with one particular outcome of sexual activity: reproduction. The underlying nature of the exchange symbolized by the wedding ring is explained when one reluctant groom-to-be, the Marquess of Dain, is maneuvered into marrying his heroine: "We shall be wed [...] on the same terms any other man would insist upon: exclusive ownership and *breeding rights*."[10] The wedding takes place "on a bright Sunday morning on the eleventh day of May in the Year of Our Lord Eighteen Hundred Twenty-Eight [...] before the minister of St. George's, Hanover Square" and the Form of Solemnization of Matrimony according to *The Book of Common Prayer*, which would have been used at this wedding, gives high priority to "breeding rights," saying of marriage that "first, It was ordained for the procreation of children."[11]

Wedding rings, however, are seldom mentioned in romance novels, and rarely in any detail. Eight of the ten rings in the romance novels I will examine are engagement rings, and none are wedding rings.[12] This parallels the primacy of the engagement over the wedding in the genre as a whole: Pamela Regis lists "the betrothal" as one of "the eight essential elements of the romance novel" and "the wedding" as merely an "accidental — optional" element.[13] Whereas a wedding ring is given as part of a communal event which, if depicted in a romance novel, demonstrates that "society has reconstituted itself around the new couple," most of the rings analyzed here have a much more personal symbolism which, like each novel in the genre, "centers around two individuals."[14]

The circular bands of engagement rings appear to share the vaginal symbolism of the wedding ring, but most of them also feature a precious stone, or group of precious stones, which can be read as symbolizing the clitoris. Support for this interpretation of the various parts of the rings can be found in a passage in Lisa Kleypas's *Worth Any Price*:

> Softly he spread her, stroking his middle fingertip along the tender seam, brushing the rosy nub of her sex each time. He smiled slightly as he saw bright patches of color appear on her face and chest. "The Chinese call this the jewel terrace," he whispered. Gently his finger slipped inside her, advancing only an inch, circling softly.[15]

The "rosy nub" of the clitoris sits like a jewel at the top of the "terrace" or seam. This seam, once penetrated by the hero's finger, reveals itself to have a shape which can be outlined by "circling" motions.

The glitter of the band and the jewels set into it seem to symbolize the heroine's sexual allure and the magic or mystery of the process of falling in love. In Jennifer Crusie's *Bet Me*, Min's glitter is most apparent when she is receiving sexual pleasure. When she and Cal kiss, she experiences the "same hot, glittery rush she got every time," and although it may explode "behind her eyelids," its source appears to be further down her body: "the glittering heat flared low just like always."[16] Not all the novels make explicit the fact that the glitter derives from the HooHa, the organ which is to be found "low" in the heroine's body, but a great many of them describe the glitter. In Melissa McClone's *If the Ring Fits ...*, for example, the heroine's "curly auburn hair flowed like silk past her shoulders and *glimmered* beneath the light of the crystal chandelier [...] she curtsied and flashed a *dazzling* smile at dignitaries and royalty."[17]

This special sexual allure, or glitter, may also be described through metaphors of magic and heat. In Kleypas's *Worth Any Price*, Nick observes that "Charlotte Howard was the most *bewitching* woman he had ever met."[18] That the witchcraft is sexual in nature is clear from the fact that Nick has an "instant reaction to her — he had never experienced such visceral response to a woman."[19] The metaphors of magic and heat are given literal form in two rings. The eponymous ring in McClone's *If the Ring Fits ...* acts as a magical matchmaker. It was made:

> centuries ago, [when] a de Thierry prince swore he would never marry because he could not find a woman he loved. Not even among the most beautiful maidens or European royalty. His worried mother had to ensure her son marry and produce an heir. She had an enchantress cast a magic spell over the engagement ring. The spell guaranteed the ring would only fit the prince's one true love.[20]

When the ring is placed on Christina's finger "it almost felt like heat was emanating from the gold band. [...] When the ring touched her skin, a buzz of electricity shot up her arm."[21] The "heat" and "buzz of electricity" perhaps suggest the sexual attraction that Christina and Richard will come to feel for one another. The "heat" generated by this magical ring matches that of another eponymous ring, the Monkcrest engagement ring, in Amanda Quick's *With This Ring*. It too seems to have magical powers because when Beatrice holds it, it is so hot it "nearly scorched her skin."[22] Leo may not describe Beatrice's sexual allure as "magic," perhaps because of his "disdain for the occult sciences," but he nonetheless has to admit that "there was no logical explanation for the unwilling fascination he felt. It was as if she secretly practiced some form of mesmerism on him."[23]

Heroines are not the only women to possess special HooHas, and a few of the HooHas previously encountered by the hero may even have been somewhat glittery, as is demonstrated by two secondary characters: the heroine's sister in Jessica Hart's *Mistletoe Marriage* and Gemma Bradshaw in Kleypas's *Worth Any Price*. Gemma is very much at ease with masculine behavior: "All men relaxed in Gemma Bradshaw's agreeable presence. One could tell just by looking at her that she didn't mind coarse words or booted feet on the table, that she loved a good joke and was never shy or disdainful. Men adored Gemma because she so clearly adored them."[24] That Gemma has a Glittery HooHa is suggested not only by her appeal to men but also by her name, Gemma, which is derived from the Latin word for "jewel," and by her surroundings. She has created a golden, glittering setting for herself: in her suite of rooms she has a "gold-papered bedroom" and the "sideboard in the receiving room was laden with a collection of *glittering* crystal decanters and glasses."[25] In *Mistletoe Marriage*, Bram was once unrequitedly in love with Sophie's sister because she "was the most beautiful girl he had ever seen. She had an ethereal golden loveliness [...] few men were immune to her appeal."[26] Her Glittery HooHa ensures that when she is present "it was impossible to look at anyone else, [...] he had felt [...] dazzled by her sweetness and her beauty."[27]

It is also possible for the glitter of the heroine's HooHa to have been recognized by other men. Jessica Trent, like her grandmother, is

> not merely a beauty, monsieur. This is *la femme fatale*. The men plagued them so, they could scarcely attend to their meal. [...] Fortunately [...], Mademoiselle Trent exercises great restraint upon her own charm. Otherwise, I think, there would have been bloodshed. Two such women... [28]

The term "femme fatale" is used repeatedly to describe Jessica's special, sexual appeal to Dain, as well as to other men, and it glitters: when she chooses not to exercise "great restraint upon her own charm," she leaves in her wake an "instantly *bedazzled* Frenchman."[29] In few romance novels, however, is the specialness of the heroine's vagina made quite as explicit as in Dorie Graham's *So Many Men....* Tess McClellan has the "gift of sexual healing," a gift which "works when we make love" and because of the magical powers of her HooHa, Tess is a "man magnet" constantly surrounded by her coterie of ex-lovers.[30]

Not every woman who glitters is given a ring, however. The distinction possessed by the heroine's HooHa is not merely that it possesses some sexual attraction or "glitter" for the hero, but that "no matter how many HooHas he might see, never will there be one as Glittery as hers..."[31] In Firestone's terms, "he holds a special high place in his mental reserve for 'The One.'"[32] In romances the hero and heroine's feeling of having discovered "The One" is mutual, as is made explicit in Crusie's *Bet Me*. Cal experiences it when "her eyes met his for a long, dark, hot moment, and this time that glint was there, and sound faded to silence, and every nerve he had came alive and said, *This one*," and Min when "he kissed her hard [...] glitter exploded behind her eyelids. She felt his hand on her waist [...] and her blood surged, and the rush in her head said, *THIS one*."[33]

Each ring symbolizes the special status of the relationship between the man who gives it, and the woman who receives it. As Bryan in Roslyn Hardy Holcomb's *Rock Star* states, "Sure, I've given women stuff before, but usually it was, you know, a part of the deal [...]. With you, it's different, you're different."[34] The individual design or history of each ring also tends to underscore the uniqueness of the monogamous relationship entered into by the couple whose union it symbolizes. In *If the Ring Fits ...* "the spell guaranteed the ring would only fit the prince's one true love" and in *With This Ring* the Monkcrest engagement ring is similarly understood to be a guarantee that the wearer is the giver's true love: "The earls give that ring only to the women they love" and "It is given only once in a lifetime."[35]

In two of the ten novels the fact that the rings symbolize both love and sexual attraction is emphasized by the way in which they are contrasted with objects which depict a woman merely as an object of lust. In Kleypas's *Worth Any Price* a miniature portrait of the heroine in an enamelled case is contrasted with the ring which celebrates the special bond between the hero and heroine. When Nick first meets Charlotte she is little more than a sex object to him, as symbolized by the miniature which contains her portrait:

> With an expertise born of habit, he pressed the catch of the enameled case and flipped it open. Settling on his back, he stared into Charlotte's exquisite little face. [...] Desire filled his cock and caused it to stiffen unmercifully. His lashes lowered slightly as he continued to watch the tiny painted face, and his hand slid down to the aching jut of his arousal.[36]

Nick subsequently returns this miniature to Lord Radnor, a secondary character obsessed with Charlotte. The symbolism is clear: for Radnor, Charlotte is only an object to be desired and controlled by him. He believes he has "*created*" her (129) and has literally paid for her: "The Howards had made a bargain with the devil, trading their daughter's future for the financial benefits Radnor could provide" (23). Charlotte, however, refused to be treated as an object to be disposed of by others and escaped from both Radnor and her parents before she could be forced into marriage. In Charlotte and Nick's relationship, the miniature, which symbolizes Charlotte as object, is replaced by the ring which symbolizes their emotional as well as physical union. The

> ring was a huge, dome-shaped sapphire, a blue that nearly approached the dark, sparkling depth of her husband's eyes. The gem was set in gold, with a ring of smaller diamonds surrounding it. What made the sapphire so remarkable, however, was the star that danced on the silky surface of the gem, appearing to slide across it with the light [281].

The jewel is one which both of them played a part in choosing. In its color the sapphire reminds Charlotte of Nick, and in its form it seems to symbolize the way that Nick perceives Charlotte. Like the star, which could perhaps be perceived as a flaw but is what makes the stone "so remarkable," for Nick, Charlotte's "little imperfections made her beauty unique and endlessly interesting" (233). Lord Radnor, who wants only the painted perfection of Charlotte's image, does not give her a ring, and neither does he accept or celebrate the flaws which make her personality unique. Instead he wishes to change her: "He planned to destroy every *facet* of the person she was and replace her with a being of his own creation" (37, emphasis added). Charlotte contrasts Radnor's possessive, critical obsession with Nick's love and acceptance: "My *flaws* don't matter to him [...] You demanded perfection from me — something I could never attain" (372, emphasis added).

Chase's *Lord of Scoundrels* also depicts a relationship in which a painted item symbolizing the heroine's status as a sex object is replaced by a carefully chosen ring. In Chase's novel this item is a watch bearing a picture of a woman.

> "When you turn this knob," he said, demonstrating, "as you see, her skirts divide and there, between her legs, is a —" He pretended to look more closely. "Good heavens, how shocking. I do believe that's a fellow kneeling there." He held the watch closer to her face.[37]

The symbolism of the watch is clarified yet further when Jessica misunderstands Dain and "'I am not a pocket watch,' she said tightly. She told herself she ought not feel in the least surprised that the cocksure clodpole proposed to settle matters by making her *his mistress*."[38] In fact, by this stage in the novel he is proposing to make her his wife, and when he later offers her a ring it is as "a tribute [...]. A bloodred stone for the brave girl who'd shed his blood. And diamonds flashing fiery sparks, because lightening had flashed the first time she'd kissed him."[39]

Engagement rings like the one chosen by Dain can carry such complicated, personalized symbolisms because unlike wedding rings, which tend to be fairly plain and homogeneous in design, the variety of engagement rings gives far greater scope for choice and individuality. A particularly striking and unusual illustration of this point can be found in Crusie's *Bet Me*, in which Cal

> picked up a doughnut and turned to Min. "Minerva Dobbs, I love you and I always will. Will you marry me?"
> "This is so sudden," Min said, grinning at him.
> "We got an audience, Minnie," Cal said. "You in or not?"
> "I'm in," Min said, and he took her left hand, spread her fingers out, and slipped the doughnut over her ring finger, knowing with a certainty he'd never felt before that this was exactly the right thing to do.
> "I'll get you a better ring later," he said.[40]

Later "Cal bought Min an engagement ring made of six perfect diamonds set in a circle. It looks nothing like a Krispy Kreme, but Min knows."[41]

Personalized symbolisms can be found in other descriptions of the rings given to romance heroines. Bram's choice of ring for Sophie demonstrates that he "know[s] Sophie very well" because the "deep glow of the rubies against the cool luster of the pearls, bound together with warm old gold in an unusual, asymmetrical setting" matches her perfectly.[42] As Melissa tells Sophie, this choice of ring is "just right for you — unconventional and warm and colorful" (132). By contrast, Sophie's ex-fiancé's unsuitability and the extent to which he failed to understand and appreciate her are made apparent by the conventionality of the engagement ring he chose for her and its lack of personalization: he bought her "a diamond" engagement ring (120) purely because he believed that was "what a real engagement ring should be" (132). Even the magic royal engagement ring in McClone's *If the Ring Fits ...*, a ring which is a family heirloom and was therefore not chosen by the hero, is described in a way which may recall aspects of the couple it is bringing together. It has as a "center stone, a diamond [... which] glimmered under the overhead lights. The ring was almost medieval-looking with a wide filigree gold band inlaid with rubies, emeralds and sapphires."[43] Christina's "curly auburn hair" (5) is not dissimilar in color to that of the rubies, and she has "emerald eyes" (5). As for the sapphires, they perhaps match the prince's "piercing blue eyes" (113), while the gold is the same color as his "thick, sun-bleached wavy hair" (12–13).

The ring need not be expensive, however, in order to possess a deeply personal, emotional significance. The "colored plastic ring" that Mason offers Tess is the plainest and cheapest of all the rings under discussion in this chapter.[44] Perhaps because the magical nature of Tess's healing HooHa has been stated so openly, there is less need to express this symbolically in the form of a highly glittery and valuable ring. However, Mason's choice of ring and the impulsiveness with which he decides to acquire it do demonstrate his acceptance of the lesson, in how to have fun and be more spontaneous, that Tess has been teaching him at an amusement arcade.

Rings, or some aspects of them, may also symbolize the overcoming of "the reasons that this heroine and hero cannot marry" which Regis terms "the barrier."[45] In Margot Early's *A Family Resemblance* the existence of the barrier is explicitly referred to: "an obstacle lay between them."[46] In this novel it takes the form of the hero's need to climb mountains:

"many climbers he knew loved being in the mountains more than anything. More than love. More than sex. More than their own offspring. Was he any different?" (63). When he can finally answer that question in the affirmative, Joe brings Sabine and her children "rocks from K2" (373), but from "Camp Two [...] not from the top" (373). The provenance of the rocks is therefore proof of his decision to abandon the climb to the summit, and evidence that he no longer loves mountaineering more than Sabine and the children. The rocks are thus a symbol of Joe's decision to turn his back on the challenges of high-altitude mountaineering in order to take up the "challenge to stay alive, to live as a family man, to raise children, to keep a marriage together" (351). The ring he gives Sabine contains gemstones which share this symbolism because although they were not acquired at Camp Two, these "rocks" are

> "Black emerald, [...] peridots and aquamarine, all from Pakistan."
> Finn laughed suddenly. "You *did* bring her rocks" [376].

The gemstones which symbolize Joe's acceptance of a new challenge have a "gold setting" (376) and his married life will be set in Sabine's hometown of Oro, Colorado which literally means "colored gold."

The engagement ring in Laura Abbot's *The Wrong Man*, although it will be given "a new setting" to mark its change of ownership, has a primarily familial rather than personal significance but it is precisely because of this that the ring can represent the overcoming of "the barrier" in this novel.[47] Libby and Trent divorced many years ago because she "had unrealistic notions of what a husband should be like" (191) and he was unable to be "the ideal loving husband, who would father the beautiful children that would make up our perfect family" (191). Now older, wiser, widowed, and the father of a little girl, Trent hopes they can try again, but Trent's mother-in-law, Georgia, is hostile to Libby. After the first meeting between Libby, Trent, his daughter, and her grandparents, Libby wonders, "Was there even a chance to forge a family out of tonight's cast of characters? And had Trent truly changed?" (210). Georgia's hostility and Libby's doubts about Trent form "the barrier." The engagement ring offered to Libby and accompanied by Trent's promise that "this time we'll be a family" (288) is a symbol that "the barrier" has been overcome. It is a gift from both Trent and Georgia: "It belonged to her mother. She had a neighbor send it overnight. She wants you to have it. So do I" (288). Libby acknowledges its significance with "We *are* a family at last" (288).

Each of the rings described in these ten romance novels indicates that the hero and heroine have found their "One" and may also symbolize the sexual attraction between them, commemorate their triumph over "the barrier," recall a moment of particular importance to their relationship, or reflect aspects of the personality and appearance of the heroine, the hero, or both. That the rings in romance novels can be endowed with such rich emotional and sexual symbolism would no doubt surprise earlier critics of the genre. Janice A. Radway, for example, wrote that "the genre's characteristic attention to the incidental features of fashion [...] clearly serves to duplicate the homey environment that serves as the stage for female action in the 'real' world." [48] However, as the present chapter demonstrates, some of the seemingly "incidental features of fashion" included in romance novels may repay closer scrutiny. In this respect romances resemble another, older, popular genre, of which Edith Rogers noted that

> the imagery and the tropological aspect of ballad language are often passed over, since the symbols

are apt to retain also their denotative, obvious, meaning. In other words, the literal image is not displaced by, but coexists with, the figurative image. When a girl is said to be combing her hair, we may confidently imagine a girl combing her hair; when she is said to reject the gift of a costly gown, we are correct in assuming that she does just that; and, thus, we may easily fail to discern consciously any second meaning in her actions. Subconsciously, however, we do get the message: later we know somehow the intentions, expectations, emotions, sufferings, strengths, or failings of that girl, even though the explicit information in the ballad was only about actions and tangible, visible objects.[49]

In romance novels a ring, given by the hero to the heroine, may retain its "denotative, obvious, meaning" as an engagement ring and also reveal a great deal about the donor, the recipient, and their relationship, for, as Jessica Trent observes in *Lord of Scoundrels*, "the selection of a gift requires the balancing of a profoundly complicated moral, psychological, aesthetic, and sentimental equation."[50]

NOTES

1. Helen Fisher, "The Drive to Love: The Neural Mechanism for Mate Selection," in *The New Psychology of Love*, ed. Robert J. Sternberg and Karin Weis (New Haven: Yale University Press, 2006), 88.

2. Lisa M. Diamond, "Emerging Perspectives on Distinctions Between Romantic Love and Sexual Desire," *Current Directions in Psychological Science* 13, no. 3 (2004): 116, and Fisher, "The Drive to Love," 102.

3. Shulamith Firestone, *The Dialectic of Sex: The Case for Feminist Revolution* (New York: Bantam, 1971), 148 and 150.

4. *Ibid.*, 148–149.

5. Lani Diane Rich quoted in Jennifer Crusie, "Modern Literary Terms: The Glittery HooHa," Argh Ink, 9 April 2007, http://www.arghink.com/2007/04/09/the-glittery-hooha-an-analysis/. I wish to thank Lani Diane Rich and Jennifer Crusie for their support and encouragement. Had it not been for Lani's explanation of the term and Jenny's posting of it on her blog, I would never have written this essay. Lani also provided me with further details concerning the provenance of the "Glittery HooHa": the term "glittery hoo-hoo" seems to have been coined at *Television Without Pity* on the sixth of January 2004 by a poster named phxchic in the context of a discussion about advertising (see http://forums.televisionwithoutpity.com/index.php?showtopic=3100820&st=180&p=846765&#entry846765). It was then used to describe certain female characters in soap operas and on 5 October 2006 the following definition was produced by another poster, Bill C: "A **GHH** (*glittery hoo-ha*) refers specifically to the almost magical tendencies of certain female characters' genitalia to entrance men, intimidate other women, and/or otherwise control the known universe (or at the very least allow the woman possessing it to almost literally get away with *anything without repercussions*)" (see http://forums.televisionwithoutpity.com/index.php?showtopic=165519&st=30930&p=6226296&#entry6226296).

6. I have only analyzed romances in which a hero and heroine enter into a monogamous relationship with each other. Further research would be required to determine whether rings are present and have similar symbolisms in romances with homosexual pairings or ones in which the protagonists find happiness in a permanent polyamorous relationship.

7. Thomas D. Hill, "Androgyny and Conversion in the Middle English Lyric, 'In the Vaile of Restles Mynd,'" *ELH* 53, no. 3 (1986): 464.

8. Bruno Bettelheim, *The Uses of Enchantment: The Meaning and Importance of Fairy Tales* (1976; rpt., London: Penguin, 1991), 271–272.

9. Angus McLaren, *Impotence: A Cultural History* (Chicago: University of Chicago Press, 2007), 52.

10. Loretta Chase, *Lord of Scoundrels* (New York: Avon, 1995), 140–141. Emphasis added.

11. *Ibid.*, 170, and *The Book of Common Prayer* (London: Oxford University Press), 202.

12. The romances discussed in this paper are relatively few in number since limitations of space compelled me to focus on novels in which the symbolism was particularly clear. They do, however, include historical and contemporary romances and both category romances and single titles. Among their number are three winners of the Romance Writers of America's RITA awards: Loretta Chase's *Lord of Scoundrels* won a RITA in 1996 in the Best Short Historical category; Lisa Kleypas' *Worth Any Price* won a RITA in 2004 in the Best Short Historical category; and Jennifer Crusie's *Bet Me* won a RITA in 2005 in the Best Contemporary Single Title category.

13. Pamela Regis, *A Natural History of the Romance Novel* (Philadelphia: University of Pennsylvania Press, 2003), 30.

14. *Ibid.*, 38, and "About the Romance Genre," Romance Writers of America, http://www.rwanational.org/cs/the_romance_genre.

15. Lisa Kleypas, *Worth Any Price* (New York: Avon, 2003), 202.

16. Jennifer Crusie, *Bet Me* (New York: St. Martin's Press, 2004), 241, 104 and 299.

17. Melissa McClone, *If the Ring Fits ...* (2000; rpt. Richmond, Surrey: Harlequin Mills & Boon, 2001), 5. Emphasis added.

18. Kleypas, *Worth Any Price*, 38. Emphasis added.

19. *Ibid.*, 30,

20. McClone, *If the Ring*, 56.

21. *Ibid.*, 14.

22. Amanda Quick, *With This Ring* (1998; rpt. New York: Bantam, 1999), 312.

23. *Ibid.*, 21 and 24.

24. Kleypas, *Worth Any Price*, 4.

25. *Ibid.*, 18 and 7. Emphasis added.

26. Jessica Hart, *Mistletoe Marriage* (Richmond, Surrey: Harlequin Mills & Boon, 2005), 14.

27. *Ibid.*, 15.

28. Chase, *Lord of Scoundrels*, 41.

29. *Ibid.*, 55. Emphasis added.

30. Dorie Graham, *So Many Men ...* (Don Mills, Ontario: Harlequin, 2005), 8, 139 and 82.

31. Rich quoted in Crusie, "Modern Literary Terms."

32. Firestone, *The Dialectic*, 148.

33. Crusie, *Bet Me*, 44 and 104–105.

34. Roslyn Hardy Holcomb, *Rock Star* (Columbus, MS: Genesis Press, 2006), 131.

35. McClone, *If the Ring*, 56, and Quick, *With This Ring*, 344 and 351.

36. Kleypas, *Worth Any Price*, 40. Further references will be included parenthetically.

37. Chase, *Lord of Scoundrels*, 33.

38. *Ibid.*, 140.

39. *Ibid.*, 166. Both the giving of the ring and the wedding occur in London at roughly the center-point of the novel. London, and the events which take place there, act as a pivot between the first section (set in Paris, where Dain leads a debauched, loveless existence) and his return to his ancestral home in Devon, where, with Jessica's help, he can confront his past and come to both accept love from others and reciprocate it. The three locations reflect three stages in Dain's character development and are symbolized by three objects: Paris by the watch which represents lust; London by the ring which demonstrates Dain's acceptance of marriage and a change of lifestyle; and finally Devon by the icon of a Madonna which Jessica gives him and which symbolizes his acceptance of fatherhood and a change in his view of his mother.

40. Crusie, *Bet Me*, 381.

41. *Ibid.*, 391.

42. Hart, *Mistletoe Marriage*, 132 and 116. Further references will be included parenthetically.

43. McClone, *If the Ring*, 14. Further references will be included parenthetically.

44. Graham, *So Many Men*, 184.

45. Regis, *A Natural History*, 32.

46. Margot Early, *A Family Resemblance* (2006; rpt. Richmond, Surrey: Harlequin Mills & Boon, 2007), 234. Further references will be included parenthetically.

47. Laura Abbot, *The Wrong Man* (2004; rpt. Richmond, Surrey: Silhouette, 2005), 288. Further references will be included parenthetically.

48. Janice A. Radway, *Reading the Romance: Women, Patriarchy, and Popular Literature* (1984; rpt. with a new Introduction, Chapel Hill: University of North Carolina Press, 1991), 195.

49. Edith Rogers, "Clothing as a Multifarious Ballad Symbol," *Western Folklore* 34, no. 4 (1975): 261.

50. Chase, *Lord of Scoundrels*, 25.

8

The More the Merrier? Transformations of the Love Triangle Across the Romance

Carole Veldman-Genz

French theorist René Girard calls the triangle "a model of a sort, or rather a whole family of models [...] They always allude to the mystery, transparent yet opaque, of human relations."[1] A persistent novelistic constellation, the love triangle freezes impulses of desire into a fixed, schematic set of erotic positions. However, the triadic configuration is by no means a mechanical model; instead, it is a dynamic structure, capable of producing plural textual effects. For the legendary Arthur, Guinevere, and Lancelot, triangular desire had tragic consequences; in Shakespeare's *A Midsummer Night's Dream*, the love triangle is employed for comic effect; in Jane Austen's work, the triadic structure provides romantic conflict. And for scholars of popular romance fiction, the love triangle is a particularly apposite topic of investigation, since it allows glimpses at generic shifts and development.

Admittedly, the love triangle is not a narrative essential of the romance plot; for example, it does not appear in Pamela Regis's list of eight elements that define the genre. Nonetheless, popular romances abound with love triangles and have done so for some time. In 1984, Rosalind Coward records that the existence of a rival is "almost obligatory" in romances.[2] In the same year, Janice Radway draws on Margaret Jensen's research to state that "98 percent of her sample of Harlequins [...] included either a male or a female rival."[3] In the mid-nineties, Kay Mussell observes that almost all romantic scenarios feature "a man, a woman, and another woman."[4] After twenty years of romance reading, previous work as a romance editor, and research on the genre as a university lecturer, I can corroborate these views. Without doubt, most popular romance authors have used the love triangle device at one time or another—but for different reasons and to differing effects.

This chapter explores the plurality of those textual effects: the ways a single structural device serves contrasting contextual specificities and hegemonic variables. My aim is to offer a discriminating insight into the narrative possibilities of romances. As my use of the plural "romances" indicates, I am not concerned with any singular or monolithic meta-text of *the* romance. Of course, I do not deny the existence of *a* romance genre—at least insofar as it is understood as an epistemological horizon of expectation for readers and a socio-symbolic model of writing for authors.[5] Nonetheless, critics have focused far too long on the ostensibly homologous praxis of the romance, portraying it as a "frozen and repetitive form,"[6] a "deeply conservative, even regressive"[7] genre. Accordingly, I oppose any reductive and a-historical homogenization of the romance, and instead propose a more fine-grained approach that looks at romances as relational discourses whose definitions contain evolving and heterogeneous practices. I believe that the love triangle serves as an ideal interpretative tool for this purpose.

Infused with emotion and rich conflict, the triadic constellation stages the romantic scenario in ways that are narratively variable and ideologically telling. In what follows, the love triangle emerges as a sensitive register processing a whole spectrum of generic variations. My critical trajectory first introduces the existing literary theory on the triangle; then it looks in detail at three types of romance where the constellation's potential for change can clearly be seen: romances governed by the conservative logic of oppositional splits, romances influenced by popular feminism, and, lastly, pioneering examples of the genre that venture into new romance territory and expand generic boundaries.

The Triangle in Theory: Mimeticism and Homosociality

This section is dedicated to the two most influential literary theories of the triangle — René Girard's concept of mimeticism and Eve Kosofsky Sedgwick's notion of homosociality.[8] In *Deceit, Desire and the Novel* (1961), Girard argues that the novelistic tradition of European high culture continually replicates a tripartite structure of mimetic, or imitative, desire. In the Girardian drama, an individual subject does not desire spontaneously or independently. Rather, an object is desirable only insofar as it is desired by another person whom the subject has chosen as a role model. No form of desire points directly from subject to object, because every exchange between the two is invariably mediated via a more important third pole. This third pole, the "mediator," functions as a rival who triangulates, heightens, sustains, and ultimately legitimizes the desire. All desire is thus a *désir selon l'autre*— a desire according to the other. All action is motivated by the obsessive rivalry and fascination between subject and mediator. In the mimetic economy, the object of desire loses its concrete value, receding more and more into the background until the only relationship of consequence is that between subject and rival. "No resolution of the deadlock is really satisfactory," Girard explains. "The only tolerable situation is for rivalry to go on. The triangle must endure."[9]

Girard bases his theory of the triangle on readings of literary texts ranging from Greek drama, and Shakespeare, to Proust, and Joyce. The mimetic economy "reappears *as such* only in the greatest writers, reproduced with clockwork accuracy," he observes.[10] Only those "secret sharers"[11] of the mimetic truth are "capable of seeing that the sexual side of the matter is far from being primary and must be subordinated to mimeticism."[12] In contrast to such excellence, Girard places the "romantic" writer who upholds the "illusion of spontaneous desire" and therefore can never achieve "novelistic depth."[13] "[N]ovelistic genius" in turn is "won by a great struggle against these attitudes we have lumped together under the name 'romantic' because they all appear to us intended to maintain the illusion of romantic desire and of a subjectivity almost divine in its autonomy."[14] It goes without saying that contemporary romance writers fall into that latter, debased category. Stepping back from Girard's argument, we can see that the mimetic diagram invariably blocks out certain areas of human experience that give precedence to the optimistic affirmation of human instinct and autonomy. Such an affirmation is crucial to popular romances that focus precisely on the relational exchanges apparently unworthy of Girard's investigation. Here, the object of desire remains the principal pole of desiring activity and the libidinal subject-object relation functions as the main axis of importance. Individual agency is perceived as the effective locus of direct and autonomous motivational processes, giving expression to what Girard might term a *désir selon soi*—a desire that is a self-sufficient and spontaneous manifestation of an individual's preferences. The plot of romances depends on the existence of this independently desiring subject. The optimistic patterns of the genre — the belief that *amor omnia vincit*— appear irreconcilable with the open-ended pessimism of the mimetic model. There is no place, then, for romances in the Girardian canon.

The analytical fissures in Girard's model become particularly apparent when one notes that the mimetic truth is predominantly communicable by a handful of male writers who uphold literary standards. Despite Girard's claim that mimetic "rivalry [...] occurs in an absolutely symmetrical way in both sexes," his canon traces proto-triangles in which two active males compete for an apparently passive female.[15] With the exception of Flaubert's *Madame Bovary*, Girard does not consider women as desiring subjects. Masculine desire is the narrative motor that propels the Girardian plot and provides the emotive point of reference for the reader. The mimetic model thus occludes female desire, female subjectivity, and processes of identification governed by female points of view—all features innate to the "gynocentric"[16] plots of popular romances.

In *Between Men: English Literature and Male Homosocial Desire* (1985), Eve Kosofsky Sedgwick draws attention to the gender blindness governing Girard's model, calling the Girardian love triangle a "deadly symmetry from which the historical accidents of gender, language, class and power detract."[17] Sedgwick's own concept of homosociality, however, bears significant, and deliberate, similarities to Girard's theory. We are dealing with the same male-based triangle, an analogous (all-male) spectrum of desire and a similarly elitist formulation of the literary canon. Like mimeticism, homosociality describes the ways men bond with each other through a female object of desire or exchange. The male/female/male triangle is exposed as a nurturing ground for homosocial bonding — which Sedgwick defines as not homosexual, but blatantly homophobic. Patriarchal power and institutions are shown to be organized around a ritualized traffic in women in which the "contemptible female figure is a solvent" who binds together two men, so that they will be able to "exchange power and to confirm each other's value."[18] This homosocial set-up, Sedgwick argues, has shaped the entire European literary canon since the Renaissance and, more impressively, structures the whole "heterosexual European erotic ethos."[19] Once again, the male/female/male triangle shapes and canonizes literature.

Sedgwick's theory blocks out the romance genre on all accounts. Thoroughly male-focused, the mechanics of the homosocial triangle are alien to the female-orientated plots of contemporary romances. A "female" genre *par excellence*, the romance is typically gendered feminine, both in terms of its heroine-centered plots as well as its authors and readership.[20] Using gendered phrases such as "women's genre," "female genre," or "feminine discourse" might seem outdated in the age of suave vanguardism expected from every self-respecting feminist cultural critic nowadays. Nonetheless, considering the contextual/historical/formulaic baggage that comes into play when discussing romances, I find that the use of the gendered "f-word" (feminine) is unavoidable, just as I must acknowledge the unapologetically gendered attributes of the genre. Granted, making assumptions about what exactly constitutes a female/feminine genre opens up my analysis to the accoutrements of essentialism. With this in mind, we must, of course, remain vigilant against pernicious and unexamined concepts of common gender sensibility and sensitive to differences between women. Coming back to Sedgwick's argument, it is axiomatic that the mass-produced and irrevocably feminized romance must be disqualified from any participation in Sedgwick's highly masculinized, high-culture canon — a canon that deftly eliminates any author focusing on subject matter other than homosociality or depicting triangles other than the male/female/male one. True to form, Sedgwick is aware of the gaps in her argument, freely conceding that gender is "expected to alter the structure of erotic triangles."[21] Unsurprisingly, though, she does not spare the time to investigate these non-homosocial structures, since to do so would mean to damage, if only schematically, the canonized masculinist triangle she is intent on elaborating.

This chapter, then, examines what René Girard refused to investigate and where Eve Kosofsky Sedgwick left off. In my readings of romances, I explore both the critically acclaimed male/female/male triad and the previously ignored female/male/female triangle. I highlight the feminocentric potential these structures display in a genre centered upon female desire, subjectivity, and women's authority/authorship. Published over the last thirty years, the texts I have chosen illustrate a variety of romance types — short series romances, longer single titles, as well as the short-story format. With varying historical and contemporary backdrops and including erotic, paranormal, and horror plots, this diverse and plentiful selection should lend itself, I hope, to a differentiated approach to the genre.

The Good and the Bad:
Dichotomous Politics in Romances

Love triangles frequently depend on a logic of oppositional splits. When this occurs, the same-gender participants of the triad are played off against one another and cast into the molds of the "good" / "bad" lover. In the case of the male/female/male triangle, this means that the romance heroine is caught in the intermediary position between two men. Structurally, of course, this resembles the triad described by Girard and Sedgwick. Yet, in the romance scenario, the heroine is no passive object of exchange, but an independently desiring subject whose desire propels most action and whose point of view governs reader identification. Her romantic quest is informed by a process of selection in which she decides who is the "good" / "bad" suitor. Her choice expresses a confident and determining female gaze and a knowing, autonomous subjectivity.

In Lisa Kleypas's contemporary romance *Sugar Daddy* (2007), heroine Liberty Jones is torn between childhood idol Hardy Cates and tycoon Gage Travis. The two men are cast as opposites, "different in almost every way, education, background, experience."[22] The bittersweet puppy love between Liberty and Hardy overshadows all her adult relationships. This changes when she meets Gage. The romance between Gage and Liberty progresses until triangulation asserts itself. Hardy reemerges, having transformed himself from white trailer trash to self-made millionaire. As soon as the second man enters the erotic economy, the heroine's subjectivity comes under threat: Liberty finds herself "in the middle of a tug-of-war between two ruthless men" (347). Put into the terminology of the love triangle, this means that the gynocentric romance plot is threatened by the impending imposition of a mimetically/homosocially informed triad, which would transform the actively desiring heroine into a passive object of exchange. At this juncture, the female-centered romance plot asserts itself. The heroine's selection of one man over another articulates an individual agency that remains untainted by mimetic/homosocial relations: for Liberty, it is about "[m]aking a real choice" (357). Her point of view holds the authority to impose the dualistic patterns that will decide who the "good" suitor is. When Hardy uses Liberty's insider knowledge of Gage's firm to advance his business, he is immediately relegated to the role of "bad" suitor. All Liberty and he shared is "childhood history" (361), whereas the relationship with Gage is built on "love" (360). As soon as the dualistic patterns are imposed, the erotic tension of the love triangle is dispersed; the heroine's romantic quest has ended.

A similar selective process shapes Christina Dodd's *In My Wildest Dreams* (2001). This historical romance faithfully transposes the plot of Billy Wilder's movie *Sabrina* (1954) into a mid-nineteenth-century setting. Celeste Milford is the young governess who returns from the Distinguished Academy of Governesses to find her affections shifting from handsome Ellery Throckmorton to his surly older brother Garrick. Once again, the two rivals are cast as opposites. Where lighthearted Ellery has "blond, blue-eyed allure," Garrick is "plain, dark and somber."[23] Like Kleypas's heroine, Celeste harbors a lifelong infatuation: "She had wanted Ellery forever, and she didn't understand her own confusion, her appalled attraction to stodgy old Garrick" (173). While the novel includes other romantic barriers — for instance, Ellery's sweet-natured fiancée Hyacinth — the initial romantic tension originates from the heroine's inability to choose between the two brothers. As she learns to distinguish between the "right" and "wrong" suitor, her determining gaze functions as a selective, bifurcating mechanism that breaks up triangulation. Ellery is not so much vilified as he is belittled as a weak-minded, if appealing, womanizer. Searching for "nothing less than her soulmate," Celeste determines that "Ellery was not that" (247). Garrick, on the other hand, has "shown her that the dream of Ellery she'd cherished for so many years was nothing but a chimera" (249). As in Kleypas's novel, the breakup of triangulation involves an authoritative expression of choice on the heroine's part. As Celeste states, "I choose you, Garrick Throckmorton, I choose *you*" (370).

In romance novels, then, the dualistic structures of the male/female/male triangle harbor the potential for female determination and agency. This is not so much the case for the female/male/female counter-model. Here, the logic of oppositional splits involves the heroine not as a commanding subject but as part of a dualistic couple system with a distinctly patriarchal flavor. As with the masculinized triangle, the imposition of dualistic categories encourages the breakup of triangulation. Yet, whereas the "wrong" suitors of the male-based triangle are not necessarily vilified, the women of the female-based triangle frequently undergo more stringent assessments. Arranged as moral/sexual/social opposites (the "good" / "bad" woman), the two female figures structurally orbit around the male whose determining gaze holds definitional power. This doubling of women into opposites—good/bad, virgin/whore, sane/mad—functions as a zoning method that circumscribes women antithetically, thereby perpetuating female rivalry. As Patricia Duncker observes, this is "precisely how patriarchy works, either on the page or in the world: by dividing the women."[24]

Clearly, the imaginative practice involved offers a thoroughly antiquated representation of womanhood; it negates female diversity and replaces it with starkly polarized, and therefore manageable, female images. Much of a hero's brutish behavior can be explained away by the staple excuse of him having suffered at the hands of a "bad" woman. In Linda Howard's contemporary romance *Duncan's Bride* (1990), second wife Madelyn fights the hero's bitterness about his first marriage to April. The divorce settlement has financially ruined his farm and his emotional scars originate from the "dirty deal" he got first time around.[25] Although the vilified April is vindicated in a surprise turnaround — after her death, she returns the divorce settlement "in a gesture of fairness too long delayed"[26] — the romantic resolution depends to a large degree on the imposition of dualistic categorizations. The heroine spends much of her time trying to prove she is the "good" lover and "not his first wife."[27]

Considering the outdatedness of the gender system involved, it is unsurprising that this type of female/male/female triangle is frequently employed in older or more formulaic examples of the genre. In Catherine George's Mills & Boon *Devil Within* (1984), heroine Claudia contrasts the hero's "selfish, cold" first wife Elaine.[28] This dualistic depiction of femininity echoes in the equally retro-sexist rhetoric: the romantic resolution articulates the heroine's deep satisfaction of marrying "one of those chauvinists who consider woman's place in the home."[29] Isabelle Holland's *Darcourt* (1977) portrays a similar super-male hero who "will not be disobeyed."[30] Once again, we find an unsettling, if revealing, marriage of sexism and dualism. *Darcourt* features a leprous, mad and "diabolical" first wife whose textual presence is only conveyed through indistinct glimpses or "odd, eerie" laughs — not unlike Brontë's (in)famous Bertha Rochester.[31] Cast into a position of oppression, the second woman becomes an easily eradicable linguistic non-presence — a stereotypical madwoman, who, as Helen Small rightly says, "sums up virtually everything feminism might wish to say about the suppression of women's speech."[32]

The pairing of sane heroine and deranged rival is a regular feature in popular romances and particularly indicative of traditionalist impulses in the genre. The first installment of Jude Deveraux's hugely successful Velvet quartet, the medieval-set *The Velvet Promise* (1981), maps out the triangle between Deveraux's favorite heroine Judith Revedoune, her warrior husband Gavin, and Gavin's longtime mistress, the beautiful but cruel Alice. The two women are physical, moral and, it turns out, mental opposites, as different as "fire and ice."[33] For much of the plot, the hero remains convinced of his affection for Alice. The romantic resolution requires the breakup of triangulation and Gavin's gradual unmasking of Alice's true — i.e. insane — nature. During his romantic quest, the hero must learn to exercise his determining/bifurcating gaze. In front of his eyes, Alice transforms from "sweet-natured woman" to the "caricature of the woman he thought he knew."[34]

Amanda Scott's medieval romance *Lord of the Isles* (2005) replays the same erotic scenario. Here, sisters Cristina and Mariota are rivals for the affections of warrior hero Hector. The women are, once again, cast as opposites: plain Cristina is "naught" beside the younger, beautiful Mariota.[35] Though enamored with Mariota, Hector is tricked into wedding and bedding the older sister. Most of the tension stems from his inability to reconcile himself to his fate and, in broader terms, impose the dualistic structures that would replace the unstable triad with romantic coupledom. Triangulation is dismantled in a gradual process that sees Hector first witnessing Mariota's "childish, disobedient and annoying" flirtations and finally diagnosing her "mad."[36] Again, the dualistic juxtaposition of the two women allows the rival's structural elimination from the text and heralds the end of the romantic quest.

Sisters and Brothers: Relational Discourses in Contemporary Romances

This section focuses on romances that move away from the dichotomously conceptualized love triangle towards a triad that affirms relational dynamics. Such triangles refute the traditionalist binarism of the "good" / "bad" lover in favor of a discourse in which same-gender and heterosexual bonds coexist harmoniously within the bounds of the romance plot. Here, the breakup of triangulation is not brought about by the imposition of oppositional categories but by more affirmative and inclusive strategies. The "bad" lover is replaced by a more sympathetic character, who is in turn pitied, befriended, or harmoniously put to rest. Love in these romances is not necessarily singular and original, but an emotion that might and will be re-experienced. For the male/female/male triangle, this involves a more expansive symbology of love and a rejection of male rivalry. For its gender-reversed counterpart, it implies an assertion of female-female bonds or, as I argue, a popular-culture appropriation of the Second-Wave feminist ideal of sisterhood.

In some cases, the positive re-visioning of the female rival is an unconvincing and tacked-on send-up. In Catherine Coulter's medieval romance *Rosehaven* (1996), for instance, the dualistic schematization opposing heroine Hastings and "silver-haired bitch" Marjorie is so insistent that the rival's belated conversion — Marjorie selflessly saves the heroine's life — is "beyond [...] comprehension."[37] When the de-vilification of the female rival is successful, however, it marks a welcome adjustment to the stodgy binarism of the "good" / "bad" woman. This can happen even when the novel trades on the familiar opposition between sane heroine and insane rival. In Maggie Osborne's *A Stranger's Wife* (1999) and Karen Ranney's *Heaven Forbids* (1998), the formerly unbreachable mental rift between rival women is healed. Forging bonds with her mad predecessor, the heroine of Osborne's novel promises, "not to forget that my change in fortune came about because of your possible misfortune."[38] In Ranney's text, heroine Kathryn accepts her own involvement in bringing about her rival's madness and suicide, refusing to wipe out her presence "as if she never lived."[39]

These changes in the heroine's relationship with her female rival are often accompanied by changes in the hero. No longer an impenetrable emotional cipher (for heroine or reader), the hero is vulnerable, and invites readerly engagement and identification. As romance writer Nora Roberts in an interview with Kay Mussell states, it "is now at least as much his story as hers."[40] Sandra Brown's *Texas! Chase* (1991) and Nicole Jordan's *The Heart Breaker* (1998) feature such sensitized heroes and textualize the widowers' grieving and healing processes. Brown's hero "shared a special love" with his first wife Tanya and the heroine is not interested in "taking [her] place."[41] Jordan's hero Sloan McCord will always feel a "haunting sense of loss" at the death of his first wife.[42] In these romances, the notion of erotic singularity — the once-in-a-lifetime love — is replaced by a more inclusive romantic conceptualization. Rather than resolve the triangle by imposing oppositional categorizations, these novels resolve it through a harmonious integration of characters. The potential female rival is not forgotten but put to rest, her blessing and goodwill a given.

Equally vulnerable heroes, the men of the male/female/male triangle need not be cast as opposites. They may be best friends, as in LaVyrle Spencer's Western romance *Twice Loved* (1984). Here, the triadic relations between heroine Laura, second husband Dan, and supposed-to-be-dead first husband Rye have always been based on friendship. It "had always been the three of them, forever comrades."[43] When sailor Rye finds his place usurped by his best friend, "[t]hey were no longer three [...] but two plus one" (82). While rivalry takes hold of the men, the bonds of friendship ultimately prove stronger in times of need. Dan and Rye both feel "the tether of lifelong sanguinity binding them together with a strength that superseded their rivalry for the same woman" (338). There is a slight homosocial element to this triangle; yet again, the heroine's determining gaze commands reader attention and her selection imposes erotic exclusivity. For Laura, Rye would always be "her first choice" (240). A romantic hierarchy is undeniably at play — Rye is the "better" lover — but the whole triangular economy is informed by an inclusive discourse of love. The heroine loves "two men, each in a different way" (142).

In Penelope Williamson's historical Western romance *Heart of the West* (1995), love is also not a singular emotion, but one that can be experienced doubly, even synchronously. Heroine Clementine loves both husband Gus and his wild cowboy brother Zach. The triangle is eventually resolved — Gus dies and Clementine is free to love Zach alone — but across the novel, her twofold affections seem a matter of conscious choice rather than mere indecision. In the heroine's words, if she had to "live over again, I would do all of it, *all* of it, in the exact same way."[44] Clementine's multiple affections shade over into other, non-romantic, feminocentric bonds. In a striking scene, all women of the settlement protest against the polluting mining company as if they were "of one mind and one heart."[45] Clementine finds more "sisters" in local dance-hall owner Hannah and Chinese mail-order bride Erlan — the wording inevitably recalling the sisterhood metaphor of Second-Wave feminism.[46] These ties of female sociality are a recurrent topos of contemporary romance fiction. Susan Elizabeth Phillips's contemporary romance *Fancy Pants* (1989) celebrates female sociality in the "bond of love and friendship" existing between the hero's first wife Holly Grace and heroine Francesca.[47] In Jude Deveraux's historical romance *River Lady* (1985), the two rivals Leah and Kimberly shift from being opposites — "a whore and a virgin" — to being, in Kimberley's words, "best girlfriend[s]."[48] In Penelope Williamson's *The Passions of Emma* (1997), heroine Emma finds the "dearest, best friend in the world" in potential rival Bria, while Bria knows Emma "as well as I know myself, for we are the same in our deepest places."[49]

This affirmation of female collectivism is indicative of the ways in which romance has managed to incorporate many themes of liberal feminism without jettisoning its central narrative of courtship and triumphant happily ever after. Of course, these romances stage female bonding on an individual — rather than political/social/organizational — level. The examples of love triangles discussed here offer a popularized and de-politicized discourse of solidarity, which is not harnessed to an obvious political project and does not share the radical potential of feminism's wider agenda. But they do, I maintain, recuperate "the most compelling themes evoked by feminism," female collectivism and sisterhood.[50] These popular-culture texts are interesting particularly because they are structured both by familiar romance formulas as well as an engagement with feminism. Despite the limitations of the mainstream media logic, the romances disseminate, in broad and accessible strokes, feminist beliefs and ethics. In turn, those beliefs have had a demonstrable impact on how romance authors deploy the plot device of triangulated desire.

The More the Merrier: The Love Triangle in Romantica

In the novels discussed so far, the intra-gender bond has always been secondary to the main romantic relationship. Whether love was singular or plural, there could only be one primary (heterosexual, monogamous) relationship at the end of the romance. In all cases, the breakup of triangulation was a prerequisite for the balanced mutuality of pair bonding; only the declaration of monogamy brought narrative closure. This generic staple is revisited in the romantica[51] novels I discuss in this subsection. Blending *ars erotica* and romance, romantica combines a romance-driven plot — one in which the happily-ever-after is a narrative essential — with plentiful and graphic sexual scenes, sexually explicit language, and erotic constellations that may go beyond coupledom and heteronormativity. All the novels I discuss here feature ménage-à-trois-style erotic constellations in which the triangle ceases to be an obstacle to romantic closure; indeed, the threesome replaces the dyadic pairing as romantic ideal.[52]

If one believes the marketing strategies of erotic romance publishers, romantica re-envisions an autonomous female sexuality. The website of one of romantica's market leaders, e-publisher Ellora's Cave, plays up to women's entitlement to sexual pleasure and proclaims that the premise of romantica is that "women's sexual experiences are legitimate, positive, and beautiful."[53] British publishing house Black Lace describes its venture in similar semi-feminist terms: "We never underestimate female sexuality,"[54] it announces on its website, projecting the Black Lace publishing environment as a woman-defined space where books are written "by women, from the female point of view, and with women's desires and tastes in mind."[55] There is, of course, nothing new about promoting the female body as a key site of femininity or coding it as sexually receptive — those are age-old practices that have dominated our visual and textual landscapes for centuries. With romantica, however, the difference lies in interpretation; now sexually rapacious femininity is given weight and is available for reading as an emblem of independence and self-pleasure. The constructions of femininity on offer speak of a "sexual subjectification" that takes female pleasures (even occasionally deviant or conflicting pleasures) seriously.[56] Female sexuality has thus become "active, recreational, material, independent, consumerist and consumed, a key site of conflict, resistance and division."[57]

Emma Holly's Black Lace erotic romance *Ménage* (1998) features a strong, desirous, and self-possessed heroine whose sexuality has broken free from traditional passivity. Emancipated workaholic Kate Winthrop is older than her two grad-student lovers and clearly "the master of [her] flesh."[58] The heroine's romantic quest goes hand in hand with a journey of sexual discovery in which "three healthy animals [rub] against the boundaries of love."[59] Although Kate ends up marrying one of her lovers, the "precarious balance of three" is part of the happy ending and expressly continues with her "permission."[60] Here, the threesome is not an introductory step towards hedonistic sexual anarchy; instead, the romantica ménage functions as a committed and sexually exclusive structure that rivals dyadic coupledom in terms of romance.

In Rachel Bo's contemporary romantica *Double Jeopardy* (2004), heroine Kendall Aaronson enters a "long-term, permanent relationship" with Sutter Campbell and Joshua Reed.[61] Over-weight — or, in Bo's words, "voluptuous, rubenesque" (12) — and older than her lovers, Kendall functions as the provider for the trio. She is thus cast in a position of power that typifies romantica's focus on strong women. The connections between the three lovers are supernaturally strong. They share not only "triple orgasms" (122), but a "joined consciousness" (18) that allows them to communicate telepathically. The triangle functions as the only structure allowing complete romantic expression. As Sutter explains, "Josh and I have always known there was something — some*one*— missing [...] You're a part of us" (15). The triadic relationship is legitimized in a semi-religious ceremony in which the two men become

Kendall's "husbands" (117). The novel thereby revises received notions of wedlock and espouses an innovative re-visioning of love and marriage. Three-way love, although not universally accepted, is presented as an authentic and liberating articulation of autonomous preferences: "We have to be true to ourselves," Kendall states (123): "[T]here are people now who don't approve of the three of us. But there are quite a few who do. They understand that we don't choose who to love. Love chooses us" (145).

For the heroine of Mardi Ballou's "quickie"[62] *Reunions Dangereuses* (2006), being in a ménage à trois is "the most natural and desirable situation."[63] Pam Holland is, once again, a "proudly round, generously curved" heroine, who enters into a three-way relationship with "average bisexual vampire[s]" Dean Morley and Jake Ardlow.[64] Admittedly, the premise of the story asks for a suspension of disbelief and the short-story format undoubtedly leaves little room for plot and character development. Generically, however, there are interesting developments at stake that deserve investigation. Ellora's Cave offers themed books — for instance, "Interracial," "Rubenesque," "Gay/Lesbian," "Menage or more" and themed lines such as "Sophisticate," featuring older women and younger men. This means that marginalized groups usually unheard of in romances are afforded representation and given a voice, thus allowing for greater diversity in media representations of women and men. The depiction of older, over-weight heroines in erotic romances suggests a wider concern with female difference (physical embodiment, age, sexual orientation, ethnicity, etc.) that disputes homogenizing romantic conventions that would allow for only some types of heroines: thin, young, and white. Here, bigger women and women with wrinkles have sexual identity and subjecthood. The texts' dismissal of standardized romance heroine body types should be read against postfeminist fare such as *Bridget Jones's Diary* or *Sex and the City*, in which female bodies, in order to be desirable, are in constant need of (self-) discipline, continuously supervised and worked on. The sexually desiring and desirable woman of romantica may be older, fatter, blacker, and more hedonistic than anyone else in romance. The emancipatory potential of this intervention should not be underestimated.

This diversity of heroines echoes in the diversity of sexualities (and of sexual subjectivities) featured in romantica ménage novels — i.e. in the celebration of bisexuality. Set in Regency England, Samantha Kane's *At Love's Command* (2007) is part of a series that envisions a whole subculture of idealized bisexual triangles. Depicting three full-blown romantic ménages, the novel presents male bisexuality not simply as the norm for most male characters, but as a definitive indicator of value. Only the ménage provides romantic closure, "[h]appiness, peace, stability."[65] The participants of the triangles "live a dream" marked by a utopian anachronism in both morality and diction.[66] Modeled on modern slang, the characters' graphic language inside the bedroom jars against the Regency setting and draws attention to the Third Wave feminist erotic liberalism that underlies the sexualities of the ménage structure, if not romantica as a whole.[67] These are typically Third Wave feminist quests for sexual satisfaction in which "no sex toy" shall be left "unturned and no sexual avenue unexplored."[68] The characters' pursuit of erotic fulfillment and romantica's emphatic prioritization of sexual pleasure resonate with an ethic of acceptance which foregrounds "pleasure over the *politics* of pleasure."[69]

The male/female/male ménages of romantica sharply contrast the homophobic implications of Sedgwick's homosocial model. Indeed, the male-male sexual encounter functions as a trigger for female sensuality. Viewed from a distinctly female, authoritative point of view, the depiction of male homosexuality elicits female pleasure; it is usually integral to the heroine's — and the female reader's — quest for erotic titillation. Kane's heroine is "shocked by the intensity of the desire that swept through her as she watched the two men kiss. It was the most arousing thing she had ever seen."[70] It seems that gay eroticism is for women what "girl-on-girl" eroticism is for men: a self-gratifying, voyeuristic experience, controlled by the gendered gaze of the onlooker and all the more pleasurable because it involves participants "other-than-me." In ménage romantica, the male body is eroticized in the same ways the female body has been objectified for centuries. This is the case textually — in the graphic depictions of gay sex and the "sexy" male body — as well as visually. Ellora's Cave covers typically feature scantily-clad, pinup-style men who are obviously constituted as objects of desire. The eroticized presentations of male bodies are clearly marked and marketed as visually exciting — an unmistakable gender-reversal of standard pornographic imagery. It remains to be seen whether the overt fetishization of the male body transforms romantica into a cutting-edge genre, seeing that the male body remains restricted to the predictably young, slim, and muscular mold. Undeniably, however, this representational practice diversifies the visual landscape and codes male bodies so that they can be looked at and desired. The active and sexualizing female gaze that these covers imply and invite opens up positions of authority and desire for women readers: positions from which to control and take pleasure in the erotic scenarios on offer, whether or not they explicitly feature female characters.

Romantica has proven particularly responsive to shifting social conceptions of female sexuality, and particularly flexible in opening the genre of romance to the new structures and plots these shifting conceptions imply. The erotic romance allows for the articulation of modes of organizing sexual relations that are not necessarily heteronormative; it offers a forum for the articulation of "illicit" or formerly non-romantic identities and structures, i.e. the older overweight woman, the bisexual man, the romantic threesome. That such articulation might facilitate a wider acceptance of these identities and structures by mainstream culture is not at issue here. Although mainstream publishers have become increasingly interested in the erotic romance product, most initial generic experimentation occurs in niche markets (e-publishing or specialized erotica).[71] This niche positioning has allowed for rapid generic evolution, including changes in format (the romantica "quickie"), characterization (the overweight/black/older heroine; the bisexual hero) and subject matter (the ménage romance). When romantica deploys the familiar structure of the love triangle, we can see the genre of romance push outward, revising and reviving itself. However overdetermined the triadic constellation may seem in the canons explored by Sedgwick and Girard, it proves remarkably flexible — as plot and as cultural construct — when popular romance fiction is added into consideration. This flexibility is indicative of the pluralistic unity and the contextually charged dynamism infusing the romance genre as a whole. As the changing fate of the love triangle attests, generic boundaries are not fixed but constantly in motion, sites of revision rather than immutable inscription.

NOTES

1. René Girard, *Deceit, Desire and the Novel: Self and Other in Literary Structure* (1961; rpt. Baltimore: Johns Hopkins University Press, 1976), 2–3.
2. Rosalind Coward, *Female Desire* (London: Palladin, 1984), 193.
3. Janice A. Radway, *Reading the Romance: Women, Patriarchy and Popular Literature* (1984; rpt. with a new Introduction, Chapel Hill: University of North Carolina Press, 1991), 122.

4. Kay Mussell, "*Paradoxa* Interview with Janet Daily," *Paradoxa: Studies in World Literary Genres* 3, nos. 1–2 (1997): 217.

5. I draw on Tzvetan Todorov's idea of genres as dynamic, socio-historical entities, which serve as "horizons of expectation" for readers and "models of writing" for authors (*Genres in Discourse* [1976; rpt. Cambridge: Cambridge University Press, 1990]), 80, 18. See also Mary Gerhart's description of genres as "epistemological because they are constitutive of meaning" (*Genre Choices Gender Questions* [Norman: University of Oklahoma Press, 1992], 9).

6. Coward, *Female Desire*, 178.

7. Sarah Goodwin Webster, "Romance and Change: Teaching the Romance to Undergraduates," *Paradoxa: Studies in World Literary Genres* 3, nos. 1–2 (1997): 233.

8. For other explorations of the love triangle, see H. M. Daleski, *The Divided Heroine: A Recurrent Pattern in Six English Novels* (London: Holmes & Meier, 1984); Jean E. Kennard, *Victims of Convention* (Hamden, CT: Archon, 1978); Terry Castle, "Sylvia Townsend and the Counterplot of Lesbian Fiction," in *Sexual Sameness: Textual Differences in Lesbian and Gay Writing*, ed. Joseph Bristow (London: Routledge, 1992), 128–147.

9. René Girard, *"To Double Business Bound": Essays on Literature, Mimesis, and Anthropology* (Baltimore: Johns Hopkins University Press, 1978), 66.

10. René Girard, Preface to *The Secret Sharers: Studies in Contemporary Fictions*, by Bruce Bassoff (New York: AMS, 1983), xiv.

11. *Ibid.*, xiv.

12. René Girard, *Things Hidden Since the Foundation of the World*, trans. Stephen Bann and Michael Metteer (1978; rpt. London: Athlone, 1987), 338.

13. Girard, *Deceit*, 28, 146.

14. *Ibid.*, 28–29.

15. Girard, *Things Hidden*, 337.

16. Annette Kuhn, "Women's Genres: Melodrama, Soap Opera, and Theory," in *Feminist Television Criticism: A Reader*, ed. Charlotte Brunsdon, Julie D'Acci and Lynn Spigel (1984; rpt. Oxford: Clarendon Press, 1997), 145.

17. Eve Kosofsky Sedgwick, *Between Men: English Literature and Male Homosocial Desire* (New York: Columbia University Press, 1985), 27.

18. *Ibid.*, 160.

19. *Ibid.*, 16.

20. I do not rule out the possibility of male romance readers and writers. Kay Mussell claims that the romance is read by a great number of closet male readers (Mussell, "Janet Daily"). Clover Williams and Jean R. Freedman estimate the number of male romance writers using female pen names to be as high as 30 percent. See Clover Williams and Jean R. Freedman, "Shakespeare's Step-Sisters: Romance Novels and the Community of Women," in *Folklore, Literature and Cultural Theory: Collected Essays*, ed. Cathy Lynn Preston (London: Garland, 1995), 135–168.

21. Sedgwick, *Between Men*, 23.

22. Lisa Kleypas, *Sugar Daddy* (London: Piatkus, 2007), 337. Further references will be included parenthetically.

23. Christina Dodd, *In My Wildest Dreams* (New York: Avon, 2001), 8; 3. Further references will be included parenthetically.

24. Patricia Duncker, *Sisters and Strangers: An Introduction to Contemporary Feminist Writing* (Oxford: Blackwell, 1992), 25.

25. Linda Howard, *Duncan's Bride* (1990; rpt. Waterville, ME: Thorndike, 2004), 280.

26. *Ibid.*, 318.

27. *Ibid.*, 280.

28. Catherine George, *Devil Within* (London: Mills & Boon, 1984), 87.

29. *Ibid.*, 285.

30. Isabelle Holland, *Darcourt* (London: Collins, 1977), 52.

31. *Ibid.*, 222, 57.

32. Helen Small, *Love's Madness: Medicine, the Novel and Female Insanity* (Oxford: Clarendon, 1996), 26.

33. Jude Deveraux, *The Velvet Promise* (New York: Pocket, 1981), 45.

34. *Ibid.*, 370, 371.

35. Amanda Scott, *Lord of the Isles* (New York: Warner, 2005), 43.

36. *Ibid.*, 211, 305.

37. Catherine Coulter, *Rosehaven* (New York: Jove, 1996), 269, 361.

38. Maggie Osborne, *A Stranger's Wife* (New York: Warner, 1999), 70.

39. Karen Ranney, *Heaven Forbids* (New York: Zebra, 1998), 263.

40. Kay Mussell, "*Paradoxa* Interview with Nora Roberts," *Paradoxa: Studies in World Literary Genres* 3.1 (1997): 157.

41. Sandra Brown, *Texas! Chase* (London: Warner, 1991), 8, 110.

42. Nicole Jordan, *The Heart Breaker* (New York: Avon, 1998), 347.

43. LaVyrle Spencer, *Twice Loved* (New York: Jove, 1984), 38. Further references will be included parenthetically.

44. Penelope Williamson, *Heart of the West* (1995; rpt. London: Signet, 1997), 359.

45. *Ibid.*, 405.

46. *Ibid.*, 404.

47. Susan Elizabeth Phillips, *Fancy Pants* (London: Futura, 1989), 313.

48. Jude Deveraux, *River Lady* (New York: Pocket, 1985), 93, 275.

49. Penelope Williamson, *The Passions of Emma* (New York: Warner, 1997), 283, 303.

50. Amy Farrell Erdman, *Yours in Sisterhood: Ms. Magazine and the Promise of Popular Feminism* (Chapel Hill: University of North Carolina Press, 1998), 36.

51. Romantica is a copyrighted term for the line of erotic romances published by Ellora's Cave (and used by Pocket Books when it publishes that imprint's anthologies). Ellora's Cave defines romantica as any work of literature that is both romantic and sexually explicit in nature. In this article, it is used synonymously with erotic romance.

52. In this section, I only discuss male/female/male triangles. The predominantly female heterosexual readership of romantica seems to prefer the ménage scenarios of the masculinized triangle. This is suggested by the dominance of the male/female/male triangle in the catalogues of erotic romance publishers, which presumably reflect reader feedback and sales potential. Why this is the case is beyond the scope of this article, but perhaps romantica author Katherine Cross sheds some light on this development when she comments, "M/M/F takes the excitement and eroticism of M/M and makes it accessible to women. It's really the best of both worlds — two hot guys who are into each other but who are also interested in me" ("Talking to the Author Katherine Cross," *Seren's Scribblings*, 28 July 2007, http://serensscribblings.blogspot.com/2007/07/talking-to-author-katherine-cross.html).

53. "What is Romantica©?" Ellora's Cave, http://www.jasminejade.com/t-romantica.aspx.

54. "About Black Lace," Black Lace, http://www.blacklace-books.co.uk.

55. Esther Sonnet, "'Erotic Fiction by Women for Women': The Pleasures of Post-Feminist Heterosexuality," *Sexualities* 2, no. 2 (1999): 173.

56. Rosalind Gill, "From Sexual Objectification to Sexual Subjectification: The Resexualisation of Women's Bodies in the Media," *Feminist Media Studies* 3, no. 1 (2003): 100.

57. David T. Evans, *Sexual Citizenship: The Material Construction of Sexualities* (London: Routledge, 1993), 41.

58. Emma Holly, *Ménage* (London: Black Lace, 1998), 68.

59. *Ibid.*, 15.

60. *Ibid.*, 270.

61. Rachel Bo, *Double Jeopardy* (Akron: Ellora's Cave, 2004), 60. Further references will be included parenthetically.

62. "Quickies" is a trademarked term used by Ellora's Cave for short-story format erotic romances.

63. Mardi Ballou, *Reunions Dangereuses* (Akron: Ellora's Cave, 2006), 36.

64. *Ibid.*, 13, 17.

65. Samantha Kane, *At Love's Command* (Akron: Ellora's Cave, 2007), 77.

66. *Ibid.*, 198.

67. Romantica's overt celebration of sexual identities and female subjectivity should be placed within the cultural context of Third Wave feminism, in particular its engagement with erotica, female empowerment and sexuality. The pleasure-orientated, sex radical attitudes of Third Wavers are discussed for example in Astrid Henry's chapter "Taking Feminism to Bed: The Third Wave Does the Sex Wars" in *Not My Mother's Sister: Generational Conflict and Third-Wave Feminism* (Bloomington: Indiana University Press, 2004), 88–114.

68. Debbie Stoller, "Sex and the Thinking Girl," in *The BUST Guide to the New Girl Order*, eds. Marcelle Karp and Debbie Stoller (London: Penguin, 1999), 84.

69. Melanie Waters, "Sexing It Up? Women, Pornography and Third Wave Feminism," in *Third Wave Feminism: A Critical Exploration Expanded Second Edition*, ed. Stacy Gillis, Gillian Howie, and Rebecca Munford (Basingstoke, Hampshire: Palgrave Macmillan, 2007), 258.

70. Kane, *At Love's Command*, 160.

71. Avon launched its Red line in June 2006; Kensington its Brava line in 2001 and its Aphrodisia line in 2006. Harlequin launched its Blaze line in 2001 and its Spice line in 2006.

9

"Why would any woman want to read such stories?": The Distinctions Between Genre Romances and Slash Fiction

Deborah Kaplan

Both scholarly and informal writing make unexamined comparisons between the romance novel and slash fiction (fan fiction which pairs same-sex couples romantically or erotically). Catherine Salmon and Donald Symons defend this comparison extensively, even going so far as to call slash a subgenre of women's romantic fiction.[1] The comparison has become one which can be stated *sans* defense in most writing on slash without provoking comment; no serious scholar questions the mapping from slash to romance. Scholars might question how exactly slash works within the romance genre: whether it reconfigures romance, exists at romance's boundaries, or is merely an undifferentiated subgenre.[2] However, they don't question the essential connection between the genres.

The comparison usually carries with it a whiff of scorn for romance, if not for slash. Romance, it is to be understood, is a simplistic and static genre composed entirely of bodice-rippers, and slash fiction is either more of the same or is essentially the same but somehow improved. If a slash fan calls the comparison into question in an informal critical essay, it will only be to point out the so-called inferiorities in romance as compared to slash; sure, the basic structure is the same, the essay will assert, except that slash is less misogynistic, less formulaic, and has richer characterizations. Both groups of critics (those who assert that slash is a subgenre of romance, and those who assert that romance is a poor cousin to slash) will often preface their statements with disclaimers about how they are not readers of romance novels except inasmuch as was necessary to do their research; Donald Symons introduces his discovery of slash with "I had forced myself to read a few romance novels."[3] As Rosemary Auchmuty says about critics of romance, "Many who have never read one are quite prepared to denigrate the genre without regard for evidence or truth."[4] Indeed, many who have never read any more romances than were necessary to produce a scholarly paper are prepared to assert romance's similarity to slash fiction. Moreover, when scholars of slash discuss romance, they invariably weight their analysis heavily toward romance as defined by Janice Radway's dated and oversimplified *Reading the Romance*, without taking into account the more modern romance scholarship.

This chapter argues that this collapse of slash into a special case of genre romance fails to take into account the generic markers that clearly distinguish the two. Whatever set of structural elements one sees as defining romance fiction — Janice Radway lists thirteen "functions" in her narrow study, while Pamela Regis and jay Dixon have more recently offered shorter, more flexible accounts — when we examine slash fiction for these elements we find them transformed, replaced, or markedly absent. I focus on a number of slash stories intentionally written in the style of Harlequin or Mills & Boon romances. These stories reveal a synthesis of slash fan fiction and genre romance which highlight both the similarities and differences of the genres. For comparison, I also examine the same-sex love story created by the genre romance author Suzanne Brockman, published in her line of mainstream romantic suspense novels. By calling attention to the genuine similarities but also the very real distinctions between romance and slash, this chapter allows for a deeper understanding of the tropes of romance, moving beyond the infamous Harlequin and Radway formulas to a closer reading of how those tropes play out.

Defining Romances

In order to distinguish between romance tropes and the tropes of slash stories, I must use some kind of working definition of "romance." Finding such a definition is nontrivial; as jay Dixon's study clearly illustrates, even the romances of one publisher, Mills & Boon, changed drastically throughout the 20th century, responding to changing social mores and the demands of the market. Pamela Regis discusses the difference between formula and genre, claiming that the wide genre of romance cannot be accurately described in a single formula.[5] Rather than identifying a limited formula or recipe to define a romance, Regis starts with a very broad definition —"a romance novel is a work of prose fiction that tells the story of the courtship and betrothal of one or more heroines" (23)—and follows it up with eight essential but extremely broad necessary narrative events. For Regis, every romance novel must contain:

1. Society Defined: a definition of the society to be confronted during the courtship.
2. The Meeting: the meeting of heroine and hero.
3. The Barrier: the reasons the heroine and hero cannot marry, often including societal strictures, economic situation, alternate lovers, or internal barriers.
4. The Attraction: the reason the couple must marry.
5. The Declaration: explicit declarations of love from both hero and heroine.
6. Point of Ritual Death: the moment when union seems impossible.
7. The Recognition: information which will overcome the barrier.
8. The Betrothal: marriage is not necessary as long as permanent commitment is clear.

Additionally, Regis identifies three other elements as frequent: the wedding or party, the exile of a scapegoat, and the conversion of the wicked (27–39). There are other elements of romances which frequently occur but are not necessary. These elements vary widely by time period, publisher, subgenre, and even author. For example, Radway's thirteen functions of the romance novel, while not common to all romances, do appear frequently in erotic historicals of the 1970s and 1980s. Many narrative themes occur with some regularity. Conflicts between the city and the country, for example, are common in both historical and contemporary romances, while conflicts between the heroine's and hero's careers might occur in many contemporary romances but not in historicals. While none of these regular narrative themes are required, these and many others do occur with enough frequency to be recognized.

It would be naïve to ignore the gender switch from the heterosexual love story of the genre romance to the homosexual love story of slash. Virtually all critics of romance explore the interaction of a man and a woman as central to the romance plot. Gender here is vital both to an understanding of the narrative and to the reader's response to the text. Pamela Regis cites Deborah Chappel as arguing that the gender politics of Janet Dailey specifically create "ungendered space" and "androgynous" landscapes (166). David Shumway stresses that "narrative patterns that take marriage as a defining category cannot have the same meaning for those whom that category excludes,"[6] i.e. homosexuals. Even Stephanie Burley, with her homoerotic interpretation of romance, still sees romance as "rein[ing] in its inherent homoerotic implications in order to present a would-be-coherent ideology of heterosexuality."[7]

Though romances have moved their treatment of homosexuality from the mid-century fear and loathing to a growing twenty-first-century acceptance and sympathy,[8] the homosexual character still falls outside the essential heterosexual plot. Over the last several years, a growing number of small (predominantly e-book) presses, such as Ellora's Cave and Torquere Press, have been publishing same-sex romances, almost entirely featuring male/male relationships. However, same-sex romance from mainstream presses is nearly unheard of. Suzanne Brockmann's 2007 novella *All Through the Night*, the twelfth entry in Brockmann's "Troubleshooter" series, is the first mainstream romance by a major press which focuses on the romance of two male characters. Given the essential heteronormativity of the romance plot, and given the established romance pattern of homosexual as (either positive or negative) other, it is significant for a same-sex relationship to be mapped onto the heterosexual narrative of the romance. As I will show, the slash stories and the Brockmann novel both map same-sex couples onto the stereotypical gender roles of the heterosexual partnership to varying degrees and with different results.

Harlequin Challenges: Imperfect Copies

Fan fiction — unpublished, unofficial stories written in the worlds of pre-existing television shows, books, movies, and other source texts — comprises a huge array of styles, genres, and tropes. Slash fiction is one subset of fan fiction, in which pre-existing characters are written as having erotic or romantic same-sex tensions, encounters, or relationships, often but not always originating in perceived homoerotic subtext of the source material. Slash stories come in a multitude of flavors, including angst-ridden character pieces in which a romantic or sexual interest is never requited, plotless erotica, epic tales of domestic tranquility, and many more. Given this wide variety of potential story structures, it is extremely odd that simplistic statements equating this genre with the romance novel stand unquestioned. Even more than the conventions of romance, fan fiction tropes have changed over time and across fandoms (communities organized around a given source text), and it is a mistake to characterize all erotic and romantic fan fiction by the conventions that prevail in a particular fandom and a particular time. However, even in those slash stories where the tropes of romance hold most true, slash still clearly has its own identifying generic markers which distinguish it from romance. One of the many sub genres of slash fiction is that of the "Harlequin story." Stories of this type are intentionally written to follow the so-called romance formula. This formula is usually derived either from the publicly posted guidelines on the Harlequin website or from the back copy material on a Harlequin, Silhouette, or Mills & Boon title. It would seem logical that if any slash stories would share the same tropes and structures as romance novels, it would be these, which are purposely written to mirror the style of romances. However, a close reading of some of these stories reveals a multitude of differences, highlighting the distinct genre characteristics of both romance and slash.

A Harlequin fan fiction challenge in the *Stargate: Atlantis* fandom asked participants to write fan fiction featuring the characters of the television show *Stargate: Atlantis* (SGA) in a Harlequin-like plot. The resulting stories follow the tropes of genre romance with varying success. Some mimic the plot of a specific Harlequin title extremely closely but leave out many of the subtleties of romance characterization. Others develop along more general themes associated with romance novels, incorporating setting (Old West), character roles (boss and secretary), or initial conflict (marriage of convenience). Almost without exception, the completed stories develop conflict along different lines than do romances, and although this structural difference is likely influenced by length, it is also evidence of distinction between the genres of slash and romance. In fact, these differences are most pronounced in those stories which most successfully synthesize the two genres, forming a blend which brings to light the differences in structure, relationship politics, power dynamics, and characterization. Studying these amalgams of genre illuminates specific characteristics that transcend categories while highlighting the textual subtleties of both genres of fiction.[9]

Some differences between slash and romance are readily apparent in the Harlequin challenge stories: the gender of the characters; the single point of view of the fan fiction stories as opposed to the more common shifting point of view of romances[10]; the explicitly emotional model of romances as opposed to the less emotional mode of fan fiction; and the rarity in slash of that romance necessity, the formal declaration of love.[11] In other ways, the challenge responses do share traits with many romances: they have happy endings; disparate wealth and power between the two main characters; and contrived character occupations. Of these, only the happy ending is required of a romance novel as we (following Regis) have defined it. The wealth and power division and contrived occupations — common in many romances, but not necessary — are explicitly absent in the majority of *Stargate: Atlantis* fan fiction and in the television show itself, yet almost universally present in the Harlequin challenge responses.[12] Far from revealing innate similarities between the genres, these distinguishing characteristics which resemble features of many romances are contrived by the very nature of the community challenge. It's these forced similarities which call attention to some of the more subtle distinctions.

Harlequin Challenge Examples

Casspeach's "Animal Husbandry"[13] is a slash novella pairing McKay and Sheppard in an alternate-universe Western setting. Sheppard is a poor rodeo rider, trying to succeed as a stud farmer, and McKay is a wealthy city vet. In order to pay for treatment for his injured horse, Sheppard must work for a sexually voracious woman who manipulates him into dangerous rodeo work. Though he is sexually and romantically attracted to McKay, Sheppard's stubborn independence prevents him from letting the wealthy vet learn about his financial state. "Animal Husbandry" is chock-full of romance conventions, including the conflict between city and country, the destruction of Sheppard's social identity when he sacrifices his financial independence to care for the horse, the barrier in the form of the sexually dangerous foil, and the comforting friendship of another couple dispensing relationship advice and affectionate disgust as necessary.[14]

"Animal Husbandry" reveals some of the difficulties of mapping the strict heterosexual pattern of romance onto a same-sex pairing. Sheppard primarily takes on the stereotypically female role in this story: the narrative focus is exclusively his; he is stubbornly hiding poverty; he must resist the sexual advances of someone who holds economic power over him; he loses his social identity and regains it when his romance is complete; and after proving his independence he is financially rescued by McKay, who gives him the wherewithal to realize his dream. However, Sheppard does not exclusively take the heroine's position. It is Sheppard who approaches physical standards of masculinity. It is Sheppard who organizes a bachelor party, helps at a barn raising, is an athletic rodeo rider, and is badly injured without complaint. It is Sheppard, not McKay, who needs to be socialized to accept help and affection. In other words, in characterization, Sheppard takes on the romance's male role, but in place in the plot arc, he frequently takes the female.

This gender-mapping I present here is forced and artificial. Many frequently occurring traits of both the romance hero and heroine are present in neither Sheppard nor McKay. Neither character is concerned about the fast growth of their sexual relationship, for example. More significantly, McKay, unlike either member of a typical romance couple, has negligible character growth, reacting primarily to Sheppard's worries rather than expressing any of his own. In the less explicitly emotional mode of fan fiction, it is perfectly normal to have character growth or epiphanies for only one character, or to have the emotional development of the relationship left unspoken, shown rather than told. But the structured and symbolic language of the romance requires explicit declarations as well as implicit ones: one of Regis' few necessary elements of a romance is The Declaration (34–5). The novella fulfills six of Regis' eight necessary narrative elements perfectly, if in a low-key manner. But elements which require explicit statement of emotion — The Recognition and The Declaration — are absent. In fact, The Declaration is actively rejected; the story concludes with "a kiss [Sheppard] could only hope would tell Rodney the things he couldn't find the words for." The conclusion of "Animal Husbandry," so satisfying within a fan fiction world accustomed to "cold pricklies," leaves a romance reader hanging, waiting for the explicitly stated happy ending.

In Astolat's "No Refunds or Exchanges,"[15] a slash novellette about the romance of Sheppard and McKay, the two male characters embody many aspects of the stereotypical heterosexual romance couple in the "marriage of convenience" romance plot.[16] McKay is the wealthy adventurer who orders a mail-order spouse to provide domestic service on the intergalactic frontier. Because McKay, who wanted a woman, forgets to specify gender, and because he is Canadian and can legally marry a man, the mail-order bride company sends him John Sheppard as a partner. Sheppard — who is excellent at the requisite domestic tasks — clearly takes on the stereotyped female role. Throughout the story, however, his masculinity is constantly emphasized, especially in contrast to McKay's. To begin with, the limited point of view is consistently McKay's, leaving him as the more likely filler of the heroine role, although his initial callousness and his insistence on not being seen as a rapist are more stereotypically masculine. Sheppard's discomfort with being the sexual bottom causes the first conflict in the relationship, opening up questions both of actual and desired gender roles, although mapping penetrative and receptive sexual acts onto male and female gender roles is admittedly extremely problematic. Sheppard's physical masculinity, his military background, and his calm, laconic demeanor are all male hero tropes. The household chores of cooking and cleaning, Sheppard's most feminine activities, are masculinized as Sheppard honorably fulfilling the terms of a business arrangement, and are used to highlight another stereotypically male attribute: his brilliance at math. Even as a mail order spouse, Sheppard is still what McKay thinks of as an "insane galactic space hero." Yet in more subtle ways Sheppard's feminine characteristics are emphasized. Though his brilliance at math surpasses even McKay's, that brilliance is based on intuition, not logic. He doesn't know how to do a mathematical proof, he "just went with [his] gut." Following feminine stereotypes, he uses his genius to improve Rodney's life, using extraordinary empathy combined with his intuitive brilliance to know how Rodney organizes his papers, the better to clean his apartment.

In other ways the gender characteristics that Sheppard and McKay take on are simply too complex, too shifting and genderqueer, to easily pin down. At the story's climax, Sheppard proves his feelings for McKay by bottoming in bed. Perhaps by doing so he is taking on a stereotyped female role. Perhaps he is taking part in the romance's very masculine transformation of the hero, in which the heroine teaches positive effeminate behaviors to the hero in order to make him a perfect man. But perhaps it is neither, and instead simply an instance of the modern slash fan fiction convention that for healthy romantic and sexual relationships, both partners must take turns topping in bed. Both characters are the first and only men to penetrate each other, which plays into one common slash convention that the characters aren't gay, they're just men who love each other.[17] But in the context of romance genre conventions, it makes them both simultaneously masculine (the taker of virginity) and feminine (the virgin). Slash and romance conventions play off one another intertextually to create something which is difficult to pin down.

Like "Animal Husbandry," "No Refunds or Exchanges" depicts a Sheppard who finds a career path in the romance heroine mode, as his personal success depends on finding career independence by his own talents but with the support of the societally powerful McKay. Sheppard has been brought over to be a mail-order bride in order to provide domestic duties for McKay: cooking and cleaning. He is exquisitely good at domestic duties, and extremely thorough, but in the course of his tidying McKay discovers that Sheppard is also a mathematical genius. Through a series of accidents and serendipitous events, Sheppard is offered those duties to which he is most well-suited: flying and working with ancient technology. As with "Animal Husbandry," the figure who best matches the heroine role pairs up with a much wealthier romantic partner, and uses that romantic partnership, not to stop working, but to find more difficult and fulfilling work; and as with the earlier story, this model is only possible because of the restructuring of the social arrangements from the source material of the *Stargate: Atlantis* television show. Interestingly, however, "No Refunds or Exchanges" finishes with professional roles very similar to those in the source text: scientist and soldier/pilot.

"No Refunds or Exchanges" follows Regis' structure perfectly except where explicit statement of emotion is required. Like "Animal Husbandry," the absence of explicit statements, of explicit declarations of love, is not just passive but active. Though McKay declares his love for Sheppard, when McKay asks Sheppard if he loves him, Sheppard "stopped and glared and smacked Rodney upside the head" as his only answer. The Recognition and Betrothal, too, are implicit rather than explicit. A skilled reader of fan fiction knows that a near death experience followed by a happy sex scene means that Sheppard has come to recognize what McKay means to him, and has returned to McKay to live out the rest of his life as a happy mail-order husband in a mutually loving relationship. In other words, a fan fiction reader sees The Point of Ritual Death, The Recognition, The Declaration, and The Betrothal. A romance reader, however, used to seeing these narrative elements made explicit, won't see the fulfillment of the structure. Only an experienced reader of fan fiction can successfully read a genre-compliant romance in Astolat's novelette.

Speranza's "Last Will and Testament"[18] uses themes of genre romance to turn reader expectations completely upside down. In this novella, McKay and Sheppard meet as adults and have a one night stand. The next day, they discover they might be brothers. Despite their misgivings, they continue the sexual relationship during a tense roadtrip, even as it becomes increasingly clear that they do, in fact, share parents. There are multiple romance themes at work here. The first is that of the victory of love over law. The adventure McKay and Sheppard have is seemingly a fully masculine journey to fight lawlessness: an astrophysicist and an air force pilot in a buddy movie, careening across North America while shooting at and being shot at by the bad guys, culminating in their employment by a top-secret military installation. Two men in occupations fully associated with masculinity have an adventure based on subverting lawlessness and coming home to government endorsement. Yet at the same time, they blithely participate in one of society's most ingrained taboos, all while violating multiple laws (against incest and against military homosexuality). This is a clear victory of the rule of love over the rule of law.

One of the ultimate victories of love over law, for jay Dixon, is the attraction to the inappropriately, possibly incestuously close romantic partner such as a step-sibling, in a relationship which is not taboo in modern society but may be taboo or illegal during the setting of a historical romance.[19] Here, the incest taboos are played out explicitly; that the Sheppard and McKay of "Last Will and Testament" are not just step-siblings but actual brothers only emphasizes the conflict. Romance heroes often feel instinctive passion for a heroine who at first seems to be completely unavailable. Often this unavailability is surmountable (such as the wrong social class, the appearance of working for the enemy, or an old family feud). Other times, more unassailable taboos seem to be in play, and must be revealed as false before the romance can develop (such as the heroine initially disguised as a boy, or the initial appearance of incestuously close relationships). "Last Will and Testament" subverts expectation by treating an obstacle of the second class as if it were of the first, by treating a usually unassailable taboo — incest — as something that can be ignored by a couple willing to fly in the face of societal convention. The experienced reader of *romances* knows that, since McKay and Sheppard are the romantic couple, their blood relationship must not, in fact, be real; the evidence pointing to their fraternal relationship must be incorrect.[20] But the experienced reader of *fan fiction*, in which there are large communities which happily pair incestuous couples, knows no such thing. The incestuous pairing in the world of fan fiction can be treated as just one more surmountable difficulty, one more place in which the barriers placed on the romance are falsely instituted by a prejudiced society.

The metaphorical incest theme of many romances is here made concrete. The incest increases the Oedipal tensions some see in the romance genre. In "Last Will and Testament," McKay resembles his unremembered mother in looks, career, and temperament, and Sheppard likewise resembles his never-met father. Through their budding relationship, each man builds a relationship with the parent he never knew. In fact, the relationship cannot be complete until the Oedipal tensions are happily resolved, incest and all. McKay and Sheppard have no substantial tension between them in their adventure, no personal feelings keeping the romance from resolving happily. Instead, the barrier keeping them from being completely happy — although not keeping them apart — is their unresolved emotions about the unknown parents. Only when McKay is given evidence that both his parents cared for and understood him can he be fully happy with Sheppard as romantic partner and mother replacement.

While "Last Will and Testament" brings these romantic themes to the forefront with its unexpected incest, it still follows fan fiction conventions of emotional tension. McKay never declares his love for Sheppard, even internally, as would be necessary in a romance. Moreover, though the story concludes without angst, the closeting required by the incestuous nature of their relationship precludes the completely happy restoration to society a romance requires. In this way, "Last Will and Testament" subverts both the tropes of romance and some recurring conventions of SGA slash fiction: because most SGA stories take place off world, many of them create a happy non-homophobic land where alternative sexualities (if not incestuous relationships) are accepted. The characters in this Harlequin story, however, live on a modern day United States military base, where condemnation of an incestuous homosexual relationship is likely — and yet the story allows for a happy ending, never delving into angst because it never discusses the unresolved problem of societal acceptance.

When this essay was first conceived, it was only possible to speculate about how many of the differences between slash fiction and romance are merely due to the changes inherent in mapping a same-sex pairing onto the heterosexual love story. However, in October 2007, a mainstream same-sex romance by award-winning novelist Suzanne Brockmann was published by a major U.S. publisher in a non-segregated line. Brockmann's best-selling and acclaimed "Troubleshooter" series is published by Ballantine, not by a romance publisher, but is nevertheless accepted in the romance journalistic press as mainstream suspenseful romance. Most of the books in the Troubleshooter series consist of an A-plot featuring the primary hero and heroine and a B-plot which explores the romance of secondary characters. Moreover, most of the books also feature couples introduced in previous volumes in the series, as well as individuals who will be paired up in later volumes. Early on in the Troubleshooter series, the gay FBI agent Jules Cassidy is introduced. Having a gay secondary character in a mainstream romance is no longer unheard of. However, over the course of three entries in the Troubleshooter series (*Hot Target, Force of Nature, All Through the Night*), Jules's own romance with male actor Robin Chadwick develops. The romance of Jules and Robin culminates in a novella dedicated to their wedding. While *All Through the Night* doesn't stand alone as a romance novel,[21] the story arc of Jules and Robin running through these three novels and concluding in a stand-alone novella can be analyzed as a mainstream romance starring gay characters.

The Jules/Robin love story, except for having The Meeting in *Hot Target*, follows the complete Regis narrative arc as the B-plot in *Force of Nature*. Multiple barriers prevent their betrothal: Robin's alcoholism, his closeting, and the kidnapping of both men by a skinhead/terrorist alliance. Each of these barriers leads to an appropriate Point of Ritual Death (Robin's alcoholism and the YouTube movies which both out Robin and reveal him as an alcoholic, and the suspense plot when each man thinks the other has been killed). Each moment of Ritual Death leads to an appropriate recognition (Robin's long-awaited self-recognition as an alcoholic, both men's realizations that their career aspirations mean nothing compared to their love for one another). The romance as formulated in *Force of Nature* is so completely and perfectly structured as not to need any further exploration. Nonetheless, Jules and Robin return in their own novella. *All Through the Night* is the story of Jules' and Robin's wedding, and while it doesn't exactly lack any of the elements Regis requires for romance, several of them are present far less organically than they are in *Force of Nature*. The Declaration of love, for example, while it comes repeatedly in the face of a series of contrived barriers (Jules's feared death in Afghanistan, a stalker's attempted murder of Robin, Jules's jealousy, Robin's being made late to his own wedding by a comedy of errors), is never really in doubt, thus weakening the narrative impact. The Recognition to overcome barriers is still present, but no barriers outside of potential death are likely to prevent this happy wedding from happening; the moments of recognition merely increase the overall loving tenderness of the A-plot couple — a tenderness which is far more explicit, more warm and fuzzy, than any seen in the slash Harlequin challenge stories.

The gender roles of these two androgynously-named heroes compare fruitfully with the gender roles which were so difficult to pin down in the slash stories. It would be disingenuous and highly inaccurate to describe Jules as the romance's "man" and Robin as its "woman." Both characters are often described as physically extremely male, while both also have the so-called civilizing female characteristics, the gentling androgyny, which romance heroes often acquire in their quest. Both men weep in the course of *All Through the Night*, for example (as does the heterosexual hero of the B-plot). And even in the gender roles between the two men, there are clearly places where Jules is given a more traditionally female gender assignment. He's substantially shorter, for example, and it's Robin who first proposes marriage. But throughout *All Through the Night*, Jules and Robin are assigned roles which helped them to fit into the structure of a conventional romance novel. It's not that Robin is made into a woman in terms of his gender characteristics or his sexual role. At one point, he specifically makes it clear to a reporter that answering questions of who is top or bottom is completely irrelevant to their love story.

Nonetheless, in the structure of the romance, Jules is the FBI agent who goes to Afghanistan and is almost killed, while Robin stays home in the protective arms of the Navy SEAL wives (though even while Robin is being made into the wife waiting at home, the novella stresses that he is not weeping as visibly as the female wives whose company he keeps). Jules is the jealous partner in the relationship, and Robin is frequently emotionally warmed by Jules's possessive hand on his back. Jules is the armed federal agent hunting down a stalker, and Robin is the spunky but untrained hostage at risk. In case there were any questions, the text makes their roles in the story explicitly clear: "despite the fact that Robin was taller, Jules was the alpha in their relationship. And Robin loved it, loved him."[22] Robin even asks Jules if he can take his name after the wedding, a gesture all the more emotionally fraught because Robin is an actor, one of the rare careers where it is difficult even for women to change their professional names after marriage. Yet Robin makes it clear that he is changing his professional name as well. Their relationship has a clear alpha, and the alpha and beta roles of this relationship are not fully disassociated from gendered stereotypes.

All Through the Night manages to assign Jules and Robin into clear alpha/beta — and thereby, hero/heroine — roles without ever feminizing Robin or overly-masculinizing Jules. The characters take their appropriate roles in the story without needing to change their gender presentation. In the slash stories, the roles the two heroes take are never so clearly defined. Even though many of the story structures come straight from specific romance titles, and *not* mapping the character roles on the hero and heroine is more difficult than just doing so, most of the slash stories make a point of problematizing the hero/heroine mappings. Perhaps the slash authors are reacting against earlier claims that slash feminizes one member of a romantic pairing,[23] while the romance author has no such claims to react against.

When Robin and Jules marry, they "use fairly traditional vows, adjusting the words only slightly."[24] This is consistent with the portrayal of these two male heroes throughout their otherwise-traditional genre romance plot lines. The ways in which their story does not resemble the other romances in the Troubleshooter series are incidental, such as the replacement of fear of commitment with fear of outing as a potential barrier. It's far too early to draw general conclusions about mainstream same-sex romance, but Jules's and Robin's story, at least, follows the narrative structures of genre romance almost completely. Brockmann's same-sex romance reveals that there is nothing inherent in same-sex relationships which would cause deviation from genre tropes. Like Robin and Jules' vows, the words of this romance have only been adjusted slightly.

The slash Harlequins, on the other hand, deviate in some fairly substantial ways from traditional romance genre conventions. More accurately, in those slash stories in which the tropes of romance should ostensibly prevail, the genre conventions of fan fiction take precedence over the genre conventions of romance. The slash convention for understated emotions, for example, is directly in opposition to the explicit declarations required by the romance. Slash is its own genre, with all the wealth and breadth of any other, and this convention for understated emotions is no more inherent in all fan fiction than rape or time travel or a Regency setting are inherent in all romance. But in one small subsection of the genre — that produced by the portion of SGA slash fandom that participated in that particular Harlequin challenge in 2005 — understated emotions are an extremely commonly used method of prose crafting. In this challenge, which brought together conventions from the two distinct genres of slash and romance, the interaction created something which stood partway between them both. As the slash and romance genres speak, barter, challenge, and flirt with each other on this fertile meeting ground, new insights emerge about each genre, and new genres are probably being born.

NOTES

1. Catherine Salmon and Donald Symons, "Slash Fiction and Human Mating Psychology," *Journal of Sex Research* 41, no. 1 (2004): 7.
2. See Catherine Driscoll, "One True Pairing: The Romance of Pornography and the Pornography of Romance," in *Fan Fiction and Fan Communities in the Age of the Internet*, ed. Karen Hellekson and Kristina Busse (Jefferson, NC: McFarland, 2006), 79–96; Anne Kustritz, "Slashing the Romance Narrative," *The Journal of American Culture* 26, no. 3 (2003): 14; Patricia Frazier Lamb and Diane L. Veith, "Romantic Myth, Transcendence, and Star Trek Zines," in *Erotic Universe: Sexuality and Fantastic Literature*, ed. Donald Palumbo (New York: Greenwood Press, 1986), 235–55; Salmon and Symons, "Slash Fiction," 7.
3. Catherine Salmon and Donald Symons, *Warrior Lovers: Erotic Fiction, Evolution and Female Sexuality* (New Haven: Yale University Press, 2003), 2–3.

4. Qtd. in jay Dixon, *The Romance Fiction of Mills & Boon, 1909–1990s* (Philadelphia: UCL Press, 1999), ix. Future references will be included parenthetically.

5. Pamela Regis, *A Natural History of the Romance Novel* (Philadelphia: University of Pennsylvania Press, 2003), 23–25. Further references will be provided parenthetically.

6. David Shumway, *Love: Romance, Intimacy, and the Marriage Crisis* (New York: New York University Press, 2003), 8.

7. Stephanie Burley, "What's a Nice Girl Like You Doing in a Book Like This? Homoerotic Reading and Popular Romance," in *Doubled Plots: Romance and History*, ed. Susan Strehle and Mary Paniccia Carden (Jackson: University Press of Mississippi, 2003), 146.

8. See Dixon, *Romance Fiction*, 162–3.

9. Like earlier flawed studies of romance, my analysis is limited by the texts I choose to examine. My study does not claim to speak for all of slash fiction, but only for one small group of stories in one time period of the LiveJournal-based *Stargate: Atlantis* slash fan fiction community.

10. This is evidence of an aesthetic change in both genres in which both have been moving further apart from each other in recent years. When Henry Jenkins wrote *Textual Poachers: Television Fans & Participatory Culture. Studies in Culture and Communication* in 1992, he could say, "Slash stories often play with shifting points of view and the construction of shared subjectivities" ([New York: Routledge, 1992], 199), but by 2006, fanwriter JaneDavitt observes that point of view shifts are mostly gone from fan fiction ("Pov Shifts? Bring Them On!" 28 April 2006, http://janedavitt. livejournal.com/503862.html). Meanwhile, romance novelist Laura Kinsale documents the romance genre shift towards multiple viewpoints in the 1980s ("The Androgynous Reader: Point of View in the Romance," in *Dangerous Men and Adventurous Women: Romance Writers on the Appeal of the Romance*, ed. Jayne Ann Krentz [1992; rpt. New York: HarperPaperbacks, 1996]).

11. The lack of explicit emotion in fan fiction and, as a byproduct, the absence of formal declarations are also recent aesthetic developments, characterized by some slashers as the debate between "warm fuzzies" and "cold pricklies" (Julad, "Anyone Who Had a Heart ... " 10 May 2005, http://julad.livejournal.com/71396. html). Linda Barlow and Jayne Ann Krentz, discussing romance, characterize the same debate as being between a patriarchally imposed masculine set of literary standards and a feminine writing style densely packed with symbolic codes ("Beneath the Surface: The Hidden Codes of Romance," in *Dangerous Men and Adventurous Women: Romance Writers on the Appeal of the Romance*, ed. Jayne Ann Krentz [Philadelphia: University of Pennsylvania Press, 1992], 15–29). It's important to note that Barlow and Krentz's essay is problematic, making mass generalizations about romance that aren't even supported by Krentz's own work and relying on essentialist gender understanding of readers to explain textual codes. Other romance scholars also refer to the essential nature of the explicit declaration, however, with Lisa Fletcher using it to introduce her entire study: "My readings of historical romance novels seek to show the extent to which 'I love you' is necessary to the telling of each and every romance. 'I love you' is the romantic speech act because romance cannot proceed without the promise of its utterance. It is impossible to imagine a romance fiction which does not depend on the force of these three little words" (*Historical Romance Fiction: Heterosexuality and Performativity* [Aldershot: Ashgate, 2008], 1).

12. Arguably, this construction of power and occupation was demanded by the wording of the challenge for which these stories were created: "how about the one where rodney is really, really rich and powerful and he sees john the independent girl [...] rodney is a fashion model nursing a broken heart, when he meets an arrogant pilot and they crash land!" (Cesperanza, "Admin Post: The Harlequin Plot Challenge," Sga_flashfic, 27 August 2005, http://community.livejournal.com/sga_flashfic/149489.html).

13. Casspeach, "Animal Husbandry," 14 January 2006, http://www.casspeach.com/sga_fic/animal.html.

14. For discussion of the city/country convention, see Dixon, *Romance Fiction*, 45 and 48. For discussion of the sexually dangerous foil, see Regis, *A Natural History*, 32–3.

15. Astolat, "No Refunds or Exchanges," http://www.intimations.org/fanfic/stargate/No%20Refunds% 200r%20Exchanges.html.

16. For discussion of the marriage of convenience plot, see Dixon, *Romance Fiction*, 155.

17. So common as to have its own unwieldy acronym, WNGWJLEO, which stands for "We're not gay, we just love each other" ("We're Not Gay; We Just Love Each Other," fanlore, http://fanlore.org/wiki/WNGWJLEO.)

18. Speranza, "Last Will and Testament," http://www.trickster.org/speranza/cesper/Testament.html.

19. Dixon, *Romance Fiction*, 79.

20. Lisa Fletcher discusses this tension between early evidence and eventual conclusion in her study of heterosexual cross-dressing romances: "this retrospective logic is a standard *modus operandi* in the romance genre: a happy ending draws our attention back to all those hints in the text that, despite appearances, the hero loved as he should all along" (*Historical Romance Fiction*, 60).

21. Brockmann has apologized for not giving Robin and Jules a dedicated novel, explaining that she

tried to end *Force of Nature* with the two characters unhappy so she could begin the next novel as a complete romance, but the characters took over and would not let her conclude their B-plot before their declaration of love ("Thoughts on Force of Nature," http://www.suzannebrockmann.com/fon_happened.htm).

22. Suzanne Brockman, *All Through the Night* (New York: Ballantine, 2007), 131.

23. See Joanna Russ, *Mommas, Trembling Sisters, Puritans & Perverts* (New York: The Crossing Press, 1985); and Patricia Frazier Lamb and Diane L. Veith, "Romantic Myth," 235–55.

24. Brockman, *All Through the Night*, 273.

10

Borderlands of Desire: Captivity, Romance, and the Revolutionary Power of Love

Robin Harders

Of all the motifs in genre romance, captivity is one of the most ubiquitous and diverse. While one of the most popular and enduring romantic captivity scenarios is that made famous in Edith Hull's 1919 novel *The Sheik*, in which the beautiful "civilized" heroine is captivated body, soul, and heart, by the "wild" desert-living sheikh, captivity has many permutations and purposes in the genre.[1]

In Jo Goodman's *Only in My Arms*, Apache-raised Ryder McKay escapes hanging with the unintentional assistance of Mary Dennehy, who evolves from Ryder's reluctant captive to his passionate ally.[2] Linda Howard, in *Midnight Rainbow*, plays it a little differently, bringing Grant Sullivan into Costa Rica to rescue Jane Greer from her captivity at the hands of a wealthy criminal, requiring Grant to steal her away and make her *his* captive.[3] Michelle Reid riffs on the stereotypical sheikh story in *The Sheikh's Chosen Wife*, with Sheikh Hassan ben Khalifa Al-Qadim imprisoning his estranged wife, Leona, on his yacht until he can convince her that he loves her and does not care about her apparent inability to conform to traditional cultural expectations by giving him a biological heir.[4] Elizabeth Asher, the heroine of Jeanne Allan's *No Angel*, really turns the tables, convincing her brothers to kidnap the reluctant Andrew Harcourt and bring him to a remote cabin where Elizabeth can convince him that she is ready to be the kind of wife who travels to remote, even dangerous, locations with an oil engineer husband.[5]

There are a number of reasons for the widespread appearance of the captivity device in romance, but one of the least discussed and most important is the literary link between the wildly popular genres of Anglo-American Indian captivity narratives and romance, a relationship that tracks into and through sentimental and sensational fiction of the eighteenth and nineteenth centuries, across the ocean between England and America, and over numerous cultural assumptions about the superiority of Anglo-American patriarchy. Early American narratives have been largely read as patriarchal, Puritan, colonialist propaganda,[6] and for the most part, discussions about the relationship between these narratives and genre romance are premised on the belief that captivity scenarios reinforce rather than upset prevailing racial, cultural and gender hierarchies.

However, a close look at early American captivity narratives and their literary endurance suggests a much more dynamic and interesting exercise in negotiating difference, an opening up of narrative spaces through which traditional hierarchies can be interrogated and challenged. The implications for romance are provocative and substantial: the more traditional social values the genre consistently celebrates — monogamous, heterosexual love, marriage, domesticity, the nuclear family — do not have to be mere performances of Euro-American patriarchal supremacy, but can be subversive, even revolutionary, in their contemplation of a new social reality, one that changes the couple's position relative to traditional social and cultural norms.[7]

From Captivity to Captivation

When the English Puritans set sail for the New England colonies, they did so not with minds open to empirical discovery, but rather with what Tzvetan Todorov explains as the "'finalist' strategy of interpretation," namely, "the ultimate meaning is given from the start."[8] This "meaning" was that of religious sanctuary interpreted through the Old Testament, as "God's dealings with ancient Israel becoming a blueprint for how He would deal with his new English Israel."[9] Charismatic and influential Puritan ministers like John Cotton, Increase Mather, and Cotton Mather provided the foundational authority for such interpretive fatalism, and they made the most of Old Testament language and law for the purpose of keeping their flock pure and devoted. As early as 1676, Increase Mather was chastising and admonishing the Puritan colonists for wayward and backsliding behavior, such as *Pride in respect of Apparel*:

> People in this Land have not carried it, as it becometh those that are in the Wilderness, especially when it is such an humbling time as of late years hath been. [...] A proud Fashion no sooner comes into the Country, but *the haughty Daughters of Zion* in this place are taking it up, and thereby the whole land is at last infected. What shall we say when men are seen in the Streets with monstrous and horrid *Perriwigs*, and Women with their *Borders and False Locks* and such like whorish Fashions, whereby the anger of the Lord is kindled against this sinful Land! And now behold how dreadfully is God fulfilling the third chapter of Isaiah. *Moreover the Lord saith* (if the Lord say it who dare slight what is said) *because the Daughters of Zion are haughty, therefore he will discover their Nakedness.* Hath not the Lord fulfilled this threatening when the *Indians* have taken so many and stripped them naked as in the day that they were born. *And instead of a sweet smell there shall be a stink*, Is not this verified when poor Creatures are carried away Captive into the Indians filthy and stinking *Wigwams*, yea, when so many English are feign to crowd together, till it becomes loathsome and unsavoury?[10]

Colonists were taken captive for several reasons — e.g. as potential adoptees to replace tribal losses,[11] for negotiation and ransom in various wars with the French and English — but for the Puritans, at least, the political dimensions of captivity were secondary to the spiritual lessons such an experience could impart.

Echoing Increase Mather's language above, in 1699, his son, Cotton, offered the example of Hannah Dustan, who actually scalped her captors during her escape, an action that would be wholly "uncivilized" and heathen, except that Dustan "took up a Resolution, to Imitate the Action of Jael upon Sisera: and being where she had not her own *Life* secured by any *Law* unto her, she thought she was not Forbidden by any *Law*, to take away the life of the Murderers, by whom her *Child* had been butchered."[12] Mather goes on to admonish, "*the Lord is punishing of us, for our Leaving of his Ordinances*," and that "it may be *For this Cause*, is the Singular *Distinction* and *Protection*, which the CHURCHES of our LORD have Enjoyed throughout the whole progress of our Calamity."[13] Mather and his faithful know that Dustan's actions are not those of a "civilized" Puritan woman; consequently, he must place her outside the scope of the *Law*, usurping any legal or moral transgression with the lawful actions of a Biblical exemplar, to legitimize Dustan's actions while at the same time using her experience to warn and chide those to whom she is witnessing. God, through those ministers like Mather, was always watching and judging, and depending on how clearly your experience reflected your purity and devotion, your "story" could bring you safely back into the community or cast you out into the spiritual and literal *Wilderness*.

The captivity narrative was, therefore, a critical form of witnessing for the captive. Not coincidentally, it was also an immensely popular literary phenomenon, "the first coherent [American] myth literature,"[14] as Richard Slotkin calls it, in its construction of the civilized white captive fighting for survival against the swarthy wild heathen. This dynamic echoes through American and English art and literature from the seventeenth through nineteenth centuries, through the novels of James Fenimore Cooper and Nathaniel Hawthorne, through the poetry of Longfellow, and the paintings of John Vanderlyn, among countless others. By the eighteenth century, stories of American Indian captivity were so popular in England and America that Daniel Boone's narrative was attached to John Filson's 1784 *Discovery, Settlement, and Present State of Kentucke*, a glorified real estate advertisement encouraging further Western settlement and expansion.[15] Boone is a prototype of the iconic American frontiersmen, an image that, in turn, figures prominently into the construction of a white, masculine American national identity. That his captivity would be used to encourage settlement demonstrates a bit of the powerful fascination captivity narratives engendered, both in the colonies and abroad.

The early, archetypal captivity stories, though, such as Mary Rowlandson's 1682 narrative, establish an important pattern that later narratives reconstruct, replay, and renovate, without ever losing the core genre element of an immersion in a "radical otherness"[16] that is ultimately self-defining. How the self is ultimately defined is key, of course, and within a strict Puritan context, that definition must align with the overarching narrative of symbolic community redemption via strict adherence to doctrinal authority. To that end, most of the early narratives feature female captives and were edited by men, because women could not minister. The tone of these narratives is often sermon-like, which seemed to reinforce the valid spiritual and legal authority of white men and to affirm the vulnerability of women as fallen mortal sinners. As Michael Sturma explains, captivity narratives "often reflect deeper anxieties and desires," and "[t]he white female captive in particular often symbolized the conflict between wilderness and civilization."[17] Successful return and redemption of the captive into "civilization" validates the holy mission of the Puritan colonies, and it is the work of the male editor to deliver the captive safely back into the fold.

There is a practical difficulty in the narrative to negotiate the *experience* of captivity with its prescribed lesson in a way that satisfies the prurient curiosity of the reader (and thus ensures the narrative's popularity) but also maintains strict cultural, religious, and/or racial boundaries between captive and captors. As Stephen Greenblatt insists, we must "resist the drift toward normalizing what was *not* normal" in the initial meetings of Europeans and indigenous Americans, which created an "incommensurability," laid over by "conventional intellectual and organizational structures," which "greatly impeded a clear grasp of the radical otherness of the American lands and peoples."[18] Once these encounters become more "anticipated," routine, and recorded, however, they also become more "porous,"[19] Greenblatt observes, characterized by a certain level of hybridity:

individuals and cultures tend to have fantastically powerful assimilative mechanisms, mechanisms that work like enzymes to change the ideological composition of foreign bodies. Those foreign bodies do not disappear altogether but they are drawn into what Homi Bhabha terms the in between, the zone of intersection in which all culturally determinate significations are called into question by an unresolved and unresolvable hybridity.[20]

As Robert Young argues, "[f]ixity of identity is only sought in situations of instability and disruption, of conflict and change," and because colonial and imperialist strategies require a "dislocation of [...] peoples and cultures" and long-term interactions between different cultures, attempts to establish cultural and racial purity become simultaneously more overt and more frustrated.[21]

In Cotton Mather's brief story of Hannah Dustan, that "zone of intersection" is the place in the narrative where Dustan scalps her captors. Mather assiduously attempts to cut off any path of interpretation but his own — that because Dustan was in the *Wilderness*, she was governed by a different *Law*, although not the law of the "savages" (i.e. "creatures of the wilderness" characterized by capricious and ungovernable passions who are therefore ungovernable), even though her behavior mimicked that expected of her "heathen" captors. However, by calling such attention to the act, Mather inadvertently marks the boundary crossing, even as he tries to keep Dustan within the narrow borders of Puritan exegesis.

In longer narratives, especially narratives that though edited still claim to express the voice of the captive, in between zones are more prominent and plentiful, especially in the most popular texts. Mary Rowlandson's narrative,[22] for example, went through no fewer than five editions in England and the colonies, between 1682 and 1720.[23] Rowlandson describes an arduous three months among the Narragansett in Massachusetts during King Philip's War in 1675, a captive for ransom in the year-long Anglo-Indian conflict.[24] Her captors are capricious and "barbarous creatures," and Rowlandson seems to relish in relating the gory details of warfare, as well as points of foreignness between her and the indigenous peoples, all of which the narrative uses to reinforce the Puritan theme of God's punishment. When she notices that the Indians are able to find plentiful food, it is because "our perverse and evil carriages in the sight of the Lord, have so offended Him, that instead of turning His hand against them, the Lord feeds and nourishes them up to be a scourge to the whole land." During the first week or so, Rowlandson eats little, although she retains her Bible, which nourishes her in different ways.

As her captivity extends, however, Rowlandson must eat foods that she would never have considered palatable:

> In the morning I went to the same squaw, who had a kettle of ground nuts boiling. I asked her to let me boil my piece of bear in her kettle, which she did, and gave me some ground nuts to eat with it: and I cannot but think how pleasant it was to me. I have sometime seen bear baked very handsomely among the English, and some like it, but the thought that it was bear made me tremble. But now that was savory to me that one would think was enough to turn the stomach of a brute creature.

It is, in fact, often other women who are kind to her in this way and who offer her food and other domestic comforts. One woman lets Rowlandson sleep in her wigwam, where she "laid a mat under me, and a good rug over me." Another gave her the piece of bear she finds "savory" (and note the shift between past and present tense in the passage above).

Most often these kindnesses are overtly attributed to God, even as the reader notes how Rowlandson seems to be adapting to her changed conditions with alacrity:

> During my abode in this place, Philip spake to me to make a shirt for his boy, which I did, for which he gave me a shilling. I offered the money to my master, but he bade me keep it; and with it I bought a piece of horse flesh. Afterwards he asked me to make a cap for his boy, for which he invited me to dinner. I went, and he gave me a pancake, about as big as two fingers. It was made of parched wheat, beaten, and fried in bear's grease, but I thought I never tasted pleasanter meat in my life. There was a squaw who spake to me to make a shirt for her sannup, for which she gave me a piece of bear. Another asked me to knit a pair of stockings, for which she gave me a quart of peas. I boiled my peas and bear together, and invited my master and mistress to dinner; but the proud gossip, because I served them both in one dish, would eat nothing, except one bit that he gave her upon the point of his knife.

The narrative is very careful about placing these markers of difference in between Rowlandson and those experiences revealing the intimacies of everyday life to which Rowlandson is becoming somewhat acculturated. That these points of cultural crossing tend to occur in the domestic space is particularly significant because that is the space in which Rowlandson is defined within her "civilized" community and may also be the places in which Rowlandson's own voice speaks out from behind the editor's.

In any case, Rowlandson becomes a strong participant in the micro economy of the tribe — bartering for food by offering her own domestic skills, giving her labor to them in return for what she needs for sustenance. These cultural exchanges represent a remarkably equitable arrangement given her continued insistence that she is humble and denigrated. Further, the more details she provides about her life among her captors, the more she is engaged in that life as a member of this "Other" community, and the closer she brings the reader to that space of cultural crossing, captivated but not captive.

By the late eighteenth century, the Indian captivity narrative had become one of the most popular forms of American literature, and its themes reflected the burgeoning political values and alliances of the new country, as well as the evolving view of women as symbolic of home and hearth.[25] New Hampshire widow Jemima Howe's captivity narrative nicely demonstrates this new image of patriotic womanhood. Despite the fact that women were becoming more literate and therefore more engaged in political life,[26] Howe does not write her own story; instead, David Humphreys writes it into his 1788 biography of Revolutionary War hero General Israel Putnam. Howe was captured in the 1756 French and Indian raid on the British Fort Dummer and was held in and around Montreal for four years before her redemption by Albany Colonel Phillip Schuyler and Putnam (both former captives themselves). Humphreys sentimentalizes Howe as a "mild daughter of sorrow," a "handsome" woman to whom "[d]istress, which had taken somewhat from the original redundancy of her bloom and added a softening paleness to her cheeks, rendered her appearance the more engaging."[27] In other words, she is softer and more maternal, and Humphreys explains that the "same maternal passion, which, sometimes overcomes the timidity of nature in the birds when plundered of their callow nestlings" brings Howe out of her own domestic nesting to relate the story of her sufferings (75–6).

Among those are the attentions of a lecherous French officer who "forcibly seized her hand and solemnly declared that he would now satiate the passion which he had so long refused to indulge" (77). Howe employs her "prevalent female weapons," including tears and attempts to struggle, and he then threatens to kill her. Her vulnerability is a calculated function of Putnam's paternal strength and wisdom, for "[t]hough endowed with masculine fortitude, [Howe] was truly feminine in strength and must have fainted by the way, had it not been for the assistance of Major Putnam" (80–81), who is possessed of "native courage, unshaken integrity, and established reputation as a soldier" (iv). Howe is the sentimental republican heroine, strong enough to resist rape or other forms of moral or political impurity, but still in need of strong, paternal protection.[28] And Putnam's "native" strength is not the strength of those native to the now-American territory, but 'natively American,' a powerful semantic conversion in creating a new American mythology. Critical to this myth is that the American man (both individually and collectively as a nation), not God, now symbolizes safety and civilization, which he will bring to the land and against his enemies, protecting the loyal and vulnerable women and children. Howe is symbolic of that vulnerability both in the narrative itself and in its telling—even her voice is sheltered by both Putnam and Humphreys, and when she finally does tell what she claims to be her "genuine and correct" story some years later, it is in yet another narrative written and edited by a man and subsumed into a history of New Hampshire, where Howe lived much of her life.[29] For all of the admonishing language the Puritan ministers regularly employed, the domestication of eighteenth and nineteenth century women has largely shaped the Anglo American patriarchal hierarchy with which we contend in Euro-American sentimental, sensational, and romantic fiction.

Love, Liberty, and the Pursuit of Domesticity

While the more than three hundred extant American Indian captivity narratives offer extensive testimony of the public's lasting appreciation for this genre, it is perhaps surprising that by far the most popular is Mary Jemison's, edited by James Seaver and subsequently republished in more than thirty editions between 1824 and 1967.[30] The surprise here is related to the fact that Jemison's narrative is that of a woman who willingly abandoned her white family and culture to live out her life among and as Seneca.

In Crevecoeur's *Letters from an American Farmer*, James laments that "thousands of Europeans are Indians, and we have no examples of even one of those aborigines having from choice become Europeans."[31] James wonders why it is that "children who have been adopted when young [...] can never be prevailed upon to readopt European manners?"[32] He reasons that "[t]here must be in their social bond something singularly captivating and far superior to anything to be boasted of among us," because over time and "[b]y the force of habit, [Europeans become] at last thoroughly naturalized to this wild course of life."[33] That this "wild course" can become "natural" to the European reflects that porous nature of cultural interaction Greenblatt articulated, and while James might be a fictional farmer, his observations are not. Europeans, especially women and children, did abandon "civilization" for life among the Indians, sometimes through captivity, but also through desertion from the English army and other means.[34]

Mary Jemison, the young daughter of Irish immigrants, was taken in a Shawnee raid in 1755. Her immediate family was killed after the raid, but she was saved for adoption into a Seneca family who lost a son in battle.[35] She became very fond of her "sisters," married twice within the tribe, and raised her Irish-Seneca children. At the end of the French and Indian War, she encounters a Dutchman who hopes to redeem her to the English for a bounty. Afraid of the Dutchman, Jemison "carefully watched his movements in order to avoid falling into his hands" (59) and is so desperate that she hides for three days "in an old cabin at Gardow, and then went back trembling at every step for fear of being appre-hended" (59). Ironically, redemption to the white world by a white man becomes, for Jemi-son, captivity, subverting the traditional cultural and gender hierarchies these narratives often seem designed to serve.[36]

Still, Seaver makes a point of claiming that this now-elderly woman is still known as "The White Woman" and "the friend of the distressed" (viii), insisting that she "speaks English plainly and distinctly, with a little of the Irish emphasis" (xi), after decades with the Seneca and even though "[h]er habits, are those of the Indians" and "[h]er ideas of reli-gion, correspond in every aspect with those of the great mass of the Senecas" (xiv). Ironically, Seaver's emphasis on Jemison's whiteness highlights her alienation from Euro-American communities, demonstrating her preference for Indian life and her adoption of Seneca cul-ture. And it is not an easy life. Jemison's narrative is full of hardship and war, with armed conflicts and harsh winters and two of her sons meeting violent deaths.

More significantly, Jemison does not identify as American; at one point she notes that while "our Indians were in their first battle with the Americans [...] my daughter Nancy was born"(67). Seaver tries to fashion Jemison as a sentimental white heroine, but, as Annette Kolodny points out, "Jemison's story insistently emerges" against Seaver's intentions.[37] Jemi-son consistently refers to "our Indians" (67) and "our tribe" (63), and forgets how to read English: "[a]fter the revolutionary war, I remembered the names of some of the letters when I saw them; but have never read a word since I was taken prisoner" (23). This is a significant marker of her acculturation into an oral tradition and a distancing from the very narrative Seaver fashions of her life.

As Michelle Burnham argues, "Cultural exchange produces a supplement [...] the pro-duction of cultural difference" that is evident in the affective characteristics of captivity nar-ratives, namely "the process of sympathy, which requires a crossing of the boundary between reader and text."[38] That is, as the captive moves more fully into that cultural difference, so does the reader, as long as her sympathy remains with the captive. The popularity of Jemi-son's narrative demonstrates how powerfully her figuration occupies that in between space of cultural hybridity. Similarly, her story remains captivating precisely because she has become an insider to Indian culture and therefore functions as a sort of cultural translator to those who only vicariously share her experiences but continue to retell her story.[39]

To the contemporary reader, most unadapted captivity narratives may seem pedantic, dogmatic, and dry, but their influence on the development of eighteenth- and nineteenth-century literature is substantial. As Nancy Armstrong argues,

> During the period when Richardson's *Clarissa* was enthralling European readers, accounts of Euro-peans held captive in America flooded into England from the colonies. English readers consumed these captivity narratives almost as avidly as they did sentimental fiction, and they consequently knew exactly what kind of story would ensue once they recognized it as the testimony of a captive woman. [...] Once created, furthermore, the appetite for narratives of this particular kind never diminished with the rising popularity of fiction on both sides of the Atlantic.[40]

In fact, Pamela Regis names Richardson's 1740 novel *Pamela* as the first best-selling romance in English, characterizing it as "the story of the courtship, betrothal, wedding, and triumph of lady's maid Pamela Andrews to Mr. B, the master for whom she works."[41] Armstrong pushes in the opposite direction, arguing that in *Pamela*, "Richardson tapped into the power of this written testimony by turning a series of exemplary letters into a kind of captivity narrative" (375). More generally, while Regis links the burgeoning genre of sentimental fiction to the romance novel, Armstrong explicitly links the evolution and popularity of sentimental fiction to the New England captivity narrative:

> In the last chapter of *The Imaginary Puritan*, moreover, Leonard Tennenhouse and I found unmistakable traces of a distinctly New England genre, the captivity narrative, in eighteenth-century British fiction (196–216). We argued, in a nutshell, that sentimental fiction borrowed from the following cluster of narrative ingredients from its New England cousins: (1) a lone heroine whose self-determination and cultural value are under assault from members of a tribal culture, (2) an individual who manages to hang onto her values and identity by transcribing personal experiences under extreme circumstances, and (3) a written account that testifies to the captive's unwavering desire to return to an English home.[42]

Although I am arguing for a more troubled reading of New England captivity narratives, I think Armstrong and Tennenhouse's observations about how captivity narratives influenced sentimental fiction work in reverse, as well. That is, some of the eighteenth- and nineteenth-century captivity narratives mirror different tropes of sentimental fiction. Jemima Howe's idealized republican mother, for example, represents what Lori Merish calls "feminine consent," by which the "superior enlightenment of American men" is demonstrated through feminine agency, specifically the "elevated social position" and "taste" of women.[43] While Mary Jemison's narrative suggests the way sentimental fiction can "evince [...] a solid social realism that also constitutes a critique (even if sometimes covert) of the patriarchal structure" of society,[44] Jemison's rejection of Anglo-American society and the laborious, difficult details of her life among the Seneca paint a much less idealized picture of roughly the same historical period.

What sentimental fiction specifically innovates is the meditation on courtship, love, and marriage. As Cathy Davidson argues, "An unstated premise of sentimental fiction is that a woman must take greater control of her life and must make shrewd judgments of the men who come into her life," because choosing a good marriage was one of the most significant choices a woman could, and hopefully would, make.[45] And like those moral lessons some of the early captivity narratives sought to impart to a potentially wayward community, inherent in the sentimental tradition was a strain of moral instruction on the dangers of certain choices and behaviors. Richardson's introduction to *Pamela* made his intentions explicit:

> Publish then, this good, this edifying and instructive little Piece for their sakes. The Honour of Pamela's Sex demands Pamela at your Hands, to shew the World an Heroine, almost beyond Example, in an unusual Scene of Life, whom no Temptations, or Sufferings, could subdue. It is a fine, and glorious Original, for the Fair to copy out and imitate. Our own Sex, too, require it of you, to free us, in some measure, from the Imputation of being incapable of the Impressions of Virtue and Honour; [del. 8th] {and to shew the Ladies, that we are not inflexible while they are so.}[46]

Where captive heroines like Rowlandson, Howe, and even Jemison are drawn as virtuous because of spiritual, national, or culture providence, the sentimental heroine is expected to be virtuous for the sake of virtue, and more specifically for her chances at legitimate marriage and motherhood. As Davidson notes, the eighteenth century had a "huge social interest in women's sexuality, which was fetishized into a necessary moral as well as a social and biological commodity."[47] Such is also the case for many seventeenth- and eighteenth-century captivities, as exemplified by Mary Rowlandson's narrative, in which she emphatically indicates that "not one of [the Indians] ever offered me the least abuse of unchastity to me, in word or action," despite the other incidents of violence that pepper the text. The virtuous captive is she who does not consort sexually — consensually or otherwise — with her captors. That quite a few women did, in fact, choose to remain in their tribe of capture makes this prohibition against miscegenation even more important, and for captives like Mary Jemison, their narrative redemption comes in the form of marital fidelity, devoted motherhood, industrious habits, and the arduous life of living among the Indians.

Still, stories like Jemison's were outright bestsellers, vehicles, perhaps, through which the reader could cross borders and boundaries without the attendant challenges and sacrifices, where she could imagine the kinds of desires that are carefully disguised in the surface narrative. In the case of sentimental fiction, women often read the novels communally, and Davidson argues that these novels dramatize various marriage scenarios (and their consequences) for women to test and contemplate safely.[48] Still, it is interesting that the biggest bestsellers were often books like Hannah Webster Foster's *The Coquette,* featuring the well-born and educated Eliza Wharton, a woman who is so "tenacious of [her] freedom" that she disdains marriage to a man who will afford her "tranquility and rational happiness" for "those delightful amusements and flattering attentions which wealth and equipage bestow," setting in motion her moral and physical degradation and ending in her ignominious abandonment and death.[49]

In novels like Foster's, the figure of the uncivilized Indian has been replaced by the figure of the seemingly civilized seducer (like Howe's inappropriately amorous French officer). Eliza is attracted to the inappropriate man because "[h]is person, his manners, his situation, all combine to charm my fancy; and to my lively imagination, strew the path of life with flowers" (Letter X). Yet she does not want to abandon the values society insists are critical to her happiness: "My sanguine imagination paints, in alluring colors, the charms of youth and freedom, regulated by virtue and innocence. Of these, I wish to partake" (Letter XIV). At the same time, she is hesitant to marry her respectable suitor, Reverend Boyer: "I recoil at the thought of immediately forming a connection, which must confine me to the duties of domestic life, and make me dependent for happiness, perhaps too, for subsistence, upon a class of people, who will claim the right of scrutinizing every part of my conduct; and by censuring those foibles, which I am conscious of not having prudence to avoid, may render me completely miserable" (Letter XIV). Eliza's dilemma is complicated, because while she is not outright rejecting the life society expects of her, she is understandably reluctant to abdicate what little autonomy she has for the sake of social propriety, which, as she astutely recognizes, is intimately connected to the judgment and scrutiny of strangers. She *wants,* and in that experience threatens to give way to appealing emotions and desires that alienate her from the staid duty of complacent domesticity. That Eliza ends up falling so far from any path to happiness (she has a stillborn son out of wedlock, doubling the misery and the implicit punishment) likely made her plight sympathetic to some moderately well-born, moderately-educated female readers, who were themselves attempting to negotiate the Scylla and Charybdis of autonomous desire and the social prescription for female virtue. While Richardson seems to tolerate no gray in his black and white virtue-and-vice moral paradigm, Foster seems to understand something that female readers of Mary Jemison's captivity narrative would likely also discern: namely that any happiness gained on the borderlands of social acceptability came at a steep cost. For Jemison, that cost included various losses and crises due to military aggression, tribal displacement due to increasingly rapid Western settlement, and the negative effects of alcohol (to which many Indians became addicted). Although Jemison is lauded as a moral exemplar, her choice to live outside the protection of the colonial and national governments is one of great hardship. For Foster's Eliza Wharton, there isn't really an in-between space where she can find some measure of lasting happiness without completely losing respectability, even as her fate subtly indicts the patriarchal social rules that ordained it.

Beyond Civilization and its (Dis)contents

Diversity is essential to sentimental fiction, in part because of its contemplation of the various choices women could and could not make, which partially explains its overlap with other genres, especially romance. Still, eighteenth and nineteenth century sentimental novels are not generally identified as romantic. Except, that is, for Jane Austen's *Pride and Prejudice*, which is often identified as the literary prequel to genre romance.

Unlike Eliza Wharton, Elizabeth Bennet succeeds in a match that satisfies both social respectability and autonomous desire. The romantic innovation in Austen's novel is the construction of a character like Darcy, whose own multi-faceted desire and love for Elizabeth reveals him to be intelligent, tolerant, and unconventional without being socially suspect. Austen's novel also contains a critical element of the sentimental novel in the portrayal of Wickham's unsavory seduction of Lydia Bennet. And again, unlike Eliza Wharton, Lydia Bennet is saved from total, impoverished social humiliation by the novel's true hero, Darcy, who pays off Wickham's debts and facilitates a proper marriage between Wickham and Lydia. On one level, this change of fortune reinforces the very social rules that troubled Eliza Wharton. However, the transformation of Lydia and Wickham's very improper relationship into a respectable and conventional marriage suggests that sexual desire itself is not untoward.

The conversion of Lydia and Wickham's relationship is critical in discerning the complex literary relationship among the captivity narrative, sentimental fiction, and romance, all of which converge in Edith Hull's 1919 novel, *The Sheik*, a sentimental captivity romance that is arguably the first genre romance novel.[50] It certainly seems to serve as the prototype for the sheikh romance in film and literature, echoing through novels like Violet Winspear's *Blue Jasmine*—which replicates numerous elements of Hull's story—as well as other genre romances.[51]

In the context of British colonial history, it is no surprise that the deserts of the Middle East would become the new "wilderness" for England, as World War I resulted in previously unrealized British control over the Ottoman Empire, Egypt, and other Arab states. But with that stronger control also came anxieties, conflicts, and novelties similar to those between the English colonists and North American indigenous peoples in previous centuries. Moreover, women's travel writing was growing in popularity in the opening decades of the twentieth century, and the most "exotic" destinations were particularly coveted by both female travelers and readers:

> Travel to remote regions was especially transgressive for many Western women of the nineteenth and early twentieth centuries who sought both escape and pleasure abroad. These women, themselves "Other" to masculine concepts of biology, thought, emotion, and sexuality, found the authority they were denied at home by becoming experts of an exotic area. The Otherness they found served as a vehicle for inscribing something new, even something unspoken about themselves.

Writing about foreign bodies in a strange land compelled a woman writer to consider the position of her own body as a foreign object and to make choices about the presentation of that body on paper.[52]

As Kelley explains, this self-referential consideration of the writer's body shaped the textual geography of the narrative such that women's "quests were less about opening new territories for their country and more about opening new spaces for themselves and their readers at home."[53] Although the historical and ideological contexts are different, the narratives of female captives like those of Rowlandson and Jemison demonstrate the same dynamic of contemplating the "Otherness" of an "exotic" culture from a position of Otherness.

The doubling of this perspective is crucial, because it positions the female narrator as cultural mediator, located both within dominant cultural values and yet in many ways Other to those values. Her voice, itself an articulation of a minority viewpoint on at least two levels, must navigate both her own Otherness and that of her hosts (or captors, depending on the context of the narrative), simultaneously repositioning the reader, as well, as both insider and outsider, depending on the reader's gender, race, and cultural identity. As Reina Lewis argues, the subjective position of the white woman in the East, especially, "gives the woman writer or artist the chance to avail herself of a colonial superiority that may well elude her in the colonial field itself but can be appropriated, by proxy, in the textual domain of an Orientalized Europe."[54] Consequently, women were "challenging the positionalities open to" them in "active disruption/production of the fictions that culture seeks to normalize" through "intervention into cultural codes."[55] Identity is thus relational and in flux, depending on the social, cultural, and narrative context.

Within the traditional Indian captivity narrative, the voice of a male "editor" may overlap or even overlay that of the female captive in crafting the moral of the tale. Still, the reader can often detect a divergence of voice in many of the personal details provided by the captive — Rowlandson's focus on food, for example, or Jemison's discussion of her husbands and children — that the editorial shaping cannot erase. As female authorship becomes more popular, the patina of patriarchy is still present but can sometimes be more directly challenged. The overt merger of the captivity narrative and the sentimental romance in novels like *The Sheik* and *Blue Jasmine* provides an opportune narrative context in which to contemplate and potentially subvert white Anglo patriarchy.

In spite of the fifty years between them, the remarkable similarities between Hull's novel and Winspear's Mills & Boon/Harlequin category romance create a kind of direct lineage for the now-common sheikh romance, and, by extension, the popularity of the captivity motif in genre romance. Hull and Winspear both introduce beautiful blonde heroines with no apparent interest in marriage or the respectable English men who pursue them. Hull's Diana insists, "'When God made me He omitted to give me a heart.'" Winspear's Lorna yearns only for the desert, and "[t]he only male person she had even been close to had been her father, and only in the last year of his life" (8). Diana shares this passion, promising, "I like wild places." Both are now fatherless, and neither heeds the warning of a paternalistically-minded brother who cautions against a sojourn in the desert. Both also defy the admonitions of their local guides and venture too far beyond civilized society, resulting in capture by a sensually ruthless sheikh.

Here the stories diverge slightly, as Diana suffers more physical violence from her sheikh, who has "the handsomest and cruelest face that she had ever seen," and whose "possessive passion" results in "savage kisses" that "w[ere] like a narcotic, drugging her almost into insensibility" except for the fear she felt "for the first time in her life." When the sheikh dropped her off in his tent, leaving her to prepare for his lusty attentions, Diana knew "[s]he could only wait and suffer in the complete moral collapse that overwhelmed her. [...] 'Oh, God,' she sobbed with scalding tears that scorched her cheeks. 'Curse him! Curse him!'" With "no mercy to be hoped for," despite "abject prayers" and "grovel[ing]," Diana cannot convince Sheik Ahmed Ben Hassan to spare her virginity. At first Diana is moved by the "passionate fierceness" of her desire to die, but ultimately the sheikh's fierce possession of her body and her attention transforms her desire to die into a romantic desire to be deeply loved by Ahmed, as she now loves him.

Lorna's captor, Kasim ben Hussayn uses a more complicated coercion technique to maneuver Lorna into physical and emotional submission. Even though he appears to be "arrogant as the devil" (29) to Lorna and insists, "'I prefer what I take to what I am given,'" namely this little "tiger-kitten who has not yet been tamed" (37), Prince Kasim bullies and threatens but does not physically violate. Like Ahmed, he keeps his "desert captive" in his tent and tries to get her to wear native dress, but unlike Ahmed, he appears a bit more ambivalent toward Lorna. In one conversation he tells her that "'[a] real woman [...] enjoys her fear of the man who is unafraid of her,'" explaining that he "handles" her "'as one handles a spirited filly, so that she feels the tension of the rein and won't lose her head'" (86–87). He tells her how much he likes her pride, even as he strips her old life away and works to undermine her resistance without having to resort to physical force. His ambivalence matches Lorna's, and their courtship is a less physically violent rendition of Diana and Ahmed's, although the trajectory of the romance itself is quite similar. Both men are also eventually revealed to be of European heritage — both have Spanish mothers and English or French biological fathers — making their attachment to the desert Arab life voluntary and their Otherness cultural rather than racial.

One might call Winspear's book more "romantic" than Hull's, even though the basic structure of the tale is the same. In both the heroine is held captive, stripped of her Western dress and other accoutrements of "civilization," won over to complete physical and emotional adoration of the sheikh, only to fear they will never fully possess the man who insists he is incapable of love. Both heroines are described as "wild" or even animalistic by the sheikh, who seems to be practicing his own sort of taming of the women, which further complicates the superficial civilization/wilderness dynamic. In both books the sheikh almost dies, leading to mutual declaration of love and ready assimilation (aka taming) by the heroine into the hero's adopted culture. Hull's text includes a second captivity for Diana by the sheikh's stereotypically evil enemy, "the Arab of her imaginings" with his "swollen, ferocious face" and "broken, blackened teeth." By the time the "robber Sheik" threatens Diana with rape and worse, Ahmed appears to be a savior rather than a marauder, and the reader's sympathies are clearly meant to be engaged with him over this outlaw, "savage" Other. In the terms of the traditional Indian captivity narrative, the robber sheikh is the "bloody savage" while Ahmed is the "noble savage." Except that Ahmed turns out not be "savage" at all, merely noble, both in position and in his ultimate protection of and commitment to Diana.

Both novels also demonstrate the complexity of the mediating perspective. Diana and Lorna are, as women, Other to both the English males of their home society and to the Arabs in their current environment. Like Eliza from *The Coquette*, they feel similarly Other to traditional notions of marriage within cultural expectations, and their captivity removes them further from those traditional expectations and behaviors. Captivity ultimately gives way to captivation by a man who is himself Other to the Arab culture, even as he has fully adopted it as his own, rejecting his European breeding. And the very context of "civilization" changes depending on the character's perspective — to the English women, the sheikhs are wild, but to the sheikhs, it is the women who appear untamed. Thus in marrying the sheikh, Diana and Lorna ironically fulfill the superficial expectation of marrying someone of European blood, but, like their husbands, they acculturate as Arab, which places them in a position of mediation among several signifiers of cultural identification, hybrids who seem to be initiating a different paradigm of love and marriage. Where women like Eliza Wharton or Mary Jemison must pay handsomely for their alienation from Anglo patriarchal norms, the happily ever after construct of the genre romance provides another, much more satisfactory path for Diana and Lorna, but one that does not force them back into their original culture.

The pairing of the sheikh and the English or American woman is central to many sheikh romances, a pattern that seems to lend substance to critiques of the books as Orientalist fantasy. Emily Haddad argues that the sheikh captivity device "serves to reaffirm the cultural stereotype of the dominant Arab man holding 'his' women in virtual enslavement," which she argues is further affirmed when the hero rescues the heroine from either "the grip of a villain or sandstorm."[56] For Haddad, captivity functions as a device intended to generate necessary romantic conflict, one in which "[b]ondage gives way to bonding," while "the structure of captivity remains, transmogrified as marriage" (49), reaffirming rather than undermining traditional patriarchal values filtered through racial and cultural stereotypes casting men as conquering savages who are ultimately tamed by their prey. While I agree with Haddad's critique of the Orientalist aspects of these romantic fantasies, I would argue that neither the stereotypes nor the culminating marriage invalidate the subversive potential of these texts. And as Reina Lewis avers, "The contradictions of women's challenges to imperial power indicate the splits within imperial discourse and its imperial subject" as opposed to "Said's monolithic Orientalist discourse."[57] That the cultural shifts in romance are largely imagined does not necessarily mean that the resulting figurative hybridity is any less powerful within the context of the narrative and in the space between the text and the reader. Indian captivity narratives could offer readers a vicarious spiritual or physical trial of the captive removed from her civilized life, and sentimental and sensational fiction presents the consequences of various romantic possibilities. Genre romance, though, offers a further possibility, namely an imagined in-between space in which blood does not trump acculturation, and where desire and love can blend both blood and cultures.

Moreover, the captivity scenario in romance does not only function to secure marriage, nor does marriage necessarily mean lasting happiness. In Michelle Reid's *The Sheikh's Chosen Wife*, Hassan and his English wife Leona have been estranged for a year, their marriage troubled by Leona's inability to conceive Hassan's heir. Hassan is unwilling to let the marriage go, however, so he concocts a plan to capture her and isolate her on a yacht until he can convince her to come back to him. But Leona believes that her inability to conceive a child, let alone a son, will ultimately imperil Hassan's power in the region, and she further understands that the tribal elders will not accept alternative forms of conception or adoption, but will insist Hassan instead take a second wife. The challenge here is to negotiate a solution that maintains balance among Hassan's duty, his modern desires and choices, and the traditions that still hold political and cultural dominion. Interestingly, it is Hassan who is willing to do whatever it takes to hold on to Leona as his sole wife, even if she cannot have children, while still maintaining his duty and his family's political security.

If the construction of the captivity motif is meant to perpetuate traditional cultural and gender roles, Hassan's approach to Leona's fertility issues presents a challenge to those, as he explicitly refuses to equate her value as a woman with her ability to procreate:

> "Coming to terms with being a failure is not something I wanted to share with anyone," she murmured dully.
> "You are not a failure," he denied.[58]

He continues later in the book: "'Children are a precious gift from Allah,' Hassan interrupted, dark head somberly bent over his task. 'But so is love. Very few people are fortunate enough to have both, and most only get the children. If I had to choose then I would choose, to have love.'"[59] The fantasy element here is that the captivity functions not to force the heroine to submit to the dominant hero, but rather to liberate her from traditional expectations and a sense of personal value dependent on sustaining the traditional cultural patriarchy. That the culturally miscegenated couple remain accepted within this traditional context further demonstrates its porousness and susceptibility to hybridization.

In this context, a different process of Otherizing is taking place, as well. Both Hassan and Leona face a potentially alienating situation, and both are aware that without a miracle (which the reader often knows is imminent, even if the characters do not), they will be forging a new path, a hybrid reality to which the reader connects through the emotional bond of love and desire the couple share. In other words, it is the traditional romantic bond that allows the couple to take a risk that would otherwise not be possible.

In Love We Trust

While the conservative origins of romance are arguably manifested most strongly in the requirements of the happy ending, the use of the captivity motif in concert with the happily ever after can provide a challenge to the domestication of love and desire. In Louise Allen's category Roman-set historical romance *Virgin Slave, Barbarian King* and Elizabeth Vaughan's single-title paranormal romance *Warprize*, for example, the hero and heroine come from very different worlds, and their union represents an overt hybridization of those cultures rather than the assimilation of one by the other. It is in this manifestation that the captivity motif may have the most subversive potential in romance.

Virgin Slave, Barbarian King is a heavily idealized narrative through which the heroine realizes that her cultural assumptions and sense of superiority are completely backward. Her veneration of all things Roman as the height of civilization is turned completely around by her discovery that the "barbarian" Visigoths are actually more "civilized" in the ways that matter to her. Such a narrative has an antecedent in popular literature and even in the captivity narrative—Daniel Boone's famously misanthropic rejection of Anglo society later in his life comes to mind—and it often relies on the same romanticized notions of cultural superiority that produce the opposing view. However, within the romance context, the reversal serves an interesting purpose in generating a couple who will take an active part in shaping a society different from that of either the hero or heroine's.

When Julia Livia Rufa is captured by Wulfric, she rails at the notion that she will be a slave, exclaiming, "'I am a noblewoman!'"[60] She wonders if he would let his pet wolf "savage" her should she try to escape (38), and realizes that "[f]or the first time in her life [...]

her status meant nothing" (42), which disorients her. Wulfric orders her to manage the domestic chores, including cooking, cleaning, and washing the clothes, which she refuses to do (most of which she doesn't know how to do), along with rejecting the native clothes he gives her to wear. In some ways the Goth encampment is the mirror image of Julia's Roman society, but this time she views things from the perspective of a domestic "slave," ironizing the Western cultural narrative of domestication.

However, Julia's position is hardly degraded to the level that Roman servants were (Julia does not even know the name of the servant who accompanied her into town and was murdered in front of her), something that forces her to adjust her own cultural attitudes. It is only a matter of days before Julia refuses to escape when she has the chance, because her attraction to Wulfric — "[a] bronze god, [... h]e was more alive than any man she had ever seen" (79) — becomes part of her growing sense of place within the camp. In many ways, Wulfric is the socially and culturally progressive version of Hull and Winspear's sheikhs, a man who leads with natural authority, who possesses an innate sense of civility, who commands the respect of animals and children (although his pet is a wolf rather than a dog), and who terrifies and excites Julia at the same time. Like the sheikhs he is autocratic when he chooses, telling Julia, "'You cannot be free now [...] — you are mine'" (99–100). And yet after their first kiss, when Julia tries to insist that Wulfric "'forced [her]'" (175), and he tells her to "'behave like [the virgin she is]'" (175), it is clear that both are merely repeating the dialogue given to them via so many captivity romances — Julia is in no danger of being raped and Wulfric does not possess the same chauvinism toward women common in Rome. They rehearse the types and mimic the formula, but their behavior conforms more to the example of Mary Jemison's captivity narrative than *The Coquette* or even *The Sheik*.

In taking her captive, and then captivating her, Wulfric liberates Julia well beyond what she could have expected as a respectable Roman noblewoman. In fact, one of the consistent themes in Allen's novel is the balance between freedom and responsibility, a universalized democratic ideal. Julia and Wulfric are even equal in their view of each other. Julia sees Wulfric as "like his wolf, domesticated until roused, then a killer" (98), while he sees her as akin to "an exotic animal, half-tame, half-wild" (81). This is a kinder, gentler *in between* world than that of *The Sheik*, and its progressivism requires not merely that Julia will take up Goth ways, but rather that Wulfric's visionary leadership will create a society that merges the best of both societies and cultures. Wulfric, who at one point tells Julia that his long hair is "sacred to our kingship" (199), is ultimately willing to cut it in the Roman style to retrieve her after she has been returned to her parents' home, telling Julia, "'I want to go north to Gaul [...] to buy land, not wait for it to be given. [...] to settle, learn to live with my Roman neighbors'" (191). In this way, both Julia and Wulfric are offered as examples of change and hybridity, their own happiness as a couple intertwined with a new social reality that is not yet defined, leaving open myriad possibilities for them both and transforming the love relationship into a socially subversive union.

Elizabeth Vaughan's *Warprize* is a bit more complex in its dualistic cultural view. The initial political dynamics between Xylara's people and Keir's are similar to those between the English and the Native Americans, with Keir's "Firelanders," as they are known to the Xy, viewed as nomadic tribal people of a savage and inferior culture next to the urbanized Xy. When Keir demands XyLara as his Warprize, her half-brother, the current king, tells her to prepare for slavery and forced subjugation to the Warlord Keir. With this expectation,

Lara moves into Keir's camp, terrified and frustrated that everyone calls her "Warprize" instead of Lara and indignant at the fact that she is monitored everywhere and ordered to take only what Keir gives her.

Where Allen's book basically inverts the cultural dynamics of the captivity narrative, Vaughan provides us with an unreliable narrator through whom we experience the captive's dual cultural reality. Like Wulfric, Keir has a new vision for the future, understanding that the continued vitality of his people depends on their political and social evolution, but to the Xy, Keir's people are "Devil riders," tainted by rumors that "they ate their dead, and tore the hearts out of their kills. That they were black, and yellow, and blue, and that their eyes glowed with madness."[61] Lara never fully accepts this idea, viewing her transfer to the Warlord as part of her royal duty and seeing it not as captivity, *per se*, but as a political bargain that would save her people. In a sense, her transfer as Warprize is a captive redemption in reverse; however, since we know that Keir and Lara will fall in love, we can anticipate that his world will ultimately become her *true* home. That inevitability is prefigured in Keir and Lara's first anonymous encounter, which makes Lara recognize that she "had never felt more alive. My whole body seemed newly aware of itself" (45), when Keir holds her against an alley wall, asking her for information about his wounded men, imbuing her with a sense of vitality and self-awareness even as he restrains her.

One of the most interesting things about Vaughan's novel is that despite Lara's willingness to accompany Keir to his camp, she narrates the story much in the way a captive would. At one point she suffers a crisis of identity, realizing, "I wasn't really Xyian anymore, was I? I wasn't really anything, was I?" (176) still believing that her position as Warprize makes her nothing more than a slave. It is not until quite late in the novel that Lara discovers the truth of her position:

> "Lara, a true warprize is a rare thing. We value them, for our people have found that the warprize brings a new way of thinking, of doing things. It makes us better, stronger, when we are exposed to new ways and new ideas. You cannot fake a true warprize, nor pick one, nor force one. They happen maybe once in five generations, and we see it as a benediction from the elements themselves, even for the upheaval that they bring" [240–241].

Lara's self-understanding changes radically at this point, as she can finally reject the denigrated role of slave and embrace the esteemed role of the warprize. The Warprize is unique, she is new, she is not of the world she enters, and no longer of the world she left. This knowledge gives Lara an opportunity to *redefine herself*, and with that knowledge she takes the initiative and seduces Keir, sealing their bond through her own volition, redeeming herself, in a sense, and giving herself freely to the people she had been serving and learning to love and admire for many months. That she had been allowed to serve as a healer (introducing a substantive aspect of her own culture), that her independence had been tolerated with great amusement, that she was guarded and protected and offered great deference had never registered for Lara, so certain she was of her enslaved status.

It is still possible to argue that Lara's status mirrors that of the domestic ideal, the woman as nurturer, as sacrifice, as cultural go-between — that her elevation is a naturalization of her femininity, an essentialization of her subjugated superiority. But that interpretation is challenged by the active role Lara takes in a culture where women routinely serve as warriors and where motherhood is somewhat disconnected from the process of giving birth. As in so many of these other texts, there is a strong tension here between Lara's freedom to choose her fate and the fatedness of her relationship with Keir. She ultimately relinquishes the role of Xyian Queen in order to be with Keir, but her resignation of one kind of power will likely enable her to enjoy more freedom traveling with Keir's people, who are not politically joined but not culturally unified with the Xyians. Like Mary Jemison, Lara does not return home, and like Julia Rufa, her romantic union is a promise of change for everyone. In other words, the "bonding" in *Warprize* can be seen as aspiring to a new and unknown social reality rather than affirming a traditional domestic model, with the love between Keir and Lara itself transgressive and transformational.

In *Bound and Determined*, Christopher Castiglia argues that captivity narratives "offered American women [...] an adventure story."[62] He goes on to trace the genre into territory often explored by scholars of romance:

> As it evolved from a religious document of the seventeenth to a feminist plot of the twentieth century, the captivity narrative allowed women authors to create a symbolic economy through which to express dissatisfaction with the roles traditionally offered white women in America, and to reimagine those roles and the narratives that normalize them, giving rise ultimately to a new female subject and to the female audience on which she relies.[63]

Castiglia's insight into the "symbolic economy" of captivity is important, especially given the ways in which women have often been seen as property, in fiction and society. In the captivity romance, the heroine is allowed to desire and to choose, and once she chooses love, her adventure is often one that marks a significant cultural challenge or change, a shift that cannot be wholly accommodated within the old paradigm. The promise of long-term happiness is not only for the couple, but for the reader, as well, reinforcing the wisdom of cultural and social hybridity.

While romance persists in idealizing the institution of marriage, the nature of the union as either socially conservative or socially transformational is not uniform throughout the genre. That captivity narratives are themselves often transgressive, for example, does not necessarily guarantee the successful subversion of social prejudices against women, and in fact, the multiple levels and directions of transgression can sometimes reinforce those judgments and expectations. It is the possibilities for subversion and examples of narrative and social transgression I have tried to highlight here, as a way of starting a new conversation about how the idealized worlds depicted in romance are grounded in contemporaneous social reality and yet also invite new perspectives on how a culturally hybridized model of love and desire can challenge and change those realities that keep us captive to our own cultural prejudices and paradigms.

NOTES

1. Sheik, sheikh, and shaikh are all used in various texts under discussion, but outside of how the word appears in a book title, I will be using sheikh.
2. Jo Goodman, *Only in My Arms* (New York: Zebra, 2004).
3. Linda Howard, *Midnight Rainbow* (Toronto: Harlequin, 1986).
4. Michelle Reid, *The Sheikh's Chosen Wife* (Toronto: Harlequin, 2002).
5. Jeanne Allan, *No Angel* (Toronto: Harlequin, 1991).
6. See, for example, Christopher Castiglia, *Bound and Determined: Captivity, Culture-Crossing, and White Womanhood from Mary Rowlandson to Patty Hearst* (Chicago: University of Chicago Press, 1996).
7. Given the chronological and generic breadth of this essay, it is intended merely as an introduction, although I try to raise numerous implications for more in-depth work on the ways in which romance is capable of challenging dominant norms of race, gender, and nation-building.
8. Tzvetan Todorov, *The Conquest of America*, trans. Richard Howard (New York: Harper Torchbooks, 1987), 17. Speaking of Columbus, Todorov says, "There is nothing of the modern empiricist about Columbus:

the decisive argument is the argument of authority, not of experience" (17). Todorov's argument applies to many religious exiles, as well, who came to the colonies with rigidly structured paradigms into which they expected their new surroundings to fit. Columbus was convinced he would see the magnificently outrageous creatures featured in Mandeville's travels and other sensationalized narratives, and the Puritan colonists were not much better educated about what they should expect in North America.

9. Reiner Smolinski, Introduction to *An Earnest Exhortation to the Inhabitants of New-England (1676)* by Increase Mather, ed. Reiner Smolinski (Lincoln: University of Nebraska Electronic Texts in American Studies, http://digitalcommons.unl.edu/etas/31/), 2.

10. Increase Mather, *An Earnest Exhortation to the Inhabitants of New-England (1676)*, ed. Reiner Smolinksi (Lincoln: University of Nebraska Electronic Texts in American Studies, http://digitalcommons. unl.edu/etas/31/), 8–9.

11. See, for example, Anthony F.C. Wallace, *The Death and Rebirth of the Seneca* (New York: Vintage Books, 1969), 150–185, where he discusses the way the Iroquois, in particular, adopted captives to replace members lost through colonial wars and inter-tribal conflicts.

12. Cotton Mather, *Decennium Luctosum*, vol. 3 of *The Garland Library of North American Indian Captivities*, ed. Wilcomb Washburn (New York: Garland, 1976), 142–43.

13. *Ibid.*, 206.

14. Richard Slotkin, *Regeneration Through Violence: The Mythology of the American Frontier, 1600–1860* (Middletown, CT: Wesleyan University Press, 1973), 95.

15. John Filson, "Life and Adventures of Daniel Boon," vol. 14 of *The Garland Library of Narratives of North American Indian Captivities*, ed. Wilcomb Washburn (New York: Garland, 1978). Boone's narrative is particularly interesting because by the end of his life he apparently eschewed the company of white settlers in favor of the Indians, presaging the shift in the late nineteenth century from portraying Native Americans as "bloody savages" to "noble savages." Both terms are profoundly Anglo-centric, characterizing the indigenous peoples as either a horrific threat to white settlement or an expression of white guilt over the violence done to Native Americans in the settlement and expansion of the American nation.

16. Stephen Greenblatt, *Marvelous Possessions: The Wonder of the New World* (Chicago: University of Chicago Press, 1991), 54.

17. Michael Sturma, "Aliens and Indians: A Comparison of Abduction and Captivity Narratives," *Journal of Popular Culture* 36, no. 2 (2002): 330–31.

18. Greenblatt, *Marvelous Possessions*, 54.

19. *Ibid.*, 54.

20. *Ibid.*, 4.

21. Robert J. C. Young, *Colonial Desire: Hybridity in Theory, Culture, and Race* (New York: Routledge, 1995), 3–4. See Also Jennifer DeVere Brody, *Impossible Purities: Blackness, Femininity, and Victorian Culture* (Durham: Duke University Press, 1998) for a discussion of the ways in which nineteenth-century culture and literature produced and reproduced fictions of racial purity that were always challenged by the existence and pervasiveness of miscegenation and the children of such unions. As Brody argues, "Hybridity and purity are related terms that must be thought of as shifting and mutually constitutive representations — purity is impossible — every mention of the related term, hybrid, only confirms a strategic taxonomy that constructs purity as a prior (fictive) ground" (11–12). See also Theodore Allen, *Invention of the White Race, Volume I: Racial Oppression and Social Control* (London: Verso, 1994) for a discussion of the British creation of whiteness as both a result and a tool of slavery and economic oppression, especially in the West Indies.

22. Mary Rowlandson, *Narrative of the Captivity and Restoration of Mrs. Mary Rowlandson (1682)*, Project Gutenberg, http://digital.library.upenn.edu/webbin/gutbook/lookup?num=851.

23. Nancy Armstrong, "Captivity and Cultural Capital in the English Novel," *Novel: A Forum on Fiction* 31, no. 3 (1998): 374.

24. See Richard Slotkin, *So Dreadfull a Judgment: Puritan Responses to King Philip's War 1676–1677*, ed. Richard Slotkin and James K. Folsom (Middletown, CT: Wesleyan University Press, 1978) for an extended analysis of King Philip's War.

25. See Mary Beth Norton, *Liberty's Daughters: The Revolutionary Experience of American Women, 1750–1800* (Boston: Little, Brown, 1980) for a strong analysis of the patriotic mother figure.

26. Norton points out that women both had more control over the domestic sphere after America boycotted British goods (164), and were more politically aware and engaged (161).

27. David Humphreys, "An Essay on the Life of the Honorable Major-General Israel Putnam," in vol. 19 of *The Garland Library of Narratives of North American Indian Captivities*, ed. Wilcomb Washburn (New York: Garland, 1977), 74. Further references will be provided parenthetically. Howe later told her story again, to Reverend Bunker Gray in the 1792 "A Genuine and Correct Account of the Captivity, Suffering, and Deliverance of Mrs. Jemima Howe," and there was even another version of her story published in 1815,

"The Affecting History of Mrs. Howe" (rpt. in vol. 19 of *The Garland Library of Narratives of North American Indian Captivities*, ed. Wilcomb Washburn [New York: Garland, 1977]), but there is no indication it is connected as much to Howe as to the anti-American sentiments of the anonymous British author who used and embellished sections of Humphreys's narrative.

28. Note the pun on "native" in this description of Howe, reflecting Humphrey's casting of Putnam as intrinsic to the American soil rather than the indigenous peoples and naturalizing the project of nation building and all of its various forms of violence.

29. Jemima Howe, "A Genuine and Correct Account of the Captivity, Sufferings and Deliverance of Mrs. Jemima Howe," ed. Rev. Bunker Gray, in vol. 19 of *The Garland Library of Narratives of North American Indian Captivities,* ed. Wilcomb Washburn (1792; rpt. New York: Garland, 1977).

30. This number does not include the various adaptations of Jemison's story, including a number of children's books, one of which is Lois Lensky's *Indian Captive: The Story of Mary Jemison* (1942; rpt. New York: HarperCollins, 1995), a 1942 Newbery Honor book.

31. St. John De Crevecoeur, *Letters from an American Farmer*, ed. Albert E. Stone (1782; rpt. New York: Penguin Books, 1981), 214.

32. *Ibid.*, 213.

33. *Ibid.*, 214.

34. James Axtell, *The European and the Indian: Essays in the Ethnohistory of Colonial North America* (New York: Oxford University Press, 1981), 304. See also Slotkin, *Regeneration*, 97–8. Slotkin notes that between 1677 and 1750 at least 750 captives were taken. Of those on record, three hundred were redeemed through ransom, ninety-two died in captivity, and at least sixty were converted to Indian ways and chose to stay with the tribe (98).

35. James Everett Seaver, *A Narrative of the Life of Mary Jemison* (1824; rpt. New York: Garland, 1977). Further references will be provided parenthetically.

36. Jemison's choice of a Seneca man over a white man also flips the paradigm Jessica DeVere Brody notes in *Impossible Purities*: "[i]n the 1860s, the image of miscegenation promoted by a range of discourses was that of the black woman and the white man. This couple's coherence was sustained by sexual theories that labeled the prior union (between black man and white woman) sterile and literally 'impossible,' and the latter (between white man and black woman) fecund and, in some cases, not only possible but desirable — especially for economic gain" (8). While there was often a distinction drawn between miscegenation between Native Americans and whites, with Jefferson commenting positively in *Notes on The State of Virginia* on the red-white mix of color, the supposition that white women should marry white men was persistent and reflective, perhaps, of the fact that white men would, especially when slavery was legal, be mixing their blood with that of black women, often to produce additional slaves.

37. Annette Kolodny, *The Land Before Her: Fantasy and Experience of the American Frontiers, 1630–1860* (Chapel Hill: University of North Carolina Press, 1984), 68–81. Kolodny does a rather straightforward feminist reading of the text, arguing that the main concern of the "female captivity narrative" was to negotiate the unhappiness and anger associated with the masculine drive towards westward expansion. For Kolodny, "these narratives offered models of the kind of passive forbearance that some readers were themselves practicing — and on a recognizable terrain" (34). Kolodny goes on to subordinate the issue of transculturation via miscegenation to the idea that "to accept a white woman's intimacy with the Indian was, as well, to accept her intimacy with the forest spaces he inhabited" (70). Kolodny sees the tension in the narratives as located between white men and women who struggled for a place within the American landscape.

While Kolodny's overall argument about the frontier as a place in which white male identity was constructed is valuable, her reading of Jemison ignores some very important aspects of the narrative which complicate her overall model. To ignore the issue of transculturation is, I think, to diminish the subversive authority of the text and to diminish the importance of cultural identity in the narratives overall. Kolodny does, to be fair, argue that Jemison's narrative "represented the first text in American literature to move a real world white women beyond the traditional captivity pattern to something approaching the *willing* wilderness accommodations of a Daniel Boone" (80).

38. Michelle Burnham, *Captivity and Sentiment: Cultural Exchange in American Literature, 1682–1861* (Hanover NH: University Press of New England, 1997), 20–21, 44.

39. A cursory search on Amazon reveals the latest re-publication date as January 2011.

40. Armstrong, "Captivity," 374.

41. Pamela Regis, *A Natural History of the Romance Novel* (Philadelphia: University of Pennsylvania Press, 2003), 63.

42. Armstrong, "Captivity," 373.

43. Lori Merish, *Sentimental Materialism: Gender, Commodity Culture, and Nineteenth-Century American Literature* (Durham: Duke University Press, 2000), 19.

44. Cathy Davidson, *Revolution and the Word: The Rise of the Novel in America* (New York: Oxford University Press, 1986), 123.

45. *Ibid.*, 113.

46. Samuel Richardson, Introduction to *Pamela*, ed. Sheridan W. Baker, Jr. (Los Angeles: William Andrews Clark Memorial Library, University of California, 1954), http://www.gutenberg.org/files/24860/24860-8.txt.

47. Davidson, *Revolution*, 110.

48. *Ibid.*, 113.

49. Hannah Webster Foster, *The Coquette, or The History of Eliza Wharton* (Boston: William P. Petridge and Company, 1855), http://digital.library.upenn.edu/women/foster/coquette/coquette.html.

50. E.M. Hull, *The Sheik* (1921), http://www.gutenberg.org/dirs/etext04/sheik10.txt.

51. Violet Winspear, *Blue Jasmine* (Toronto: Harlequin, 1969). Further references will be provided parenthetically. There is also a Japanese comic version of the book published in 2007, and even apparently a Japanese stage production in 1983 (http://en.wikipedia.org/wiki/Violet_Winspear).

52. Joyce Kelley, "Increasingly 'Imaginative Geographies': Excursions into Otherness, Fantasy, and Modernism in Early Twentieth-Century Women's Travel Writing," *JNT: Journal of Narrative Theory* 35, no. 3 (Fall 2005): 357.

53. *Ibid.*, 358.

54. Reina Lewis, *Gendering Orientalism: Race, Femininity, and Representation* (New York: Routledge, 1996), 38.

55. *Ibid.*, 41.

56. Emily A. Haddad, "Bound to Love: Captivity in Harlequin Sheikh Novels," in *Empowerment Versus Oppression: Twenty-first Century Views of Popular Romance Novels*, ed. Sally Goade (Newcastle: Cambridge Scholars, 2007), 45.

57. Lewis, *Gendering Orientalism*, 41.

58. Reid, *The Sheikh's Chosen Wife*, 37.

59. *Ibid.*, 132.

60. Louise Allen, *Virgin Slave, Barbarian King* (Toronto: Harlequin, 2007), 38. Pages provided are ebook page numbers. Further citations will be provided parenthetically.

61. Elizabeth Vaughan, *Warprize* (New York: Tor, 2005), 6–7. Further citations will be provided parenthetically.

62. Castiglia, *Bound and Determined*, 4.

63. *Ibid.*

Patriotism, Passion, and PTSD: The Critique of War in Popular Romance Fiction

Jayashree Kamble

[I]n order to be consequent, the will to read literary or cultural texts as symbolic acts must necessarily grasp them as resolutions of determinate contradictions. [...] The type of interpretation here proposed is more satisfactorily grasped as the rewriting of the literary text in such a way that the latter may itself be seen as the rewriting or restructuration of a prior historical or ideological *subtext*, it being always understood that that "subtext" is not immediately present as such, not some common-sense external reality, nor even the conventional narratives of history manuals, but rather must itself always be reconstructed after the fact.[1]

Romance novels make up a genre in which the familiar narrative impulse of describing a courtship and marriage completely permeates the form it has assumed and becomes the source for regaining the lost Lukácsian "immanence" or "totality of being" in a bourgeois universe.[2] In the process of attaining this end, romance novels also play out the "determinate contradictions" brought on by the clash of incompatible worldviews that often stem from differing economic systems. The warrior romance, in which one or both protagonists are combatants in some form of military or political conflict, stages the determinate contradiction posed by the discourses surrounding two imperatives: the bourgeois social one of preserving companionate marriage and the political one of preserving a version of democracy under advanced capitalism. In attempting to confer a "totality of being" on protagonists who are soldiers via a courtship and marriage that takes precedence over duty to the nation and its defense policy, the warrior romance reconstructs the social unconscious that is in fact a critique of American patriotic aggression.

The primary element of romance fiction that serves as a conduit for this social unconscious is the romance hero — specifically, the hero involved in direct combat or espionage — who serves to document the conflicting twentieth and twenty-first century ethos surrounding these concepts. In reading the genre through the romance hero, I draw on Mikhail Bakhtin, who suggests that mask-wearing by the protagonist of a novel is a result of the form's constant awareness of the demands of the changing present, of the shifting forces of new circumstances that dramatically alter a society's understanding of its own world and that of another. This excess of reality has to be gathered up by the novel hero's multiple masks (unlike the static epic hero who only deals with a fixed unalterable past).[3] It is unsurprising therefore that in a world where global armed conflict is a staple of the media (and thereby a significant filter through which one encounters the world), one of the masks that the romance hero wears is that of the soldier. The trope of the warrior hero is significant because it not only demonstrates the working of the mythology of patriotic heroism in the last century and the current one, but it also participates in an analysis of the actions of soldiers, at home and abroad.

The warrior hero has been tied to the rhetoric of democracy and patriotism to varying extents. He is typically aligned with the capitalist, democratic nation and his devotion to his country (or some symbol of it) becomes the marker of his moral strength. But this mask also embroils the hero in larger questions about the logic and ethics of his work or their effect on him and his immediate world. Some examples of such a hero in novels from the 1980s onward can highlight the conflicts in these texts that reflect an ongoing conversation in the U.S. about war and its consequences.[4] The trope of the hero as warrior includes men who are career soldiers, mercenaries, or spies, individuals engaged in the mission of defending freedom and safeguarding the capitalist, democratic nation's security. In other words, in this face of the romance hero, the genre carries an awareness of the militaristic fervor of the twentieth and early twenty-first century. But in using heroes that range from Vietnam vets to warriors in historical romances (whose plots allegorize America's latest armed conflict), many novels waver between employing a "support our troops" rhetoric and agonizing over the post-traumatic stress and moral impoverishment that soldiers experience as a result of combat. This History — Jameson's conception of the absent cause that we can unearth from narrative — and its social reception can be retrieved through this hero.[5] The warrior is thus evidence of the form's inordinate sensitivity to contemporary reality in the U.S.

The hero dons the mask of the warrior as romance novels attempt to fathom the spikes in a jingoistic nationalism as voiced by the state — and almost on the heels of it, to challenge the alignment of armed aggression with democracy and capitalism that has progressively become a commonplace in the U.S. These debates in the genre range from the 1980s' arguments about Communism to the 1990s' Gulf War rhetoric about rescuing other nations from an individual's tyranny (though at great cost to the American psyche and moral character). Since the 9/11 terrorist attacks, the conversations have begun to include attempts to determine the "enemy" and distinguish between war, paranoia, revenge, and racism. It is in sifting through these competing voices contained by the genre, through the "rifts and discontinuities within the work" that the warrior hero romance can be revealed to be a "heterogeneous and [...] schizophrenic text."[6]

Unable to fully reject the notion of going to war (since political rhetoric in the U.S. has fused American military offensives with the concepts of democracy and freedom), yet aware of its daily fallout, romance novels solve the problem by insisting on the American soldier's right to a long, happy marriage. Put differently, the genre's fundamental narrative imperative of lifelong romantic happiness gives rise to the warrior romance, with its wariness of a patriotic fanaticism that can only result in individual isolation, death, and widowhood. As often as romance novels venerate the hero who fights in the name of the country and of democratic capitalism, they also negate such an ideal, warning against his rampant zeal that may cost the nation its soldier and the man his conscience — and the hero his romantic happy ending. The genre cannot permit threats to its plot arcs of love and life and develops narratives to combat the nationalist imperative that challenges its axiomatic identity. Through such a narration of political history, warrior romances become an "ideological act

[...] with the function of inventing imaginary or 'formal' solutions to unresolvable social contradictions,"[7] namely, the opposition between allegiance to the nation and a personal one to couplehood within the nuclear family.

American category romance series like Silhouette and other imprints in the 1980s and the 1990s have regularly included warrior heroes who are laudable for their selflessness; this attitude views the hero through Cold War ideology's representation of an American soldier as unquestionably well-intentioned. The novels present his dogged dutifulness as commendable but problematic, however, because it contravenes the romantic plot. Nevertheless, despite a condemnation of the government that imposes its poor decisions on him and the worry that the soldier's actions will cost him a happy family life, the belief in the worthiness of American missions retains its force in many cases even up to the early 1990s.

Though few romances even after the first Gulf War directly question the validity of the fight to "free" beleaguered populations and bring them democracy, many reveal the narrative fissures that are better concealed in the 1980s romances. They include a stronger humanist critique of war, returning repeatedly to the diagnosis of Post-Traumatic Stress Disorder.[8] In this critique, the depiction of the soldier-hero is usually sympathetic and commendatory, and the narrative questions war because of the toll it takes on the hero's body, his psyche, and his emotional relationships. The novels decry American offense policy in a back-handed fashion by reviewing its human cost while praising the individuals who must enforce it and whose lives are directly affected by it. But there is also a secondary "rebellious tendency"—to use Herbert Marcuse's term[9]—that emerges in some romances at this time: not just an awareness of the unscrupulousness of any jingoistic, albeit democratic, government, but also a fear that such a government will instill that unscrupulousness into its otherwise heroic military and intelligence personnel. Since the first Gulf War, in other words, the genre has started to reflect the worry that strategies employed against the enemy might be directed against the domestic population as well. The concern over the deterioration of the American soldier's values has become even more evident since the War on Terror in Afghanistan and Iraq. Romances published following 9/11 are increasingly critical of an "us versus them" rhetoric, too. They identify this binary as a threat to the romantic arc of the narratives because it traps the hero in an inconclusive bloodbath. This impulse to challenge U.S. policy is far from universal, however, and always competes with an affirmative impulse that is disinclined to question nationalistic ideology. Warrior romances, whose heroes *are* American heroes in and out of uniform, thus grapple with the patriotism that undermines their happiness.

Many of Linda Howard's romantic-suspense thrillers, which she began writing in the 1980s, are classic examples of warrior romances. In these novels, the critique of war shows itself as a concern over what the heroes are being asked to sacrifice in the line of duty (typically, the bourgeois values of affective individualism and companionate marriage). Novels like these demonstrate a fundamental opposition between two cogs in the mechanism of power established for the preservation of the bourgeoisie—allegiance to the democratic, capitalist state, and allegiance to the nuclear family. For instance, *Diamond Bay* introduces a protagonist who places himself on the line for America's safety in a secret nonstop war.[10] The story of a soldier (though not in uniform), the plot is a fictionalized representation of Cold War rhetoric, venerating espionage as a legitimate defensive strategy. But there is a counter-narrative to this flag-waving in the novel, which stems from the conviction that this ideology is incompatible with marriage and family life and is therefore undesirable.

Rachel Jones rescues Kell Sabin, a Vietnam vet and high-ranking CIA administrator, after he is nearly killed in an ambush by terrorists (whose names mark them as East European). But the plot involves more than the hero staying alive and killing the enemy; it is highly invested in promoting his right to romantic attachments. The latter need injects an aberrant note in the text's endorsement of America's dual mission of defending itself and saving the world. Kell believes that national security, and the safety of his loved ones, must take precedence over his personal happiness; he therefore rejects Rachel's overtures even after he falls in love with her, thus threatening the romance arc of the novel. In this case, the devotion to the nation runs counter to the genre's formal imperative of a happy ending. Kell leaves the woman he loves in obedience to the ideology that national defense is the primary good (though its exact enemies are unclear), but the pull of the heroine and the promise of family soon outweigh that master narrative and Kell eventually gives in to his personal needs and returns to marry Rachel. By the end of the novel, he has distanced himself from active conflict, choosing to focus on marriage and parenthood. It is this narrative, the *raison d'être* of romance novels, which finally triumphs over the one about saving the nation at any cost. The novel may thus be conservative in terms of its conviction in the wedded state as the highest good but its allegiance to the genre actually overrides the claims of the patriotic imperative and thus makes it politically subversive. In this instance, it appears that the genre is more willing to cleave to cultural rather than political bourgeois myth.

A different narrative of the warrior romance novel's "contact with the inconclusive present and future"[11] of United States defense policy emerges in the 1990s through the inclusion of heroes who are not just dangerous to America's enemies but also to its own people. The development shows the genre expressing a "rebellious tendency" that reexamines the nation's "heroism," a departure from its earlier tendency of keeping soldiers unmarked by any suspicion that they are being corrupted by their mission. While possessing significant courage, loyalty, and uprightness, these 1990s heroes employ questionable methods for maintaining domestic security and policing international politics. Driven by their commitment to protecting the country, they act in charming ways while concealing exploitative tactics. It is through such a hero that Linda Howard's *Loving Evangeline* exhibits an awareness of the problematic manner in which the U.S. might conduct its security operations.[12] The narrative is propelled by CEO Robert Cannon's suspicion that the defense software that his company developed for NASA is being sold illegally to another country's affiliates by marina-owner Evie Shaw. The acuity that Robert—who has some influence in the world of intelligence gathering—shows in his business dealings is seen to be doubly fierce when he directs it toward punishing the suspected saboteur of the political system that he is invested in shoring up. Robert enters Evie's world intent on proving her guilt in international espionage and when he finds himself attracted to her, he seduces her without any scruples. In the course of the novel, he inserts himself into her life as her lover while also working on ways to drain her finances so she would be forced to make another sale and get caught in the act. When the two finally learn the truth about each other—Evie finds out about his duplicity just before he discovers she is innocent—Robert appears puzzled by her vehement rejection of him. He wonders why she will not forgive him even though she understands that national security takes precedence over everything, including the loss of the home she was forced to sell: "It wasn't the house. As much as that had hurt her, she had understood his explanation; he had seen that in her eyes. Balanced against national security, her house was nothing."[13] The text suggests here that even unethical acts are acceptable under the ideology to which Robert subscribes since they are undertaken due to the needs of national security. Evie seems to believe this theory as well because her refusal to forgive him is not based on the fact that he is responsible for sabotaging her home and car, foreclosing on her mortgage, and believing that she is a traitor — it is based on Robert's emotional remoteness and inability to declare his love. In light of the very real damage Robert has done to her life and livelihood, Evie's disappointment at his linguistic inadequacy feels jarring and disproportionate, even in a genre that is concerned with love. Evie's unexpected reaction to learning about Robert's treachery is a fissure in the text, a conundrum that works to bring to the fore an ideological flaw and undermines the novel's ostensible primary stance. Her lack of anger at being treated as inconsequential in the face of national security — with its implication of unquestioning subservience to the ideology that American defense supersedes all other values — is odd enough that it serves to highlight the problematic nature of Robert's behavior as an American Hero.[14] Evie's acceptance of the legitimacy of the motivation behind his Machiavellian strategy, and his own lack of repentance is so striking that it actually draws attention to the magnitude of his scheming and calls into question the ideology that breeds such callousness.

In a way, love and mendacity function as shadow narratives for patriotism in novels like *Loving Evangeline*: the narrative of love serves to excuse the patriotic cause (by shifting the focus from the latter's problematic working onto itself), and the narrative of mendacity calls the patriotic cause into question.[15] Though the romance genre by definition must allow the hero and heroine's reconciliation and happy ending, it is far from certain in novels like *Loving Evangeline* if the civilian affected by the actions of the political system (via the hero) has actually acquitted that very system of wrongdoing. In this way, though the novel does not confront the whitewashing of actions done in the name of protecting the country, it contains potential critiques of the actant; the disgust and anger one may feel at his professional ethics is present, albeit displaced onto the stock figure of the emotionally dangerous romance hero in a private drama.[16] Such a narrative tendency in this and other similar novels acts as a counter to the entrenched strategy of pro-national security rhetoric that was developed during the Cold War and has come to dominate the media today. Even if it is not a consciously subversive stance, it is a critical indication of the fact that even a seemingly conservative cultural form like romance fiction is sensitive to the flaws of prevalent ideologies.

Following the First Gulf War, however, the affirmative tendency of internalizing the rhetoric that America must save other nations from a "tyrant" appears to be on an upswing, as seen in Gaelen Foley's *Knight* series (set during the Napoleonic Wars). The setting lends itself to being read as an allegory, with England standing in for the U.S., Napoleon for America's enemies, the liberal Whig party for the less jingoistic Democrats, and the Tories for the Republicans.[17] These historical referents are recounted in terms that conjure the Cold War opposition between the Western and the Soviet bloc but are also infused by more recent events. Much of the series was published after 9/11 — although some of it was probably written before the event, through the lens of Cold War rhetoric — and developed alongside the War on Terror and post–9/11 policies about the "Enemy" who must be destroyed in order to protect the U.S. and other nations. In *Lord of Ice*, Lord Damien Knight — the name attests to his devotion to duty and honor — seems to unequivocally support the fight against "tyranny."[18] An army captain and a patriotic Tory, he dislikes the Whig party because "[it] had protested the expense and duration of the war — as though England could realistically have ignored what was happening just a few miles across the Channel, Napoleon swallowing the Continent whole" (207). As an actant, this hero stages arguments reminiscent of Cold War fears of the Red Scare, which have built up to recent versions of American war ideology (including its dismissal of objections voiced within the country to America's aggression abroad). Damien's alignment with the patriotic cause (as defined by a longstanding rhetoric that supports American military action and despises its opponents) is unmistakable.

At the same time, irrespective of the hero's avowed position, the counter-movement that persistently resists the claims of the holy war of democracy manifests itself in the novel's depiction of his shattered psyche and inability to fulfill his conjugal promises. A decorated veteran against Napoleon's armies, Damien has not survived the war unscathed. When the novel opens in 1814, Napoleon has been imprisoned and Damien is back in England, but having lost several of his soldiers to enemy fire and seen his horse ripped open before him, he suffers from severe mental distress (that a contemporary reader might recognize as PTSD). Tormented by flashbacks, he withdraws from his family, afraid that he is capable of murder at these moments. The fear that he has brought the savagery of war home with him haunts him for much of the novel. In the following excerpt, he recalls how the sound of festive fireworks in London was enough to bring to life his memories of battle:

> For a full five or six minutes, he had lost track of reality, a horrifying state of affairs for a man so highly trained to kill.
> When he thought of how easily he could have hurt someone, it made his blood run cold [18].

Further descriptions of his mental state highlight his trauma:

> He did not want to admit it, but the ghastly dreams of blood and destruction were even more frequent now, as though his addled brain could not unburden itself of its poisons fast enough. The rage in him was a frozen river like the ice-encrusted Thames that wrapped around his property. He knew it was there, but the strangest thing was he could not quite ... feel it. He could not feel much of anything. Six years of combat — of ignoring terror, horror, and heartbreak — had that effect on a man, he supposed [18].

It is no coincidence that PTSD has such a key place in the novel, the condition having taken a greater hold of the cultural imagination after the first Gulf War led to several reports on it.

While Damien's torment gestures toward flaws in the grand narrative of patriotic war and salvationist warfare, Miranda, the ludic heroine, throws into greater relief the one-sided ideology with which Damien has aligned himself. Aided by her affection and comic deflation of his high-mindedness, he marries and turns away from his violent past (thus acknowledging the flaws in his earlier political choices). Even when he receives word of Napoleon's escape from Elba, he initially refuses to rejoin the army as it threatens his dreams of a peaceful married life. (Here, as in Linda Howard's novels, the critique of war rests on how it infringes on soldiers' family lives and upsets their emotional balance.) He changes his mind almost immediately, however, and Miranda reacts to his decision with anger and disbelief, reminding him of the psychological abyss into which the last combat pushed him:

> "Damien, I can't let you do this," she said with forced calm, though her voice trembled. "I cannot lose you. It took all of your strength and my love to find your way out of darkness the last time. I almost lost you to it. If you go back and expose yourself to all that violence and bloodshed again, it might happen all over again, and this time I may not be able to save you."
> "It is my duty."
> "I am your duty! I am your wife! You are my husband, and I need you here!" [386].

Her arguments contest his dogged, even self-destructive, devotion to the nation. He insists that he must set aside his bride and his plans for a bucolic existence, and risk his own life for England's safety (and that of the Continent), explaining, "I have to finish this [...] I fought too hard, sacrificed too much to see that Corsican monster once more on his throne" (386).

The sentiments Damien expresses belong to an American ideological tradition going back at least to World War II, and one that former President George W. Bush frequently invoked, as in this 2005 Veterans Day address:

> Once again, we face determined enemies who follow a ruthless ideology that despises everything America stands for. Once again, America and our allies are waging a global campaign with forces deployed on virtually every continent. And once again, we will not rest until victory is America's and our freedom is secure. [...] Franklin Roosevelt refused to accept that democracy was finished. His optimism reflected his belief that the enemy's will to power could not withstand our will to live in freedom. He told the American people that our liberty depended on the success of liberty in other lands. And he called on Americans to defend that liberty, and millions answered the call. Within four years, America would recover from the devastation of Pearl Harbor. Within four years, we would fight and win a world war on two fronts.[19]

The Veterans Day address is part of a narrative of American patriotism as an ongoing battle between its high ideals and their enemies. It conflates the country's opponents in World War II with contemporary "determined enemies who follow a ruthless ideology that despises everything America stands for," relying on the notion of "freedom" to justify the "global campaign." Despite the presence of similar beliefs in *Lord of Ice*, the knowledge that subscribing to this narrative means a return to trauma haunts the novel. Foley offers love as the antidote to Damien's PTSD, an antidote that enables him to go back to the battlefield; but even devoted aficionados of the genre must doubt the narrative that love can overcome his memory of a line of infantry men getting decapitated by canon fire or of him executing his own soldiers for raping and pillaging the fallen enemy.[20] In including these bleak and shameful incidents, the novel reveals an ambivalence toward its own espousal of noble causes, and is no more than marginally convincing in the claim that Damien's wife (and the children she bears him) can erase his trauma. In fact, Miranda serves as a reminder of the voices that do not accede to the hegemonic drama of the "good" war.

The genre continues to grapple with two seemingly irreconcilable impulses regarding American defense strategy: the inability to directly challenge national policy on America's role in international politics, and an awareness of the popular disenchantment with America's military actions. There are occasional examples of warrior romances that conceive of a symbolic attainment of the goal of American security without the potential sacrifice of morality on the part of actual U.S. armed forces, i.e., of the conscience of the nation itself. The two conditions must be achieved in order to appease both the anxiety that America is a potential terrorist target as well as the constant fear that the nation is protecting itself at the cost of teaching soldiers to adopt the very methods they are publicly fighting against. This ideological conflict is best seen in the work of author Suzanne Brockmann, who began writing novels starring FBI agents, Navy SEALs, and mercenaries in the 1990s, and is a significant contributor to the war/espionage romance. While her protagonists find themselves facing some of the same choices mentioned so far, their allegiance to the state-prescribed versions of truth and justice is highly nuanced.

In *Gone Too Far*, for instance, Brockmann tackles racial profiling as a problematic weapon in America's counter-terrorist arsenal.[21] The novel starts with an ostensible equation of race and criminality in a manner that seems to align with some of the most egregious security screening and intelligence gathering protocols adopted after 9/11, mainly toward men of color. But it then explodes this equivalence by demonstrating the folly of overlooking the homegrown, Caucasian terrorist even as it proves the goodness of an Arab character. This refusal to participate in the flawed mythology of American patriotism is also exemplified in Brockmann's FBI agents and soldiers, who are ethical even when they could use excessive force to get desirable results. In 2007's *Force of Nature*, FBI agent Jules Cassidy refuses to kill a terrorist — the same man who is suspected of having murdered Cassidy's lover — in cold blood, electing to take him into custody instead. Brockmann's work is thus much less an affirmation of predominant political ideology than might be suspected of novels in the warrior romance category.

It is also noteworthy that while Brockmann's novels, too, contain the tactic of countering war rhetoric by either proposing relief for the traumatized hero or questioning the mendacious, ruthless one, neither serves as a way out of an ongoing external conflict. In other words, Brockmann's work participates in a conversation on war without employing romance as a way to avoid examining its ongoing demands on both the physical and psychological wellbeing of all concerned — soldiers and civilians. The character of Max Bhagat, the head of the FBI's counterterrorist branch in Brockmann's *Troubleshooter* series, for instance, is seen struggling with his love for a woman over the course of several books before marrying her. His reluctance to give in to his feelings stems, among other things, from the demands of his job. Unlike Linda Howard's characters, however, Max continues to work in war zones after he is married.[22] In this manner, Brockmann acknowledges the fact that the conflict in which the U.S. is engaged cannot be ignored through the happy end of a romance, and neither can it be left unevaluated. In other words, Brockmann's protagonists retain their attachment to preserving the country's safety but the narratives continue to raise questions about the right-wing policies that promote national paranoia and individual prejudice by naturalizing government-backed bigotry.

There are indications that other romance authors are following her lead and reassessing the defensive project in innovative ways as well. The theme of an on-going fight to keep the world safe for mankind has made its way into the fantasy romance sub-genre, such as in Sherrilyn Kenyon's *Dark Hunter* world, which adds its own twist to the warrior romance. First, these novels address the fear that the good soldier may have lost his moral compass, going as far as mentioning non-combat civilian slaughter; even when they diffuse that fear — a seemingly affirmative move — they cleverly use that revelation to contravene the rhetoric that encourages war against a monolithic Enemy. Instead of constructing a one-sided portrait of their opponents by employing labels that never need questioning, Kenyon's heroes are constantly forced to make individual assessments of the other side, partly because they themselves were once seen as the "Enemy."

The series' premise is that Apollo created a race of superhuman beings called Appolites but later cursed them so that they can only survive past the age of twenty-seven if they consume human souls. To fight these daimons, Artemis has created the Dark Hunters, an army of former humans who were killed in horrific circumstances and cried out for vengeance as they died. In return for their wish, she bargained with them for their souls, and they are bound to serve her, and protect humans. Each novel in the series not only relates a Dark Hunter's love story but also recounts events from his mortal life. The tales are often angst-ridden, even melodramatic, the tone likely stemming from the strain of trying to reconcile the drastically opposed twin narratives of supporting armed conflict and recounting its devastating effects on everyone involved in the fray. As in several examples discussed so far, the series is aware that the two narratives pose a "determinate contradiction" between a "rightful" war and a happy home. It goes a step further, however, and shows via its centuries-old battle-weary characters that an unexamined "us versus them" ideology in support of abstract causes leads to endless conflict and misery. Since the Dark Hunter army is a heterogeneous group, composed of warriors who were often enemies when they were human, each one has never forgotten what it feels like to be unjustly labeled the Other, the hunted. The experience has hampered their romantic happiness and is thus treated by the series as undesirable — for them and for all other characters, including whoever is currently the "Enemy." Its symbolic resolution does not stop at marriage then, suggesting, in addition, the necessity of individualizing each soldier and his struggles — even if he appears to be the "Enemy." In this way, the narratives serve to destabilize the binary of "us and them" perpetuated by the rhetoric of the Cold War and 9/11.

While the previously-discussed novels by Linda Howard and Gaelen Foley do not address the larger ideological problem of accepting received wisdom about who represents a threat in their novels, Kenyon's *Dark Hunter* series acknowledges the narrowness of this view. The soldiers in this war are not allowed to avoid the *man* who exists within the enemy soldier. In fact, the protagonists must reevaluate the warriors on either side of the conflict from time to time. This suggestion that the policy of unilaterally labeling someone an enemy is inadequate, even flawed, is a new approach to recasting the debate on war and American policy in the romance genre.

Though the series does adopt the humanist critique of war seen elsewhere in the exhortation to save the soldier from pain, it expands it to suggest that the soldier on the other side may not be quite as demonic as the hero may have been led to believe. This tendency signals a disagreement with how the Bush administration was reshaping itself and molding public perception on how enemies can be mistreated for the greater good. Even as the narrative in the *Dark Hunter* series seems to be primarily about rescuing the nation's soldiers from being mistaken as monstrous so that they can achieve companionate marriage, it often encompasses figures who have originally been marked as a threat, too. Thus, at different moments, the series introduces a character who the novel's hero first identifies as a villain but is then forced to see as heroic (and deserving of love) as well. In *Kiss of the Night*, for instance, the perception of the character of Urian undergoes a sharp change.[23] As the son of one of the worst enemies of the Dark Hunters, he has been raised to kill the heroes of the series. But he is sympathetically drawn, emerging as someone who is loyal to his own cause (as the heroes are to theirs), and has suffered great losses himself. Once he is released from his one-dimensional status of "enemy," it becomes difficult for the Hunters to objectify him as inhuman, as an abstract idea — like "Terror"— that must be destroyed. In the same novel, some of the Hunters also happen to meet other Appolites that they think of as potential enemies, but who are not in fact evil; they are revealed to have chosen to die at twenty-seven rather than turn daimon. Every such plot element blurs the Hunter/daimon distinction, escaping the polarized rhetoric that divides the world into America and its enemies. In forcing the warrior hero to rethink his own beliefs, the series calls for a politics that seeks and evaluates evidence of wrongdoing rather than blindly believing in labels.

As seen in the examples above, the popular romance genre acts as a resonating membrane that refracts the most vocal ground-swells of popular feeling on the offensive and defensive stances taken by the United States since its establishment as a Superpower — and the quieter challenges to them. In the symbolic act that is each romance text lie conflicting narratives: on one side is a systemic conviction in America's mission to protect capitalist democracy, freedom, human rights, and so on, and on the other, the concern that this mission means using good men as cannon fodder and punishing innocents (thus disturbing the narrative of love and family). In other words, warrior romances often contain the awareness that the conflation of concepts such as patriotism toward a civilized nation and the ruthless methods used to display that patriotism is untenable. This awareness shows itself in the text as the threat of the breakdown of the sanity and moral framework of the individuals that make up the nation's army, and also in the devastation it wreaks on family and the alleged foe. The warrior romance thus contains an unmistakable trace of affirmative culture and government-inspired propaganda, such as in its endorsement of America's need to confront the shadowy enemies of abstract noble causes. But it also contains an undercurrent of doubt and despair at the seemingly endless conflict that this engenders. Even as the genre — especially the *Dark Hunter* series — expresses solidarity with the cry of "Support Our Troops," its utopian longing for a wedding and a family for the soldiers resounds with the desire to "Bring the Troops Home."

NOTES

1. Fredric Jameson, *The Political Unconscious: Narrative as a Socially Symbolic Act* (Ithaca: Cornell University Press, 1981), 80–81.

2. For Lukács's use of the terms "immanence" and "totality of being" in this sense, see Georg Lukács, *The Theory of the Novel: A Historico-Philosophical Essay on the Forms of Great Epic Literature* (Cambridge: MIT Press, 1971), 34, 38, 56, 71, 102. Lukács proposes that forms of art are now burdened with the task of attempting to deal with the loss of a sense of completeness, a result of our fragmented reality; as he explains in a well-known formulation, "The novel is the epic of an age in which the extensive totality of life is no longer directly given, in which the immanence of meaning in life has become a problem, yet which still thinks in terms of totality" (56).

3. Mikhail Bakhtin, *The Dialogic Imagination* (Austin: University of Texas Press, 1982), 36.

4. The genre is less critical of this alignment in the early decades of the twentieth century, with an unquestioning allegiance to nationalistic heroism frequently visible in the romances that were published in the United Kingdom through series like Mills & Boon. But the British myth of the righteous war began eroding in the 1980s, leaving little room for glorifying the hero (despite the initial patriotic zeal that resulted from England's victory over Argentina in the Falklands). The character of the warrior hero does persist, however, in American romance publishing.

5. Jameson, *Political Unconscious*, 100–102.

6. *Ibid.*, 56.

7. *Ibid.*, 79.

8. This condition had been recognized earlier as "shell shock," "battle fatigue," and "combat-stress reaction" in relation to soldiers. Around the time of the Vietnam War, the U.S. Army had refused to recognize veterans suffering from PTSD as deserving of economic compensation, but the situation has now been changed, thanks in part to the diagnosis of PTSD as a psychiatric disorder in the Diagnostic and Statistical Manual of Mental Disorders in 1980 ("Post Traumatic Stress Disorder," Wikipedia, http://en.wikipedia.org/wiki/PTSD.) Widespread references in the media to this condition since then have familiarized the public with its causes (mental and physical trauma) and symptoms (shock, nightmares, depression, anxiety, etc).

9. Herbert Marcuse, *The Aesthetic Dimension: Toward a Critique of Marxist Aesthetics* (Boston: Beacon Press, 1979), 10.

10. Linda Howard, *Diamond Bay* (New York: Silhouette, 1987).

11. Bakhtin, *Dialogic Imagination*, 37.

12. Linda Howard, *Loving Evangeline* (New York: Silhouette, 1994).

13. *Ibid.*, 234.

14. *Loving Evangeline* was first published under the Silhouette Intimate Moments imprint as part of the "American Hero" collection.

15. While there are innumerable instances in which literary texts critique a system through characters who subvert state strategy, *Loving Evangeline* does the same but in a more unusual fashion. By having Robert use mendacity as casually as he does, *Loving Evangeline* actually succeeds in problematizing its own hero — and thus uses him to negate his cause, all underneath its affirmative guise.

16. In deploying the notion of the "actant" I am borrowing again from Jameson's analysis of Heathcliff as a "donor who must wear the functional appearance of the protagonist in order to perform his quite different actantial function," which is to be the "mediator or catalyst, designed to restore the fortunes and to rejuvenate the anemic temperament of the two families" (*Political Unconscious*, 127). An actant here is a character who is nominally a protagonist but allows "an impersonal process, a semic transformation" to occur (127).

17. The historical setting itself is a chronotope for depicting contemporary conflicts, employing embattled spaces from the past. It affords distance from the present, which helps the genre tolerate the strain of the contradictory positions on current defense policy that it finds itself having to acknowledge. But the distance does not override the novels' contact with present circumstances. Bakhtin has identified this acute consciousness of the present, even when the past is being referenced, as one of the defining traits of the novel form. Whether set in Europe (particularly during the Napoleonic wars) or in America (during its various pre-twentieth century conflicts), historical romances are infused with traces of the contemporary debates on espionage and military confrontations.

18. Gaelen Foley, *Lord of Ice* (New York: Ivy Books, 2002). Further references will be provided parenthetically.

19. "President Commemorates 60th Anniversary of V-J Day," The White House, http://www.whitehouse.gov/news/releases/2005/08/200508301.html.

20. The latter is a reference to the 1812 storming of Badajoz during the Spanish campaign in the Napoleonic War. English troops plundered the town for two days before officers brought the rampage under control. Damien is one of these officers and vividly remembers having to hang his men when they abandoned their role of honorable warriors.

21. Suzanne Brockmann, *Gone Too Far* (New York: Ballantine, 2003).

22. Max and Gina meet in *Over the Edge*, struggle with their feelings in *Gone Too Far* and are finally allowed a happy ending in *Breaking Point. All Through the Night*, which was released in 2007, however, documents one of the more dangerous incidents in Max's career following their wedding.

23. Sherrilyn Kenyon, *Kiss of the Night* (New York: St. Martin's Press, 2004).

12

Straight to the Edges:
Gay and Lesbian Characters and
Cultural Conflict in Popular Romance Fiction

Kathleen Therrien

Although scholars have explored the ways in which the romance engages with issues of gender, sexuality, and power, little attention has been paid to gay and lesbian characters within the scholarly work on the romance genre,[1] perhaps because most critics are concerned primarily with issues of power in relationships between men and women and between women and patriarchal culture. The gap may also be due, at least in part, to the fact that although they do exist, there are relatively few lesbian and gay characters in romances; critics working in an already-marginalized field may feel reluctant to focus upon one of its more marginal aspects.[2] I, however, would like to reverse the pattern and explore this textual marginality itself.

The marginality of gay and lesbian characters within romances is not only a product of their relative scarcity. It is also caused by the fact that mass-market romance novels are, *per se*, heterocentric: they revolve around the loves, concerns, and experiences of heterosexual couples. Therefore, although gay and/or lesbian characters may figure prominently in the overall plot of a romance novel, their concerns and relationships are, in the end, peripheral to the heterosexual love plot.[3] Gay and lesbian characters may also, however, be read as literally marginal, in the sense that they function to visibly and explicitly mark out the territory of, and set boundaries upon, cultural conflicts staged within the heterosexual romance narrative.

To see how this works, one crucial element of the romance's internal structure — and of its relationship to and work within culture — must be addressed. Like all texts, romances are shaped, however implicitly, by the contesting ideologies circulating throughout the cultures they are produced in. One voice or set of ideas may dominate any given text, but other, frequently oppositional, voices also weave through it, presenting readers a refracted vision of the complex, conflicted culture wherein the text was produced.[4] The heterosexual romance narrative is, therefore, frequently a site where competing ideologies, refracted and subtextual as they may be, are brought into conflict.[5] But it is also a place where these conflicts may be ultimately, if only imaginatively, negotiated out "safely." That is, some culturally resistant ideas — such as greater agency and/or sexual freedom for women — may be voiced and validated within the world of the text, but some dominant and apparently contradictory ideas, such as the absolute centrality of marriage for all women and the rightness of at least some basic class and gender privileges, may also be validated. Thus, the romance is, as Janice Radway suggests, a "profoundly conflicted form"[6] within which certain forms of power and privilege may be challenged and imaginatively rearranged, while others are reinforced and re-inscribed. Romances are therefore ultimately "both/and" texts — giving with one hand what they take away with the other, they are both resistant and recuperative, yielding some cultural ground while firmly re-establishing other borders.[7]

In some romances, gay and lesbian characters serve as markers of what ideological territory will — or emphatically will *not*— be contested, shifted, or conceded. Texts that fall into the "*not*" category suggest, implicitly or explicitly, that while ongoing ideological conflicts will, and should, shake up some power relations and alter some of the ways that men and women function within culture, other power relations and cultural norms should be left unchanged. Specifically, these texts posit that no matter how much power relations between men and women change, heterosexual partnerships are still and should remain primary and exclusively validated. Gays and lesbians (and their relations with others) function, in these novels, as the markers of how far is "too far," of how much change is dangerous, of the places where ideological negotiations break down. Not surprisingly, strikingly homophobic images and feelings may be evoked and deployed in their depictions. Diana Gabaldon's *Outlander* and Julie Garwood's *Honor's Splendour*, both popular books by best-selling authors, are examples of texts that use genuinely grotesque images of gay characters to mark out forbidden territory — and to attempt to contain the (at least potentially) resistant political energies that they unleash.

In Gabaldon's well-loved novel, the villain, Black Jack Randall, functions as the personified limit of ethical behavior: he is cruel, spiteful, sexually sadistic, and abusive of all of the power he has — personal, physical, and institutional. He is also primarily sexually oriented toward men.[8] As such, he marks the limits of textual challenges to dominant thinking and cultural practice: it may be acceptable to sleep with and even marry someone else when you're already married (as the time-traveling heroine, Claire, does), the text implies, but not to sleep with a person of the same sex; you may make an unconventional partner choice in terms of age (as Claire does in marrying a man who is ten years younger than herself), but not in terms of gender. And while you may be forgiven and reform if you beat your wife (as the hero, Jamie, does once), you cannot be forgiven if you are a sexual sadist — especially if you are male and your victims are men.

It could be argued, as Mary Novak suggests, that "sadism is Randall's main pathology, and his sexual inclination is relatively incidental."[9] Read this way, he may be seen simply as a man who has taken his gender and class privileges too far, thereby validating Claire's challenges to gender norms and making Jamie, who generally does not abuse his culturally-granted power (and who comes to regret it when he does), look progressive by comparison. I would argue, however, that Randall's monstrosity is written as inextricable from his sexuality, so he cannot be dismissed as a psychotic who just happen to be gay. This reading is supported by a scene in which Claire is able to avert Randall's attempt to rape her by refusing to scream: When, instead of screaming, she tells Randall to "[g]et stuffed," her refusal to exhibit fear renders him impotent (379). She then realizes that "[h]e wasn't going to enjoy it *unless* I screamed — and possibly not then" (379). While her initial thought in that passage suggests, rightly, that Randall needs to inflict fear and pain to be sexually satisfied, her follow-up realization suggests that sex with *her*, even if she is terrified and in pain, will not be satisfying to him.

For example, in one of *Outlander's* most disturbing scenes, Jamie, who is a prisoner, offers himself to Randall, who oversees the prison, in order to guarantee Claire's safety; Randall accepts his offer, but with a condition: he tests Jamie's sincerity, as he puts it, by driving a nail through Jamie's already broken hand "with four solid blows" (721) of a mallet. The text immediately pairs this sadism with sexuality: "[Randall] took Jamie's chin in his hand and turned his face up. 'Now kiss me,' he said softly, and lowered his head [...]. Randall's face when he rose was dreamy, eyes gentle and faraway" (721–22). It is clear that the text condemns Randall's abuse and sadism in and of themselves, but the text also obviously links Randall's abuse to his sexuality.

Later, Jamie makes it clear that one of the most disturbing aspects of his imprisonment and abuse is that Randall was able to, as he puts it, make him "r[ise] to his touch" (793). Again, Jamie's feelings of shame and horror at his own response to his abuser are completely understandable in and of themselves. But the facts that he responded physically to another man, and that he recognizes that Randall is, in his own way, in love with him, clearly compound his self-directed, self-destructive disgust.

Randall's abusive sexual behavior and twisted "love" for Jamie certainly help, by comparison, to normalize and even valorize Claire's feelings of attraction and love, which are transgressive since she is married to someone else and is ten years older than Jamie. And Randall's abuses of power, which are explicitly linked to the political project of the English attempt to control Scotland, are set as contrast against Claire's own attempts to re-arrange gendered power relations (and, starting in the series' second novel, to rewrite history itself). The text, then, deploys Randall to validate the behavior of the hero and heroine and to set firm boundaries upon what is and is not acceptable, in terms of behavior and cultural change, in the world of the text.[10]

In Garwood's *Honor's Splendour*, this technique is deployed in a more overtly political way. Like many of Garwood's early historical romances, this text critically explores the position of women in cultures where most power resides in the hands of men. But while the heroine, Madelyne, and the hero, Duncan, struggle over gender-based allocations of agency, power, and privilege, the overbearing and occasionally imperious Duncan always looks heroic in comparison to the text's monstrous villain, Louddon, who could be read as a relatively straightforward and rather progressive depiction of the evils of culturally-sanctioned misogyny. His villainy is, indeed, coded in a manner that reveals a deep and clearly feminist unease with power relations between the sexes: drawing upon the power that he, as a brother and a politically powerful man, has access to, he psychologically terrorizes and physically abuses his step-sister Madelyne,[11] orders a minion to rape a woman who loves him, and uses women as disposable pawns in political games. In the opening scene of the novel, Madelyne bluntly states that she does not believe that Louddon will rescue her from danger because, in his eyes, she has no value.[12]

However, Garwood's other primary means of coding Louddon's villainy is far less progressive. Louddon is clearly pathological, and his sadism and violence are inextricably interwoven with what the novel presents as an additional pathology, his homosexuality. He has been attracted to only two women in the course of his lifetime: his stepmother, whom he killed when she rejected him, and Madelyne, whom he believes "could well be his second chance at proving himself a man" (46)—although such "proving" would be very much against her will. The text therefore tightly connects his lack of "normal," exogamous attraction to women to his violence toward and exploitation of others. His sexuality is also linked directly with his ethical corruption and abuse of political power: Madelyne, for example, knows that "Louddon's hold on the king was said to be unusual; Madelyne had heard it said that they were special friends. [...] Marta [...] had taken great delight in revealing the vileness of their relationship" (22).[13]

The construction of Louddon's character is, in many ways, at odds with the feminist discourses within the text. After all, a text that challenges assumptions about the gendering, sexuality, and access to power of straight women and men might also challenge assumptions about gays and lesbians, or at least seem uneasy with them. Functionally, however, the homophobic discourse deployed in the text serves to recuperate and contain at least some of the critiques leveled by feminism, and is therefore, in the most literal sense of the word, conservative. If one cultural border is shaken, the text promises, another one will be reinforced. This substitution serves to maintain the power of heterosexuality within hegemony, so that even if the power relations and gender roles within heterosexuality are mixed up a bit, straight men, by virtue of being straight, will still have privileged access to power.[14] And while the heroine may be a key agent in this mixing-up of gendered power relations, puzzling Duncan with "the blatant way she disregarded his position" (208) as lord of his manor and literally challenging the traditions of patriarchy by insisting that "[h]is father had been wrong [to rule] rigidly in order to protect his position as lord" (268), her defiance of normative standards looks mild and downright inviting by comparison to Louddon's.

In fact, convention-defying Madelyne even becomes physically ill at learning that men like her stepbrother "could act intimately with other men" (23), a scene which bluntly underscores the text's differing stances toward their transgressive behaviors. Furthermore, cultural change should never, the text implies, celebrate or empower someone like Louddon, for he and those like him will do horrible things with their power. Specifically, they will injure women — thus, the text ultimately pits two struggling groups, women and gay men, against each other; the liberation of women, the text's dynamic suggests, is contingent upon the continued disempowerment of gays.

As these examples suggest, it is clear that some romances use despicable gay and lesbian characters to create margins — to place limits upon the extent or acceptability of resistance and cultural change — and that the sexuality of these characters is seen as problematic, threatening, and unacceptable. This happens often enough that two writers for the All About Romance website, Mary Novak and Candy Tan, wrote online essays criticizing the practice. Novak engages critically with writers' use of what she calls the "Multi-Pervert Gay Villain Cliché," and while she defends Gabaldon, she does suggest that writers lean on homosexuality as a "shorthand" for evilness and pathology, a move that simultaneously presupposes and reinforces cultural validation of that equation.[15] Tan argues against what she calls the "Completely Despicable Gay Über-Villain"[16] trope and notes that the average historical romance is likely to associate non-vanilla non-heterosexuality with "everything evil including (but not limited to) pedophilia, psychosis, misogyny, incest, sociopathy, bestiality, abusive tendencies and bad personal hygiene."[17] She also argues that these portrayals are clearly linked to "the super-conservative values that underlie mainstream romance."[18]

Other romances, however, such as Amanda Quick's *Deception*, Susan Wiggs' *Lord of the Night*, and Emma Holly's *Beyond Innocence* and *Beyond Seduction*, do something very different: they use sympathetic gay and lesbian characters as signposts to mark how much change *must* occur and how far it must extend. Instead of serving as fences or margins that contain the texts' disruptive ideas and protect certain concepts and structures, these characters both mark and occupy boundary positions, or culturally-established margins, that the texts suggest must be transcended—and, in the end, perhaps, eradicated—for substantive and necessary reform to occur.

In Quick's *Deception*, for example, the hero, Jared, struggles with dominant conceptions of masculinity. Scion of an adventurous family, he certainly appears to be an archetypical pirate hero: "From his long, wind-whipped black hair and velvet eye patch to the dagger he wore strapped to his thigh, he was an awe-inspiring sight [...] he radiated a supple sense of strength and masculine grace."[19] But he is much more interested in building up the family fortune and protecting their shipping line than in swashbuckling; his watch and his appointment journal are his weapons of choice in dealing with a world he often finds "chaotic and unstable" (18). His family, however, berates him for not carrying on their tradition of derring-do: his father, Magnus, calls him "a dull man o' business," and when Jared replies, "I am a dull man of business, sir," Magnus retorts, "It's enough to make a father weep" (19). Though he has effectively assumed the sanctioned role of "man of business," Jared still feels that he is, on some level, a failure as a man because he does not also match another culturally-dominant and (literally) patriarchally-valorized vision of masculinity.[20]

Jared has also internalized the judgments cast by his former fiancée, Demetria, who rejected his physical affection. Although he caught her in the arms of a female friend, he does not understand that she is a lesbian, a woman-identified and woman-loving woman, not a straight woman who rejected him and only turned to another woman because he was not macho or sexy enough. This misunderstanding leads him to feel very ambivalent about sex and himself in general: "The few [affairs] he had had over the years had left him feeling restless and dissatisfied. He suspected his partners had felt very much the same. As Demetria had taken pains to point out, once one got past his title and expectations, there was nothing very interesting left to discover" (47).

Demetria is certainly not kind to Jared, but he is not aware that part of her anger stems from her resentment at being trapped in an even more confining role than he is. As a "nearly penniless" (243–44) woman in a patriarchal, class-based society, and a lesbian in a straight world, Demetria does not even have the hero's gender- and class-based prerogative to turn away from convention and proceed, albeit uneasily, in her own way. Instead, she attempts to negotiate the competing pressures she faces and at least secure financial security, freedom from heterosexual relations, and a cover for her ongoing affair with her lover Constance by marrying a wealthy, much-older man who, according to rumor, "cannot even consummate his recent marriage" (149)—a situation which still makes her sex life a scandalous public spectacle.

The interconnection between homophobia, misogyny, and oppressive gendered expectations of men is shown perhaps most clearly in one of the ironies Jared faces: many in the *ton* know that he found his fiancée with a lover, and they wonder why he did not call the third party out for a duel. Demetria's brother, among others, think that he is weak and cowardly—unmasculine—for not taking to the field of honor. The lover, however, was Constance, a woman, and if Jared did call her out, Constance and Demetria would be exposed as lesbians within a highly homophobic society—and the already-insecure Jared would be exposed as a man who, in his society's eyes, was so "unmanly" that he lost his fiancée to a woman; as Constance tells Olympia, "It is difficult enough for a man to discover his intended with another man. It is even more awkward for him to discover her with another woman" (377). In the perfect storm generated at the intersection of oppressive dominant ideologies, everyone loses.

Unlike Jared, the novel's heroine, Olympia, has no trouble understanding and accepting Demetria and Constance's relationship, for she herself was raised by her lesbian aunt and her partner, "blossom[ing] beneath the gentle nurturing she [...] received from Aunt Sophy and Aunt Ida" (91). She recognizes the young women's romance without ado, saying, "It has been obvious to me from the first that you and Demetria enjoy a special friendship, just as my aunts did" (377). The positive language she uses — "enjoy" and "special friendship" — is resonant with the positive experience she had growing up.[21] Olympia is able to draw upon her past with her aunts to help both Jared and Demetria come to terms with their past — and their present; in the process, nearly all of the relationships in the text reach a more comfortable state.

In fact, the resolution of the romance plot is actually contingent upon recognition of and resistance to homophobia, both as an abstract concept and as an ideological force that informs interpersonal (and intrapersonal, in Jared's case) relations. The text insists that the central heterosexual couple can never be truly happy until they understand, have made peace with, and can comfortably co-exist with the primary lesbian character, and the hero's own self-acceptance is linked to his acceptance of his former love's lesbianism. The culturally-sanctioned homophobia that marginalizes and oppresses the lesbian characters is represented as part and parcel of the ideologies of gender and power that cause problems for the hero and heroine; challenging one, of necessity, involves challenging the other.

This process may be connected to what Annamarie Jagose posits as a key element of the gay liberation movement: "Gay liberation advocated a radical transformation of social values, arguing that gay liberation would be secured only after sex and gender categories had been eradicated."[22] *Deception* certainly does not go so far as "eradication" in its challenges to dominant ideologies of sex and gender. The process of Jared's self-recognition, for instance, may be seen less as a rejection of masculine gender roles *per se* than as a rejection of the idea that only certain categories of masculinity have value[23] — and that those categories are mutually exclusive (that is, that one cannot be methodical, brave, and nurturing at the same time). But the novel does suggest, in an intriguing mirror-image inversion of the process that Jagose describes, that the liberation of straight persons from at least the most stringent restrictions imposed by gender categories will be secured only when gays and lesbians are liberated (or, at the very least, when their oppression is recognized and their right to liberation acknowledged). If "gayness" and "straightness" are, in fact, mutually constitutive categories, then this makes perfect sense; a change in one term will by necessity change the other, and, conversely, one cannot change if the other remains static. In this text, then, the lesbian characters clearly do not function as the boundary of change that must not be crossed; rather, in the text's logic they mark the boundary that must be crossed if true progress on at least some issues is to be made.[24]

In its exploration of gender, sexuality, and masculinity, *Deception* also, interestingly, shies away from addressing issues of male homosexuality. But Susan Wiggs's *Lord of the Night* does, and in doing so presents an even more explicit challenge to elements of dominant gender and sexual ideology. While investigating a murder (which involves castration), the hero, a powerful Venetian official named Sandro, automatically assumes that the victim was killed by his male lover, Florio; after all, Sandro thinks, Florio is "strange" and "sick,"[25] so he must be capable of killing. He speculates that "Florio and Moro might have had a lovers' spat. Florio, already ambivalent about his own manhood, was possessed by a sick impulse to emasculate his lover" (39). Sandro comes to change his views, however, through his interactions with Laura, the heroine.

Sandro, at first, simply cannot accept or understand the fact that Laura and Florio are friends; when Florio says of the deceased, "I loved him," the shocked investigator "glanced sharply at Laura; surely she could not understand this. Yet she sat gazing in heartfelt sympathy at her strange friend" (38). Sandro is even more shocked when he learns that Laura underwrites her budding career as a painter by working as a courtesan. He informs her, imperiously, that she should "find [her]self some likely merchant" (47) and marry, dismissing her argument that she wishes to support herself and her career by snarling, "How can you be a painter if you have no self-respect?" (47). Sandro simply assumes that all "deviant" sexual behavior is pathological and that all who engage in it must have internalized some form of self-hatred. In this light, the scene in which Florio and Laura first respond to Sandro's questioning is quite powerful: before the eyes of a civic official who is empowered to pronounce judgments of "right" and "wrong" upon actions, Florio and Laura express their affection and love for each other (and Florio his love for his partner), refusing to accept the marginalized, pathologized positions that Sandro and others would assign them to.

Sexuality is not the only grounds for marginalization and injustice within this novel, however. It is remarkably explicit in both its depiction of power imbalances based upon gender and class and its insistence that such arrangements are ultimately destructive both to individuals and communities. For example, of Laura's struggle to be accepted as an artist by the Venetian Academy, the painter Titian says bluntly, "My lord, there is nothing more frightening to men than a woman who is their superior" (79). And the damage wrought by behaviors licensed by classist and misogynist ideologies is quite literally embodied in the character of Magdalena, who was actually born male. Her mother, Celestina, had become pregnant by the future Doge, who then left the city to go to war; when she approached her lover's father for help, he arranged for her to be raped by "the Trentuno [, ...] the sons of the noblest clans of la Serinissima and beyond" (180). Celestina was so psychologically damaged by the experience that she castrated her infant son, raised him as a daughter, and molded her into a murderous instrument of vengeance.

Celestina had been assaulted because the old Doge considered a union between her and his son unsuitable and wished to inflict "punishment" upon her (336). Laura, too, is nearly assaulted by her generation's version of the gang, and in both cases the attacks are arranged by men who wish to punish women for what they consider violations of acceptable conduct. The text therefore brings together two forms of "justice" that are actually injustice: Sandro's assumptions about and near-arrest of Florio (because he is different from what he is, according to dominant norms, supposed to be) are held parallel to the vigilante Trentuno's assumptions about and assaults upon women[26] (because they are different from what they are, according to dominant norms, supposed to be).[27] Homophobia is held parallel to misogyny; classism is certainly also an element in both cases. And just as it suggests that one element of this triad cannot be combatted or addressed without the others, for all are ultimately products of marginalizing hegemonic ideologies that serve to protect arrangements of power, the text also implies that change must take place both in institutions and "on the street," for the two are mutually reinforcing and rooted in the same discourses and ideologies.

The resolution of the romance plot hinges upon Sandro's recognition that his assumptions about sexuality, power, gender, and class may not be true, and in illustrating his learning process, the text weaves women's rights and gay rights inextricably together.[28] Like *Deception, Lord of the Night* is a fraught text; its rather radical positions on sexuality, gender, and class are counterweighted with what is, in many ways, a very conventional alpha-male, older-man plot that ultimately valorizes at least some power and class structures. In the end, for example, Sandro does not need to give up his position as a nobleman because he has married a commoner; Laura is, instead, named a "True and Special Daughter of the Republic" (342) by the Doge, a rather jarring dodge that enables the text to re-contain its critique of class and power by suggesting that allowing "special" individuals upward mobility is the solution to class-based oppression. But it does not back away from the position that heterosexuals need to change their views of gays just as the hero (and dominant culture as a whole) needs to change his view of the heroine and women in general. In fact, the text suggests, one is not really possible without the other.

A more recent romance suggests even more forcefully that gay rights must be established and maintained even as it adheres to some of the most traditional, conservative elements of the romance genre — and employs some of its most common, even clichéd, plot elements, such as the high-handed alpha male/penniless heroine trope. In Emma Holly's *Beyond Innocence*, the hero, Edward, tries to manipulate the heroine, Florence, to his own ends, specifically by trying to get her to marry his brother Freddie — who needs to get married fast because he was caught in his bedroom with one of his footmen and is being threatened with exposure and legal prosecution.

Edward loves and wants to protect his brother, but he has difficulty accepting the idea that Freddie is genuinely attracted to and sexually oriented toward men. Assuming that Freddie's dalliance with the footman was a one-time aberration in an otherwise straight life, he reacts strongly when Freddie suggests that it wasn't:

> "It's the calves," [Freddie] said in a weak attempt at humor. "Never could resist a man with a good pair of legs."
> Something strained in Edward's chest. He sat, abruptly weak in the knees. "Freddie, if I believed for an instant you meant that, I'd slit my bloody wrists."
> Freddie's head came up, clearly startled by his brother's tone. [...] "'Course I don't mean it," he said. "You know me. Can't pass up a quip. We'll call it temporary insanity."[29]

Freddie's family and his friends, positioned within very homophobic ideologies, have trouble seeing him as a kind, strong, decent, good-humored *gay* man, and they struggle to recognize and accept his homosexuality as inextricably part of his identity.

Although Freddie denies his physical attraction to men with good legs in an attempt to salvage his relationship with his brother, the text itself does not marginalize or gloss over Freddie's sexuality. He is not portrayed merely as a cuddly, asexual teddy bear of a fellow, as much as other characters (such as his brother) — and, perhaps, some readers — might like to see him that way. Freddie's sexuality is instead presented as a source of erotic pleasure that does not need to be hidden, denied, or condemned. His aunt, for example, has some trouble accepting the fact that he is in fact a gay person (as opposed to a straight man who had a moment of "temporary insanity"), but she doesn't blanch at his sexual activities *per se*: When Edward asks if everyone is, in fact, calling Freddie "the footman's scourge," Aunt Hypatia says, "Well, I can think of one footman who isn't. From what I hear, they were having a lovely time before that wretched beermaker burst in. [...] I've seen things a good deal more shocking than young Freddie's peccadillo. Done them, for that matter."[30]

Freddie's sexuality is also a key part of his own passionate romance sub-plot: he falls madly in love with Nigel, the family steward, and the scene where Florence catches them kissing is written as erotically and attractively as any of the straight love scenes. While this is stunningly unusual within the genre, it's not at all surprising given Holly's previous work: she has written erotica for the Black Lace series, and much of it, such as the novel *Ménage*, features male characters together in erotically written, explicit sex scenes.

Ultimately, this text ends up reversing the pattern seen in the "Gay Uber-Villain" romances discussed previously: while those texts used "multi-pervert gay villain clichés" to contain challenges to dominant ideologies and power relations between the sexes, *Beyond Innocence* uses a set of alpha-male plot clichés to contain its challenges to traditional ideologies of sexuality — of which, not coincidentally, there are many. The gay men are certainly not the only ones having passionate and interesting sex outside of marriage in this novel. And while the novel implicitly argues for greater sexual freedom for all, like *Deception*, it also champions the importance of family and emotional commitment — for all. The gay couple end up as happily partnered as the straight couple; in the novel's conclusion Florence and Edward bring their young daughter to visit Freddie and Nigel's home. In this text, contrary to dominant conservative assumptions, homosexuality is not in opposition to or dangerous to romance or families; instead, it builds relationships and is only divisive and problematic when heterosexuals marginalize and condemn it.[31]

In fact, one could argue that the novel is actually quite conservative in the sense that it deploys not only the traditional alpha-male plot but also the traditional teleology of romance to contain its challenges to dominant ideologies of sexuality. In other words, while one set of cultural norms — those that stigmatize and condemn sexuality that is not straight, marital, and purely vanilla — are challenged, another set — those that valorize some traditional gender norms and monogamous, long-term partnerships as the one and only true happy ending for everyone — are re-invoked and valorized. Change will only go so far.

Holly's novel *Beyond Seduction*, however, goes further. Nic, the hero, is a painter (and reluctant marquis) whose friends include two painters, Sebastian and Evangeline, who, Nic says, "consider what they have an 'open' marriage."[32] Nic's connection to them and their bohemian community is multivalent; he is a fellow artist, and he too delights in rejecting dominant mores. But he is also linked to Evie and Sebastian by deeper ties, both sexual and emotive. While the text does not describe his sexual activity with men *per se*, it makes it clear that Nic enjoyed and was comfortable with his unconventional sexual relationships, and he does not downplay or apologize for them. He tells the heroine, Merry, "Yes, we were all intimate together" (218), and when Sebastian proposes a *ménage à quatre*, saying of himself and Evie, "Hell, Nic, we both think she's adorable" (223), Nic is not outraged or defensive. And while he has clearly shifted his primary orientation to monogamous heterosexuality, he does not attempt to efface the other facets of his sexuality. For example, after he and Merry are separated, Sebastian makes him an offer:

> "Evie and I thought that you might be in need of entertainment. We met a young tenor at the opera the other night. He came for dinner. An adventurous lad." He cocked his head. "Perhaps you'd like to help us make him sing."
> The flush that moved through Nic's body was more reflex than desire. With a sense of detachment, he let himself remember how it was to tangle too many limbs to count, to be mindless flesh, to forget oneself in drunken laughter and faceless warmth.
> Unfortunately, he also remembered how disconcerting it was to catch a stranger's eye in the throes of pleasure, and how empty one could feel when the pleasure drained away [253].

Nic's rejection of Sebastian's offer is based on his emotional state and desire for deeper intimacy with his heroine, not his attitude toward the sexual situation *per se*. Similarly, when Sebastian offers to "[k]eep it just the three of us" (253) instead, realizing that Nic needs connection with people who love him, Nic's refusal is based on his fear of "stepping into a pit of [emotional] quicksand" (253). "Too old for those games" (253), he says, referring to the volatile dynamics of Seb and Evie's relationship, not the sex.

Clearly, the text challenges the assumption that monogamous, heterosexual marriage is the only type of relationship wherein sexuality can be a healthy, positive element, but it also reinforces the idea that sex is best when connected to emotional closeness. In turn, it also suggests that sex can add an element of additional intimacy and connection to both same-sex and opposite-sex friendships. For example, though he is no longer sleeping with him, Nic treats Sebastian with affection and physical tenderness; when he and Sebastian reminisce, he "brushe[s] his friend's jaw with the back of his fingers" (156). He also explicitly tells Merry that when he came to London after the death of his best friend (for which he feels responsible), Sebastian and Evangeline "welcomed [him] back to the human fold" (218) and recalls that after his involvement with them, an affair with another bohemian friend, Anna, "had made him sane" (218). For Nic, sex, affection, and friendship are inextricably linked, and when he recalls his involvement with his three friends, he thinks, "A love that generous, that lifesaving, should never cause regret" (156).

Like *Deception*, *Lord of the Night*, and *Beyond Innocence*, *Beyond Seduction* contains characters whose sexual orientation must be accepted in order for true and necessary change to occur. In Nic's case, only by knowing himself, accepting himself, and making willful, personal, non-socially-dictated choices about his own sexuality is he able to heal his wounds and build functional, emotionally stable relationships with Merry, his mother, and his half-brother. The same dynamic holds true for the heroine, Merry, who discovers through the course of her relationship with Nic that her own sexuality is far from vanilla: she is comfortable posing nude for a painting, and she thoroughly enjoys having sex with Nic on a balcony. When they are finished she realizes that Sebastian has been watching them: "Her body tightened and heated, a response she could not control. She might hate herself for it but she could not reason it away" (206). Her flash of self-hatred is quickly replaced by acceptance and realization, though: "Attraction doesn't matter, she thought. It doesn't dictate what I do" (207). Like Nic, she recognizes that she can claim ownership of her sexuality, acknowledging it in all of its complexity, enjoying even some of its unexpected and/or culturally-deplored elements, but also making thoughtful, constructive choices about how she deploys it.

Her acceptance of her own sexuality, in turn, allows her to understand and accept others: while she is not sexually interested in women, for example, she is "more intrigued than offended" (223) when Sebastian says that he and Evie both find her appealing. She tells Nic that the fact that he is "a man who has no limits" (218) makes him, in her eyes, admirable, attractive, and "very brave" (218). Merry's linking of sexual self-acceptance and bravery here is crucial, for she herself uses unconventional sexual choices—becoming the nude subject, then mistress, of a notorious painter—in order to make agentive, resistant choices in the face of power. She "ruins" herself to avoid marrying a good friend at her mother, Lavinia's, coercive insistence. Interestingly, Merry refuses him simply because, in her eyes, he is a friend, not a lover, and she does not want to marry without love or create a partnership that will be emotionally unequal and eventually cause suffering. She values marriage and commitments, and the process of discovering her sexuality and accepting others' intensifies this: after hearing that Sebastian and Evie are actually married, she thinks, "Marriage was a promise to forsake all others. Or it ought to be. She hadn't realized that she believed that but she did" (202). For Merry, ultimately, discovering and accepting variants of sexuality, both her own and others', is part of the process of creating a self and relationships that are not based upon or dictated by economics, social norms and expectations, and/or gendered, hierarchical power arrangements.

This process is highlighted by the way in which Merry's trajectory is contrasted to her mother's. Lavinia had once engaged in an extramarital affair with Althorp, a sadistic, arriviste friend of her husband's. When he threatens to reveal the affair, Lavinia's fear of exposure leads her to acquiesce to his demands that she force Merry into marrying his son. Exposure of the affair itself, however, is not the only thing Lavinia fears. She and Althorp had a BDSM relationship, and her dread of public knowledge of that element of the relationship is clearly linked to her reluctance to truly see and accept her own sexuality: when he says, "I see you've forgotten how you trembled with excitement when I made you crawl to me on your knees, how you moaned when I took you so forcefully you'd be tender inside for days. [...] You were made for me, though you haven't the courage to admit it" she thinks, "It wasn't true. She would not let it be. He was sick and depraved and she was nothing like him!" (271).

Filled with self-loathing, Lavinia lies to and about her family, exploits her culturally-sanctioned parental authority, and alienates Merry, all in an attempt to keep her sexuality a secret. But her sexuality *per se* is not presented as the problem; rather, the text suggests that it is the marginalization and condemnation of BDSM sexual desires and practices, combined with a double standard that judges women's sexual activity far more harshly than men's, that creates the fear that drives Lavinia. Her inability to accept herself—her fear of being what she sees as "sick and depraved"—and her knowledge of how others would judge her lead her to make decisions that nearly destroy her family. Therefore, although she is the villain of the story, Lavinia is presented quite differently from Randall and Louddon: her sexuality is not both a marker and an element of her villainy and therefore to be condemned; rather, it is condemnation of her sexuality that, at least in part, leads to her corruption and damaging choices.

In their own way, then, these LGB-positive romances may be read as truly "conservative." They ultimately center upon the creation and maintenance of healthy, functional, heterosexual relationships, and they suggest that to protect—to conserve—these relationships, recognizing and combating homophobia is crucial, since, they argue, all ideologies that license unequal access to and abuse of power are a) interconnected and b) vectors of destruction that threaten both individuals and stable, long-term, monogamous relationships—and families in general. In fact, these novels suggest that same-sex and heterosexual partnerships may ultimately best exist in a symbiotic dynamic. As conservative writer Andrew Sullivan notes, "The image of two men or two women in a marriage could, I think, be a vivid symbol to many heterosexuals of what true equality in a marriage could be about, and it could help many heterosexual women further realize their dignity and equality in a relationship of mutual love and commitment. [...] I don't exactly see this as a social or human disaster."[33]

In his essay "Straight with a Twist," Cal Thomas argues that "any large-scale reconfiguration [of heterosexual identification] is unlikely without the participation of those women

and men who are themselves the putative subjects of heteronormative paradigms of identification and desire but who, for whatever reason, are 'able to relish, learn from, or identify
with' queers and queer theory."[34] I would argue, at the risk of oversimplifying his larger
argument, that a version of this pattern holds within the gay-positive romances under discussion here: that learning from, acting in solidarity with, and, perhaps, empathizing or
identifying with gay and lesbian characters help the heterosexual characters learn to recognize
and resist not only homophobia but also the inequities within dominant ideologies of gender
and heterosexual relationships. The heroes' and heroines' encounters and negotiations with
gay and lesbian characters — and, as in Nic and Merry's cases, with their own sexuality —
finally make visible to them their own location, and participation, in patterns of oppression
and reveal the damage it can cause to self, others, and relationships, ultimately freeing them
to make choices that lead to strong, monogamous partnerships. In the ideological balancing
act that lies at the heart of the romance, then, the most seemingly radical novels may be,
in the end, the most "old-fashioned" of all.

NOTES

I would like to thank the Middle Tennessee State University Faculty Research and Creative Activity
Committee for their support, which helped me in the process of revising what was initially a conference
paper (presented at the Popular Culture Association annual meeting in 2002) into an essay. I would also
like to thank Will Thomas, Alfred Lutz, and Elvira Casal for their support and feedback at various points
during this project.

1. For example, Pamela Regis' *A Natural History of the Romance Novel* (Philadelphia: University of Pennsylvania Press, 2003) features a full chapter on Jayne Ann Krentz, who also writes as Amanda Quick, and
examines *Deception* (which will be discussed here) at some length. However, Regis does not discuss the lesbian characters in that text, despite the fact that they play a prominent role in the novel.

2. Intriguingly, there has been thoughtful discussion of gay and lesbian characters in the para-academic
space of some online forums, such as All About Romance (http://likesbooks.com) and the Teach Me Tonight
blog (http://teachmetonight.blogspot.com).

3. It could, of course, be argued that, whether they are actually present in the text or markedly absent
from it, marginal gay and lesbian figures are actually essential to the construction or conceptualization of
any straight narrative, since, as many critics and theorists have pointed out, the two terms (heterosexual/
homosexual, center/margin) may be seen as mutually constitutive. "[H]eterosexuality," as Diana Fuss points
out, "typically defines itself in critical opposition to that which it is not: homosexuality"; she also argues
that "[t]he philosophical opposition between 'heterosexual' and 'homosexual,' like so many other conventional binaries, has always been constructed on the foundations of another related opposition: the couple
'inside' and 'outside'" ("Inside/Out," *Inside/Out: Lesbian Theories, Gay Theories*, ed. Diana Fuss [New York:
Routledge, 1991], 1).
Furthermore, Alexander Doty notes, "I want to suggest that within cultural production and reception,
queer erotics are already part of culture's erotic center, both as a necessary construct by which to define the
heterosexual and the straight (as 'not queer'), and as a position that can be and is occupied in various ways
by otherwise heterosexual and straight-identifying people" (*Making Things Perfectly Queer: Interpreting
Mass Culture* [Minneapolis: University of Minnesota Press, 1993], 3–4).

4. Drawing particularly upon the work of Raymond Williams and Michèle Barrett, I have chosen to use
the term "refractive" for the relationship between text and culture because while there is a clear relationship
between texts and the culture within which they were produced, this relationship is neither simple nor
direct (reflective); "refraction" suggests that, like a beam of light passing through water or a lens, ideas and
forces "passing through" a novel can be seen — but not in their original form. See Michèle Barrett, "Ideology
and the Cultural Production of Gender," in *Feminist Criticism and Social Change: Sex, Class, and Race in
Literature and Culture*, ed. Judith Newton and Deborah Rosenfelt (New York: Methuen, 1985), 65–85.

5. John Storey's discussions of hegemony may provide a differently-oriented, but useful, perspective on
and exploration of this dynamic: for instance, in his second edition of *Introduction to Cultural Theory and
Popular Culture* (Athens: University of Georgia Press, 1998), he notes that from a neo–Gramscian perspective,
"Popular culture [...] is a terrain of exchange" (14) in which dominant and oppositional cultural forms and

ideologies are negotiated—a "site of struggle between the forces of 'resistance' of subordinate groups in society, and the forces of 'incorporation' of dominant groups in society" (13–14).

6. Janice Radway, *Reading the Romance: Women, Patriarchy, and Popular Literature* (1984; rpt. Chapel Hill: University of North Carolina Press, 1991), 14.

7. Though his argument focuses more upon the preservation of hegemonic equilibrium than mine does, I have found Raymond Williams' work in "Base and Superstructure in Marxist Cultural Theory" very useful in conceptualizing this process: for instance, he posits that "[t]he arts [...] contribute to the dominant culture and are a central articulation of it. [...] They express also and significantly some emergent practices and meanings, yet some of these may eventually be incorporated, as they reach people and begin to move them. [...] In this process, of course, the dominant culture itself changes, not in its central formation, but in many of its articulated features" (In *Rethinking Popular Culture: Contemporary Perspectives in Cultural Studies*, ed. Chandra Mukerji and Michael Schudson [Berkeley: University of California Press, 1991], 419–20).

8. Diana Gabaldon, *Outlander* (New York: Dell-Bantam Doubleday Dell, 1991). Further references will be provided parenthetically. Mary Novak states that Gabaldon herself has said that Randall is bisexual, but the texts suggest that his primary orientation is clearly toward men ("The Multi-Pervert Gay Villain Cliché," At the Back Fence Issue 106, *All About Romance*, 15 November 2000, http://www.likesbooks.com/106.html).

9. Novak, "The Multi-Pervert."

10. Gabaldon's portrayal of problematic same-sex orientation is reinforced by a more minor character, Sandringham, who is described by the Jamie and his friends as an "arse-bandit" who repeatedly attempted to corner and rape the hero when he was young and who repeatedly traded political favors for sex with other men (*Outlander*, 482–86). His sexuality is clearly linked to his corruption and abuses of power, although he is not nearly as villainous as Randall, and when Jamie tells the story of his pursuit he treats it like a joke.

To be fair, Gabaldon's series does contain one positive gay character, John Grey, a very decent man who ends up being a friend and ally of Jamie and Claire. (He even eventually gets three mystery novels of his own.)

11. Though Madelyne initially believes that she is Louddon's half-sister, she later discovers that she is, much to her delight, not related to him by blood at all.

12. Julie Garwood, *Honor's Splendour*, (New York: Pocket Books, 1987), 17. Further references will be included parenthetically.

13. The text's depiction of King William II is slightly more sympathetic; Duncan, for instance, has some respect for him even though he "knew well enough what the king's preferences were [and] had guessed long ago that Louddon was more than a clerk in William's court" (257–58).

14. Diana Fuss' "Inside/Out" offers a number of useful insights for understanding some of the complex dynamics in romances that deploy the gay-villain theme; for example, she notes that "heterosexuality secures its self-identity and shores up its ontological boundaries by protecting itself from what it sees as the continual predatory encroachment of its contaminated other, homosexuality" (2) and explores the fraught ways in which homo- and heterosexuality constitute and challenge each other.

15. Novak, "The Multi-Pervert."

16. Candy Tan, "The Completely Despicable Gay Über-Villain," At the Back Fence Issue 106, *All About Romance*, 15 November 2000, http://www.likesbooks.com/106.html.

17. For a very different take on a similar phenomenon, see Gayle S. Rubin's discussion of the ways in which non-mainstream sexual practices are judged and marginalized in "Thinking Sex: Notes for a Radical Theory of the Politics of Sexuality," *The Lesbian and Gay Studies Reader*, ed. Henry Abelove, Michèle Aina Barale, and David M. Halperin (New York: Routledge, 1992), 3–44. Of particular interest here is her argument that "[l]ow-status sex practices are vilified as mental diseases or symptoms of defective personality integration. In addition, psychological terms conflate difficulties of psycho-dynamic functioning with modes of erotic conduct. They equate sexual masochism with self-destructive personality patterns, sexual sadism with emotional aggression, and homoeroticism with immaturity. These terminological muddles have become powerful stereotypes that are indiscriminately applied to individuals on the basis of their sexual orientations" (12).

18. Interestingly, Tan notes that she found the Über-Villain that pushed her over the edge while reading a novel about "freeing and exploring one's sexuality"; this supports, I think, my argument about the marginal/recuperative function of many gay romance villains ("Completely Despicable").

19. Amanda Quick, *Deception* (New York: Bantam, 1993), 25. Further references will be included parenthetically.

20. See the opening chapter of Gail Bederman's *Manliness and Civilization: A Cultural History of Gender*

and Race in the United States, 1880–1917 (Chicago: University of Chicago Press, 1995) for a very helpful discussion of the construction and negotiation of multiple (and often competing) codes of "manliness" and "masculinity."

21. In fact, the text pointedly counterposes their parenting against the actions of several of Olivia's culturally-coded "normal," straight relatives. When her Uncle Dunstan served as her guardian, for instance, he "followed her into a room and closed the door [...] telling her how pretty she was and [...] reach[ing] for her with his great sweaty hands" (90). His wife, responding to Olympia's screams, "said nothing, but the next morning, Olympia found herself on her way to the next relative on the list" (90).

22. Annamarie Jagose, *Queer Theory: An Introduction* (New York: New York University Press, 1996), 59.

23. Jagose also quotes Steven Seidman's statement that "[l]iberation politics aimed at freeing individuals from the constraints of a sex/gender system that locked them into mutually exclusive homo/hetero and feminine/masculine roles" (59).

24. *Deception* is not the only Quick novel featuring sympathetic lesbian and gay characters. In *Seduction* (New York: Bantam, 1997), for instance, the hero's aunt Fanny and her partner, Harriette, are depicted as a loving couple who are accepted by the hero and heroine. At one point the two older women even provide pointed commentary on assumptions about sexuality. They discuss the memoirs of The Grand Featherstone, a notorious courtesan who disparages the sexual performance of her lovers:

"According to Featherstone, most men are rather boring in bed," Fanny said. "Thus far she has not had a good word to say about any of her admirers."

"Perhaps the more interesting lovers have paid the blackmail she is said to be demanding in order to be left out the *Memoirs*," suggested a young matron.

"Or perhaps men, in general, simply do not make interesting lovers," Harriette observed calmly. "More tea, anyone?" [106].

25. Susan Wiggs, *Lord of the Night* (New York: HarperPaperbacks, 1993), 39. Further references will be included parenthetically.

26. While the Tretuno is not an "official" institution of the city, it is recognized as a tradition (181) by all of the characters and carries the immunity granted by the participants' class status.

27. Madgelena may seem to function as a boundary figure here: she may be read as suggesting that all unjust "justice"—in this case, vigilantism—must be rejected, even when it is committed in response to injustice; resistance can only go so far. However, I would argue that she also serves as a marker of the necessity of social change: the violence against women perpetrated by the men of the Trentuno ultimately also devolves upon men—Celestina's son and the rapists and their families themselves—so, in the end, everyone, male and female, suffers from culturally-sanctioned violence.

28. As Karin Quimby suggests in her reading of the popular sitcom *Will & Grace*, narratives of straight women's (idealized) friendships with gay men may serve as sites wherein more traditional heterosexual relations can be critiqued, arguing that the very popular sit-com, and other shows and films that feature the gay-best-friend plot, address "straight women's desire for relationships with men that exist outside the norms proscribed by the heterosexual contract. [...] Could it be that these [shows and films] signal the most recent manifestation of straight women's dissatisfaction with the norms of masculinity and the kinds of relationships that such gendered conventions demand?" ("*Will & Grace*: Negotiating (Gay) Marriage on Prime-Time Television," *The Journal of Popular Culture* 38, no. 4 [2005]: 715).

29. Emma Holly, *Beyond Innocence* (New York: Jove, 2001), 1–2.

30. *Ibid.*, 31.

31. The text also explicitly rebuts a set of theological presumptions often deployed in negative portrayals of homosexuality. When Freddie says, "I know people say it's unnatural, Florence. I know they say it's a sin," Florence draws upon her background as a vicar's daughter in order to think through the situation and reassure him, saying, "I don't think you're a sinner [...] Maybe if I didn't know you, I would, but I've always thought you a good, kind man. My father used to say God weighs each man's sins in private. We can't presume to know what's on the scales" (204).

32. Emma Holly, *Beyond Seduction* (New York: Jove, 2002), 202. Further references will be included parenthetically.

33. Andrew Sullivan, "Dialogues: Gay Marriage," *Slate Magazine*, 4 April 1997, http://www.slate.com/id/3642.

34. Calvin Thomas, "Straight with a Twist: Queer Theory and the Subject of Heterosexuality," in *Straight with a Twist: Queer Theory and the Subject of Heterosexuality*, ed. Calvin Thomas, Joseph O. Almone, and Catherine A. F. MacGillvray (Urbana: University of Illinois Press, 2000), 24.

13

"You call me a bitch like that's a bad thing": Romance Criticism and Redefining the Word "Bitch"

Sarah Wendell

Bitch.

No, really.

Bitch!

What — or who — comes to mind upon reading that word? That pushy woman in line at the bank who uses her purse, her breath, and her body weight to assert physically that you've taken her spot in line, and thus you should move your ass immediately? Or the woman who dumped you after a four-month relationship because she decided her happiness was more secure without your involvement? The lady next door who leans out the window and asks you to please keep the noise down during your last party? Or perhaps a blonde, female candidate for the Democratic nomination for the 2008 Presidential election? Is a bitch a woman or a man? Is it someone who annoys you, who demands that you do things her way? Is it a person, usually female, who is uncompromisingly firm, assertive or aggressive, and who takes no crap from anyone? Who, or what, is a bitch?

I, Sarah Wendell, am a Bitch. Specifically, I'm Smart Bitch Sarah[1], co-owner and author of a website that reviews romance novels and discusses feminism, politics, cover art, mantitty, David Hasselhoff, plagiarism, ethics, and orgasms. On a given day, it might feature a heuristic discussion of pubic wigs and socialism. Our site is called *Smart Bitches, Trashy Books*. My co-pilot at the site is Smart Bitch Candy. The readers who frequent our site and participate in discussions therein are "the Bitchery." Our discussions are long, often fractious, and can stretch on for hundreds of comments, but since 2005, our site has actively and continually redefined what it is to be a Bitch. To make a broad, sweeping assessment of our own importance, our site has reclaimed, subverted, and redefined the term "Bitch" into a description of confident intelligence that is erudite and fierce, argumentative, and above all affirming of the idea that being a Bitch is a Good Thing, particularly within the context of romance novels and their readers.

Putting the Bitch Back in Romance

Romance novels themselves, and the community of writers and readers that create and promote them, are not necessarily known for Bitchy behavior. Romance novels are among the most purely women-centered genres of literature. They are written mostly by women for women, and yet often appear to reinforce deeply traditional roles for women. There are gender tropes left, right, and center, from the expectations and variations of virginity that plague the average romance heroine regardless of time period, to the alpha male requirements enforced upon heroes. The sexuality in romance novels often and frequently embraces a theme of deflowering, with an inexperienced female being introduced to the wonders of the hero's masterful wang and experiencing the birth of her own autonomy and sexual agency under the sheltering wings of her manly hero.[2] Even as women write and retell with variations the traditional romance plotline which ends with a happy ending for both the male and female protagonists, the plotlines themselves can sometimes read as repeated written reinforcement of patriarchal authority over women: a woman needs a man in order to find fulfillment.

If one examines the romance writing community solely by the titles of the books and the initial marketing of the industry product — judging the genre by its cover, so to speak — it is a facile matter to dismiss romance as merely reinforcement of the virgin/whore mythology that feminist scholars have long argued imprisons women in untenable and powerless roles. However, as romance readers can attest, many romance novels eagerly and deliberately subvert that mythology, even as they appear to embrace it. Recent and detailed examinations of the subversion of the virgin/whore mythology by romance novels and the emerging classifications of hero archetype, particularly Pamela Regis's *A Natural History of the Romance Novel,* reveal that the patterns of self-actualization represented in romance novels contradict any accusations of suppression and discrimination against women, and instead reveal that romance novels tell and retell stories of female empowerment and fulfillment, both within and in spite of traditional expectations of women in society.

Much as the novels are dismissed, so are the women who write them. The individuals writing romance novels are most often women operating their own independent businesses as writers, who work as entrepreneurs within the publishing industry, represented by agents and editors of both genders, within a lucrative industry that sells writing by women to an eager consumer base made up mostly of women. Yet ask any romance author about comments from shoppers during bookstore signings, or from colleagues and extended family, and you'll have a buffet of backhanded compliments and insults from which to choose. Most romance authors have had to defend their careers against accusations of writing pornography for women and field comments about writing "those books." Alas, not much has changed since the late 1800s, when Nathaniel Hawthorne's knickers were in a twist about the "damned mob of scribbling women" whose books sold so well that their works blocked more deserving writers from entering the market. Women who write romance are part of a $1.7 billion annual industry that is looked down upon by many, even as the profit of the romance genre provides financial support to publishing houses reporting losses each quarter. Beneath the surface of the genre that is dismissed and denigrated is a financial powerhouse of female entrepreneurship that is also dismissed and overlooked.

And yet, there is one part of the romance writing community, online and off, wherein there is precious little subversion, and a sad lack of any feisty challenge to the existing standard of gender roles: romance novel reviewing. Because the genre itself is beneath the notice of mainstream reviewers such as *The New York Times, The New Yorker,* and other magazine and newspaper print reviewers, romance novels have been reviewed almost exclusively within their own community, in print publications such as *Romantic Times* (now *RT Book Reviews*), *Affaire de Coeur,* and independent websites such as "All About Romance" (likesbooks.com) which started operation in 1997. A pattern emerges, however, when one examines the grading, phrasing, and overall conclusions of those reviews: the grading curve is skewed to the positive. While there are negative grades, most books rate higher than average. While *Romantic Times* will give a one-star review, for example, the bulk of their reviews are between three and four-and-a-half stars on a scale of one to four-and-a-half. To put it plainly: there is a deliberate pressure to "be nice" when one is a writer, author, or reviewer in the romance novel genre. Authors rarely criticize other authors publicly, and that conduct applies to reviewers as well, it seems.

The origin of the romance review culture is a mystery — a big, pink mystery — and is likely a combination of factors. First, until recently with the advent of blogs and personal websites, romance was a self-contained community of authors, publishers, media professional devoted to the genre, and readers. But without blogs, the readers didn't have much of a voice outside of direct communication with authors. Because romance is beneath the notice of most literary review establishments, only the publications dedicated to the genre itself were examining the quality thereof, and if those magazines were relentlessly positive, which they were, no exacting criticism had any room to flourish. And of course authors who read within the genre couldn't endanger their own careers by offering their own critical opinion: professional courtesy demanded a "be nice" mentality and fostered an attitude of "if you don't have anything nice to say, don't say anything at all."

Thus, when we began our site, the established communities of romance readers online operated within a strange dichotomy. On the one hand, readers would grumble about how romances are dismissed as plebian dreck, or that they receive neither respect nor adequate attention from the media outlets who are continually distracted by the sex and the appearance of Fabio on the cover. But then, should anyone (read: us, for example) begin to examine individual romance novels critically, pointing out narrative flaws or questioning the sexual authority of a heroine who subsumes her identity completely into the hero's by page 4, these same readers and writers would cry that romance is just silly escapist fun and certainly doesn't need to be subjected to harsh criticism. By reviewing romances critically, we are already at odds with these readers, because romances, in our opinion, *should* be subjected to thorough examination, both from an irreverent and a critical perspective.

However, we also remain at odds with the rest of the population that disdains romance novels, and greets the sight of us reading a romance with the phrase "But you're so smart! How come you read *those* books?" To be completely frank, the only appropriate response we could conjure up was to be bitchy in every sense of the word and refute both the critics of the genre and those who insist that the genre shouldn't be held to critical standards. We are offensive for telling those who insult our reading material that they could kiss off, and we are irritating to those who wring their hands at the idea that anyone would call into serious question why in the name of God's green earth any hero would rape a heroine because her father screwed him over in a business deal twenty-five years ago.

That, in a nutshell,[3] is how our site came to be. We wanted to review romances. We didn't think there were enough realistic examinations of the genre that subjected it to much-needed criticism while also celebrating what made romance novels such satisfying reading material. We wanted to be a community and haven for readers of romance who love the genre and were tired of taking shit for it from both sides. No quarter would be given to snide comments from those who didn't read the genre, nor to any self-righteous outrage from readers who were mad because we said their favorite author's new release sucked donkey wang. Thus we named our site *Smart Bitches Who Love Trashy Books* in an effort to play with both the dismissal of the romance genre as "trashy" and the dismissal of outspoken, cursing, opinionated women as "bitchy."

Initially, there was some outrage because we were unabashedly snarky and a lot more forthcoming than established romance reviewers regarding our opinions on the books we were reading, particularly when those books failed to meet our expectations. We were saying loudly and frequently that some romance novels sucked and should never have been published, which was an outrageously mean and shocking idea to a community that had never really confronted reader opinion stated so frankly and so publicly. At one point, we came up with a drinking game that required a chugging of one's beverage should a commenter state that we've gone too far, or that we should be banned from the internet because of our conduct online.[4]

Conversely, however, we also encountered relieved gratitude from readers who were finally able to discuss what they didn't like about a particular novel. For example, Candy, my partner in Bitching, wrote in February 2005 that Lucy Monroe's *The Real Deal* was "excruciating to read on all levels. The writing style veered from hilariously purple to hilariously wooden, the characters were poorly-recycled archetypes at best, and the plot was completely humdrum when it wasn't busy being implausible."[5] This wasn't exactly revolutionary review writing, except that so many other print and online romance reviews, from *Romantic Times* to All About Romance gave *The Real Deal* very high grades. *Romantic Times* gave the book four stars out of five, and All About Romance gave it "Desert Isle Keeper" status, the highest grade possible at that site.[6] Candy's review, however, brought out comments from those who hadn't liked it and felt alienated in any attempts to discuss why they hadn't liked it. Jac wrote after Candy posted her review, "Thanks for the honest review of this book. Finally. Someone who tells it like it is. It was getting a bit tiresome listening to everyone kiss-ass (can I say that here?!) to the author about her 'oh-so-fantastic' book when it really truly sucks."[7] Other readers echoed that sentiment with comments like "I thought I was the only one who hated this book," and "I thought it was just me!"[8]

While we expected some disgust from readers who disagreed with our decision to name ourselves Bitches or to call the genre "trashy," we didn't expect, but were utterly pleased to find, that due in part to our irreverent and Bitchy title and monikers, our site attracted a community of readers, writers, and publishing professionals whose commentary on our blog entries was unique to the internet. While we do battle the occasional troll, our site has created by fiat an unspoken code of behavior that dictates a style of argument which avoids personal and direct attack of the writer but instead invokes a sophisticated language and manner that invites further discussion. Since our site has been online, several discussions have illustrated that code of behavior, and revealed how, in a relatively short amount of time, being a Bitch on our site has come to serve as a shorthand for conducting an assertive, intelligent, and respectful debate.

Bitch Is the Word

Bitch, let it be said, is a marvelously interesting word. Historically and linguistically speaking, there are few words that can be ascribed only to women when used in the pejorative sense. Words like "whore," "slut," and "cunt" are particularly useful, but few words have the effortless shorthand definition and linguistic explosive-consonant-laden punch of "bitch." First recorded in the year 1000 as referring to female dogs, and in the year 1400 as referencing a woman[9], the word has since become both a noun and a verb.[10] In the Online Etymology Dictionary, the slang definition encompasses both the verb form, which means "to gripe or complain," and the noun form: a "lewd [...] spiteful or overbearing [...] highly objectionable or unpleasant [...] difficult" woman, or conversely, a man who is "sexually contemptuous," a derivation from the female insult.[11] What a delightful pairing: weak men and strong, assertive, perhaps aggressive women are "bitches." The weak male, who is charged by gender expectations to be aggressive, and the aggressive woman, who, according to those same standards, is meant to be subservient, weak, and submissive, are the maligned parties using a word that formally refers to a "female dog."

According to the etymology webzine *Take Our Word for It*, the use of the word "bitch" to refer to a female is "simply a metaphor: comparing lewd women to female dogs, which, if left to their own devices, will bear pups rather frequently, suggesting sexual promiscuity."[12] The more contemporary usage of "bitch" referring to a "malicious or treacherous woman" is traced by Francis Grose's *1811 Dictionary of the Vulgar Tongue* which defines the word as "the most offensive appellation that can be given to an English woman, even more provoking than that of 'whore.'"[13] But wait, there's more! According to AskOxford.com, an online language repository of questions and answers from the creators of the Oxford English Dictionary, "Bitch" can refer in the informal sense to "a woman whom one considers to be malicious or unpleasant" or, comfortingly, in "black English" as simply, "a woman — used in a non-derogatory sense."[14] Take a look at that one again: it's *non*-derogatory, according to AskOxford, because "bitch" is simply another word for "woman." Either the word has lost some of its negative power due to repeated sustained use, or it's even more dangerous because it's synonymous with "woman," and therefore drags the word "woman" itself into derogatory territory by association.

The further one delves in to the etymology of the word "bitch," the more twisted, confusing, and ultimately powerless and powerful the word itself becomes, not because it is pejorative, but because it is acceptable usage in many social and professional situations. From a foundation based in metaphoric slurs alluding to promiscuity and aggressive behavior, the word has since become somewhat tame: one can say the word "bitch" in some television broadcasts and during live radio broadcasts on the air. While each individual network has a set of Standards and Practices guidelines that determine what words can be used during which time of day on a television program, the U.S. Federal Communications Commission allows the use of the word "bitch" and does not issue fines to networks if the word is used. When I was asked to participate in a sports-talk radio show based in Houston, Texas, in May 2008, I asked the producers if I could use the full name of our website, and refer to myself as "Smart Bitch Sarah." "Absolutely," they said: "You can say 'bitch' on the air. It's a female dog."[15] But when I was interviewed by *The Today Show* in late July 2008, I was not permitted to use the word at all, nor mention the full name of our website as some of their affiliate stations would be outraged.

Thus, in a lexical and political sense, the word "bitch" is more than merely outrageous. It's exceedingly powerful precisely because its layered meaning combines with a persistent social acceptance. It is a derogatory term for women that ties up in five letters and one syllable all the negative stereotypes and limitations placed upon women. It's a metaphor for promiscuous canines with unguarded and accessible vaginas and a propensity toward frequent procreation, and a term for sexually unacceptable men. "Bitch" is a truly amazing, terrible, offensive, and creative word. Its history and depth are taken for granted by those who use it. We love it, each and every letter.

Taking Back the Bitch

Third Wave feminism, the activities and examinations of feminists beginning in the early 1990s, often focused on the power of specific words, and sought to reclaim them from derogatory to self-affirming and celebratory use. In efforts to inspire activism among young women who grew up with the rewards of earlier feminist activism, and to a large extent take them for granted, Third Wave feminism advocates for reclaiming words because "it's better to change the meaning of a sexist word than to censor it from everyday speech."[16] As Inga Muscio notes in her memoir *Cunt*, English is already a language of power, "because it represents the victors of history's present telling."[17] Therefore, undermining that power by grabbing a word and twisting it to suit a purpose is an action filled with ballsy courage: "seizing this language and manipulating it to serve your community is a very powerful thing to do"[18] because, as a language of international commerce, English has some considerable social, political, and economic power.

Reclaiming as an activist process has succeeding in undermining and reforming the definitions of many words that have been used by the dominant hegemony to oppress and marginalize minorities. Words like "queer" have been co-opted by gay men and women to celebrate their homosexuality, and today several universities in the United States, including Smith College, have courses of study formally called "Queer Studies."[19] Words that range in power from "geek" and "nerd" to "gaijin" and "nigger"[20] have been reclaimed by the communities they refer to and re-appropriated in ways that diminish their negative power, even though the context in which those terms can be used without incident and by whom some words can be said is still up for debate.[21] "Bitch" is also subject to debate as to who should use the word, and in what context. Kathleen King in an article titled "Do You Use the B-Word?" concluded, after encountering an entire display of books with the word "bitch" in the title, that "[t]he B-word implies a strong woman who speaks her mind. But as long as women (read: not men) are writing these books, many of us believe we can — and should — reclaim the term 'bitch' for ourselves."[22]

Reforming the word "bitch" into an expression of affirmation instead of a sexual pejorative begins with the usage of the word among communities of women. Reclaiming the word "bitch," however, or even using it to suit one's own purposes is not akin to trying to convince someone that they embody the negative stereotypes used against them, and that they should be pleased and grateful to be so insulted. Reclaiming and using the word "bitch" for affirmative use demands recognition for the idea that the stereotype itself is wrong and that there is nothing at all wrong or unnatural with a woman being any of the meanings of the word: so what if a woman has a great deal of sex? More power to her (and more orgasms). So what if a woman is assertive, aggressive, powerful, or even scary? More power to her (no mention of orgasms). So what if a woman decides to reject the established paradigm of female behavior and chooses to act in opposition to those dictates? Literally: more power to her! Refusing to be offended by the word itself, and using the word as often as possible in a context that redefines its meaning demonstrates a self confidence and self assurance that, coincidentally[23] works against those same established paradigms of female behavior.

Therefore, we proclaimed ourselves "Bitches" with a capital "b." Why? Many reasons. First: ego. As the hosts of the site, we use the title as a proper name. Secondly, since we're seizing the word, the capitalization serves as a visual method of claiming and reinforcing ownership. We lend the capital "B" to the community that frequents our site by calling them the "Bitchery." And third, because being a "Bitch" in the context of our site's community has a specific and distinctive meaning, one that, dare we say, capitalizes on the idea of rejecting the standard of being nice for politeness's sake and instead saying what we think for the betterment of our future reading material. Because being a Bitch in the romance community online means entering a battle on the two distinct fronts mentioned earlier: we're fighting the dismissal of romance as a genre read by stupid, undersexed women, and we're fighting against the pressure within the romance community itself to limit disagreement and self-assertion. Being a Bitch is necessary in the context of romance reviewing because we're acting against two sets of gender roles, and in turn creating a new one for ourselves. We're not being mean out of hand simply because the genre on the whole is trashy[24] and not worth the effort of working the powers of lit crit against it, but we're also not being nice to every single book that crosses our path, because some books are indeed of dubious quality and it's about time we discussed that, too. We're not heartlessly mean, we're not unilaterally nice, and we invite and revel in disagreement.

The Rules of Being a Smart Bitch

Anatomically and succinctly speaking, being a Bitch means not being an asshole. Our review style is one example: when we review a book, even if we truly, completely, and utterly *hated* the book, one underlying rule is that our response is to the book itself. I, for example, picture the author staying up until 4:30 in the morning working on that book, and know that that much effort deserves at least a thorough answer as to why I didn't like the book itself. The line between book and author, or, more broadly, between a subject under discussion and the people arguing that subject, is a very crucial boundary, and marks the border between "bitch" and "asshole."[25] When I write a review, I may shriek with rage and adverbs about the stilted dialogue, the plot that had more holes than antique socks, or the hero who wouldn't know compassion if he tripped and fell into a bucket of it, but I try deliberately to focus on the book and the flaws with the book itself. While some negative reviews, particularly those written by angry consumers on Amazon.com, accuse the author of all manner of chicanery, including not having actually written the book at hand, such comments in my opinion cross the boundary between issue and person. I'm sure no author likes to hear that a reviewer didn't enjoy the book, but in the long run, critical evaluations of the genre help the genre improve, if constructive feedback is given proper attention.[26] Our focus is the romance novel itself, not the person who wrote it.

That line we try deliberately not to cross, that boundary between the issue and the person on the other side of the argument, carries over into most of the more heated discussions on our site. Generally speaking, we as a Bitchery argue the issue and don't denigrate the person who argues the opposition so long as they keep to the code of respectful argument. This behavior code isn't earth shattering in and of itself, except in that it occurs on the internet, which isn't known as a place of calm and thoughtful communication. Because of the distance and impersonal nature of internet communication, it's all too easy for users to turn off their monitors after saying something particularly hurtful or inflammatory without personally experiencing the fallout of their comments. On our site, however, even the more heated conversations tend to toe the line of demarcation between issue-oriented discussion and personal attack. To put it simply: our users prefer to debate an issue,[27] and adhere to simple rules of fair argument. Most users will not attack the person who voices a dissenting opinion, but instead reply by explaining their own perspective. For example: new visitors to our site will find comments that read "I disagree, and here's why," rather than "You're a moron."[28]

There are exceptions to the code of fair argument. When a comment thread gets too long, it reaches what I call "critical mass," and there's no way to adequately address any comment that steps over that line between discussion and attack. In smaller comment threads, visitors whose comments edge into territory that is too personal, and too, shall we say, "asshole," are generally rebuked by other members of the community. Many, many times I've read a comment in my email that I found offensive,[29] but by the time I reached a computer to respond, three or four other people had already done so.[30]

One thread that demonstrated our argument style — and the limits of our community's ability to self-police — was what was called "the Swan Hat thread." After the 2007 RWA National Convention in Dallas, Texas, Candy wrote an entry wherein she discussed the controversy over costumes as self-promotion at the RWA Literacy Signing,[31] a charitable event that brings in local romance fans who buy books which authors personalize and sign before purchase. It's a big event, both in size, scope, and fundraising power, and in 2007, author Sherrilyn Kenyon wore a three-foot-tall feathered swan hat. This was, apparently, a controversial choice because some authors and attendees, among them Nora Roberts, felt that it was unprofessional and detracted from the professional development of the conference and the charity signing itself. Additionally, the presence of two new authors, Liz Maverick and Marianne Mancusi, for a debut line from Dorchester called "Shomi," which merged romance and manga, was also debated. Maverick and Mancusi called themselves "The Rebels of Romance" and dressed for the public and casual parts of the conference in the style of their novels' setting, which took place in an urban future. Their costumes consisted of short skirts, thigh-high stockings, corsets, bustiers, and brightly colored accessories, most of which didn't look completely abnormal as fashion choices, except that they were meant to promote the authors and the books, as well as the publisher and the new imprint. Between the costume play (or "cos play") and the swan hat, the use of personal appearance and costume to market books and author careers was a hot topic of discussion at and after the conference.

Candy's entry on 17 July 2007 defending the use of costumes[32] at the conference as promotional tools received over six hundred comments by the time we closed the thread. In the beginning, the discussion was civil, and despite the strong emotions on both sides of the debate, people explained their positions and kept their comments about their own opinions, or their responses to someone else's comments. For example, Nora Roberts said:

As for costumes, I stand by my previous statements. The young girls were very, very pretty. And very inappropriately attired — imo — as writers in a public, media-attended event. But it was the big-ass black swan that really got me.

Sherrilyn Kenyon will hate me forever for picking on this. But, I calls 'em as I sees 'em.

Lighten up. Easy to say when you're not CONSTANTLY called on to defend the genre and its readers and writers to the media, then have the media focus on the costumes so the image projected is silly women rather than interesting professionals who write Romance.[33]

Candy responded to Roberts:

I was thinking some more about the Mancusi/Maverick costumes, when I realized that if they'd pulled this at an SF/F con, I wouldn't feel any particular way about it, good or bad, but because they did it at RWA, I'm all "Woo hoo, awesome." It is, in essence, a dorky thing to do — mind you, I love me some dorkiness — but I think my positive reaction had to do with the way they subverted the romance author/reader stereotypes. They were being dorks, yes, but they weren't being dorks in a way that people typically expect romance authors to be dorks. There was, in short, dork cross-pollination, and I'm all for that, because I want people to realize that more people than they realize, with interests wider than they could ever imagine, read romance novels. I love subverting people's expectations that way.[34]

Roberts replied:

Must we feel we have to push ourselves into some out-of-the-box image — and let's be honest — must we feel we must do that to get attention? What does that say about the work?

I don't want to harp on these girls. They're young, awfully cute, and they weren't that outrageous.

But I do feel that dressing up like your characters is silly, and it smudges the lines. Why not be who you are — because that's exactly what it'll come down to anyway.[35]

Despite the presence of a major author in romance in the discussion, the issue at hand was costumes and professional appearance, and the image of romance readers and writers therein. Roberts' point was that she found the costumes to be silly, but then said specifically that her issue was not with the persons who dressed up but the idea that dressing up would be viable option for promotion: "it smudges the lines [...] why not be who you are?" Her point, and that of other commenters, was not who was wearing the costumes and what they looked like, but the decision to dress up and what it means.

MaudeClare, another commenter, wrote, "I agree with Ms Roberts on the costumes. I thought they were a bit much, and sometimes, we need to remember *tone* when we discuss issues. We don't have to be tarts or frumpy."[36] MaudeClare's decision to parallel tone within an argument about costumes as self-promotion is clever: one must consider the manner in which a message is conveyed, verbally or physically, to assure that the message itself isn't contradicted or polluted by the method in which it is communicated. To extrapolate her comment into the discussion of Bitchy behavior demonstrated in the early part of this thread, the content of the comments, and the fact that up to this point the commenters have addressed the issue itself and not the women who dressed up is important: the question is the decision, not the people themselves. So far, the debate had not crossed into personal attack.

The women themselves who wore the costumes, Liz Maverick and Marianne Mancusi, left a long comment explaining that they were in no way coerced by a marketing person or by their publisher to wear their costumes, and their decision to promote their books using costume play was a deliberate one:

On the issue of professionalism: Dressing up as manga-inspired characters was a fun way to promote our manga-inspired books. Obviously, it's not for everybody. (It is, however, completely normal at SF/F events and SF/F readers are also a target readership for these books.) But it happens to suit our personalities, our image as "rebels" and the kind of out-of-the-box books we write.

Meaning, we don't feel forced to do something "unnatural." Dressing up and having fun is part of who we are. And we certainly don't believe short skirts and thigh highs equate to being unprofessional. We just understand how to market ourselves and our books, we've taken a strong approach to branding, and we're working it.[37]

The debate continued for a few more hours as commenters debated the line between "cute outfits to get attention" and "holy crap, that hat is crazy."[38] The focus of the discussion centered more on Mancusi and Maverick as "the Rebels of Romance" and their usage of costumes to distinguish themselves as authors and their books as manga-romance hybrids, than on Kenyon's swan chapeau, and that focus made sense as the discussion was also, on a separate level, examining how and why authors market themselves along with their books — a relatively new phenomenon in the romance industry. Fellow blogger Jane Litte from Dear Author.com wrote, "Authors dressed up in short skirts and ponytails are nothing compared to the imagery that is inundating the public on an hourly basis at the grocery store and the bookstore. These women aren't selling themselves. They are selling an idea. A concept. A package. It was done for the public signing to attract readers to their table, to stand out in the masses."[39] Promotion that gains attention is successful promotion, said some, but at the same time, those detractors of romance who denigrate the genre from the position of never having read a single romance novel pick out the swan hat and the costumes as yet another reason romance is silly. One commenter, Jonquil, compared the costumes to the "naked guy at the Pride parade":

> There will always be one naked guy at the Gay Pride parade. The reporters will *always* interview and photograph (discreetly) that guy. And all the gay people pushing strollers, or doing drill-team routines in their business suits, or flaunting their respectable professional status, will be mentioned, if at all, as a sidebar. Because the frame for that story is "weird people," not "normal people having fun." And until the frame changes, it really doesn't matter what you do.[40]

What originally began as a discussion of costumes and place became a discussion of professionalism, marketing, the target audience of the convention itself, and a heuristic approach to locating romance on the spectrum of respect from within and from outside of the genre community. All that in one swan hat and two pairs of thigh-highs. The discussion maintained its level tone, even from participants on far opposite sides. The discussion was certainly polarized and heated, but it remained entirely civil.

Early on in the discussion, one published author commented, "For every perky little author who dresses like a pedophile-luring schoolgirl or wears a swan hat or shows her rack or whatever in the vague hope of becoming a bestselling author that way, there are a hundred who a) don't wear costumes, b) are fat, middle-aged and flat-chested c) don't even go to conferences, in costume or not, and d) are hugely successful."[41] That marked the first moment the line was crossed between individual and issue. Suddenly the authors in question were "perky authors dressed as pedophile-luring schoolgirls" — a personal attack and interpretation of the motive behind their apparel. But the comment was quickly rebutted. Author Alesia Holliday responded, "This is flatly offensive. Also the premise of your post is unsupported — writing good books is not a bar to being an effective marketer, as Liz's starred review in PW attests."[42] The original comment was mostly ignored in the hours following, or referred to by others as the lone example of egregious argument.

Then that commenter returned and called Mancusi and Maverick "self promoting cheesecake" and reiterated the idea that their dressing in a sexualized fashion was "about promoting sex with underage girls."[43] Despite the incendiary nature of the post, responses were civil but firm. Author Lani Diane Rich replied:

> I couldn't disagree more. First of all, whether Marianne and Liz were actually dressed like schoolgirls is up for debate. They were dressed in the style of manga, which is promotional for what they write, and accusing them of supporting pedophilia is galactically out of line. It's like saying Playboy bunnies support bestiality — that's one hell of a slippery slope you're employing there.[44]

A few people took issue with the fact that the discussion was about what two women wore, and felt that we were personally attacking them — which is ironic since the original entry that started the discussion was in favor of wearing costumes in the first place. One commenter, desertwillow, wrote, "This debate has been going on since Tuesday and it has been matured, balanced, and intelligent — for the most part. The few inappropriate comments were squelched quickly, loudly. I've gotten a lot out of most of the postings and my admiration for several members of this blog has grown. You all were so mature and wise."[45] But another commenter wrote, "Would any of you (and sheeeww there are some huge names on these comments) like to be publicly reprimanded like this in a room of ten thousand or more people? And be so embarrassed and humiliated that you can't even defend yourself? Some of the points made are rather brilliant, but I still can't help but see this as two people being paraded around the town square and then flogged."[46] The idea that the costume wearers in question couldn't defend themselves is ludicrous — they already had, and had entered the discussion several times explaining their perspective. But the idea that individuals disagreeing and discussing the marketing decisions of three authors amounts to "public humiliation" merely because they were being talked about is quite a jump, and indicative of the "Be Nice" mentality that aligns itself so closely to Being an Asshole, despite residing on the supposed opposite end of the behavioral spectrum. Whether one advocates for Being Nice and never disagreeing, or Being an Asshole and attacking personally those who disagree, the end result is the same: discussions cannot occur, and education cannot be experienced.

Because the discussion became so complex and was about clothing worn by authors promoting their books, it was alarmingly easy for some to cross the line into personal attack, and when one comment does so, readers attempting to catch up on a long thread may see one incendiary comment and read many of the other analyses of costume in that same light. It's also easy to extrapolate comments out of context and toss the entire thread under the heading of bullying, when it was in reality an analysis of marketing technique in context, plus a bonus discussion of where one buys stripy thigh-highs. But when other sites highlighted fragments of comments and used those to defend a hypothesis that we were bashing authors and promoting online bullying, the comments strayed away from the issue to defending the discussion of the issue itself. Roberts wrote, "I kinda wished I'd never clicked on those links. Bullying is brought up several times. I'm horribly sorry and not a little sick at the idea that speaking my mind, expressing my opinion that I dislike — strongly dislike — costumes at a particular event, and how I feel that reflects on the genre could be construed as bullying."[47] Robin L. replied, "I'd like to think this community's strength and value is measured by the way it handles difference and disagreement — ideally in engaged, honest, sometimes passionately raucous debate and not in mocking others for shits and giggles."[48] Robin's comments underscore the line between the issue and the person, even when the issue is what the person is wearing at the time as a method of self-promotion.

However, the amazing thing to me, as an administrator and author of the site, is that the crazy didn't start blossoming until there were over 375 comments in the discussion, and more importantly, that the really off-color comments, minus those referencing pedophiles and cheesecake, took place at other sites, not ours. Our community adhered to the rules of fair argument for the bulk of the discussion, and individuals responded quickly and firmly to comments that broke those rules. Not only did the members of the Bitchery embrace the concept of fair argument, but they immediately defended their right to do so, pointing out when outrageous accusations had no support behind them, and deliberately making room for the dissenting arguments based on facts and personal opinion.

Most discussions within the romance novel community, unfortunately, are plagued by the relentless "Be Nice" compulsion, and are unable to disagree without qualifiers ("Well, this is just my opinion, but ...") or without excusing themselves first ("I don't want to cause bad feelings but ..."). There is no room for disagreement without the automatic assumption of dismissal, distrust, and derision. The subtext of the discussions on our site for the most part remain simply but exceptionally different: "I disagree with you. This does not mean that I despise you."

The Bitches' Rules

The participation and the depth of the debate in involved threads demonstrate the creation of what I loosely term The Bitch Rules of Argument, which apply mostly in our community but can be wielded in any situation involving debate, discussion, or general dialogue. The rules are simple and few, but powerful.

Bitch Rule #1: Agree to disagree, and disagree to agree

One way in which our community is unique is that the underlying drive to convert the opposition to one's own way of thinking is almost entirely absent. Arguments begin with the assumption that anyone who argues will agree to disagree, and that a resolution may not be reached. In fact, the underlying purpose of any dialogue on our site is not about persuading the opposite party to one's way of thinking, but maintaining and sustaining the dialogue that is the foundation of the Bitchery community.

For example, in a discussion about *The Jewel of Medina*, a fictionalized account of the Prophet Mohammed and his bride Aisha, there were many individuals who identified themselves as Muslim and described how deeply offensive the book's content was, as it is forbidden to depict Mohammed and his wives as fictional characters. In the discussion on our site, no one said that the Muslim individuals shouldn't feel offended, or that they were overreacting by explaining how much of an affront they considered the author's work. There wasn't an attempt to convert their thinking to the other side. Most of the individuals who participated were not arguing to persuade; they were stating or defending their point of view.

Parties also disagree to agree, by which I mean that their disagreement is also founded on a larger agreement. It could be that both parties adore the same author, or have the same sense of humor, or find David Hasselhoff to be among the sexiest creatures to walk the land.[49] The agreement beneath the disagreement plays out in what often seems to be a meta-discussion that exists concurrently with the argument itself. It is often humorous, as well as conciliatory, suggesting that through the disagreement there is a baseline of respect so long as both parties keep to the established rules of argument. For example, in the midst of the discussion about *The Jewel of Medina*, one of the first to explain why the book was potentially offensive was a young Muslim woman who posted under the name "shewho-hashope." More than a few commenters challenged her explanation as to why the book was potentially offensive and chastised her for using sarcasm. But the underlying foundation of agreement allowed for a good dose of humor. When one commenter joked that there ought to be an extension of Godwin's law[50] to include references to the terrorists seizing freedom of speech, shewhohashope responded, "Screw the Iranian government. Let's get married!"[51] Certainly proposals of gay marriage among Muslims and non–Muslims should be a prime feature of any discussion of free speech and defining the boundaries of cultural overreaction. Even though the thread was fractious and involved several very personal subjects, this commenter and others maintained their sense of humor and a sense that, despite widely polarized viewpoints, the participants weren't enemies. It's more than mere respect: it's an agreement to participate in each discussion with the understanding that we're part of the community for a reason (a common love of romance novels) and that in the next debate, we might be on the same side.

Rule #2: Apologize sincerely, but not condescendingly. Admit when you're wrong.

Apologizing is something women are accused of doing far too much — and yet online, apologies and admissions of incorrect assumption are few and far between. People on other sites frequently begin comments with a condescending, "I'm sorry, but ..." which is not at all the same thing.

At our site, apologizing and saying the other three magic words, "You were right," is a powerful demonstration of confidence. We apologize when we are wrong, but we do not ever apologize for having opinions. We can have a balls-to-the-wall, knock-down, drag-out, no-holds-barred discussion of the most minute of minutiae, but when one party crosses the line and begins personally attacking the other party, more often than not, the site regulars who realize they've crossed the line apologize for doing so. Sometimes, even the guests to a new discussion do as well. Ziggy, who joined the *Jewel of Medina* discussion after it was brought to her attention on a Muslim community site, also argued that the book was offensive. When another person took issue with her temperament in a comment, Ziggy replied, "I may be mistaken, in which case I totally apologize for losing my temper."[52] Likewise, when two longtime visitors to the site began arguing back and forth about international perceptions of American cultural attitude, one of them edited her own comment to redact a few lines of sarcasm she later regretted[53] and apologized[54] for having been sarcastic in the first place. Rather than deleting what she had said, she used HTML coding that rendered the redacted portion as if it were crossed out, allowing it to be read, along with the apology that followed: a visual statement of "I was wrong, and I amend my statement accordingly."

That's it, really: there are only two main rules of Bitch conduct. Agree to disagree, and apologize when you're an asshole.[55] Simplistic, yes, but revolutionary. In our perspective, being a Bitch means that you have the confidence to disagree but can do so respectfully, with the acknowledgement that the other party is a member of the same community and therefore worthy of consideration. Being a Bitch is also an entirely new gender role for women, because it doesn't fit on the nice/mean continuum, nor does it resemble the traditional definition of the word "bitch." Because the word "bitch" is used by men to denigrate women and used by women to limit disagreement and self-assertion, our reacquisition of the term is particularly crucial and deliberate. Having an opinion and disagreeing with someone directly and respectfully isn't "mean," and keeping your opinion to yourself isn't "nice" in our world. In fact, it's the opposite: disagreement is nice, and refusing to participate is mean.

If We Bitches Have Offended

This analysis likely would have had more authority and certainly less arrogance had it come from a third party instead of from one of the site's creators. However, in this account I've had the opportunity to examine the results of the past few years of running a website stemming from our decision to declare ourselves Bitches. We had no business plan when we started, no plot or nefarious agenda except to crack each other up and write about romance novels and man titty. We declared ourselves Bitches because we give a hearty finger[56] to anyone who dismisses or demeans our reading material, and we're awful in the opinion of others because we don't pull punches when we discuss in great detail what we didn't like about a plot, a particular novel, a romance trope, or the continual habit of cover models to have slack-jawed expressions of passion[57] and four-foot mullets.

Even now many of the posts on the site which I write are from the seat of my pants, so to speak, in that I don't plan ahead except to exercise the only two real authorities a blogger has: consistency and continuity. I remain humbly and deeply impressed by the manner and style in which our community chooses to argue, and find that I try to adapt that standard to my live interpersonal daily interactions. Perhaps the internet and our dependence on technology has caused us to become more distant from other individuals, or perhaps we collectively fear conflict, but disagreement can too easily be read as "I don't like you," rather than "I don't agree with you." The Bitch style combines both: "I like you, but I don't agree with you." Our Bitching standards are about the same as they were when we started the site and said, "Hey! Let's be Smart Bitches!" So far, the fallout from that decision has been, if you'll forgive me, bitchin'. Until recently, most criticism about the romance genre from inside and outside that community was dismissive and derisive. We Bitches refuse to be cowed by anyone who looks down on the romance genre and our enjoyment of it, and we self-confidently celebrate the genre, to the shock of those who deride it, even as we mock and skewer the more horrific elements of it, much to the dismay of those who celebrate it without limit.

This book of literary examination and criticism itself represents what might be the Third Wave feminist approach to the romance genre. The genre deserves to be examined with the same respect that we bring to arguments and discussions on our site, and it's about time that the critical evaluations began. That which was dismissed as plebian enforcement of traditional gender roles, the humble romance novel, has been overturned to reveal a fracture of those same roles and a casting of new characters: the romance scholar, the proud author, the fearless reader, and, of course, the Smart Bitch.

NOTES

1. I'm also *Her Grace, the Duchess of Cuntington*, but that's a different academic analysis, sort of.

2. Further examinations of these elements are in our book *Beyond Heaving Bosoms: The Smart Bitches' Guide to Romance Novels* (New York: Fireside, 2009). Shameless self promotion ends here.

3. A rather large nutshell.

4. Candy Tan, "Blog Drama Drinking Game," Smart Bitches, Trashy Books, May 18, 2007, http://www .smartbitchestrashybooks.com/index.php/weblog/comments/the_blog_drama_drinking_game_special_sb_ edition/.

5. Candy Tan, "*The Real Deal*," Smart Bitches, Trashy Books, February 7, 2005, http://www.smart bitchestrashybooks.com/index.php/weblog/comments/monroe_therealdeal/.

6. "The Real Deal," Lucy Monroe, http://www.lucymonroe.com/AbouttheBooksTRD.htm.

7. Jac, comment on Tan, "*The Real Deal*," Smart Bitches, Trashy Books, June 15, 2005, http://www. smartbitchestrashybooks.com/index.php/weblog/comments/monroe_therealdeal/#2806.

8. Ah, yes, the internet. Never doubt its fearsome power to unite any two people with any one tiny thing in common. From hating a book to finding sink traps erotic.

9. pinkolaeses, posting to "Word Etymology," on SurLaLune Fairy Tales Discussion Board, September 28, 2002, http://surlalunefairytales.com/boardarchives/2002/oct2002/wordetymology.html.

10. Which prompts me to add: "Bitch is the word, it's the word that you heard. We're the noun and the action."

11. "Bitch," Online Etymology Dictionary, http://www.etymonline.com/index.php?term=bitch.

12. Michael and Melanie Crowley, "Words to the Wise," Take Our Word for It 195:2, http://www.take ourword.com/TOW195/page2.html.

13. Francis Grose, "Bitch," *1811 Dictionary of the Vulgar Tongue: A Dictionary of Buckish Slang, University Wit, and Pickpocket Eloquence*, Gutenberg Project, http://www.gutenberg.org/cache/epub/5402/pg5402.html.

14. "Bitch," AskOxford.com, http://www.askoxford.com/concise_oed/bitch?view=uk.

15. I doubt any individual who hears the word on the radio or elsewhere thinks of dog breeding, though.

16. "Third Wave Feminism: Reclaiming Derogatory Terms," Wikipedia, http://en.wikipedia.org/wiki/ Third_wave_feminism#Reclaiming_derogatory_terms.

17. Inga Muscio, *Cunt* (Seattle: Seal Press, 2002), xxv.

18. *Ibid.*

19. "Queer Studies," Smith College, http://www.smith.edu/swg/queerstudies.html.

20. "Reclaiming," Wikipedia, http://en.wikipedia.org/wiki/Reclaiming.

21. One must often be a member of the minority doing the reclaiming to use the words in an appropriate context; Jackie Chan famously mocked this exclusion in the film *Rush Hour,* when he, a Chinese man, walked up to a black bartender, and said, mimicking his black colleague Chris Tucker, "What's up, my nigger?" Chan's character promptly found himself the target of a bar-fight. The scene's comedy was based entirely on the idea that a Chinese man should not and could not use the word "nigger" to refer colloquially to a black man. Some reformations of lexicon are, to say the least, not entirely complete, or, more accurately, not entirely accessible to all individuals who use that language. Fluency in a language does not equal admission to its communities. (*Rush Hour*, directed by Brett Ratner [1999; Burbank: New Line Cinema, 2009], DVD).

22. Kathleen J. King, "Do You Use the B-Word?" DivineCaroline.com http://www.divinecaroline.com/ article/22362/27498.

23. Not really.

24. Hence our other reclaimed word, "Trashy," in "trashy books." The title of our website is a double dismissal of those two groups mentioned. We're bitches because we're mean to those poor authors whose books we didn't like, and we're reclaiming the dismissal that our chosen genre is "trash" by examining it as a subject of critical worth.

25. That border also exists between "Bitch" and "Nice Girl," as being the latter means there is no bound-ary between the subject and the person disagreeing with you. If you disagree, it's not nice, so better to agree with everything, says the Nice Girl. That doesn't help the genre either, as we've said.

26. Proper attention to our reviews is located somewhere between "taken with grain of salt" and "hang on every one of our pearls of brilliant wisdom."

27. Perhaps "debate" is too mild a word. More like "pick the issue apart into tiny twitching pieces."

28. Or, "U R a m0ron! *LOLOLOL*"

29. As I am a Super Admin for the site, all comments on entries I write are emailed to me.

30. A few critics of our site take issue with the idea that we don't moderate, and that is simply untrue. Candy and I do not delete comments, merely because if you want to look like a douchebag, that's your

right. The comments I delete are most often spammers, or people who have linked to technologically dangerous webpages. I do read every comment, but I do not moderate in the sense that if someone disagrees with me, or disagrees with the community, I remove their comment from the thread.

I will, however, close a comment thread to additional comments once that discussion has reached, as I said, "critical mass." When the thread just simply has too much mass to balance the criticism, it's time to close the thread itself and move on to other discussions.

31. In 2010, the Literacy Signing, so named because it raises money for a local literacy charity, featured over 500 authors and raised over $62,000.

32. As well as the presence of bloggers at the convention, which was also an issue for some authors who felt that the convention was in danger of becoming a fan event.

33. Nora Roberts, comment on Candy Tan "On the Presence of Bloggers and Costumes at the RWA Nationals," Smart Bitches, Trashy Books, http://www.smartbitchestrashybooks.com/index.php/weblog/comments/on_the_presence_of_bloggers_and_costumes_at_the_rwa_nationals/#32099.

34. Candy, comment on Tan, "On the Presence," Smart Bitches, Trashy Books, http://www.smartbitches trashybooks.com/index.php/weblog/comments/on_the_presence_of_bloggers_and_costumes_at_the_rwa_nationals/#32107.

35. Nora Roberts, comment on Tan, "On the Presence," Smart Bitches, Trashy Books, http://www.smart bitchestrashybooks.com/index.php/weblog/comments/on_the_presence_of_bloggers_and_costumes_at_the_rwa_nationals/#32112.

36. MaudeClare, comment on Tan, "On the Presence of Bloggers and Costumes at the RWA Nationals," Smart Bitches, Trashy Books, http://www.smartbitchestrashybooks.com/index.php/weblog/comments/on_the_presence_of_bloggers_and_costumes_at_the_rwa_nationals/#32118.

37. Liz Maverick and Marianne Mancusi, comment on Tan, "On the Presence," Smart Bitches, Trashy Books, http://www.smartbitchestrashybooks.com/index.php/weblog/comments/on_the_presence_of_bloggers_and_costumes_at_the_rwa_nationals/#32157.

38. Yes, I'm fully aware that this is a scholarly paper and my evidence so far is about swan hats and thigh highs. Isn't scholarship awesome!?

39. Jane, comment on Tan, "On the Presence" http://www.smartbitchestrashybooks.com/index.php/weblog/comments/on_the_presence_of_bloggers_and_costumes_at_the_rwa_nationals/#32222.

40. Jonquil, comment on Tan, "On the Presence," Smart Bitches, Trashy Books, http://www.smart bitchestrashybooks.com/index.php/weblog/comments/on_the_presence_of_bloggers_and_costumes_at_the_rwa_nationals/#32214.

41. Deb Smith, comment on Tan, "On the Presence," Smart Bitches, Trashy Books, http://www.smart bitchestrashybooks.com/index.php/weblog/comments/on_the_presence_of_bloggers_and_costumes_at_the_rwa_nationals/#32211.

42. Alesia Holliday, comment on Tan, "On the Presence," Smart Bitches, Trashy Books, http://www. smartbitchestrashybooks.com/index.php/weblog/comments/on_the_presence_of_bloggers_and_costumes_at_the_rwa_nationals/#32218.

43. Deb Smith, comment on Tan, "On the Presence," Smart Bitches, Trashy Books, http://www.smart bitchestrashybooks.com/index.php/weblog/comments/on_the_presence_of_bloggers_and_costumes_at_the_rwa_nationals/#32318.

44. Lani, comment on Tan, "on the Presence," Smart Bitches, Trashy Books, http://www.smartbitches trashybooks.com/index.php/weblog/comments/on_the_presence_of_bloggers_and_costumes_at_the_rwa_nationals/#32329.

45. desertwillow, comment on Tan, "On the Presence," Smart Bitches, Trashy Books, http://www.smart bitchestrashybooks.com/index.php/weblog/comments/on_the_presence_of_bloggers_and_costumes_at_the_rwa_nationals/#32966.

46. Eva Gale, comment on Tan, "On the Presence," Smart Bitches, Trashy Books, http://www.smart bitchestrashybooks.com/index.php/weblog/comments/on_the_presence_of_bloggers_and_costumes_at_the_rwa_nationals/#32967.

47. Nora Roberts, comment on Tan, "On the Presence," Smart Bitches, Trashy Books, http://www.smart bitchestrashybooks.com/index.php/weblog/comments/on_the_presence_of_bloggers_and_costumes_at_the_rwa_nationals/#33235.

48. Robin L, comment on Tan,"On the Presence," Smart Bitches, Trashy Books, http://www.smart bitchestrashybooks.com/index.php/weblog/comments/on_the_presence_of_bloggers_and_costumes_at_the_rwa_nationals/#33236.

49. Who doesn't?

50. "As a discussion grows longer, the probability of a comparison involving Nazis or Hitler approaches one." ("Godwin's Law," Wikipedia, http://en.wikipedia.org/wiki/Godwin%27s_law).

51. shewhohashope, comment on Sarah Wendell "*The Jewel of Medina* is Now on Sale — No, Wait. Nevermind," Smart Bitches, Trashy Books, http://www.smartbitchestrashybooks.com/index.php/weblog/comments/the-jewel-of-medina-is-now-on-sale-no-wait-nevermind/#66020.

52. Ziggy, comment on "*The Jewel of Medina* is Now on Sale — No, Wait. Nevermind," Smart Bitches, Trashy Books, http://www.smartbitchestrashybooks.com/index.php/weblog/comments/the-jewel-of-medina-the-prologue/#66652.

53. Users of the site who register and login have the ability to edit their own comments.

54. snarkhunter, comment on "*The Jewel of Medina* is Now on Sale — No, Wait. Nevermind," Smart Bitches, Trashy Books, http://www.smartbitchestrashybooks.com/index.php/weblog/comments/the-jewel-of-medina-the-prologue/#66687.

55. I'm working on trademarking these concepts and enforcing them in all venues, but it seems doing so makes me more of an asshole.

56. Guess which one!

57. Or gastrointestinal distress — we're never sure which.

14

The Interactive Romance Community: The Case of "Covers Gone Wild"

Miriam Greenfeld-Benovitz

Just as it is often difficult to classify novels as romance or as particular types of romance, the romance community lacks clear boundaries. Authors, editors, publishers, and readers can be identified as one community with subgroups or treated as separate communities. The romance reader is also difficult to define. One must decide whether to look at quantity and frequency of reading, or analyze those who self-define themselves as romance readers regardless of how much or how often they read. Further complicating the problem is the notion of community. Lee Komito shares this view, describing community as a social construct that may be constructed differently in different societies: "A community is not fixed in form or function, but is a mixed bag of possible options whose meanings and concreteness are always being negotiated by individuals, in the context of changing external constraints."[1] This creates a context through which to understand the romance community and the communication among its constituents, while acknowledging the impact of external forces.

Given this definition of community, it would be impossible to study the entire romance community because the constant negotiation by individuals necessitates an understanding of all individuals who constitute the romance community. Even with a workable definition of what it means to be a member of the romance community, it does not mean that it is possible to access the entire constituency. As such, learning about the romance community means understanding a piece of the whole, fixed in a particular historical context. This does not mean that it should not be attempted. Each undertaking to understand the romance community provides another piece of the puzzle. Compiling a number of studies related to the romance community provides patterns of issues and meanings that apply to multiple segments and provide a broader understanding of what it means to be a member of the romance community. This chapter explores one sub-community of the romance community: those who post on the Smart Bitches Who Love Trashy Books (SBTB) website. By analyzing the interaction in "Covers Gone Wild" entries and the role it plays in creating and sustaining the SBTB subculture, we can learn more about the way one segment of the romance community works. What do visitors to SBTB accomplish through their participation and interaction in "Covers Gone Wild"? How do these accomplishments reflect SBTB's subculture? What implications does this have for our understanding of the larger romance community?

My own experiences as a member of the romance community led me to SBTB, and provide a context to understand the site. While I might consider myself an outsider for the most part, further reflection shows greater involvement than I initially considered. Overall, I typically read on my own and choose not to discuss my reading with others. When I first started reading the genre, I discussed the books with my friends and relied on their advice to find other romances to read. Later, stigmatization of the genre by other friends encouraged me to stop discussing romances. It was not until I became actively involved on the Internet that I started to interact with others in the romance community again. A link led me to SBTB, where I found a new way to rejoin the romance community.

These experiences tie into many ways researchers have approached romance reading. Similar to my overall experience, Mann classified romance novels as "personal" fiction.[2] It is a leisure activity operating on an individual level. Janice Radway's iconic study of the Smithton group also focused on the personal act of romance reading, although her sample consisted of women who discussed romance reading with her primary informant, Dot.[3] This connection was unexplored in the study, but has been explored in other settings. Moffitt shows how mothers and daughters use romances to communicate with one another.[4] Not only do they discuss the contents of the books, but they also apply the contents to their real-life relationships. One of the mothers goes on to say, "If you don't have someone to share it with, it's no fun."[5] The act of reading may be personal, but for some, romance reading moves beyond the book. Women's book clubs have existed for over a century, so it is not surprising that romance readers share their reading experiences.[6]

My early experiences also relate to a well-known communication model: the two-step flow. In this model, ideas flow from the mass media to opinion leaders before continuing to "less active sections of the population."[7] Romance novels are mass produced and send the same message to a large number of people. One might think of Dot as an opinion leader for the Smithton women in Radway's study. She encourages her readers to choose certain novels and avoid others.[8] Similarly, I relied on particular friends to introduce me to new authors when I first started reading romances.

Unfortunately, the stigma associated with romance reading impacted my active participation in the romance community. Romance readers face a form of stigmatization that results in various strategies to manage others' impressions of them when they interact with those outside the romance community. Strategies include readers covering book jackets, separating themselves from the "typical" reader, and even criticizing the genre they enjoy when in a situation where they could be interacting with outsiders.[9] These strategies manage other people's impressions of them and are a form of facework. Goffman pioneered the idea of "face" and "facework" in his study of social interaction, where face is "the positive social value a person effectively claims for himself" and facework refers to "the actions taken by a person to make whatever he is doing consistent with face."[10] In other words, romance readers potentially lose face by being associated with the stereotypes and criticisms linked to romance. They engage in different forms of facework as a way to avoid losing face. Therefore, one may not know that another person in a particular interactional setting is a member of the romance community. Rather than risk losing face, they may choose to avoid discussing romances and remain less involved with the romance community.

Technological developments have alleviated some of this uncertainty. The Internet reduces the risk of interacting with those critical of the romance genre because it contains a number of different types of virtual spaces dedicated to those who do belong to it. As a result, several sub-communities of the romance community have formed in various virtual spaces. It does not mean that people remain in one place or that the sites are mutually exclusive, but rather the interaction between people who visit a particular site maintain their interaction at that site. Sites reference one another, but this interaction typically leads to separate conversations at each site with little crossover. Therefore, it is possible to focus on one virtual space to understand how that segment of the romance community functions. However, one cannot simply apply traditional understandings of offline communities to virtual communities.[11] This is why Komito's social constructionist viewpoint of community is a good approach for the SBTB sub-community. The social constructionist approach to community is inherently communicative. In order to negotiate meanings, people must communicate. Ethnography emphasizes the users over the technology, a good technique for online community analysis.[12] Ethnography of communication is a theoretical and methodological approach that combines the participant focus with a way to understand a community through its communication. The approach began with Hymes' call in 1962 for an ethnography of speaking, treating speaking as an activity for the focal point of examination.[13] The method expanded following Basso's study of silence among the Western Apache because he used the techniques for speech analysis on silence.[14] Ethnography of speaking became known as ethnography of communication, but retained Hymes' basic premises.[15] It is an approach that seeks to describe a form of communication in detail (descriptive analysis) and then examine how that communicative form is part of the community's culture (interpretive analysis). Culture is one of the major components of a community, regardless of its purpose.[16] As Carbaugh delineates, studying cultural communication phenomena requires examining "those resources (patterns of symbolic action and meaning) that are a) deeply felt, b) commonly intelligible, and c) widely accessible."[17] This means focusing on forms of communication that multiple members of the community respond to, believe are significant, and have the capacity to use.

The descriptive analysis is based on a description of the structural features of communication that Hymes developed to create uniformity across studies. Much as grammar divides the parts of a sentence, Hymes' structure creates division among social units of analysis, starting with the smallest possible form of interaction up to and including the speech community, which is comparable with others' use of community.[18] Most studies utilizing this form of analysis work closely with one unit of analysis, although two are present. This occurs because a speech community is always being studied, even if only part of the community's communication is under analysis. A speech community is defined as "a community sharing rules for the conduct and interpretation of speech, and rules for the interpretation of at least one linguistic variety."[19] In this case, SBTB is the speech community. The "Covers Gone Wild" entries are a speech event, a form of communication with a distinct beginning, middle, and end.[20]

I became a member of SBTB approximately a month prior to the start of data collection and still participate on the site. The data was collected over a period of three months starting in February 2007. Due to the asynchronous nature of SBTB, the speech event could not be fully observed while occurring; responses were stretched out over multiple days. Data collection started via participant observation at SBTB for an average of two hours per week. This led to an observance of communication patterns and concentrated time spent within the archives to further examine the speech event. In addition to field notes, major posts and comments were saved. The shorter than average period of data collection led to the inclusion of archived posts from 2005 and posts from January to April 2007. During collection, the data was reviewed for primary patterns, and later data was collected with these patterns in mind. Archived posts provided the opportunity to see if the speech event evolved over time.

Ten interviews were also conducted during the end of April 2007, based on those who expressed interest and responded to arrange an interview. The respondents were all female and ranged in age from 20 to 57 (M=31.4). Only two of the interviewees were not from the United States; one lived in the Netherlands and the other in Canada. The interviewees ranged from lurkers to heavy posters at the site, and included one of the site's two bloggers. The interviews were conducted to gain a general understanding of the community and to see how members viewed the speech event "Covers Gone Wild." All of the interviews took place via an instant messaging service and lasted approximately one hour each, which excluded potential respondents who did not use the service.

SBTB self-identifies as a romance review site. Despite its description as a "website that reviews romance novels from a couple of smart bitches who will always give it to you straight," links within the site make it clear there is far more to the site than reviews.[21] SBTB is an online community through the way in which those who post and comment on the site construct it as such through their communication. In this case it is a sub-community within the larger romance community. At the time of study, the page was named "Smart Bitches Who Love Trashy Novels," but those who post on the site used the shorthand of the domain name, "http://www.smartbitchestrashybooks.com," to reference the community. This is why the site is referenced as SBTB rather than SBTN.

Since the data was collected, the site name, design, and layout have all changed, but the use of SB and SBTB remains. During the time of study, the site contained a bright pink border. There were links to the entry categories, the archive, contact information, a frequently asked questions page, and an "about us" page. On the right-hand side was a sidebar containing a number of internal and external links. Comments appeared in a separate window when the link was clicked. This new window displayed a smaller version of the header for the main page, the entry's subject line, comments, and a new comment form. The comment page format was uniform across all SBTB posts.

From a technological standpoint, SBTB is a blog used predominately by the two women who started the site. This format creates an element of hierarchy. Only the two bloggers can create and post an entry. There are a few entries where the site owners publish posts composed by other people writing as "Guest Bitches," but this does not apply to "Covers Gone Wild." As a result, site viewers/members can only make entry suggestions. This is an element of the site design and cannot be circumvented. However, the two bloggers acknowledge others' contributions when they are incorporated into posts. It places the bloggers in the role of opinion leaders for SBTB, creating a form of the two-step flow described earlier. There is also an RSS feed for the site, which makes it more difficult for those who use the feed to interact with others as they only receive the entries from the bloggers, not the comments.

Given the title of SBTB, it is important to review its meaning as it has implications for the discourse. When interviewed, SB1 defined the term "smart bitch" as a "woman who is unafraid to demonstrate her intellect by articulating defined and defended opinions, who argues fairly and respectfully but with strength, and doesn't take much crap from anyone." This definition is gendered, but it also reflects the tone and quality of the site's discourse. Only one person who was interviewed mentioned men posting on the site and expanded the term "smart bitch" to include them. Another, uncomfortable with the use of the word "bitch" outside SBTB, responded that it "supplies attitude."

The term "trashy books" leads to more interpretations. There are two themes for the term: the first relates to a perceived outside opinion that romance novels are meaningless, and the second questions that outside opinion. Not all respondents mentioned both parts, but all referenced the first. Surprisingly, two admitted to agreeing in part with the outside degradation of romance reading. In contrast, SB1 defined "trashy books" as "books dismissed by others as pop culture and meaningless fluffy brain candy but that have value and depth unappreciated by those who don't read them." Another person took the idea further, stating, "We're reclaiming the term!"

A major emphasis within the interviews was on the combination of intellect and humor. One interviewee commented, "I don't know if I stressed the importance of the wit and the humor enough [...] That's a very large part of the appeal of the site." Humor was mentioned within all of the interviews with site visitors, even those who preferred more serious discussions about the romance industry. The underlying humor is central to the speech event "Covers Gone Wild." Playing on the popular "Girls Gone Wild" video franchise, "Covers Gone Wild" mocks outrageous romance novel covers of both print and virtual romances. Initially a blog post without visitor comments, "Covers Gone Wild" developed into a speech event as time passed. What makes this particular speech event stand out is its regularity and inclusion of others, more so than many of the romance reviews. Given that SBTB presents romance reviews as the focal point of the community, it makes one wonder what participation in "Covers Gone Wild" provides the SBTB community.

Hymes developed a set of tools through which to analyze the social unit of analysis, called the components of the social unit. These components, Settings, Participants, Ends, Act sequences, Key, Instrumentalities, Norms, and Genre, combine to form the SPEAKING mnemonic.[22] Settings refers both to the physical (in this case virtual) and psychological setting.[23] "Covers Gone Wild" occurs in an individual blog entry and its subsequent comments, where the only physical space that appears is the space the entry takes on the computer screen. While there may be an influence on participation based on the physical settings where SBTB visitors and members have their computers, there is no way to access this influence beyond message content. The speech event occurs approximately once a week. The entries are classified in the archives under the heading "Covers Gone Wild! (Non-Snoop Dogg Edition)." The reference to Snoop Dogg, a celebrity known for his involvement with the Girls Gone Wild enterprise in an attempt to include more black women in the Girls Gone Wild videos, incorporates a racial element. The person or people responsible for creating the category knowingly invoke the reference, most likely in a tongue-in-cheek manner. The lack of covers with blacks being mocked likely results from the difficulty in finding romances with blacks on the cover.

According to Hymes, participants include all those who take part in the speech event.[24] The participants in "Covers Gone Wild" include the two people who run the site, as well as the various visitors and members. Comments by both bloggers appear in the main entry, with a bold name to indicate whose thoughts are whose. Other participants are the commenters. These include romance writers, editors, publishers, and readers. Occasionally someone outside the romance community posts a comment, but this is rare. These are the active readers who create conversation, or the potential for conversation, through visible participation. Those who only read the entries ("lurkers") cannot be tracked. According to Clark, those who only read blog posts and do not comment are still participants because the bloggers write their entries in a way that the readers can understand them and thus be considered a part of "Covers Gone Wild."[25] This assumes that the readers belong to the SBTB community in at least a peripheral manner. Its public setting creates the possibility, however unlikely, for overhearers — those who are not meant to receive the message and do — because those who dislike romance may potentially see the entries.[26]

The distinction between who should and should not receive the message included in the "Covers Gone Wild" entry relates to the ends. The ends of a speech event are divided into outcomes (what does happen) and goals (what's intended to happen), because the former does not necessarily stem from the latter.[27] The "Covers Gone Wild" event is meant to mock covers of romance novels. The bloggers introduce the theme for the entry and write comments about each cover. Then others respond in the comments. For example, a post in February 2005 mocked Dara Joy covers from self-published novels. For the cover of *That Familiar Touch*, SB2 commented, "If Louis XIV had been fed a non-stop diet of LSD and crack, he still would've rejected that wig as too tasteless and far-out."[28] What occurs in the responses may or may not be the bloggers' intended goals. Responses may be directed toward the bloggers ("STOP IT!! YOU GUYS ARE CRACKING ME UP!!"), other commenters ("she's right! It is her boyfriend" in response to a prior poster), or continue mocking the covers directly ("'Help me! My forehead ... it's taking over my face!'").[29] Some-times they include multiple forms of responses within the same comment. This may appear in a format similar to the following comment:

> WHAT have you all done to me? In just an hour and a half I have to talk about two serious immunological problems. HOW am I going to get the silly grin off my face by then?
> Cover #1[*A Girl, a Guy, and a Ghost*, by Patricia Mason]. I couldn't convince myself that these two people were in the same cover. He would have to be floating a few feet off the floor or else standing on a pile of dictionaries. I'm also trying to decide if he is very, very small or she is very, very large.[30]

While the intention is to mock the covers, if an outside link to other media or news is included, people may respond to the link rather than engage in "cover snark." There may also be side discussions regarding the role of authors with respect to the development of the cover for their novels. For example, one commenter writes, "OMG, Poor Linnea [Sinclair]. Oy, the infamy. This cover for Accidental Goddess wasn't her choice. Ultimately marketing people said, 'This will sell more books!' Apparently people buy books with women in scarlet latext [sic] jumpsuits, who knew?"[31] These digressions often move away from the typical humor of the speech event.

The act sequence breaks down the order in which communication occurs.[32] The act sequence for "Covers Gone Wild" is rather simple. A typical entry that starts the speech event contains the following format: introduction of the theme, followed by the first cover and comments by first one blogger and then the other, the next cover and ensuing comments, and so on until the covers for the week have all been posted with reactions to them by both bloggers. The bloggers do not communicate directly with one another because, as SB1 explained in the interview with her, "[they] can post an entry and leave it 'closed' with a date and time to go live in the future." The two live on opposite sides of the United States, so one posts her comments and contacts the other so that she goes to the site and adds her part before making the entry "live" and visible to the community. All interaction takes place within the comments. Comments may be directed at the main entry or to prior comments. The technological format requires reading through all the comments posted after a particular comment to see if someone has responded to the earlier comment, regardless of whether a commenter has opted to receive responses via email. The next "Covers Gone Wild" entry always contains new covers, signifying a new speech event.

The next components are the key or tone of a particular speech act, followed by the instrumentalities, which covers the medium and modes of communication.[33] The key is predominately humorous, with an emphasis on mocking known as "snark." Occasionally others will comment with a more informative point about the lack of author control over the covers, changing the key. These comments may be posted by the authors themselves. For example, one of the early "Covers Gone Wild" entries led to a comment by the author of the novel saying, "Hey ladies — nobody hated this cover worse than I did! Hated it, hated it, hated it! Ohhhh ... how I wish we had control over such things."[34] This shows an underlying frustration with the covers. Even the author did not appreciate the cover given to one of her novels. Furthermore, all but one of the interview respondents commented on how bad romance covers are and their connection to the bad reputation associated with romance. The one who contradicted this commented that she was probably the only author who liked "clinch covers," but acknowledged she also enjoyed the mocking that takes place. While she is not the only one who liked some of the covers that are mocked, there is still frustration with the overall treatment of romance covers. The discussion of the lack of control authors have over covers leads to a more serious tone.

While the key may be found in interaction, the instrumentalities of "Covers Gone Wild" are found within the technology. It is an asynchronous Internet website. There are written and visual elements, including links to outside sources that contain audio and visual elements. There also was one occasion where a video from YouTube was included. The environment is predominately text-based, with the visuals serving as aids to understand what is being addressed. Links also are used as ways to support an argument or explain what is being said. The instrumentalities help develop and support the norms of "Covers Gone Wild." In ethnography of communication, norms are divided into norms of interaction and norms of interpretation, where both focus on what participants should or should not do.[35] The community develops norms of interaction as guidelines for interaction. There are norms about what to discuss and when to post. The discussion-related norms indicate that one should be aware of where the responsibility for the quality of the covers being mocked lies. These norms have the added effect of not allowing the mocking to extend past the covers to the novels themselves, which suggests respect for the books, but not the way they are packaged. The lack of discourse that extends to the novels suggests that such expansion of the discussion from cover to text should not happen. When the discussion does mention the novels themselves, it usually consists of someone commenting on how much someone enjoys an author's work despite the cover. Posters have developed the tendency not to assume the author has any responsibility for the cover design. Those who do are corrected by other commenters. Multiple "Covers Gone Wild" entries mention the role, or lack thereof, the authors have with respect to the covers of their novels. This leads to another norm, that of preventing the alienation of SBTB community members through cover snark. One interviewee points out that "cover snark has to not raise the hackles of the readers; we can't feel like our own reader choices are being maligned." "Covers Gone Wild" should not result in polarizing or mocking readers, nor should it blame authors for bad cover choices. While there were entries where commenters had been corrected in their assumptions about the authors, nobody interviewed claimed that they felt alienated by any "Covers Gone Wild" entry.

A time related norm also appeared in the cover entries. There rarely were comments that appeared more than a few days after the entry was posted. In fact, none of the interviewees mentioned commenting on older entries. If the comment is posted much later then the commenter acknowledged that. For example, one comment began with "Late to the party." This comment was posted over a month after the initial post appeared. This stands in marked contrast to the comment prior to it, which was posted five days after the initial entry and contained no such discursive move.

Finally there is a norm for participation. Participation is only recognizable to the community if it occurs in the comments or if the entry mentions covers having been provided by others. Not everyone necessarily participates in the comments to the cover entries. For example, SB9 mentioned in response to a question about commenting on cover entries that she does not do it often: "I rarely have anything more to say than 'that was funny.'" This suggests that another SBTB norm encourages people to provide more substantial comments. If someone has already expressed the idea that a post was funny, others will choose not to post rather than repeat the same idea. The only exceptions were the two cover entries in early 2007 where the themes related to two events in the personal lives of the bloggers.[36] As a result, there were a number of congratulatory comments that did not necessarily acknowledge the covers at all. The congratulatory posts are personal expressions of joy and thus it is not repetitive for different posters to express their own happiness for the site's bloggers.

The norms of interpretation reveal a focus on the community's awareness of the way the romance industry works. Restricting mocking people to those appearing in the covers and those responsible for the covers being mocked not only shows the community's intelligence about romance publishing, but also shows an overall respect for romance. Not all covers are mocked. The covers that are mocked vary from old to new, include people considered good and bad authors, and even included ebook and digital covers.

Not only are community members aware of the romance industry, but they are also aware of how others may perceive it. For example, people who post in "Covers Gone Wild" retain a narrow focus and do not engage in sweeping generalizations about romances based on the covers. This suggests that they desire to limit criticism to those elements that require criticism only. SB1 went further in one cover entry, saying, "I know the cover sells the story somewhat, but this is so awful. It's almost insulting. It's beefcake for the sake of beefcake, and it's part of what gives romance novel readers a reputation for being stupid."[37]

There are also two conflicting norms that appear. One is "don't judge a book by its cover," which was even mentioned by name within one of the earlier cover mockings. The other is that you should enjoy the cover and that covers should sell the book. Even though the cover is a form of marketing, it is expected to be aesthetically pleasing. In her entry of covers she enjoyed, SB2 posts a picture for Annette Blair's *The Kitchen Witch* and writes, "Every time I walk by this book, I pick it up. Every time, I remember it flunked the 15-page test, and put it back regretfully. That, folks, is good cover design."[38] SB1 also has "the book I keep coming back to even though I've tried to read it before. [...] I might have to try to read this book again, because it's just too good-looking."[39] In the same post, SB1 mentions, "I love it when a cover is attractive enough to match my enjoyment of the contents." The tension between these two norms is never resolved, and may also relate to some of the underlying frustration expressed within these comments. To enjoy the cover and not the book leads to needing to "put it back regretfully" or wanting "to try to read this book again."

"Covers Gone Wild" could be considered a genre of its own, in that it clearly stands out as a category for interaction. Hymes defines genre as referring to categories, such as poem, lecture, letter, etc., which may coincide with speech events, but analyzes them independently.[40] The "Covers Gone Wild" posts can be considered a form of mocking, but it is difficult to say whether it still is mocking when there are cases where there are off-topic comments. A discussion of the role of an author in comparison to a publisher is not a form of mocking. "Covers Gone Wild" certainly is a native genre for which the SBTB site is known. This is demonstrated in the comments where people mention having passed along the link to the site to their friends, introducing them to the SBTB community.

The ritual related to "Covers Gone Wild" is what Hall referred to as an "everyday ritual."[41] It has a spiral-like form, influenced by the online environment. Comments build on the initial entry rather than moving forward to a particular end. It is complicated by discussions that go on a tangent unrelated to romance novels, but still manages to celebrate the fact that they are all a part of the romance community. It starts with the introduction/preliminary comments, which consists of the blog post containing the covers and the comments by the bloggers. The members/visitors then pick it up. This includes acknowledgment of the bloggers, where commenters mention their appreciation for their comments, and/or continuation, where commenters add their viewpoints on the covers. The discussion ends when people stop commenting, independent of the discourse. The asynchronous environment means there usually are comments for a few days following the posting. If it is much later then it is typically acknowledged as such. People do not know whether or not somebody else will comment after them. Therefore, the online environment removes the termination phase.

"Covers Gone Wild" is a ritual influenced by the manner of participation. This pattern celebrates the opportunity for the bloggers and visitors to come together as a community to respond to a disliked element of the romance genre. Within these posts is an awareness that romance readers are looked down on, in part due to the covers of the novels they read. In the interview, SB1 notes this and also positions the bloggers and the rest of the SBTB site as a place for people who enjoy romance novels to come together and discuss aspects of the romance genre:

> SB1: even if we all disagree with each other on every other issue that week,
> SB1: the cover snark is humorous gathering and definitely a ritual part of the site.
> SB1: we're all romance fans, but we all hate how bad the covers are on our preferred reading material

This means that the mocking is not derision of the romance genre as a whole, but a way for the community to respond to an element they dislike without having to defend the books that they enjoy. It bears some similarities to the study of Israelis' Griping Ritual, which is the way Israelis cope with major government problems.[42] "Covers Gone Wild," like griping, responds to an outside source that has potentially negative implications for participants, such as covers making people think romance readers are stupid. The ritual fails to provide a solution, but allows the community to vent about a disliked element.[43] The venting creates the spiral-like form in the comments.

While there are a number of communicative implications apparent in the "Covers Gone Wild" entries due to its similarities to the Griping Ritual and its use of humor, it is important to note its implications for the study of romance. While researchers like Regis address the derision directed towards romance and its readers, little has been done with respect to how members of the romance community deal with these issues.[44] Although Brackett examines resultant impression management between romance readers and those who do not read, this chapter shows that there is an impact on discourse within the romance community too.[45] Not only do SBTB community members discuss outside impressions in serious conversations, these impressions can also can become part of more humorous elements.

This opens the door for several different avenues of research. Like fans, this online community has developed elements that build from the romance genre and adapted it to fit their needs.[46] Its members are "smart" in their mocking of covers by limiting it to the covers, as well as incorporating humor, play, and some information about the genre into their discourse. Although not fully focused on the discussion of the genre that appears in other types of entries at SBTB, it suggests that future research of the ways people communicate with one another about reading would benefit scholarship focused on romance and other forms of audience research.

More research is also necessary to understand the complicated interplay between self and other, or in this case community and other, when it comes to how those within the romance community view themselves and perceive themselves to be viewed by outsiders. Part of this appears through the description of "Covers Gone Wild," but it seems to be a more general theme of the site beyond the scope of this study. There is also the role of humor, which could lend more depth to the analysis of a community like SBTB.

"Covers Gone Wild" appears to be an important ritual for the SBTB community. By looking at how participants engage in "Covers Gone Wild," one sees how one segment of the romance community has found a way to be a community of its own and resist stereotypes about romance readers through focused yet humorous criticism of an element of the genre they dislike: romance novel covers. The ritual demonstrates that romance readers have found a way to come together and utilize today's technological advancements to move past the risk of losing face and enjoy, not just romances, but also the romance community.

NOTES

1. Lee Komito, "The Net as a Foraging Society: Flexible Communities," *Information Society* 14, no. 2 (1998): 98, 105.

2. Peter H. Mann, "The Romantic Novel and Its Readers," *Journal of Popular Culture* 15, no. 1 (1981): 10.

3. Janice Radway, *Reading the Romance* (1984; rpt. with a new Introduction, Chapel Hill: University of North Carolina Press, 1991), 49.

4. Mary Anne Moffitt, "Leisure Fiction and the Audience: Meaning and Communication Strategies," *Women's Studies in Communication* 16, no. 2 (1993): 47.

5. *Ibid.*, 50.

6. Elizabeth Long, *Book Clubs: Women and the Uses of Reading in Everyday Life* (Chicago: University of Chicago Press, 2003), 31.

7. Paul F. Lazarsfeld, Bernard Berelson, and Hazel Gaudet, "The People's Choice: How the Voter Makes Up His Mind in a Presidential Campaign," in *The Audience Studies Reader*, ed. Will Brooker and Deborah Jermyn (New York: Routledge, 2003), 14.

8. Radway, *Reading the Romance*, 46–7.

9. Kim Pettigrew Brackett, "Facework Strategies Among Romance Fiction Readers," *The Social Science Journal* 37, no. 3 (2000): 350.

10. Erving Goffman, *Interaction Ritual: Essays on Face-to-Face Behaviour* (New York: Penguin, 1972), 5.

11. Rick Parrish, "The Changing Nature of Community," *Strategies* 15, no. 2 (2002): 260.

12. Jannis Androutsopoulos, "Introduction: Sociolinguistics and Computer-Mediated Communication," *Journal of Sociolinguistics* 10, no. 4 (2006): 424

13. Dell Hymes, "The Ethnography of Speaking," in *Anthropology and Human Behavior*, ed. Thomas Gladwin and William C. Sturtevant (Washington, D.C.: The Anthropological Society of Washington, 1962), 101.

14. Kenneth A. Basso, "'To Give Up on Words': Silence in Western Apache Culture," *Southwestern Journal of Anthropology* 26, no. 3 (1970): 215.

15. Donal Carbaugh and Sally O. Hastings, "A Role for Communication Theory in Ethnographic Studies of Interpersonal Communication," in *Social Approaches to Communication*, ed. Wendy Leeds-Hurwitz (New York: The Guilford Press, 1995), 173.

16. Amitai Etzioni and Oren Etzioni, "Face-to-Face and Computer-Mediated Communities, A Comparative Analysis," *Information Society* 15, no. 4 (1999): 241.

17. Donal Carbaugh, "Comments on 'Culture' in Communication Inquiry," *Communication Reports* 1, no. 1 (1988): 38.

18. Hymes, "Ethnography," 108.

19. Dell Hymes, "Models of Interaction of Language and Social Life," in *Directions in Sociolinguistics: The Ethnography of Communication*, ed. John Gumperz and Dell Hymes (New York: Holt, Rinehart & Winston, 1972), 54.

20. *Ibid.*, 56.

21. "Who Are We," Smart Bitches, Trashy Books, http://www.smartbitchestrashybooks.com.

22. Hymes, "Models," 65.

23. *Ibid.*, 60.

24. *Ibid.*

25. Herbert H. Clark, *Arenas of Language Use* (Chicago: The University of Chicago Press, 1992), 218.

26. *Ibid.*, 218–9.

27. Hymes, "Models," 61.

28. Candy Tan, "This Week's Covers Gone Wild: Two Snarks for the Price of One," Smart Bitches, Trashy Books, February 20, 2005, http://www.smartbitchestrashybooks.com/index.php/weblog/comments/this_weeks_covers_gone_wild_two_snarks_for_the_price_of_one/.

29. Sookie, #8; Miri, #13990; melaniemiriam, #19. Comments on Tan, "This Week's Covers Gone Wild: Two Snarks for the Price of One," Smart Bitches, Trashy Books, http://www.smartbitchestrashybooks.com/index.php/weblog/comments/this_weeks_covers_gone_wild_two_snarks_for_the_price_of_one/.

30. DS, comment on Sarah Wendell's "Can This Cover Be Saved?" Smart Bitches, Trashy Books, http://www.smartbitchestrashybooks.com/index.php/weblog/comments/can_this_cover_be_saved/#22643.

31. Ann Aguirre, comment on Wendell, "Can This Cover Be Saved?" Smart Bitches, Trashy Books, http://www.smartbitchestrashybooks.com/index.php/weblog/comments/can_this_cover_be_saved/#22616.

32. Hymes, "Models," 62.

33. *Ibid.*, 63.

34. Danelle Harmon, comment on Candy Tan's "A Cover So Bad, It's, Well, Bad," Smart Bitches, Trashy Books, http://www.smartbitchestrashybooks.com/index.php/weblog/comments/a_cover_so_bad_its_well_bad/.

35. Hymes, "Models," 64–5.

36. Sarah Wendell, "Smart Bitch Secret Baby: The Cover Snark," Smart Bitches, Trashy Books, March 9, 2007, http://www.smartbitchestrashybooks.com/index.php/weblog/comments/smart_bitch_secret_baby_the_cover_snark/; and Sarah Wendell, "More Good News — More Cover Snark!" Smart Bitches, Trashy Books, March 9, 2007, http://www.smartbitchestrashybooks.com/index.php/weblog/comments/more_good_news_more_cover_snark/.

37. Candy Tan, "Love Hurts," Smart Bitches, Trashy Books, March 13, 2005, http://www.smartbitchestrashybooks.com/index.php/weblog/comments/love_hurts/.

38. Candy Tan, "Quitcher Bitchin!" Smart Bitches, Trashy Books, July 24, 2005, http://www.smartbitchestrashybooks.com/index.php/weblog/quitcher_bitchin/.

39. Sarah Wendell, "Sarah Spreads the Luuurve™," Smart Bitches, Trashy Books, August 1, 2005, http://www.smartbitchestrashybooks.com/index.php/weblog/comments/sarah_spreads_the_luuurve/.

40. Hymes, "Models," 65.

41. Bradford "J." Hall, "Ritual as Part of Everyday Life," in *Readings in Cultural Contexts*, ed. Judith N. Martin, Thomas K. Nakayam, and Lisa A. Flores (Mountain View, CA: Mayfield, 1998), 172.

42. Tamar Katriel, "Griping as a Verbal Ritual in Some Israeli Discourse," in *Cultural Communication and Intercultural Contact*, ed. Donal Carbaugh (Hillsdale, NJ: Lawrence Earlbaum, 1990), 101.

43. *Ibid.*, 105.

44. Pamela Regis, *A Natural History of the Romance Novel* (Philadelphia: University of Pennsylvania Press, 2003), xi.

45. Brackett, "Facework Strategies," 349.

46. Henry Jenkins, *Textual Poachers: Television Fans & Participatory Culture* (New York: Routledge, 1992), 156.

15

Happy Readers or Sad Ones?
Romance Fiction and the Problems
of the Media Effects Model

Glen Thomas

A persistent pattern in criticism of romance fiction from the late 1970s until the present is the oscillation between those who condemn the genre by denouncing romance as having an inimical effect on the minds of women, while, in contrast, defenders of romance argue that reading romance does nothing of the sort. Indeed, romance fiction defenders argue, romance fiction improves women's lives because of the happiness it brings to its readers. Both of these positions are predicated upon a media effects model of reading that is fundamentally behaviorist in its theorization of the audience. This behaviorist model assumes a direct correlation between consumers and their behavior: too much television, for example, leads viewers to a position of supine passivity, if not a life of crime; children who read comics expose themselves to rare spiders in the hope of being bitten and turning into Spiderman. David Gauntlett, however, raises the prospect that the media effects model has "consistently taken the *wrong approach* to the mass media, its audiences, and society in general."[1] In this chapter, I argue that this media effects/behaviorist paradigm of understanding the romance audience is indeed inherently flawed, in that both sides of this debate construct a fantasy reader who is in one way or another dependent on romance fiction. I then suggest an alternative approach to understanding romance fiction and its consumers through a creative industries approach that seeks to uncouple this notion of readers and dependency.

The tradition of attacking the quality of romance fiction and the delusions of its readership dates back at least to the nineteenth century. This model gained traction in the late 1970s, continued into the 1990s, and persists in the present. For example, the approach of seeing romance fiction as "pornography for women" assumes a pliant, if not manipulated, reader, one who both lacks taste and is oblivious to the patriarchal web being spun by romance fiction, which prompts Ann Snitow to wonder if her discussion of the genre is offensive to romance readers, which of course it is.[2] Snitow opens her analysis with the assertion that romance novels, represented for her by Harlequin romances, are "not art," but are instead, she argues, quoting Lilian Robinson, "leisure activities that *take the place* of art" (308). Immediately apparent in this discussion is the distinction between "art" and "not art," although what constitutes art is not defined. Snitow initially concedes that popular culture is not "soma for the masses produced by a cynical elite" (308), but that a more complex relationship exists between producers of what she calls mass culture and its consumers, which, she argues, represents an important shift in critical thinking. Yet as Snitow's self-contradictory analysis progresses, two key points emerge: one, despite her stated attempts to "steer a careful course between critical extremes" (308) Snitow's adjectives betray her distaste for the subject of her argument—"pallid" (308), "pablum" (309), "Pollyanna books" (309), "cheap" (313), "know-nothing narrowness" (317), for example. Secondly, and more importantly for this discussion, Snitow's analysis is based upon a psychological model of readership, in that she sees romance as feeding "certain regressive elements in the female experience" (308) that reflect "commonly experienced psychological and social elements in the daily lives of women" (309). Her emphasis here, then, is on the psychological behavior of women and their "regressive" tendencies that find an outlet in romance fiction.

In the same way, the formidable figure of Janice Radway, whose *Reading the Romance* was at the time a landmark study of the genre, follows the same critical continuity as Snitow and Tania Modleski. Like them, Radway's approach is behaviorist in its orientation, as *Reading the Romance* investigates "the way romance reading as a form of *behavior* operated as a complex intervention in the ongoing social life of actual subjects."[3] My interest here is not in disputing Radway's method, survey sample, or attitudes, which others have done. The focus here is on the model of reading that Radway propounds, which shares the same ideological underpinnings as others who criticize romance fiction for its effects. At one point, for instance, Radway notes that her readers' drive to "read one's way out of a bad situation and to resolve or contain all of the unpleasant feelings aroused by it is so strong in some of the Smithton readers that they read the whole book even when they hate it."[4] In other words, reading romance is a psychological process that must be negotiated to defuse or resolve readers' internal conflicts, even if the readers cannot abide the words they read. Like addicts, then, readers will press on through their nausea or hangover for the bliss of release that comes with the romance hit. This approach places readers so much in the thrall of a novel's content that they are unable to let go; these books are a habit that women cannot kick. Radway's readers know that some of the books they read are bad for them, but slaves to the genre that they are, they continue to read, book after book, all the while knowing that things will get worse before they get better.

The other frequently-cited discussion of romance fiction is the chapter on Harlequin romances in Tania Modleski's *Loving with a Vengeance*, first published in 1982. Modleski refers to the formula of Harlequin romances,[5] which she sees as encouraging and rewarding female selflessness in that the heroine of the novel can "achieve happiness only by undergoing a complex process of self-subversion, during which she sacrifices her aggressive instincts, her 'pride' and—nearly—her life" (36–37). For Modleski, the novels "perpetuate ideological confusion about male sexuality and male violence, while insisting that there is no problem" (43), while simultaneously functioning as a revenge fantasy for women (45–48), yet, more contradictorily still, showing to women the path to financial and husbandly success which can only be attained by women not actively wanting such success (50). The result of all this is the practice of "pretence and hypocrisy" in "real life" for romance readers (50).

Pretence and hypocrisy are highly likely outcomes if this confusion of impulses and motivations is taken to be an outcome of reading. As with the discussions of Snitow and Radway, the dominant element to emerge here is the behaviorist understanding of romance reading, which is presented as a symptom of an internal psychological problem (if not a crisis) that manifests itself in reading these "Pollyanna" novels. Modleski concludes by arguing that romances, "in presenting a heroine who has escaped psychic conflict, inevitably increase the reader's own psychic conflicts, thus creating an even greater dependency on the literature" (57). Modleski equates romances to "certain tranquillizers" (57) that may initially relieve anxiety, but through prolonged use ultimately raise anxiety levels. What she argues for here is an iatrogenic effect of romance, in that like some drugs, romance initially has a positive effect on consumers, but the more one reads, the worse one feels. As she says, this model of popular culture as a narcotic is a commonly accepted theory, to which romances will "lend credence" (57).

This statement brings into sharp focus the ways in which romance fiction is perceived by its critics: it is the secret addiction of narcotized housewives, not unlike the headache powders of the 1950s and 1960s that gave Mother enough of a buzz to get through her day until she could get her hands on the cooking sherry in the evening. The notion of popular culture as narcotic recalls Marx's dictum about religion, whose function now, apparently, is fulfilled by television and potboilers. Modleski's Frankfurt School assumptions are brought to the fore in her conclusion that readers should not be denounced, but rather, it is the "conditions which have made [romance novels] necessary" that should be condemned (57). In this model, romance readers are imprisoned in a false consciousness that acts upon them like some form of irresistible opiate that feeds off the inherent contradictions and conflicts in women's lives, leading to extraordinary amounts of psychic energy being expended to keep women passive; Modleski finishes by suggesting that the energy women "use to belittle and defeat themselves can be rechanneled into efforts to grow and explore ways of affirming and asserting the self" (58).

These three readings of romance fiction and its readers in many ways set the standard for much criticism to follow. The psychological approach to analyzing romance reading continues throughout criticism of the genre to the present. Wardrop, for instance, examines romance through Freud and theories of sado-masochism to conclude that romance fiction depicts female empowerment that represents a wider social shift wherein romantic love becomes an egalitarian enterprise[6]; Opas and Tweedie see romances as a "magic carpet ride" for readers who are transported by the novel into a world of intense emotional experience.[7] Again, the emphasis is on readers being removed, somehow, from their psychological reality into another realm. In each of these examples, the reader is presented as "swept away" (magic carpets), "hooked" (as on drugs), or having regressive elements of their psyche fed by this "pablum." Jeanne Dubino's romance reader is romantically unhappy, so, not "finding what they want in 'real' life, millions of women turn to romances in a vicarious attempt to compensate for the lack of attention and validation they get in their own lives."[8] Dubino then roundly castigates romance fiction for helping "to condition women for subservience by reproducing, structurally, the real relations between men and women. Romances combine the desire for a man with the inscription of the reader into patriarchal heterosexual ideology."[9] In the same manner, Mary M. Talbot cautions against "the consequences for some readers of repeated doses of Mills & Boon's variety of fantasy eroticism" on the grounds that what seem to be "problematic relationships are reinterpreted as good ones."[10] Julie Bindel, whose newspaper article describes romance fiction as "Detestable Trash," refers to romance novels as "propaganda" that "feed directly into some women's sense of themselves as lesser beings, as creatures desperate to be dominated."[11] Bindel then magnanimously concludes by stating that she does "not believe in blaming women for our own oppression"; rather the fault lies with romance publishers doling out the instruments of patriarchy.[12]

The twin impulses here — to denounce the text itself and to exhort women to discard their reading material in favor of something more consciousness-raising — were for some time the attitude of the academy to popular culture generally. These attitudes are the product of broader Leavisite or Marxist impulses to account for "art" or the ideological state apparatuses that restrain the revolutionary potential of the proletariat. In response to this often trenchant criticism of romance fiction is the (much smaller) tradition of regarding romance as empowering for women, as an expression of female consciousness and desire on pages that men, by and large, do not see. It should not be a surprise that the most ardent defenders of romance fiction are authors of the genre, who regularly assail academic critics for not understanding romance.[13] In 1999, Elaine Wethington, herself an academic, sums up this issue in a somewhat plaintively entitled article — "Are Academic Opinions about Romance Novels All Negative?" — on the web site All About Romance.[14] Wethington finds the answer to her titular question to be a qualified "no," as what she refers to as "younger academics" with an interest in popular culture come to displace the "older academic view." Even so, Wethington concludes that in the romance context many academics apparently equate "enjoyment of sex scenes as indicative of a lack of education." Wethington's point is, however, both truncated and simplistic in her division of academic criticism into "younger" critics and those who are, presumably, older (yet also amusing in its own way: the image of puritanical academic feminists lecturing women on why they should not derive any pleasure from reading sex scenes matches many of the stereotypes of academics and confirms the suspicion that education merely robs life of all its joys).

Romance authors, in the main, tend to come out swinging in defense of the genre. Deborah Camp argues that the appeal of romance is timeless (sixteen centuries and still going), and that romance fiction contains a "bright thread of morality" that consistently confounds those who do not appreciate the genre; Camp divides responses to romance into "those who understand the nature of romance novels" and "critics."[15] The latter are misguided because they fail to grasp how romances "present and ponder the dreams, desires, problems and needs of women" to provide a happy ending outlet for busy, stressed, and overworked women.[16] In the same collection of essays, Helen Mittermeyer defends romance as part of a "woman's journey" through life, which most women desire to take. Those who decline this journey lack both "imagination and vision."[17] In this context, romance authors enhance the lives of women on their "journey": through depictions of courageous women who espouse "effort and determination" on what Mittermeyer terms "that righteous crusade."[18] This strenuous defense, informed by visions of legions of women on a crusade for romance, is noteworthy for its very hyperbole. There is a sense here that barbarian hordes (or "critics") are circling and must be repelled with every ounce of firepower in the romantic arsenal.

Such responses to criticism are a feature of the romance industry among authors, readers, and publishers, who defend their genre with considerable intensity. Critics of romance fiction are seen as guilty of a set of failures: not ever having read a romance novel, yet able to declaim on the field with authority; not understanding the complexities of the language of romance integral to the genre that delivers to the reader the requisite amount of pleasure[19]; failing to see that romances ease the burden of women's lives, be she "a tired factory worker or that worried mother or that elderly woman in a nursing home [who] finds something, anything, in one of my books that makes her life just a little easier or a little happier"[20]; using an inappropriate set of criteria to judge romance fiction; or refusing, as Kathleen Gilles Seidel phrases it, to "judge me by the joy I bring."[21] The joy that romance fiction brings can take many forms: Bonnie Williams argues that romance readers have better sex lives than non-readers because romance novels allow their readers to "get in the mood."[22] She cites a staggering statistic from *Psychology Today* that asserts that women who read romances "make love with their partners 74% more often than women who don't" which does suggest that men everywhere could save money on flowers and chocolates in favor of the latest release from Harlequin. Williams adds that this fact is not news for women who read romances, as readers have "long been trying to tell mainstream nay-sayers this all along." Here, no-fun critics of romance fiction have allowed their anti-libidinal prejudices to blind them to the fact that when it comes to what Caitlin Flanagan calls the whoopee hour, the behaviorist effects of romance fiction make women's lives a lot more interesting.

These defenses of romance fiction, even in this small survey, all return to the same themes. Romance novels enhance the quality of women's lives in various ways; they offer emotional and physical satisfaction to their readers; and critics of romance do not understand the genre or its readers. Critics, certainly, are seen as prigs and bores who pityingly regard romance readers as under-educated and thoroughly misled. Stepping back from the specifics of the debate, however, we can see that the genre's defenders share the underlying assumption of the genre's harshest critics that books should *do* something, whether that "something" entails enabling readers to better understand the vicissitudes of Life (the Leavisite great tradition), stripping away readers' false consciousness (a Marxist defense of more radical forms of art), or soothing readers with promises of happiness and sensual "joy" (a Marxist critique of popular culture which the genre's defenders reframe as a badge of honor). If romance readers are not glazed addicts of the genre or internally conflicted, then they are unhappy in their lives and need something to cheer them up or put them in the mood. In sum, readers are morons, unhappy, or unhappy morons. Note the language and descriptions used to defend the genre: "tired," "worried," and "elderly"[23]; "frazzled" with "little sense of control over [their] lives"[24]; enduring "a long, hard day of bringing home the bacon, cooking it, and feeding it to a hungry family"[25]; or readers whose "own lives are out of whack."[26] This is not far removed from the language of those who criticize the genre and its readers as oppressed and downtrodden. In either the pro- or anti-romance commentaries, then, readers have something wrong with them, be it oppression from a patriarchal culture (boo!) or the fact that they are tired and overworked but made happier by romance (huzzah!). Both the critical and the supportive positions, that is to say, assume a programmatic role for creative products, and both predicate their assumptions on a psychological behaviorist model of media effects that assumes a scholarly superiority to the audience, which is presented as inferior to either the commentator or the critic. The media effects model that underpins both perspectives of analysis is fundamentally flawed, so that all results here is an argument that runs in circles (yes, it is; no, it isn't; yes, it *is*).

As Gauntlett argues, as I noted at the outset, this media effects model "has consistently taken the *wrong approach* to the mass media, its audiences, and society in general."[27] This is not to say that this chapter somehow has found the "right" approach, but it functions to highlight the enervating nature of this debate and to propose an alternative. Gauntlett points out that the view of the audience in the media effects model assumes a group of people with "no selectivity or critical skills, and their habits are explicitly contrasted with preferred activities"; in this case, the preferred activities are either reading more improving literature, or engaging in activities that lead to a more rewarding life. Because of an apparent inability to do either, fulfillment must be found in a romance novel. As Gauntlett notes, the audience itself "is not well served by studies which are willing to treat them as potential savages or actual fools." One further point Gauntlett makes that is also germane to this discussion is his observation that the effects model presumes that the mass media (or mass entertainment) "presents a single and clear-cut 'message.'" The circularity of the argument over romance emerges in the debate over this single message that romance putatively presents to its readers, be it patriarchal oppression or celebratory depictions of women's lives. Both sides of the discussion argue that there is one, single, unequivocal message that romance fiction delivers to its readers; the key feature of the debate that arises is the struggle over exactly what this one message is.

For me, though, neither of these positions is satisfactory, hence the focus on romance as a creative industry. I do not dispute the inherent sexism of Western culture and the social conditions that have a negative impact on women, be those conditions discrimination in the workplace, salary differences with men, access to maternity leave and childcare, or objectification in advertising. What I am seeking to avoid, though, is the situation Gauntlett outlines, where social problems are tackled backwards, "by starting with the media and then trying to lasso connections from there on to social beings, rather than the other way around." And in that light, finger-waving hectoring and pompous condescension are not the best ways to effect social change. By the same token, this is not a criticism of romance as such: I am sure that some readers are made happy by the novels they consume, and that romantic relationships are a feature of the lives of most people.

My point here is that the focus on romance as a creative industry offers an alternative means of examining the way romance fiction functions in the creative, social, and corporate sectors as a cultural phenomenon. The creative industries concept, as Hartley argues,[28] combines—but then radically transforms—two older terms: the *creative* arts and the *cultural* industries. This change is important for it brings the arts (i.e., culture) into direct contact with large-scale industries such as media entertainment (i.e., the market). It suggests the possibilities of moving beyond the elite/mass, art/entertainment, sponsored/commercial, high/trivial distinctions that have bedeviled thinking about creativity in policy as well as intellectual circles, especially in countries with European traditions of public culture.

Hartley's point is suggestive in that it offers an alternative framework for understanding and analyzing romance fiction. Rather than the above debates over romance (empowering or oppressive? literature or junk? savvy readers or deluded dupes?), the genre can be understood as an industry with the attendant features that come with such a label. Authors are thereby producers or creative workers who provide content for publishers. Publishers offer authors the means to distribute and market this creative product to the reader (or consumer). In creative industries terms, the reader-consumer is also, more broadly, a citizen: Hartley argues that public culture and private life have become intertwined to the extent that we should now refer to the citizen-consumer.[29] In the creative industries, the citizen-consumer, or in this context, the reader-consumer, has evolved beyond the passive, sponge-like absorber of authoritative television commercials where strange men in white coats inspect the washing of cowering women to determine if their whites really are as white as they could be. Instead, as Hartley and other theorists of the creative industries point out, the citizen-consumer is best understood through the perspective of "consumption as action, not behavior."[30] In this light, reading romance is an act of consumption in which the reader-consumer participates actively and deliberately as an aspect of identity formation. This shift to the reader-consumer of romance short-circuits the debate over how reading romance can be understood because if romance reading is understood as action, the principles of selectivity and industry will inform reader engagement.

The sheer proliferation of lines or categories of romance fiction suggests that readers are selective in their choices of what they read rather than approach romance fiction as an undifferentiated product. Readers consume those novels that match their own tastes and preferences for romantic subject matter. Hence Harlequin's distinction among romances set in medical environments, various historical periods, Christian communities, or the American West, alongside a sliding scale of sexual explicitness of content that ranges from none at all (in Christian romances) to energetic encounters that feature the protagonists swinging from a chandelier. This variety in content and setting is clear evidence that not all readers like the same material. Single title publishers also offer more than one type of romance narrative: Jennifer Crusie's romantic comedies are not the same as Keri Arthur's paranormal stories of vampires and werewolves, or characters who are hybrids of both. Readers do not consume romance fiction in the manner of alcoholics who will chug down after-shave or turpentine if nothing else is available. Rather, as Henry Jenkins has shown, fans (or in this case, readers) will participate in a specific community (in this case, a specific romance community) in a process of identity formation.[31] Readers will gravitate to those romances that assist in a process of defining their identity, in the same way fans of *Buffy* or *Star Trek* select and appropriate elements of those programs in order to define themselves, as well as to participate in a community of like-minded individuals. Consuming romance is an aspect of identity formation akin to participating in a political party, joining a church, or volunteering for the Red Cross.

As the term creative industries suggests, popular culture should be seen as an industry in terms of both its production and consumption. The variety of romantic sub-genres and heat levels, and the different media in which romance can be consumed (books, films, television programs, on-line, text messages) demonstrate that the supply side of the romance industry is and must be attuned to the demands of consumers. Rather than the *caveat emptor* approach of the media effects model, I would suggest that the model here is more one of *caveat venditor*: let the seller beware. Producers of romance fiction cannot simply dump anything on the market and assume that it will sell famously and reap a fortune for all involved. Cultural products — books, films, television programs, computer games — that do not find a market are expensive failures. Any model that assumes producers can shovel up any old nonsense to a pliant public is fundamentally flawed.

I do not, though, intend for this industry focus to represent a paean to capitalism or the free market; free markets have proved to be notoriously unreliable at delivering goods and services, while capitalism is of enormous benefit to the wealthy and less favorable to individuals who lack the resources to participate in its bounty. What I again take issue with is the conception that "pablum" will be widely and instantly consumed without any input from consumers. Such an authoritarian model of production and consumption suggests a nineteenth century robber-baron mentality of "the public be damned," which, in an era of Long Tail niche marketing, overlooks the fragmentary nature of consumption patterns.[32]

The creative industries framework I am working within here, then, seeks to examine the romance producer and consumer differently from the critical positions outlined above. In the criticism discussed, the psychological model of the reader is highly behaviorist in its orientation in that consumers are held to be duped, tricked, or addicted into purchasing products that are presented to them in a top-down model of management or marketing expertise that decides what's in demand, or what people simply have to wear this season. The creative industries approach, in contrast, regards the consumer as an actor, a causal factor in creative production. This is a bottom-up approach where producers deliver to consumers what consumers want, rather than what the producer *thinks* consumers want. Creative industries theory marks a move away from a production process that culminates in this year's model from Chrysler (and you'll like it), to an alternative understanding of how popular culture is produced. It also distinguishes romance and other popular genres from, for want of a better name, literary publishing, in that for romance writers and publishers, understanding reader desires is paramount and the key determinant of the success or otherwise of a romance novel. I doubt, for instance, that the same focus on readers is true for John Updike's publishers, who promote that author's work in terms of the cultural cachet attached to winning the Pulitzer Prize and the American Book Award, rather than, say, surveying Pennsylvanian car dealers for their thoughts on the Rabbit novels.

Romance writing, publishing, and reading are complex and inter-related activities that exemplify the creative industries' focus on causal relationships among content, production, and consumption. I do not argue that romance fiction is somehow beyond criticism, and should be uncritically celebrated. As Jennifer Crusie-Smith points out when describing the romance fiction she read for her dissertation, a "lot of what I read was bad, some of it so abysmal I gave up and skimmed."[33] What Crusie-Smith describes as "abysmal" novels should indeed be criticized, and with gusto. My point here is that criticism and discussion of the readership of romance fiction needs to move beyond the circularity of the debate over a fantasy reader who is oppressed and relieved by turns, be that oppression by the heavy hand of patriarchy, or the relief that stems from feeling happier or enjoying enhanced sexual relations with a significant other. Rather than focus on the unitary fantasy reader of romance fiction, it's time to talk of readers in the plural, and how these readers' choices are one element in constructing and shaping a complex reading position and identity.

The 2007 controversy over the reception of Anna Campbell's *Claiming the Courtesan* provides an instructive case study of both the circularity of the debates over romance fiction, as well as offering a means by which the creative industries approach can be tested.[34] Campbell's novel generated considerable discussion (and some disquiet) both before and after its publication for its depiction of scenes of "forced seduction" between the hero and heroine. The key aspects in the controversy over this novel are the scenes where the hero, the Duke of Kylemore, kidnaps the heroine, Verity Ashton/Soraya, and transports her to Scotland where he imprisons and forces himself upon her. By the end of the novel, Verity and the Duke are in love and plan to marry. For the novel's critics, the plot resolution represents an endorsement of sexual violence wherein a woman loves the man who treats her abominably.[35]

At the outset, I will say that sexual violence, or violence in any form, in the human world where people have to go to work, go home, pay their mortgages, and do their grocery shopping is an abhorrent phenomenon. Few individuals in their right minds would endorse violence as a solution to life's issues or problems. However, the question about the reception of Campbell's novel is the way it is regarded as influencing readers into believing that violence against women is acceptable. Such discussions rehearse the points I made earlier in this chapter: readers cannot tell the difference between fiction and fact; readers need to be protected against material that is not uplifting; and readers are easily swayed by what they read. Of note here is that romance fiction generates such anxieties in a manner not seen in the criticism of other genres and creative products: *Pretty Woman* is not seen as advocating prostitution as a viable career alternative any more than *Othello* is seen as justifying killing one's wife over misplaced clothing accessories.

If *Claiming the Courtesan* and its reception are examined from a creative industries perspective, the following two points emerge. Firstly, this novel is a work of fantasy that cannot be read from a realist perspective. The conclusion of the novel is proof of that: a Regency-era aristocrat, even a Scottish one, would no more marry his courtesan than he would marry his cook, no matter how delicious her haggis. The novel is therefore not positioned as an instructional guide, but a work that taps into readers' fantasies. These fantasies are one element of readers' identity formation, a complex interaction among social markers such as gender, class, race, and social capital. The gap between fantasy and day-to-day lives is a considerable one that readers well recognize. The Australian satirical television program *The Chaser's War on Everything* proved this point in fewer than five minutes: one member of the cast dressed in Regency-era clothing and approached women in the street using nothing but Mr. Darcy's dialogue from *Pride and Prejudice*. None of the women approached swooned; most looked bemused if not appalled. Mr. Darcy the fictional character functions as a figure of romantic fantasy, but he is not someone whom women want to meet in the street on the way to work. The fantasies of other people may be discomforting, but as Jennifer Crusie points out in her discussion of the controversy over *Claiming the Courtesan*, there are dominant tropes of fantasy that not everyone will share, but one individual's "squick meter" cannot define or limit a genre.[36] In this context of identity formation, the same principles apply to those who so vehemently criticized *Claiming the Courtesan*: criticism of the novel is a means by which identity is, in part, constructed through the consumption of creative products. Aversion to a creative genre or sub-genre defines an individual as much as adherence to that genre. This is not to lapse into an anodyne position of "I don't like it but other people do, so that's all right," which, taken to an extreme, could be used to defend any activity from public floggings to gambling on dog fights. Rather, what emerges here, then, is a distinction between creative works that engage with readers' fantasy identifications and actions that take place in, for want of a better term, the world of real life. Readers' consumption of these creative works occurs within a social space or habitus — in effect, in this context, a habitus of romance fiction — with a series of distinctions and hierarchies of tastes, consumption patterns, and reading positions. These distinctions and hierarchies will influence the ways that creative products are read and consumed.

This self-making is a key feature of *Claiming the Courtesan* itself. The split in the heroine's subjectivity, in her switch from the courtesan Soraya to the demure widow Verity Ashton, emblematizes the process of identity formation. The Duke of Kylemore's violent re-imposition of Verity's courtesan identity thus represents wider social processes that readers engage with on a day-to-day basis: citizens in Western democracies are bombarded by authoritative demands to be someone they are not (younger, sexier, healthier, better-dressed, wealthier, and so on, *ad nauseam*). Verity's negotiation of these competing demands and her final shaping of a new identity mirrors readers' own grappling with similar forces. In the novel, the outcome is that Verity becomes someone else entirely: neither courtesan nor widow, but wife, just as the Duke of Kylemore also changes from "cold Kylemore," to an oafish brute, then to an erstwhile courtesan's husband. The utterly ahistorical conclusion to the novel represents the contemporary citizen's dilemma of, in Hartley's terms, how to construct one's self in a situation "where customary structural roles do not exert much influence over behavior or interpersonal relations."[37] One element of the novel's appeal, then, is readers' fantasy identification with this process of self-construction. Similarly, the discomfort that critics of the novel experience can therefore be seen as a reaction against the forceful imposition of an identity that readers would prefer to avoid.

Secondly, the industry perspective of creative industries examines the ways *Claiming the Courtesan* is branded and sold. Campbell received a substantial advance from Avon-HarperCollins for the novel, which was published as a Romantic Treasure (an imprint usually reserved for highly popular authors). This was unusual for a first novel by an unknown author: Avon's advance payment and positioning of the novel in the market suggest that the company expected it to sell well and thereby increase the publisher's revenue. (From this perspective, the controversy over the novel was good for business, as controversy tends to lead to greater sales.) *Claiming the Courtesan* was branded as "Regency Noir," which is described as "dark" and "sexy." This categorization of the novel and the author places it within a specific segment of the market distinguished from other romance fiction. In effect, then, Campbell and her work are branded as offering a particular reading experience in the same way as other creative products, be they Ed McBain's police procedural novels or the films of Sophia Coppola.

Within the creative milieu of romance fiction, *Claiming the Courtesan* has achieved considerable success. The novel won the *Romantic Times* award for Best First Historical romance in 2007, and was nominated for the Romance Writers of Australia R*BY (Romantic Book of the Year) Award for 2008, and for the Romance Writers of America Best Regency Historical Romance RITA for 2008. This level of endorsement within the romance writing community suggests that the novel has garnered praise from other creative practitioners within the field. Therefore, then, within the distinctions and tastes of experts within the field, this is a novel that is rated highly. While not all consumers will agree with these assessments, the approbation of prizes and nominations from within the industry represents institutional approval. Institutional and consumer tastes may not always converge (witness some puzzling Academy Award choices), but nevertheless, within the romance industry *Claiming the Courtesan* has been branded as a quality romance novel. Although it is outside the scope of this chapter, the creative industries approach here would interrogate the criteria against which novels are selected and nominated for awards, and how these awards are determined.

In sum, then, this chapter has argued that the media effects approach to romance fiction, in the debate over its either oppressive or uplifting nature, ultimately produces a stalemate within criticism. The creative industries approach, while in no way the only, or somehow "right" way to read romance, offers an alternative to what in many ways are pre-determined positions. The creative industries examines the methods and forces through which citizens' identities are shaped, and the institutional processes that bring a product to the market and how then that product is received both by consumers and practitioners within the industry. These questions of romance tastes and distinctions offer a fruitful starting point for an alternative means of analyzing the romance industry.

NOTES

This research was supported under Australian Research Council's Linkage Projects funding scheme (project number LP0777006): "The uses of romance for new demographics and multimedia platforms: A model of media innovation in international women's fiction publishing."

1. David Gauntlett, "Ten Things Wrong with the Media 'Effects' Model," www.theory.org.uk/david/effects.htm.

2. Ann Snitow, "Mass Market Romance: Pornography for Women Is Different," in *Women and Romance: A Reader*, ed. Susan Ostrov Weisser (New York: New York University Press, 2001), 308. Further references will be provided parenthetically.

3. Janice Radway, *Reading the Romance: Women, Patriarchy, and Popular Literature*, (1984; rpt. with a new Introduction, Chapel Hill: University of North Carolina Press, 1991), 7.

4. *Ibid.*, 71.

5. Tania Modleski, *Loving with a Vengeance: Mass-Produced Fantasies for Women* (1982; rpt. New York: Routledge, 1988), 36. Further references will be provided parenthetically.

6. Stephanie Wardrop, "The Heroine Is Being Beaten: Freud, Sadomasochism, and Reading the Romance," *Style* 29 (1995): 459–73.

7. Lisa Lena Opas and Fiona Tweedie, "The Magic Carpet Ride: Reader Involvement in Romantic Fiction," *Literary and Linguistic Computing* 14, no. 1 (1999): 89–101.

8. Jeanne Dubino, "The Cinderella Complex: Romance Fiction, Patriarchy and Capitalism," *Journal of Popular Culture* 27, no. 3 (1993): 107.

9. *Ibid.*, 116.

10. Mary M. Talbot, "'An explosion deep inside her': Women's Desire and Popular Romance Fiction," in *Language and Desire: Encoding Sex, Romance and Intimacy*, ed. Keith Harvey and Celia Shalom (London: Routledge, 1997), 119.

11. Julie Bindel and Daisy Cummins, "Mills & Boon: 100 Years of Heaven or Hell?" *The Guardian* (London), 5 December 2007, http://www.guardian.co.uk/lifeandstyle/2007/dec/05/women.fiction.

12. *Ibid.*

13. Certainly this is true in my experience. At the first Romance Writers of Australia conference I attended, where I passed out a survey for delegates to complete, I was given a brisk telling-off by the romance author Daphne Clair, who told me I did not know what I was talking about, but that she was willing to discuss romance with me after I had gone away and learned something about the genre.

14. Elaine Wethington, "Are Academic Opinions About Romance Novels All Negative?" All About Romance, www.likesbooks.com/elaine.html.

15. Deborah Camp, "The Role of the Romance Novel," in *Writing Romances*, ed. Rita Gallagher and Rita Clay Estrada (Cincinnati: Writer's Digest Books, 1997), 47, 48, 48.

16. *Ibid.*, 52–53.

17. Helen Mittermeyer, "Romance — A Woman's Intricate Journey," in *Writing Romances*, ed. Rita Gallagher and Rita Clay Estrada (Cincinnati: Writer's Digest Books, 1997), 57.

18. *Ibid.*, 57.

19. Linda Barlow and Jayne Ann Krentz, "Beneath the Surface: The Hidden Codes of Romance," in *Dangerous Men and Adventurous Women*, ed. Jayne Ann Krentz (Philadelphia: University of Pennsylvania Press, 1992), 15–29.

20. Diana Palmer, "Let Me Tell You About My Readers," in *Dangerous Men and Adventurous Women*, ed. Jayne Ann Krentz (Philadelphia: University of Pennsylvania Press, 1992), 157.

21. Katherine Gilles Seidel, "Judge Me By the Joy I Bring," in *Dangerous Men and Adventurous Women: Romance Writers on the Appeal of the Romance*, edited by Jayne Ann Krentz (1992; rpt. New York: Harper-Paperbacks, 1996), 199–226.

22. Bonnie Williams, "Readers of Romance Have Better Sex Lives," Articlecity, www.articlecity.com/articles/relationships/article_717.shtml. Further references will be to this article.

23. Palmer, "Let Me," 157.

24. Susan Elizabeth Phillips, "The Romance and the Empowerment of Women," in *Dangerous Men and Adventurous Women*, ed. Jayne Ann Krentz (Philadelphia: University of Pennsylvania Press, 1992), 55.

25. Camp, "The Role," 53.

26. Mittermeyer, "Romance," 55.

27. Gauntlett, "Ten Things." Further references will be to this article.

28. John Hartley, "Creative Industries," in *Creative Industries*, ed. John Hartley (Malden, MA: Blackwell, 2005), 6.

29. *Ibid.*, 17–18.

30. *Ibid.*, 24.

31. Henry Jenkins, *Fans, Bloggers, and Gamers: Exploring Participatory Culture* (New York: New York University Press, 2006), 18–19; 41–45.

32. The Long Tail was initially the subject of an essay by Chris Anderson in *Wired* magazine where he argued that the "digital entertainment market" would differ radically from traditional physical marketing.

Anderson's model is Amazon.com, which makes available to consumers an extensive list of products that are sold in small quantities instead of stocking nothing but a small number of "mega-hit" products that sell in high quantities. See Chris Anderson, *The Long Tail: Why the Future of Business is Selling Less of More* (New York: Hyperion, 2006).

33. Jennifer Crusie-Smith, "Romancing Reality: The Power of Romance Fiction to Reinforce and Re-Vision the Real," *Paradoxa* 3, nos. 1–2 (1997): 81.

34. Anna Campbell, *Claiming the Courtesan* (New York: Avon, 2007).

35. For discussion of this point, see Janet, "Review: Claiming the Courtesan by Anna Campbell," Dear Author, March 30, 2007, http://dearauthor.com/wordpress/2007/03/30/claiming-the-courtesan-by-anna-campbell; Eileen Dreyer, "Eileen the Angry," Eileen Dryer Blog, March 31, 2007, http://www.eileendreyer.com/blog/2007/03/eileen-angry.html; Sandy Coleman, "Claiming the Courtesan," All About Romance, http://www.likesbooks.com/cgi-bin/bookReview.pl?BookReviewId=6076.

36. Jennifer Cruise, "Please Remove Your Assumptions, They're Sitting on My Genre," Argh Ink, April 14, 2007, http://www.arghink.com/2007/04/14/please-remove-your-assumptions-theyre-sitting-on-my-genre/.

37. John Hartley, "Creative Identities," in *Creative Industries*, ed. John Hartley (Malden, MA: Blackwell, 2005), 113.

16

"A consummation devoutly to be wished": Shakespeare in Popular Historical Romance Fiction

Tamara Whyte

"Matthew and I will be attired as Romeo and Juliet," said Sarah, "except in our version of the story clearly neither of them die, as we are older than the teenage lovers. And besides, I cannot abide unhappy endings."[1]

In this passage from Jacquie D'Allessandro's *Confessions at Midnight,* Sarah, a minor character in the novel, demonstrates her willingness to rewrite William Shakespeare's work, especially to change the tragic ending of *Romeo and Juliet.* Many historical romance novels include similar rewritings of the Bard, and even more allude more variously to Shakespeare's writings: from a quotation at the beginning of a novel, to an animal named after Shakespeare or one of his characters, to the novel's characters attending of one of his plays, or to the heroine and hero using Shakespeare to further their courtship. The prevalence and variety of references to Shakespeare indicate a growing interest in referencing Shakespeare, first noted by Laurie E. Osborne in her essay, "Harlequin Presents: That '70s Shakespeare and Beyond."[2] Clearly, Shakespeare is valuable to romance authors, both as a source of inspiration and as a way to connect with their readers. While some of these references seem merely to draw on the Bard's cultural status, many of the allusions involve a revision of Shakespeare's plays, such as that in D'Alessandro's novel. These revisions often involve an inversion of some aspect of the original work, reversing the gender roles in speeches or plots or giving the play a new, more positive conclusion.[3]

Understanding how these revisions function requires first understanding the cultural sophistication of the readers of romances. Without knowledge of the original work, the reader could not be expected to notice and enjoy the twist, especially when female characters quote traditionally masculine speeches. Previous scholarship suggests that in these novels, a woman who knows her Shakespeare often is a "bluestocking," an overly educated woman, alienated from others, and finally ostracized from society. Laurie Osborne explains in "Sweet, Savage Shakespeare" that such a "heroine is frequently [...] an inappropriately well-educated woman often perceived as masculine and unmarriageable."[4] My research suggests, however, that while some romance novels still cast such women as bluestocking outcasts (this occurs more often in the series romances), many others depict these women as part of a group of intelligent females, fully integrated into their societies. In fact, knowledge of Shakespeare is so unexceptional for women in the romance novels I have examined, that in D'Alessandro's *Sleepless at Midnight,* the "Ladies Literary Society of London" uses the Bard as a cover for their more shocking material, Mary Shelley's *Frankenstein.*[5] Moreover, the men that the heroines interact with in any positive manner seem to appreciate their intelligence and knowledge of literature. In *Sleepless at Midnight,* the hero, Matthew, is amused when the heroine catches his Shakespearean quotation:

> "Hmm. The lady doth protest too much, methinks."
> She hoisted her chin. "As a member of the Ladies Literary Society of London, I am well acquainted with *Hamlet,* my lord. Your quote from act two, scene three, however, is in error in this case."
> "Is it? I wonder ..."
> She applied her attention to her hard-boiled egg, but found it difficult to concentrate knowing he was staring at her.
> Then he chuckled.[6]

Rather than make the heroine unmarriageable, her knowledge pleases those around her, especially the hero of the novel who clearly enjoys testing her. The right man, then, appreciates the heroine's intelligence, as do the readers of the novels.

The romance hero is even able to complete his heroine's quotation in many cases, demonstrating their compatibility. This occurs extensively in Sabrina Jefferies' *A Dangerous Love,* where quotations of Shakespeare within the text drive much of the relationship. The heroine, Rosalind, quotes Shakespeare consistently throughout the novel and verbally spars with the hero, Griff Knighton, often identifying or completing various lines. Griff even mentions their knowledge of Shakespeare when he tries to convince her they are suited for one another:

> Brushing her cheek with his lips, he lowered his voice seductively. "For one thing, you and I are very well matched. You must admit it."
> "Well matched in bed, you mean," she choked out. Curse him for his ability to fog her mind with passion.
> "Everywhere." Clasping her chin, he forced it up so she'd look into his eyes, his beautiful, devious eyes. "What do you think are your chances of finding a husband who can match your knowledge of Shakespeare quote for quote?"
> Another piece of the puzzle fell into place. Of course he knew Shakespeare. He'd been educated at Eton. Still, of all the things he might have said to convince her, that wasn't one she'd expected. It was rather crafty of him to use it, and Griff was nothing if not crafty.
> She lifted an eyebrow. "We haven't yet established that you can match me quote for quote, sir."
> He smiled at her taunt. "Then perhaps we should. Think of all the enjoyment we'll have doing so."[7]

Here, Griff depends on Rosalind to appreciate his own ability to keep up with her knowledge. In saying that she will not find someone else who can complete her quotations, he suggests she will not find anyone else to complete her. Their shared knowledge and enjoyment of Shakespeare then becomes the symbol for their shared emotions and tastes, how well they suit one another. She even acknowledges that this ability to match each other's quotes is a clever argument for them to marry. Furthermore, Rosalind is not completely convinced that he is actually capable of keeping up with her. She is clearly proud of her expertise, which requires Griff to work continually to prove his own. By making the heroine a confident woman who quotes Shakespeare, Jeffries undermines the earlier characterization of women, suggesting that the audience would appreciate the Shakespearean allusions and the portrayal itself.

Heroines playing with their knowledge of Shakespeare place women in a position of power. For example, in Kalen Hughes's *Lord Sin*, the heroine Georgianna, called George, differentiates herself from the other women by her knowledge and appreciation of Shakespeare. Her knowledge also helps her hold her own with the men in her life, leading to an amusing exchange near the end of the novel:

> "Lead on Bottom," she commanded. "I've half a mind to fall in love with you tonight."
> "Not Bottom. Surely you're not so cruel. Let me be Puck! Let me be Orsino. Let me be Petruchio."
> "I'm afraid the role of Petruchio's already taken."
> Brimstone snorted and led her down the dark Lover's Walk, the two of them weaving their way past other couples bent on more romantic assignations.
> "What about Romeo?"
> "Dead."
> "Hamlet?"
> "The lady's dead in that one. Go back to comedies."[8]

This witty repartee illustrates the intelligence of the heroine familiar with her Shakespeare. First she suggests her former suitor is the "hard-handed" (or working-class) man Oberon gave the head of an ass in *A Midsummer Night's Dream*. When he responds wishing to play a more dominant and aristocratic role, Georgiana quips that he cannot play the role of *Taming of the Shrew's* Petruchio, for he is not the man to tame her. This role is only available to the hero of the novel. When the suitor then would cast himself as a tragic hero instead, Georgiana's deadpan response cuts off his play, reminding him of the context of his allusions. Her knowledge of Shakespeare allows her to interact on a more even playing field intellectually with the gentlemen of the novel, and even above some of them, giving her the power to assign him his role in this discussion. Readers who know their Shakespeare can appreciate both the humor here and the heroine's power.

Moreover, the prevalence of references to Shakespeare may demonstrate the romance writer's understanding and acknowledgement of her audience and in particular of the amount of sophistication attained by her audience, a possibility that Osborne seems to ignore in "Romancing the Bard." Commenting on Deanna James's assertion that she hoped her inclusion of Shakespeare quotations at the beginning of chapters would help readers remember Shakespeare, Osborne states, "Since the quotations from less popular plays such as *Pericles*, *Cymbeline*, and *King John* surely escape most readers, this transformation of romance into memory quiz seems destined to put her public down."[9] Perhaps, but the inclusion of uncited quotations can imply the opposite—higher expectations of the readers of these genres. According to a 2005 survey of readers performed for the Romance Writers of America, forty-two percent of romance readers hold a bachelor's degree or higher, another seven percent have associates degrees, and fifteen percent report having postgraduate work or degrees.[10] Highly educated women, then, make up a larger part of the romance market than may be expected, particularly by academic literary critics. Quotations from Shakespeare, therefore, must be one way to appeal to this educated readership—a way that does not necessarily alienate readers without formal higher education, since Shakespeare is readily accessible throughout popular culture.

Such seems to be the intent of Eloisa James (the pen name of Mary Bly), who comments on her use of Shakespeare in her recent novel, *Desperate Duchesses*, saying, "For those of you who love Shakespeare references, there are bits here from *Romeo and Juliet, Twelfth Night, The Rape of Lucrece* and *Hamlet*—some marked and some unmarked [...] If you'd like to track down every reference, come onto my Bulletin Board and share your findings or ask for clues!"[11] James clearly believes her audience will both be interested in finding the allusions and ultimately successful in doing so. So much so that she invites her readers to join a community of similarly sophisticated women who will play the Shakespeare reference finding game together. The popularity of James's work in particular speaks to the sophistication of romance readers and the enjoyment they take from Shakespeare allusions and quotations. James, who published her first novel, *Potent Pleasures*, in 1999, and has published more than a dozen since then, refers to Shakespeare in nearly all of her work. Her more recent titles suggest the importance of Shakespeare within: *Pleasure for Pleasure, The Taming of the Duke, Kiss Me Annabel,* and *Much Ado About You.* Since James is also a professor of early modern English literature, a scholar of Shakespeare, and daughter of poet Robert Bly, her interweaving of Shakespeare has special significance: "The literature professor in me certainly plays into my romances. *The Taming of the Duke* (April 2006) has obvious Shakespearean resonances, as do many of my novels. I often weave early modern poetry into my work; the same novel might contain bits of Catullus, Shakespeare and anonymous bawdy ballads from the 16th century."[12] Acknowledging the high cultural value attached to Shakespeare and the low cultural value attached to romance novels, James relates how her husband told her to mention Shakespeare in her first public interview about her double life; however, her focus remains on the stories themselves, hers and Shakespeare's. And readers do respond to her interweaving of Shakespeare and other elements of Renaissance literature, as her books regularly appear on best-seller lists.

At the same time, for both writers and readers, references to Shakespeare and other forms of high literary culture suggest a postmodern blurring of high and low cultural forms and even, perhaps, recall the cultural situation of nineteenth-century America when Shakespeare, opera, and classical music were the "property" of all Americans regardless of social class. As Lawrence W. Levine suggests, performers would blend Shakespeare with other popular media and alter his works to suit the occasion. *Hamlet* was often the source for these "adaptations":

> Audiences roared at the sight of Hamlet dressed in fur cap and collar, snowshoes and mittens; they listened with amused surprise to his profanity when ordered by his father's ghost to "swear" and to his commanding Ophelia, "Get thee to a brewery"; they heard him recite his lines in black dialect or Irish brogues and sing most of his famous soliloquy, "To be, or not to be," to the tune of "Three Blind Mice."[13]

For such entertainment to be successful, the audience had to be familiar with the original work. Many of the references in historical romances require the kind of knowledge of Shakespeare that Levine relates, such as in Christine Well's *Scandal's Daughter,* when Gemma says, "I thought you'd vanished like Banquo's ghost"[14]; or in Julia Quinn's *The Secret Diaries of Miss Miranda Cheever,* when Miranda says, "My kingdom for a handkerchief."[15] While in some older novels, such as Georgette Heyer's recently reissued *Venetia,* the quotations are clearly marked by being printed in italics,[16] most recent historical romances seamlessly blend in these references, assuming that the reader who will understand them will find them on her own. Only periodically does the author even mention Shakespeare by name, allowing the plays or quotes to stand on their own in the works.

This blending of high and low is, of course, certainly not something unique to romance novels. Harriet Hawkins traces themes and images that appear in both high and popular literature, linking Shakespeare and Disney films as well as Arthurian legend and *Star Wars*.[17] She suggests both that overarching rules seem to guide fictions across the board and that the mixing of high and low is unexceptional. As a result, allusions to Shakespeare can heighten a moment within a popular work without damaging the original, which, in fact, may be enriched by the inclusion of the popular, allowing readers to make deeper, more complicated connections whenever they encounter the material. As Hawkins notes, "It is not the artistic tradition but the academic tradition that has erected barriers between 'high art' and popular genres, even as it has erected barricades between art and life. The artistic tradition (popular as well as exalted) tends to break all such barriers down."[18] Following Hawkins, it seems logical to conclude that in romance novels, too, the blending of the high literature of Shakespeare into the popular medium of historical romance novels can help solidify the position of the high literature and enrich the readers' understanding of the plays. Further, rather than bring Shakespeare down to the level of the masses, the inclusion of Shakespeare in this popular medium enriches the experience of both his plays and the romance novels.

Some authors refer to Shakespeare in their titles, which alerts readers to the literary allusions and sometimes the plots within, such as in James's *The Taming of the Duke*.[19] References to *The Taming of the Shrew* occur in many romances, such as: *Taming the Scotsman*,[20] *Taming the Highlander*,[21] *Taming the Heiress*,[22] *The Taming of Lord Astor*,[23] among others; there was even another *Taming of the Duke* in 2001 by Jackie Manning.[24] Most of these make little other reference to the Bard, but by referencing the familiar plot they prepare the reader for the story to come, often — and compellingly, for my purposes here — one that inverts Shakespeare's storyline. In James's *The Taming of the Duke*, the heroine does the taming. Imogen, the heroine, forces Rafe, the hero and her guardian, to give up drinking and reform his life. Rafe is clearly an alcoholic, but Imogen's unwillingness to help him drink himself to death is what places her in the position of a shrew when interacting with Rafe: these caustic words and actions keep him from remaining in his drunken state, and save his life. She repeatedly pours out alcohol before he can drink it, going so far as to remove it from the house, and continues to nag him even when others would allow him to return to his old ways. Another female in the novel even suggests such a return is inevitable and not important, something Imogen refuses to accept, chiding Rafe for his actions even as she washes his hair when he is ill. While the plot focuses on a transformation quite different than in *The Taming of the Shrew*, it presents one figure being made more desirable through the forceful efforts of another; this time the female has the upper hand. Such inversions not only focus more clearly on the females in the works, but allow these women power and position that the original story does not afford. Not content with rewriting *The Taming of the Shrew*, this work also rewrites *A Midsummer Night's Dream*, but instead of two young men needing outside influence to realign their romantic desires, it is the young women whose desires must be transferred from one gentleman to another. Once again, the plot focuses on the role of women, here making them the ones who ultimately decide who they will marry, a choice not readily available to the women in Shakespeare's work, where choice is circumscribed by fathers, brothers, or their social superiors.

Another such revision occurs in Susan Wiggs's *The Horsemaster's Daughter*.[25] From the first page, this novel demonstrates its connections to Shakespeare's *The Tempest*, beginning each section of the book by quoting the play. The book opens with, "The isle is full of noises,/Sounds and sweet airs, that give delight, and hurt not,"[26] which sets up the shift from the southern plantation in the first chapter to the island home of the heroine. The quotation at the beginning of part four, "Be free, and fare thou well,"[27] similarly sets up the action to come at the end of the novel. In Wiggs's version, however, the figure of Miranda, here called Eliza, lives isolated on an island after her father's murder. The text suggests her father was thought a magician like Shakespeare's Prospero, but he simply had a talent for training horses which he passed on to his daughter. By removing the father figure from the action, Wiggs rewrites Shakespeare's plot with a sharper focus on the sole female in the play. Eliza shares a number of similarities with Miranda, but unlike the figure from *The Tempest,* she has had to confront tragedy on her own and must therefore find her way in the world without a father's guidance. Not only does the novel draw heavily on Shakespeare's work for the original concept, it also repeatedly allows the characters to quote the play. More than the role of Prospero is changed in the retelling; Eliza faces challenges that Miranda never knew. She acknowledges her movement beyond the original play while talking to Hunter, the hero of the novel:

> After a while, he glanced at her again. "Now what?" he asked.
> "I was just thinking about *The Tempest.*"
> "That again."
> "I never really thought about the ending. But you know, the story ends before they leave the island."
> "So?"
> "We never learn what becomes of everyone."
> "Prospero goes back to his dukedom in Milan. Ferdinand and Miranda sail to Naples, where they live happily ever after as prince and princess. All the sprites and beasts are released from their enchantment. Make fast that line, will you?"
> She obeyed sulkily. He didn't understand. As long as she stayed on the island, she didn't have to worry about the way things ended. Now, thrust into this strange place, she had to make her way through unfamiliar terrain, alien and green, fraught with peril.[28]

While Hunter makes a logical assumption about where the play was headed, even he rewrites the text, as Shakespeare's work really does leave the figures while they are still island bound. Wiggs, however, brings Eliza into the world without anyone to guide her, and allows her to flourish. She helps Hunter not only with his horses, but with his children, and eventually finds true love for herself, no magic involved. This new version of the story puts the female in a more perilous position that allows her to demonstrate her strength and ability to guide her own life in a way not offered to Miranda, whose courtship was consistently monitored — even engineered — by her father. Along with this, Wiggs is able to offer the happy ending back in the real world that Shakespeare does not fully develop by taking the characters off the island and not requiring the audience to supply the happily-ever-after as Hunter does above.[29]

Often, gender role inversions are simple, such as giving the heroine famous lines spoken by males in Shakespeare's plays. Andrea Pickens uses this tactic in *The Spy Wore Silk.* Her heroine, Siena, sees the hero, Kirtland, reading Shakespeare when she spies on him:

> From the bookshelf by his bed, the earl picked a volume from the leather-bound set of Shakespeare's works, plumped the pillows, and settled between the sheets to read.
> The candlelight caught the gleam of the gilt title. *Hamlet.*
> *Good night, sweet prince.*
> She cocked a silent salute before taking the rope in hand and dropping down into the darkness. And yet, she could not quite slip away from the strange soliloquy taking voice in her own head. *To be or not to be* ... distracted by unaccountable emotions.[30]

By quoting the very play Kirtland reads and allowing Shakespeare to be caught up in her deliberations about her emotions for him, Siena demonstrates both her position as the hero's intellectual equal and their suitability for one another. Furthermore, by quoting one of Hamlet's speeches, Siena takes the role of tragic hero of the play rather than that of the female whose life is altered by his actions. She is no Ophelia, and in connecting her to the more powerful character in the tragedy, Pickens demonstrates both Siena's sense of her own capabilities and her position within society. Siena proves herself to be a woman able to control her own destiny and make decisions for herself—unlike Hamlet. She also changes the focus of the speech from a question of suicide to a debate about romantic entanglements, turning the tragedy into something more romantic.

In *How to Propose to a Prince,* Kathryn Caskie's heroine Elizabeth also quotes Hamlet's famous speech when dealing with her romantic situation: "Now, however, she was running low on ways to engage her mind and hands until sunset. Already the small house staff was growing quite exasperated with her and she could not seem to occupy herself with reading or writing letters. And resorting to sleep to pass her time was not an option. 'To sleep, perchance to dream—ay, there's the rub.' She should have listened to Shakespeare, too, for a dream had cursed her with a heart rent in two."[31] Here, as in Siena's speech, the quoted line is about the heroine's romantic desires rather than a contemplation of suicide and death. Yet, in giving the heroine the famous contemplative lines of a traditionally male figure, Caskie creates depth for Elizabeth, allowing her not only the intellectual ability of the hero, but also suggesting that she is the one with a decision to make. In both of these works, the authors rewrite *Hamlet* with their heroine as the primary focus, someone valuable and interesting, and in a more powerful position than a woman in the original tragedy. In addition, the authors focus on the romantic relationship rather than a question of suicide.

By far the most referenced Shakespearean plays in romances are the tragedies, and in situating these works within the romance setting, with the happy ending guaranteed, the authors recast these tragedies as melodrama, which is the mass media of the theater. As Frank Rahill explains,

> Melodrama is a form of dramatic composition in prose partaking of the nature of tragedy, comedy, pantomime, and spectacle, and intended for the popular audience. Primarily concerned with situation and plot, it calls upon mimed action extensively and employs a more or less fixed complement of stock characters, the most important of which are a suffering heroine and hero, a persecuting villain, and a benevolent comic. It is conventionally moral and humanitarian in point of view and sentimental and optimistic in temper, concluding its fable happily with virtue rewarded after many trials and vice punished.[32]

And while melodramas with unhappy endings exist, the basic formula mirrors that often cited of the romance novel, with the hero and heroine facing obstacles that must be overcome to finally be together. A clear moral compass exists in both these genres, making it easy to know how things *should* turn out. Tragedies, in contrast, include moral ambiguity and internal division that do not serve the purpose of these novels. When romance novelists refer to *Hamlet* or *Othello,* they do not refer to internal conflict or moral complication so much as exaggerated emotion. They turn to the tragedies to tap into their emotional content, setting up problems that can be overcome in the setting of the romance novel. The plays thus become less serious and less "tragic," the plot features heroes who can be educated out of their tragic flaws, and dangers of fate can be outwitted. Furthermore, a dark, melancholy figure like Hamlet or Othello is particularly attractive as he is the image of many of the heroes of historical romance novels, rakish men who need a good woman to help them come to enjoy life and become the man they should be.

In romance novels, one of the most popular revisions of Shakespeare's tragedies is of *Romeo and Juliet*. Many pairs of lovers liken themselves to the ill-fated pair and wish to have their passionate beginning but not their tragic end, as evidenced by the epigraph to this essay. One such revision to Shakespeare's plot occurs in Suzanne Enoch's *Twice the Temptation*. While Evangeline (Gilly) and Connoll do not come from warring families, the hero sees himself as a Romeo to her Juliet: "He still couldn't believe he'd known Gilly Munroe for only eight days. In fairy tales, or in *Romeo and Juliet*, perhaps, eyes met across crowded rooms and people fell for one another at first sight. He'd heard of such things in the actual world, but he'd never believed the accounts. Now he seemed to be one of those few who could make such claims."[33] Yet, while Connoll likens himself to Romeo who falls instantaneously in love, he refuses Romeo's tragic fate. He even claims he will not use the case of Romeo and Juliet to convince Gilly to wed him, although the very mention of the lovers does so:

> "We have known one another for a relatively short time," he agreed. "I won't bring up the fact that Romeo and Juliet married within three days of meeting, because I hardly consider them to be beacons of long-lasting love."
> Her lips twitched. "I would agree with that."[34]

Clearly, by mentioning the tragic consequences that he does not want, Connoll sets the stage for their revision of the story, love at first sight that leads to a happy ending rather than death, which, of course, it does, for such tragic endings have no place within these stories, at least for the hero and heroine.

A more elaborate revision of *Romeo and Juliet* comes in *The Return of the Prodigal* by Kasey Michaels. In her novel, the hero, Rian Becket, and heroine, Lisette, actually do come from feuding families, and that feud has already proved deadly. When they were children, Lisette's father pillaged and destroyed the Beckets's island home, murdering all but small children who hid from his crew. In the present, he holds Rian captive, hoping to find the remaining Beckets and finally destroy them. Lisette, fooled by her father's lies into believing that it was Rian's father who brutally murdered her mother, is given charge of tricking Rian into leading them to his home. Yet, over the course of the novel, she impossibly falls in love with the son of her enemy. When Rian suggests she would be a good actress, Lisette even refers to them as Romeo and Juliet: "I would make a good Juliet, don't you think? And you could be my Romeo. You die every day." [35] Her flippant reply actually brings the obvious connection of the romance novel and *Romeo and Juliet* into focus, for these lovers seemed doomed to a tragic end like their forerunners. However, instead of killing themselves for love, they end up in an extraordinarily melodramatic hostage situation where Lisette's own father holds her at knifepoint and Rian and his giant-like friend attempt a standoff against him and his voodoo priestess. In the end, it is Lisette who saves them all from tragedy, by plunging a pair of scissors into her father's chest. A chandelier then miraculously falls and the lovers are carried off to safety by Rian's friend. Rian even manages to survive a gunshot wound given at close range. Where tragedy seems certain, Michaels instead offers a highly melodramatic climax leading to this pair's happy ending.

In *Slightly Dangerous*, Mary Balogh briefly refers to *Othello*, another oft-referenced play in historical romance novels. The heroine in Balogh's romance, Christine Derrick, is courted by the Duke of Bewcastle. Late in the novel, Christine's cousin reveals that they had been watching *Othello*: "Lady Rannulf is a magnificent actress. For a few minutes I quite forgot that she was not indeed poor Desdemona about to be murdered by Othello."[36] This comment appears to be of little significance until shortly thereafter, when the duke reveals a plot which is much easier to accept with *Othello* in mind. Throughout the novel, people repeatedly single out Christine as a flirt; her own relatives even turn against her and warn the duke away from her. Christine's first husband was a jealous man who grew increasingly so during their marriage. The duke reveals that this is likely due to her best friend Justin, who spends all of his time unnecessarily defending Christine's actions. Suddenly, Christine and her relatives realize what has been going on: rather than make Christine appear innocent, Justin's defenses planted the seed in her first husband's head which spurred a deadly duel. The duke reveals Justin's plan:

> "I was told [by Justin] this morning," the duke said, "as I rode home from Alvesley with Magnus that Mrs. Derrick must not be blamed for responding to the attentions of the Marquess of Attingsborough or accused of being a flirt, since the man concerned is an experienced rake. I was told she cannot help the effect she has on men like Attingsborough and Kitredge and myself. That is just the way she is — though she is understandably ambitious to win for herself the highest-ranking title she can acquire. I was told that if he knew of hundreds of indiscretions of Mrs. Derrick's instead of dozens, he would defend her every time because that is what friends do. I was told that though Mrs. Derrick was alone for more than an hour with a gentleman the day before her husband's death, he had willingly provided her with an alibi because he trusted her."[37]

Since Justin's plan mirrors Iago's defenses of Desdemona's behavior in *Othello*, the duke's discovery seems plausible with the plot of the play already in mind. Moreover, in Balogh's version of the story, Iago is ultimately outwitted. Here, recognition of the lies comes before they can kill Christine. While Christine's first husband suffered a tragic fate, the duke's discovery allows for a new ending where he and Christine can marry and live happily ever after. *Othello* no longer holds the tragic sting of the original, but instead becomes a sensational plot open to being solved by the right sort of hero.

In fact, in Margaret Moore's *Kiss Me Quick*, the heroine, Diana, thinks of Shakespeare's villains when thinking about the hero of the work, Edmond:

> She tried again, but not only was the acting bad, this sort of pastoral farce wasn't at all to her liking. If only they could be watching *Macbeth*, or *Othello*. She had a sneaking admiration for Lady Macbeth, who certainly did not lack for energy or determination. Neither did Iago. The viscount would make a good Iago, all lean and hungry and secretive, and with such a persuasive voice. Yes, she would cast him in that part without hesitation.[38]

Diana spends much of the work writing a gothic novel and chooses Edmond as a model for her villain — connecting Shakespeare's tragedy to the melodramatic genre. And, of course, by the end of Moore's work, Edmond is no longer the villain, but a romantic hero.

Knowledge of Shakespeare's works, especially his tragedies, on the part of the readers, allows the writers to "ramp-up" the emotions involved in these novels. Invoking tragedy in melodramatic novels is then a version of what melodrama itself does, heightening the emotions of the plot in such a way that the ending is that much more emotionally affecting. Without the knowledge of the original tragic endings of these plots, such revisions would not have as much power. Along with this, many of the novels reference Shakespeare in ways that invert the original, both focusing more clearly on the female and allowing her to overcome life's obstacles. The appeal of these novels seems tied up in the desire not only for escape through fantasy, but also in the desire to be able to overcome obstacles, specifically class and social barriers, with relative ease and guaranteed success. In contemporary life, many women are faced with obstacles in having to do two shifts: working for pay and taking care of families. Even when they succeed in the workforce, they face glass ceilings or wage discrimination at work. When faced with having to do it all, all the time, who wouldn't want to use her energy and talents to reform some sexy and rakish guy who would then guarantee her happiness? Shakespearean allusions therefore not only incorporate high culture into a traditionally popular genre, but also give authors possibilities for their heroines to demonstrate their power and intelligence as they achieve their happy endings in a way that the readers can participate in through their own knowledge of the plays.

NOTES

1 Jacquie D'Alessandro, *Confessions at Midnight* (New York: Avon, 2008), 11.

2. Laurie E. Osborne, "Harlequin Presents: That '70s Shakespeare and Beyond," in *Shakespeare After Mass Media,* ed. Richard Burt (New York: Palgrave, 2002), 127–49.

3. In order to look beyond the works and usages considered previously, this study considers only historical romance novels published in 2000 or later, dealing with current trends and their significance.

4. Laurie E. Osborne, "Sweet, Savage, Shakespeare," in *Shakespeare Without Class: Misappropriations of Cultural Capital,* ed. Donald Hedrick and Bryan Reynolds (New York: Palgrave, 2000), 145.

5. Jacquie D'Alessandro, *Sleepless at Midnight* (New York: Avon, 2007).

6. *Ibid.,* 241.

7. Sabrina Jeffries, *A Dangerous Love* (New York: Avon, 2000), 270

8. Kalen Hughes, *Lord Sin* (New York: Zebra Books, 2007), 279.

9. Laurie E. Osborne, "Romancing the Bard," in *Shakespeare and Appropriation*, ed. Christy Desmet and Robert Sawyer (New York: Routledge, 1999), 59.

10. "Romance Writers of America's 2005 Market Research Study on Romance Readers," Saralee Etter, http://www.saraleeetter.com/files/05MarketResearch_1_.pdf.

11. Eloisa James, *Desperate Duchesses* (New York: Avon, 2007), 384.

12. Eloisa James, "Biography," Eloisa James: About the Author: HarperCollins Publishers: Avon Books, HarperCollins Publishers, http://www.harpercollins.com/author/microsite/About.aspx?authorid=24747.

13. Lawrence W. Levine, *Highbrow/Lowbrow: The Emergence of Cultural Hierarchy in America* (Cambridge: Harvard University Press, 1988), 13–4.

14. Christine Wells, *Scandal's Daughter* (New York: Berkley Sensation, 2007), 138.

15. Julia Quinn, *The Secret Diaries of Miss Miranda Cheever* (New York: Avon, 2007), 166.

16. Georgette Heyer, *Venetia* (London: Heinemann, 1958).

17. Harriett Hawkins, *Classics and Trash: Traditions and Taboos in High Literature and Popular Modern Genres* (New York: Harvester Wheatsheaf, 1990), 115–20.

18. *Ibid.,* 113.

19. Eloisa James, *The Taming of the Duke* (New York: Avon, 2006).

20. Kinley Macgregor, *Taming the Scotsman* (New York: Avon, 2003).

21. Terri Brisbin, *Taming the Highlander* (New York: Harlequin, 2006).

22. Susan King, *Taming the Heiress* (New York: Signet, 2003).

23. Molly Madigan, *The Taming of Lord Astor* (New York: Five Star, 2007).

24. Jackie Manning, *Taming of the Duke* (New York: Harlequin, 2001).

25. Susan Wiggs, *The Horsemaster's Daughter* (Don Mills, Ontario: Mira, 2008).

26. Shakespeare, *The Tempest* 3.2, qtd. in Wiggs, *The Horsemaster's Daughter*, 11.

27. Shakespeare, *The Tempest* 5.1, qtd. in Wiggs, *The Horsemaster's Daughter*, 377.

28. Wiggs, *The Horsemaster's Daughter*, 204–5.

29. The text also has Caliban be Eliza's beloved dog rather than a native islander enslaved by Prospero. This allows for the text to avoid any support of slavery, as one subplot involves Eliza's father being part of the Underground Railroad. This revision then not only focuses more clearly on the female, but also erases colonialism from *The Tempest.*

30. Andrea Pickens, *The Spy Wore Silk* (New York: Warner Forever, 2007), 95–6.

31. Kathryn Caskie, *How to Propose to a Prince* (New York: Avon, 2008), 301.

32. Frank Rahill, *The World of Melodrama* (University Park: Pennsylvania State University Press, 1967), xiv.

33. Suzanne Enoch, *Twice the Temptation* (New York: Avon, 2007) 129.
34. *Ibid.*, 148–9.
35. Kasey Michaels, *The Return of the Prodigal* (New York: Harlequin, 2007), 99.
36. Mary Balogh, *Slightly Dangerous* (New York: Bantam Dell, 2004), 310–1.
37. *Ibid.*, 315.
38. Margaret Moore, *Kiss Me Quick* (New York: Avon, 2003), 126.

17

The Power of Three:
Nora Roberts and Serial Magic

Christina A. Valeo

The math is simple enough: a Nora Roberts trilogy offers three times the attraction, triple the introductions, the barriers, the declarations, the betrothals, and three or more times the happy endings for her characters.[1] What smart reader wouldn't buy into a guarantee like that? Buy into it they do, and at an astounding rate. According to the official Nora Roberts website, "Every Nora Roberts and J.D. Robb title released in 2010 hit the *New York Times* bestseller list. That's keeping up a streak started in 1999," and at last count (September 2009), there were more than 400 million copies of her books in print.[2] Many of those millions come from Roberts' twenty-seven series (as of the end of 2011).[3] According to Denise Little and Laura Hayden, co-editors of *The Official Nora Roberts Companion*, "Nora [Roberts] essentially pioneered the idea of doing linked series of novels in mainstream women's publishing, and she continues to dominate it."[4] The sales have been spectacular, the readers' dedication intense. In one case Roberts extended a trilogy to a fourth novel, years later, at least in part because of readers' demand for a happy ending for the youngest of four brothers in the family.[5]

Any Roberts series offers particular pleasures to the reader because of its scope and stretch. All of the elements readers have come to expect from a stand-alone novel by Roberts are multiplied geometrically rather than arithmetically. Romance readers crave fresh beginnings and middles on their way to happy endings. The addition of the paranormal, or the mystic, or the magical in many of these series further enhances both the content and the characters in the romance in demonstrable ways. I begin by looking at the "everyday" series, usually trilogies, where the characters and the settings could be anyone, anywhere, where no readerly leap of any kind of faith is required. Even the most "ordinary" series offers additional promises and pleasures that three equally well-crafted but separate books could not deliver. Some of her series include a paranormal presence; this is usually a ghost, often an ancestor, that may have good or evil intentions toward the human characters it interacts with. In her series that I'll call "mystical," demons, fairies, gods, or goddesses from other worlds complicate the lives of the human characters, who must then take on challenges of epic proportions. Finally, in Roberts' "magic" series, her human characters themselves have incredible powers with which to respond to everything from minor accidents to ancient evil. Although it may seem that each addition makes the story that much more fantastic, I argue that Roberts' version of magic comes home to her readers in ways that make it seem well within their reach.

The "Everyday" Series

Any Roberts series, from the explicitly magical to the seemingly mundane, still manages to be more than the sum of its parts. From Roberts' perspective, creating a series likely helps her maintain her incredible annual output; she writes three or more books, but she builds only one world. She also, by her own admission, becomes attached to her characters: she has said of the MacGregor clan, the stars of one of her first and longest series, "The characters just wouldn't shut up."[6] In each of the series Roberts introduces a related cluster of characters. Many are families, sometimes intergenerational, more often siblings or cousins of the same age. Some groups are formed around friendships, lifelong or newly found. Some clusters combine friends and families in ways that instigate and energize the inevitable heterosexual pairings that result. Many of the series share similar stories: a newcomer trying to recover from hard times finds shelter and stability in the arms of a local lover; a boy and girl who have always been friends grow into a man and woman who become inseparable; lovers long separated by grief, pride, or ambition find their ways back to each other in time to realize some astounding achievement or face some ultimate challenge. On her page at her publisher's website, Roberts is quoted as saying: "Relationship has always played a key role in my books. I'm fascinated by the dynamics of family, the shared history and the way each individual grows. In my connecting books, the characters always come first."[7]

Readers, too, are drawn into those relationships. Tommy Dreiling, a romance buyer for Barnes and Noble, reports that unlike most series where sales decline in subsequent books, a Roberts series actually gains readership — as indicated by book sales — as the books appear.[8] Some of the appeal would be the same as that of any romance, multiplied by the number of books in the series. For example, there will be someone for everyone; Roberts varies the personalities, professions, and appearances of both heroes and heroines in each group enough that at least one character is bound to appeal to every reader, either as an object of attraction or as an object of identification. A series also magnifies the pleasurable version of predictability that a romance offers the reader. We know which characters will end up together long (sometimes months or years, or hundreds of pages) before they realize it themselves. Roberts has taken this game to wonderful extremes, where the drop of a name in some early chapter works like a wink to her experienced readers-in-the-know. In *The Dream Trilogy*,[9] Roberts gives us little more than a name, and a great and allusive one at that: Michael Fury. This childhood friend of Josh Templeton will have to wait two books to romance Josh's sister Laura: there are literally 720 pages between the first mention of his name in the first book and his reappearance as Laura's potential/inevitable romance in the last. As such, a series expands on the pleasure of the predictable: we know the happy ending awaits, but the heft of the books in our hands promises many more pages and twists and turns before we and the characters get there.

By the time we do finally read our way to the final books, chapters, and pages of a series, we know Roberts' serial characters remarkably well; fans and critics alike use words like "love" and "linger" to describe not the characters' feelings for each other, but the readers' feelings for characters (see Part Nine of the *Companion*, or fansites like A Day Without French Fries <http://www.adwoff.com>, for multiple examples). Some of this intensity can be attributed to Roberts' talent for characterization, as often her stand-alone characters impact readers just as powerfully.[10] However, the series format allows Roberts the room to shift focus and points of view. The characters who play merely colorful, supporting roles in the first book will have their turns as the heroes and heroines of the later books. Because Roberts uses predominantly limited omniscience as her narrative style, readers may glimpse little or nothing of a character's interiority until her or his story takes center stage. Roberts is, in this way, romancing her readers, letting an initial attraction or affection develop into a stronger bond as we know the characters better, learn about their histories, understand their motivations.

Finally, the connections between characters in a Roberts series increase the investment for all the romantic couples involved. The relations between characters, whether those of friendship or of blood, make clear their interest in each others' happy endings. Four of the six main characters of *The Dream Trilogy*, for example, were raised in the same house: Josh and Laura Templeton are siblings; Kate Powell is an orphaned cousin raised as a Templeton; and Margo Sullivan, the daughter of the housekeeper, is a close friend to both of the other heroines. That lifelong friendship is tested by her changing relationship with Josh Templeton and the family's concern when they begin living together: "It was Kate who made the single pithy comment. 'Break his heart and I'll break your face.'"[11] The close, familiar, or friendly relations among Roberts' serial characters (whether those bonds have existed for a lifetime or a few weeks) mean that each romance matters to more than just the two characters involved. If the siblings, or cousins, or life-long friends don't actually live together, they live near each other, or go into business together, so that they are part of each other's daily lives and privy to all sorts of intimate details. A friend or family member who is agitated, or thrilled, or broken by a love affair has a real impact on those close to him or her. Furthermore, Roberts often makes these familial relationships the reason for characters to be thrown together in the first place. Whether they've known each other their entire lives or met only recently, siblings often fall for each other's best friends in a Roberts romance, so any one character may be doubly concerned about the outcome of someone else's love affair. It's easy for readers to fall into the same trap, becoming more invested in the idea of three happy endings even if they are initially drawn to one character or one couple in particular. A trilogy triples the romance but compounds the love because of the characters' connections to each other and the readers' interest in all of them.

The Presence of the Paranormal

Even a dead character may be invested in the outcome of a Roberts romance. Whether the ghosts in question are departed loved ones, lingering out of enduring love and protective instincts for those still living, or ancient evil spirits still working out a long-held grudge, the paranormal element amplifies the existing structures and themes of the trilogies and series in which they appear. If the six or more main characters are already connected by blood, some may share a common ancestor who returns to haunt or help them. Often Roberts' characters share a home or a business in a location that includes a ghost; in those cases the bonds between characters are tried and tested by the thrill or the threat that a paranormal presence provides.

In the case of the Calhouns,[12] the four sisters are united by blood, location, investment, and their search for their great-grandmother Bianca's sapphire necklace, missing since her mysterious death almost a hundred years before. For the Calhoun women, the story of the necklace is both a mystery they feel compelled to solve and a promise that sustains them through difficult financial and emotional times. Several times the sisters feel their ancestor's presence guiding and protecting them, and her appearance heartens and encourages them. When jewel thieves threaten the Calhouns' lives and home, the matriarchal ghost responds in material ways to protect her descendants, to keep the family healthy and together.

In the *Chesapeake Bay Trilogy*[13] the death of the patriarch Ray Quinn begins the action and the conflicts of the series. Dead, but not gone, Ray makes an appearance to each of his grown adopted sons, Cam, Ethan, and Phillip, as they struggle to repair and then rebuild the family he has left behind. Pamela Regis observes, "Ray punctuates each romance with guidance from beyond the grave, the sort of cryptic, partial guidance that has been associated with the spirit world at least since Delphi."[14] The unity of the Quinn family is threatened by Ray's death and shaken by rumors that the boy he was in the process of adopting is really his biological child by an illicit affair. Each of the heroes must wrestle separately with the ramifications of those challenges as they relate to their own individual history and hopes, but the reappearance of their dead father provides comfort if not clarity. As each brother experiences his own interlude with the ghost, skepticism turns to understanding and an even stronger connection between them forms through the shared experience of the supernatural.

In the fourth novel Roberts turns to the story of the youngest Quinn, Seth, and once again puts the paranormal into play. It is not Ray who appears to Seth, but his wife Stella, who preceded him in death. She quickly conveys the idea that she and Ray are still watching over their family: "We figured it was time I got to play grandma."[15] Although Seth and Stella did not know each other in life, her appearance to him as his grandmother validates his place in the family and solidifies the unity among the brothers. Having a ghost around also serves as another way for Roberts to introduce more characters who are invested in the ending. When Ray Quinn returns from the dead to visit his sons, he uses that twilight time not to clear his own sullied name but to guide his struggling children. Stella Quinn's appearance to Seth is further evidence of that ongoing investment from a paranormal plane; though she did not know Seth during her life, she cares for him after her death. "'Make a good life for yourself,'" she tells him in their last visit, "'or I'm going to be ticked off at you again.'"[16]

When the Calhoun sisters discover that their great-grandmother was murdered, uncover the story of her long-lost love, and recover her missing sapphire necklace, Suzanna Calhoun Dumont understands that their actions have had an impact on their ancestor's spirit, as her ghost has had an impact on them:

> "I think she's with him now. That they're with each other."
> She smiled when Holt's fingers gripped hers. Looking around the room, she saw her sisters, the men they loved, her aunt smiling through tears, and Bianca's daughter, gazing up at the portrait that had been painted with unconquerable love.
> "It was Bianca, more than the emeralds, who brought us all together. I like to think that by finding them, by bringing them back, we've helped them find each other."
> Beyond the house, the moon glimmered on the cliffs far above where the sea churned and fought with the rocks. The wind whispered though the wild roses and warmed the lovers who walked there.[17]

In this last scene of the original four-book series, Roberts reassures her readers that there are happy endings all around, even for those lovers who have waited decades after death to realize them.

The Meddling Mystics

In what I'm calling the "mystic" type of Roberts romance, the central circle is still human; unlike the paranormal stories, however, the humans in a mystic series are interacting with characters who are no longer — or never were — human at all. The genre of these series is still fundamentally romance; the progress of the heroes and heroines over obstacles and toward betrothal is still the focus of each story. But the introduction of champions, challengers, and enemies from other planes augments the dynamics we've seen in the "everyday" series and in the ghost stories. Like the other Roberts series, the "mystic" stories celebrate connections between characters and encourage connections between characters and readers. They also add to the celebration of enduring human ties a community beyond the human one that is equally invested — for better or worse — in the outcomes of the romance.

In *The Stars of Mirtha* series[18] the mythic blue diamonds at the heart of the quest enhance the existing series' structure until it achieves epic proportions. The three heroines, Bailey James, M.J. O'Leary, and Grace Fontaine, have been best friends since college; that existing bond is tested and strengthened by the drama and danger of protecting the precious stones. But the mystical power of those rocks, Roberts suggests, is partially responsible for the instant attraction between the heroines and their newly-met heroes. In the first book, *Hidden Star*, Cade Parris, private eye, takes one look at an unknown woman who wanders into his office and thinks, "There you are, finally. What the hell took you so long?"[19] Roberts extends that sense of recognition to the gems themselves: each heroine knows "her" own diamond, the one she protects that also protects her from the murderous maniac determined to steal them for his private collection. "There's a link," Bailey surmises in the third book. "They brought me Cade. [...] Brought M.J. Jack."[20] And despite Grace's conviction that her lover Seth Buchanan wouldn't believe "in magic of any sort,"[21] Seth has a flash of a previous life and a previous, and more lethal, encounter when he confronts the villain at the end of the series.[22] The monetary value of the stones would be enough motivation for these three stories as it motivates their villain and the ensuing conflict: the supernatural element cements the ties that bind the group as it hints at a higher reward for the couples who are motivated by more than financial gain.

The only "magic" in the first two *Born in ...* books is regular, run-of-the-mill, true love between two couples who feel lucky to have found each other: glass artist Maggie Concannon and gallery owner Rogan Sweeney, innkeeper Brianna Concannon and writer Grayson Thane.[23] But Roberts adds a mystic layer to the third book when she imports Maggie and Brianna's American half-sister to the Irish countryside where the series takes place. Like the *Star* series, *Born in Shame* suggests that the couple in question have lived and loved before, or are playing out roles in the present from stories that have already taken place in the past. Murphy Muldoon, who farms the land next door to the Irish Concannon sisters, recognizes Shannon Bodine's role as soon as he sees her: "The fairy queen, was all he could think. And the spell was on him."[24] Because the first two books of the series have taken place in the everyday world, the readers share Shannon's surprise at the various layers of her love affair. Murphy isn't speaking figuratively; Shannon looks exactly like the fairy queen he has seen in his dreams. Shannon has had dreams, too, of this legendary witch and her warrior, but she's far more resistant to what she dismisses as Murphy's "Celtic mysticism."[25] When she finally paints a scene from one of those dreams as a gift for Murphy, it indicates not only her acceptance of their love, but also her acceptance of the magical Irish countryside around her, the stone circle that dances nearby, and the legendary figures who loved there before she and Murphy did. Roberts stages their betrothal scene — the last scene of the series — at the stone circle and infuses it with the mystical elements that have permeated this love story. Having decided to give up her life in New York to stay in Ireland, Shannon

> waited until morning to go to Murphy. The warrior had left the wise woman in the morning, so it was right the circle close at the same time of day.
> It never crossed her mind that he wouldn't be where she looked for him. And he was standing in the stone circle, the broach in his hand and the mist shimmering like the breath of ghosts above the grass.[26]

The mystical materials — the painting Shannon creates from the visions she and Murphy share, the witch's broach which Murphy found years before and presents as a gift to Shannon, the stone circle itself — enhance the final romance of the series and enrich this particular pairing. But they also contribute to the overall unity of the group, because accepting that layer of meaning leads Shannon to stay in Ireland near her half-sisters; also, in marrying her, Murphy will be brother-in-law to Maggie and Brianna as he has already been like a brother in feeling.

The legend that underpins the final *Born in ...* book accounts for Murphy's immediate, and Shannon's eventual, acceptance that they are meant to be together. In their case Roberts stops short of suggesting that the outcome of their modern-day romance actually rights an earlier wrong, as wrongs were righted when the Calhoun sisters laid their ancestor to rest. But in another of her Irish series, *The Ardmore Trilogy*,[27] Roberts makes clear that the choices the mortals make directly impact the fate of those immortal characters who loved before them. In the first book, *Jewels of the Sun*, Roberts hints at the supernatural when heroine Jude Murray finds her way to her ancestral cottage on instinct through a blinding storm. The paranormal elements manifest immediately as Jude sees the figure of a woman in the second story window of a supposedly-empty house. That phantom, the ghost of the lady Gwen, who lived there during her own long-ago lifetime, appears to the heroes and heroines of the trilogy who inhabit the cottage and encourages them to choose love while they can. Gwen's erstwhile lover, the fairy prince Carrick, is less subtle and confronts the human characters, raging at their reluctance and rewarding their right choices. Roberts' story connects the lovers of the past and the couples of the present, and it soon becomes clear that the choices the six mortals make will cement or break the curse that Carrick cast three hundred years previously.

Local pub owner Aidan Gallagher tells the story to Jude Murray before their own romance has officially begun. He concludes with Gwen's final rejection of Carrick at the end of her mortal life: "Her words angered him, for he had brought her love, time and again, in the only way he knew. And this time before he walked away from her, he cast a spell. She would wander and she would wait, as he had, year after year, alone and lonely, until true hearts met and accepted the gifts he had offered her. Three times to meet, three times to accept before the spell could be broken."[28] Aidan and Jude are the first to meet and to accept love; then in the second book Aidan's brother Shawn opens his eyes to the romantic potential in his lifelong friendship with Brenna O' Toole. In each romance, the ghostly Gwen and the immortal Carrick mix and meddle with the mortals, partially for the good of the human characters (Gwen), partially because their own hearts hang in the balance (Carrick). The pressure of both worlds of love and longing, the everyday and the otherworld versions, comes to a head in the romance of Aidan and Shawn's sister Darcy and the entrepreneur Trevor Magee. Both are obstinate and neither appreciates the role they've been asked to play in the enduring drama. In their declaration scene, more than their own hearts are on the line: Darcy's siblings and siblings-in-law are invested in their happiness, and Gwen and Carrick's opportunity to be together forever depends upon what Darcy and Trevor choose. According to Little and Hayden, "By the end of the third book, *Heart of the Sea*, readers are rooting as much for Carrick and his Gwen as they are for the Gallagher siblings and their loves."[29] When the third and last couple is happily matched, Roberts concludes the entire series with a scene of the mortal woman and the fairy prince happily reunited. This final scene feels integral, rather than additional, because Roberts winds the mystical thread of Gwen and Carrick's love story through the other three romances, strengthening and enhancing each individual narrative and the series as a whole.

Although it takes them a while to believe what they have heard, the three heroines of *The Key Trilogy*[30] know from the start that their quest will have supernatural interference, assistance, and results. Their charge, which they are initially paid to undertake, is to find the three magic keys that will unlock the souls of three demigoddess sisters trapped for three thousand years in the world behind the Curtain of Dreams. At first Malory Price, Dana Steele, and Zoe McCourt are only interested in the money and the challenge, but as they learn the story of these three daughters of a mortal mother and an immortal father, and of their exiled guardians Rowena and Pitte who failed to protect the demigoddesses and so must depend on the humans to intercede on their behalf, the heroines become determined to succeed at every challenge before them: true love, professional success, and epic quest. Roberts offers the typical connections of her human series: the heroes are life-long friends, the heroines start a business together, one hero and one heroine are stepsiblings. But the mystery of the quest and weight of the cause enhance those bonds, enliven the plot, and raise the stakes from six hearts in this world to three souls in the other. When the three humans find the keys, defeat their powerful enemy, and have engagement rings on their fingers, the three demigoddesses are freed. To highlight the human ability to impact the immortal world, however, Roberts structures the denouement so that each successful woman is granted a boon, and that the boon that the final heroine demands is the absolution and return of Rowena and Pitte to their homes in that other world. The god of that supernatural world agrees, accepts the fallen heroes, and blesses the human weddings to come.

For the readers, a mystical series by Roberts offers even an additional promise and pleasure. In them Roberts tells stories of profound transformation, of lives and loves that go from ordinary to extraordinary literally overnight. The suggestion that the choices we humans make might matter in worlds beyond ours is powerful, important, and enchanting.

The Power of Magic

The significant difference between Roberts' magic series and her other supernatural series is her placement of true power in the hands of her protagonists. In the paranormal or mystical environments, human characters will interact with or react against secondary characters with superhuman capacity as they protect or seek magical objects, but they remain themselves entirely human in their abilities. The magic series change those boundaries and insist upon fluidity between the natural and the supernatural, the everyday and the magic. When Nell Channing first meets Mia Devlin in the *The Three Sisters Trilogy*,[31] Mia's generosity and goodwill lead Nell to conclude, only half-jokingly, "'You must be my fairy godmother.'" Mia responds, "'You'll find out soon enough I'm far from it. I'm just a practical witch.'"[32] This magical series is peopled with practical witches, humans with stunning power and abilities, with the accompanying risk and responsibility, whose searches for love and success are complicated by their magical gifts and obligations.

If unity among the central characters is important in the everyday, paranormal, and mystical series, it is paramount in the magic series. To the regular plot constraints that require that three — or six — characters work as a team, Roberts add the power of the number three in magic systems. To break the curse that haunts Three Sisters Island in *The Three Sisters Trilogy*, it requires the presence and power of all three women. If Nell can't find a safe place to grow and heal, if Ripley's reluctance to practice the Craft remains, if Mia's vision continues to be obscured by her long-standing grief over lost love, if any one of them is "lost" in any way, history will repeat itself and they will die broken and alone as their predecessors — the Island's creators and founders — did before them.

As we saw in the paranormal and mystical series, there are higher-than-human stakes in the magical series. If Nell, Ripley, and Mia fail, individually or collectively, more than their own lives will be lost: the Island itself, created as a sanctuary by three witches escaping from the Salem persecution three hundred years earlier, will be swamped by an ancient evil and swallowed by the sea. These higher stakes, other lives in the balance, are typical of a Roberts magic series; in some cases, as with *The Circle Series*,[33] the fates of this world and others may depend upon the choices and actions of the central characters.

As the scope of a series multiplies the potential twists and turns of a stand-alone story, the magic in a series multiplies the possible complications. The heroines and heroes who literally wield greater power have a correspondingly greater impact on the people and places that surround them in their stories. The conflict of the tales is typically instigated by some other mystical or magical presence, often before the time of the current story, but the real options the magical human characters have in their range of responses to that dilemma make for exciting and action-packed romance. On their way to finding love and the requisite "happily ever after," the Donovans experience their share of magical moments.[34] Morgana Donovan nudges a shy teenager toward a prom date, Sebastian Donovan finds a kidnapped toddler, and Anastasia Donovan saves a dying child. The point of the stories may be romance, but the magic adds a supernatural wrinkle to what otherwise might be conventional character-building. We find out that Morgana has a soft spot for romance beneath her professional, polished demeanor; we see Sebastian as a dedicated champion for the young and powerless; we see Anastasia's profound sympathy for others have an extraordinary impact on the lives of those around her. But we also see three individuals who, in these cases, "out" themselves and their gifts in order to do good in their communities. Roberts and her magic characters regularly remind us of the historical and modern persecution that can pursue people who are perceived to be drastically different from the rest of society, so the choice of magic characters to share their talents echoes and enhances the typical romance choice of one individual making him- or herself vulnerable to another.

In many ways Roberts' magical characters are exactly the same as typical romantic leads: they must learn to know and trust themselves on their way to knowing and trusting a life partner. But the magical element in these series makes those "essential" and predictable romantic steps fresh for the reader. *The Three Sisters Trilogy* may have at its heart Nell's personal quest for security and strength, but on the way she learns to magically stir the air and celebrate a Sabbat, an important Wiccan holiday or day of observance. Ripley's acceptance of Mac as a life partner is integrally connected to her acceptance of her own magical abilities and of Mac's academic interest in and personal fascination with all things supernatural. Like many strong-willed heroines, Ripley has a temper, especially in the face of injustice. Unlike most other heroines, Ripley's temper can call lightning down to sink a sailboat, or damn her own soul if she loses control in a fit of self-righteous rage. We may see from the opening chapters of the third book, or even the chapters of the two books before it, that Mia and Sam are meant to be together. But few love relationships must wrest themselves away from the lure and heartbreak of the silkies, few lovers can truly sense and see each other over the distances of miles and years. The magical elements make the requisite parts of a romance fresh for the reader; a basic ingredient like an "obstacle" can take on new scope. They also highlight the importance of love as the solution for human hearts and apocalyptic threats. In a Roberts series with magic, love can actually save the world.

With their supernatural strength and magical means, the heroines and heroes of Roberts' magic romances may seem worlds apart from the everyday lives of average readers. But when Roberts turns to magic, she often uses Pagan belief systems like Wicca, a choice that makes even the most incredible gifts seem just a step away from a version of the everyday. Roberts' readers may or may not believe in the ability of human beings to heal through herbology, or nudge attraction along through crystals, or manipulate the elements. But much of that magic — real or imagined — relates to the everyday work of humanity, making it easier to suspend disbelief. Many of Roberts' characters, male and female, have enormous gifts in various domestic arts. They cook brilliantly and effortlessly; they decorate their homes beautifully, whatever their income or budget. They care for loved ones, often children, in empathic ways that skillfully heal both physical and emotional wounds. In ways that would be obvious, if not conscious, to many of Roberts' readers, the magic her characters work is simply an unspecified number of steps away from the everyday "arts" which everyone must practice.

Roberts' series, for example, often highlight the holidays. Halloween and Christmas may seem an enormous theological leap from Samhain and Yule, and perhaps they would be for most of Roberts' readers. But many who celebrate Halloween and Christmas keep their own seasonal rituals during those festivities and speak of those holidays as "magical" times. Roberts also seems to suggest that even daily routine contains some "practical magic." The love and care Brianna Concannon expresses in making tea for family, friends, or guests is in some ways just a couple of degrees different from the Wiccan lore — and magic — that Anastasia Donovan pours into a brew to nurture her exhausted cousin Morgana who is pregnant with twins. In their section on herbalism in *A Witches' Bible*, Janet and Stewart Farrar warn about the potency of herbal healing, but also acknowledge that "Anyone who can make a pot of tea can make an infusion."[35] The love and care with which Zoe McCourt cleans and decorates the home she shares with her son in *The Key Trilogy* varies in some substance from the careful placement of crystals or candles by Mia Devlin or Sebastian Donovan, but not much in motivation. Characters' homes in a magic series are sanctuaries in both metaphorical and literal ways. In *The Heart of Wicca,* Ellen Cannon Reed explains, "Because we see the world with different eyes, we also find magic in everything else we do, and we can put magic into everything we do. Vacuuming the house can be a magical cleansing of negativity. Cooking can involve blessing the food, and so forth."[36] If there can be magic in these simple domestic tasks, Roberts' stories suggest, the possibility of magic in anyone's life waits right there next to the possibility of true love.

Amy Berkower, Roberts' agent for her entire writing career, observes that Roberts' books "provide an escape into a world populated by likable people whose lives are filled with the kind of romance that may be rooted in fantasy, but isn't so removed from the lives of everyday people."[37] Berkower's claim rings true, even for those series that reach from "fantasy" to the fantastic. In *The Key Series,* Malory, Dana, and Zoe inadvertently open a portal for evil to walk through as they dabble with a Ouija board. The magical Rowena appears on the scene in time to crack the board and close the door, but then chastises the three human heroines for, essentially, playing with fire. Zoe explains that they thought perhaps they were witches, a reasonable enough assumption in the storybook world where they find themselves, perhaps an extraordinary idea in the everyday world of the reader. But Rowena's response goes a long way to explaining the appeal of a Roberts series: "every woman has some magic."[38] In the ways that she makes the magical seem possible, and more important, the practical seem magic, Roberts proves Rowena exactly right.

Roberts may make magic explicit in only some of her series, but the message of empowerment permeates all of them. Her stories are peopled by powerful women and so suggest that women are powerful. While only some of her characters practice magic in the sense of Wicca or wands, all of them, Roberts argues, practice a potent magic when they care for homes, and gardens, and loved ones. Plot lines that seem fantastic feel affirming for readers who, having come to expect that true love is possible, can begin to believe in the power of magic as well.

Notes

I am indebted to Alexandra Robert Gordon, Carol Shillibeer, Logan Greene, and Rachel Toor for suggestions and support. Thanks also to Sarah S. G. Frantz and Eric Murphy Selinger for their vision and advice.

1. For these and other "essential elements" of a romance novel, see Pamela Regis, *A Natural History of the Romance Novel* (Philadelphia: University of Pennsylvania Press, 2003).

2. "Did You Know?" Nora Roberts, http://www.noraroberts.com/aboutnora/funfacts.html.

3. Roberts' series include the *In Death* series, over thirty-two books and nine novellas or short stories so far, which she writes under the name J.D Robb.

4. Denise Little and Laura Hayden, eds., *The Official Nora Roberts Companion* (New York: Berkley, 2003), 319.

5. *Chesapeake Blue,* the fourth novel in the *Chesapeake Bay* "Trilogy" (New York: Jove, 2002).

6. Little and Hayden, *The Official Nora Roberts Companion,* 48.

7. "Nora Roberts," Penguin.com, http://us.penguingroup.com/static/packages/us/noraroberts/books/books.htm.

8. Susan C. Stone, "An Interview with Tommy Dreiling," in *The Official Nora Roberts Companion,* ed. Little and Hayden, 361.

9. *Daring to Dream* (1996), *Finding the Dream* (1997), *Holding the Dream* (1997).

10. Part Ten of the *Companion* includes internet reader polls of favorite characters, relationships, kisses, and so on. The series dominate the charts, but not to the utter exclusion of the individual novels.

11. Nora Roberts, *Daring to Dream* (New York: Jove, 1996), 254.

12. This Silhouette series nicely represents Roberts' range of romance: she wrote each of the four titles for a different Silhouette line (Little and Hayden, 47): *Courting Catherine* (1991), *A Man for Amanda* (1991),

For the Love of Lilah (1991), *Suzanna's Surrender* (1991). In a fifth and later novel, a sister-in-law is brought into the fold and given her own romance (*Megan's Mate,* 1996). See *The Calhoun Women* (New York: Harlequin, 1996).

13. *Sea Swept* (1998), *Rising Tides* (1998), *Inner Harbor* (1999), *Chesapeake Blue* (2002).

14. Regis, *A Natural History*, 195.

15. Nora Roberts, *Chesapeake Blue* (New York: Jove, 2004), 109.

16. *Ibid.*, 347. *The Garden Trilogy* (*Blue Dahlia* [2004], *Black Rose* [2005], *Red Lily* [2005]) introduces an ancestor who is truly "ticked off." Though her intentions toward the living characters are more malignant than benign, she is also laid to a peaceful rest at the end of that series.

17. Nora Roberts, *The Calhoun Women* (New York: Harlequin, 1996), 506.

18. *Hidden Star* (1997), *Captive Star* (1997), *Secret Star* (1998).

19. Nora Roberts, *Hidden Star* (New York: Silhouette, 1997), 13.

20. Nora Roberts, *Secret Star* (New York: Silhouette, 1998), 166–67.

21. *Ibid.*, 168.

22. *Ibid.*, 280–81.

23. *Born in Fire* (1994), *Born in Ice* (1995). The third is *Born in Shame* (1996).

24. Nora Roberts, *Born in Shame* (New York: Jove, 1995), 71.

25. *Ibid.*, 160–62, 148.

26. *Ibid.*, 351.

27. *Jewels of the Sun* (1999), *Tears of the Moon* (2000), *Heart of the Sea* (2000).

28. Nora Roberts, *Jewels of the Sun* (New York: Jove, 1999), 101–02.

29. Little and Hayden, *The Official Nora Roberts Companion*, 313.

30. *Key of Light* (2003), *Key of Knowledge* (2003), *Key of Valor* (2004).

31. *Dance Upon the Air* (2001), *Heaven and Earth* (2001), *Face the Fire* (2002).

32. Nora Roberts, *Dance Upon the Air* (New York: Jove, 2001) 23.

33. *Morrigan's Cross* (2006), *Dance of the Gods* (2006), *Valley of Silence* (2006).

34. *Captivated* (1992), *Entranced* (1992), *Charmed* (1992). Later extended by a fourth book, *Enchanted* (1999). See *The Donovan Legacy* (New York: Silhoutte, 1999).

35. Janet and Stewart Farrar, *A Witches' Bible: The Complete Witches' Handbook* (Custer, WA: Phoenix Publishing, 1996), 221.

36. Ellen Cannon Reed, *The Heart of Wicca: Wise Words from a Crone on the Path* (York Beach, ME: Samuel Weiser, Inc. 2000), 103–04.

37. Denise Little, "The Mind of an Agent," in *The Official Nora Roberts Companion*, ed. Little and Hayden, 53.

38. Nora Roberts, *Key of Light* (New York: Jove, 2003), 278.

Works Cited

Abbot, Laura. *The Wrong Man.* 2004. Reprint, Richmond, Surrey: Silhouette, 2005.

"About Black Lace." Black Lace. http://www.blacklace-books.co.uk/.

"About the Romance Genre." Romance Writers of America. http://www.rwanational.org/cs/the_romance_genre.

Adorno, Theodor. "On Popular Music." In *Cultural Theory and Popular Culture: A Reader,* 2d ed., edited by John Storey. Athens: University of Georgia Press, 1998.

"The Affecting History of Mrs. Howe." 1815. Reprint, *The Garland Library of Narratives of North American Indian Captivities,* Volume 19. Edited by Wilcomb Washburn. New York: Garland, 1977.

Alberts, J.K. "The Role of Couples' Conversations in Relationship Development: A Content Analysis of Courtship Talk in Harlequin Romance Novels." *Communication Quarterly,* 34 (1986): 127–142.

Allan, Jeanne. *No Angel.* Toronto: Harlequin, 1991.

Allen, Louise. *Virgin Slave, Barbarian King.* Toronto: Harlequin, 2007.

Allen, Theodore. *Invention of the White Race, Volume 1: Racial Oppression and Social Control.* London: Verso, 1994.

Anderson, Chris. *The Long Tail: Why the Future of Business Is Selling Less of More.* New York: Hyperion, 2006.

Anderson, Jennifer. *Mills & Boon: Love and Oppression.* Broadway: New South Wales Institute of Technology, 1981.

Anderson, Rachel. *The Purple Heart Throbs: The Sub-literature of Love.* London: Hodder and Stoughton, 1974.

Androutsopoulos, Jannis. "Introduction: Sociolinguistics and Computer-Mediated Communication." *Journal of Sociolinguistics* 10, no. 4 (2006): 419–38.

Armstrong, Nancy. "Captivity and Cultural Capital in the English Novel." *Novel: A Forum on Fiction* 31, no. 3 (1998): 373–98.

Astolat. "No Refunds or Exchanges." http://www.intimations.org/fanfic/stargate/No%20Refunds%20Or%20Exchanges.html.

Axtell, James. *The European and the Indian: Essays in the Ethnohistory of Colonial North America.* New York: Oxford University Press, 1981.

Bach, Evelyn. "Sheik Fantasies: Orientalism and Feminine Desire in the Desert Romance." *Hecate* 23, no. 1 (1997): 9–40.

Bakhtin, Mikhail. *The Dialogic Imagination.* Austin: University of Texas Press, 1982.

Ballou, Mardi. *Reunions Dangereuses.* Akron: Ellora's Cave, 2006.

Balogh, Mary. *Slightly Dangerous.* New York: Bantam Dell, 2004.

Barlow, Linda, and Jayne Ann Krentz. "Beneath the Surface: The Hidden Codes of Romance." In *Dangerous Men and Adventurous Women: Romance Writers on the Appeal of the Romance,* edited by Jayne Ann Krentz, 15–30. Philadelphia: University of Pennsylvania Press, 1992.

Barrett, Michèle. "Ideology and the Cultural Production of Gender." In *Feminist Criticism and Social Change: Sex, Class, and Race in Literature and Culture,* edited by Judith Newton and Deborah Rosenfelt, 65–85. New York: Methuen, 1985.

Basso, Kenneth A. "'To Give Up on Words': Silence in Western Apache Culture." *Southwestern Journal of Anthropology* 26, no. 3 (1970): 213–30.

Bederman, Gail. *Manliness and Civilization: A Cultural History of Gender and Race in the United States, 1880–1917.* Chicago: University of Chicago Press, 1995.

Belsey, Catherine. *Desire: Love Stories in Western Culture*. Oxford: Wiley-Blackwell, 1994.

Benjamin, Walter. "The Work of Art in the Age of Mechanical Reproduction." In *Illuminations*, edited by Hannah Arendt, translated by Harry Zohn, 217–252. New York: Schocken Books, 1969.

Bettelheim, Bruno. *The Uses of Enchantment: The Meaning and Importance of Fairy Tales*. 1976. Reprint, London: Penguin, 1991.

Bindel, Julie, and Daisy Cummins. "Mills & Boon: 100 Years of Heaven or Hell?" *The Guardian* (London), 5 December 2007. http://www.guardian.co.uk/lifeandstyle/2007/dec/05/women.fiction.

"Bitch." *AskOxford.com*. http://www.askoxford.com/concise_oed/bitch?view=uk.

"Bitch." *Online Etymology Dictionary*. http://www.etymonline.com/index.php?term=bitch.

Blake, Susan L. "What 'Race' Is the Sheik?: Rereading a Desert Romance." In *Doubled Plots: Romance and History*, edited by Susan Strehle and Mary Paniccia Carden, 67–85. Jackson: University Press of Mississippi, 2003.

Bloom, Allan. *Love and Friendship*. New York: Simon & Schuster, 1993.

Bo, Rachel. *Double Jeopardy*. Akron: Ellora's Cave, 2004.

The Book of Common Prayer. London: Oxford University Press.

Brackett, Kim Pettigrew. "Facework Strategies Among Romance Fiction Readers." *The Social Science Journal* 37, no. 3 (2000): 347–60.

Brisbin, Terri. *Taming the Highlander*. New York: Harlequin, 2006.

Brockmann, Suzanne. *All Through the Night*. New York: Ballantine, 2007.

_____. *Force of Nature*. New York: Ballantine, 2007.

_____. *Gone Too Far*. New York: Ballantine, 2003.

_____. "Thoughts on Force of Nature." http://www.suzanne brockmann.com/fon_happened.htm.

Brody, Jennifer DeVere. *Impossible Purities: Blackness, Femininity, and Victorian Culture*. Durham: Duke University Press, 1998.

Brooks, Cleanth. *The Well-Wrought Urn: Studies in the Structure of Poetry*. New York: Harcourt, Brace, and World, 1947.

Brown, Sandra. *Texas! Chase*. London: Warner Books, 1991.

Burley, Stephanie. "What's a Nice Girl Like You Doing in a Book Like This? Homoerotic Reading and Popular Romance." In *Doubled Plots: Romance and History*, edited by Susan Strehle and Mary Paniccia Carden, 127–46. Jackson: University Press of Mississippi, 2003.

Burnham, Michelle. *Captivity and Sentiment: Cultural Exchange in American Literature, 1682–1861*. Hanover, NH: University Press of New England, 1997.

Butler, Judith. *Gender Trouble: Feminism and the Subversion of Identity*. New York: Routledge, 1990.

_____. "Performative Acts and Gender Constitution: An Essay in Phenomenology and Feminist Theory." *Theatre Journal* 40, no. 4 (1988): 519–531.

Caine, Rachel. *Firestorm*. New York: ROC, 2006.

Camp, Deborah. "The Role of the Romance Novel." In *Writing Romances*, edited by Rita Gallagher and Rita Clay Estrada, 46–53. Cincinnati: Writer's Digest Books, 1997.

Campbell, Anna. *Claiming the Courtesan*. New York: Avon, 2007.

Capelle, Annick. "Harlequin Romances in Western Europe: The Cultural Interactions of Romantic Literature." In *European Readings of American Popular Culture*, edited by John Dean and Jean-Paul Gabilliet, 91–100. Westport, CT: Greenwood Press, 1996.

Carbaugh, Donal. "Comments on 'Culture' in Communication Inquiry." *Communication Reports* 1, no. 1 (1988): 38–41.

_____, and Sally O. Hastings. "A Role for Communication Theory in Ethnographic Studies of Interpersonal Communication." In *Social Approaches to Communication*, edited by Wendy Leeds-Hurwitz, 171–87. New York: The Guilford Press, 1995.

Carson, Anne. *Eros the Bittersweet*. 1996. Reprint, Normal, IL: Dalkey Archive Press, 1998.

Caskie, Kathryn. *How to Propose to a Prince*. New York: Avon, 2008.

Casspeach. "Animal Husbandry." 14 January 2006. http://www.casspeach.com/sga_fic/animal.html.

Castiglia, Christopher. *Bound and Determined: Captivity, Culture-Crossing, and White Womanhood from Mary Rowlandson to Patty Hearst*. Chicago: University of Chicago Press, 1996.

Castle, Terry. "Sylvia Townsend and the Counterplot of Lesbian Fiction." In *Sexual Sameness: Textual Differences in Lesbian and Gay Writing*, edited by Joseph Bristow, 128–147. London: Routledge, 1992.

Cavell, Stanley. *Pursuits of Happiness: The Hollywood Comedy of Remarriage*. Cambridge, MA: Harvard University Press, 1981.

Cawelti, John G. *Adventure, Mystery, and Romance: Formula Stories as Art and Popular Culture.* Chicago: University of Chicago Press, 1976.

Cesperanza. "Admin Post: The Harlequin Plot Challenge." Sga_flashfic. 27 August 2005. http://community.livejournal.com/sga_flashfic/149489.html.

Chancellor, Alexander. "What's the point of being told the terrorist beast is on the prowl if we don't know when or where it will strike?" *The Guardian* (London), July 13, 2007: 5.

Chang, Jeff. *Can't Stop Won't Stop: A History of the Hip-Hop Generation.* New York: St. Martin's Press, 2005.

Chappel, Deborah Kaye. "American Romances: Narratives of Culture and Identity." PhD diss., Duke University, 1992.

Chase, Loretta. *Lord of Scoundrels.* New York: Avon, 1995.

Claire, Daphne, and Robyn Donald. *Writing Romantic Fiction.* London: A & C Black, 1999.

Clark, Herbert H. *Arenas of Language Use.* Chicago: University of Chicago Press, 1992.

Coddington, Lynn. "Romance and Power: Writing Romance Novels as a Practice of Critical Literacy." PhD diss., University of California, Berkeley, 1997.

Cohn, Jan. *Romance and the Erotics of Property: Mass-Market Fiction for Women.* Durham: Duke University Press, 1988.

Coleman, Sandy. "Claiming the Courtesan." All About Romance. http://www.likesbooks.com/cgi-bin/bookReview.pl?BookReviewId=6076.

Coles, Claire D., and M. Johnna Shamp. "Some Sexual, Personality, and Demographic Characteristics of Women Readers of Erotic Romances." *Archives of Sexual Behavior* 13, no. 3 (1984): 187–209.

Connell, R.W. *Masculinities.* Berkeley: University of California Press, 1995.

Coulter, Catherine. *Rosehaven.* New York: Jove, 1996.

Coward, Rosalind. *Female Desire.* London: Palladin, 1984.

Crane, Lynda L. "Romance Novel Readers: In Search of Feminist Change?" *Women's Studies*, 23, no. 3 (1994): 257–69.

Crevecoeur, St. John De. *Letters from an American Farmer.* Edited by Albert E. Stone. 1782. Reprint, New York: Penguin, 1981.

Crow, Anah. *Uneven.* Round Rock, TX: Torquere Press Publishers.

Crowley, Michael, and Melanie. "Words to the Wise." *Take Our Word for It* 195: 2. http://www.takeourword.com/TOW195/page2.html.

Crusie, Jennifer. *Bet Me.* New York: St. Martin's Press, 2004.

———. "Modern Literary Terms: The Glittery HooHa." Argh Ink. April 9, 2007. http://www.arghink.com/2007/04/09/the-glittery-hooha-an-analysis/.

———. "Please Remove Your Assumptions, They're Sitting on My Genre." Argh Ink. April 14, 2007. http://www.arghink.com/2007/04/14/please-remove-your-assumptions-theyre-sitting-on-my-genre/.

Crusie-Smith, Jennifer. "Romancing Reality: The Power of Romance Fiction to Reinforce and Re-Vision the Real." *Paradoxa* 3, nos. 1–2 (1997): 81–93.

Cullinan, Heidi. *Nowhere Ranch.* San Francisco: Loose Id, 2011.

"Curry House Founder Is Honoured." *BBC News.* September 29, 2005. http://news.bbc.co.uk/2/hi/uk_news/england/london/4290124.stm.

Dahl, Victoria. *The Wicked West.* Don Mills, Ontario: HQN, 2009.

Daleski, H.M. *The Divided Heroine: A Recurrent Pattern in Six English Novels.* London: Holmes & Meier, 1984.

D'Alessandro, Jacquie. *Confessions at Midnight.* New York: Avon, 2008.

———. *Sleepless at Midnight.* New York: Avon, 2007.

Dandridge, Rita B. *Black Women's Activism: Reading African American Women's Historical Romances.* African-American Literature and Culture, no. 5. New York: Peter Lang, 2004.

Danson, Lawrence. *Shakespeare's Dramatic Genres.* Oxford: Oxford University Press, 2000.

Darbyshire, Peter. "Romancing the World: Harlequin Romances, the Capitalist Dream, and the Conquest of Europe and Asia." *Studies in Popular Culture* 23, no. 1 (2000): 1–10.

Davidson, Cathy. *Revolution and the Word: The Rise of the Novel in America.* New York: Oxford University Press, 1986.

Davis, Fanny. *The Ottoman Lady: A Social History from 1718 to 1918.* Westport, CT: Greenwood Press, 1986.

Deacon, Desley, Penny Russell, and Angela Woollacott. Introduction to *Transnational Lives: Biographies of Global Modernity, 1700–Present*, edited by Desley Deacon, Penny Russell, and Angela Woollacott, 1–14. Houndsmill, Basingstoke: Palgrave Macmillan, 2010.

De Geest, Dirk, and An Goris. "Constrained Writing, Creative Writing. The Case of Handbooks for Writing Romances." *Poetics Today* 31, no. 1 (2010): 81–106.

Deveraux, Jude. *River Lady*. New York: Pocket, 1985.

———. *The Velvet Promise*. New York: Pocket, 1981.

Diamond, Lisa M. "Emerging Perspectives on Distinctions Between Romantic Love and Sexual Desire." *Current Directions in Psychological Science* 13, no. 3 (2004): 116–119.

"Did You Know?" Nora Roberts. http://www.noraroberts.com/aboutnora/funfacts.html.

Dixon, jay. *The Romance Fiction of Mills & Boon, 1909–1990s*. Philadelphia: UCL Press, 1999.

Dodd, Christina. *In My Wildest Dreams*. New York: Avon, 2001.

Dominguez, Ivo, Jr. *Beneath the Skins: The New Spirit and Politics of the Kink Community*. Los Angeles: Daedalus, 1994.

Doty, Alexander. *Making Things Perfectly Queer: Interpreting Mass Culture*. Minneapolis: University of Minnesota Press, 1993.

Douglas, Ann. "Soft-Porn Culture: Punishing the Liberated Woman." *The New Republic* 183, no. 9 (August 30, 1980): 25–29.

Dreyer, Eileen. "Eileen the Angry." Eileen Dryer Blog. March 31, 2007. http://www.eileendreyer.com/blog/2007/03/eileen-angry.html.

Driscoll, Catherine. "One True Pairing: The Romance of Pornography and the Pornography of Romance." In *Fan Fiction and Fan Communities in the Age of the Internet*, edited by Karen Hellekson and Kristina Busse, 79–96. Jefferson, NC: McFarland, 2006.

Dubino, Jeanne. "The Cinderella Complex: Romance Fiction, Patriarchy and Capitalism." *Journal of Popular Culture* 27, no. 3 (1993): 103–118.

Duncker, Patricia. *Sisters and Strangers: An Introduction to Contemporary Feminist Writing*. Oxford: Blackwell, 1992.

Dylan, Bob. "Sad Eyed Lady of the Lowlands." *Blonde on Blonde*. Columbia Records, 1966.

Eagleton, Terry. *How to Read a Poem*. Malden, MA: Blackwell, 2007.

Early, Margot. *A Family Resemblance*. 2006. Reprint, Richmond, Surrey: Harlequin Mills & Boon, 2007.

Enoch, Suzanne. *Twice the Temptation*. New York: Avon, 2007.

Erdman, Amy Farrell. *Yours in Sisterhood: Ms. Magazine and the Promise of Popular Feminism*. Chapel Hill: University of North Carolina Press, 1998.

Ervin, Clark Kent. "Answering Al Qaeda." *The New York Times*, May 8, 2007: 25.

Estrada, Rita Clay, and Rita Gallagher. *You Can Write a Romance*. Cincinnati: Writer's Digest Books, 1999.

Etzioni, Amitai, and Oren Etzioni. "Face-to-Face and Computer-Mediated Communities, A Comparative Analysis." *Information Society* 15, no. 4 (1999): 241–8.

Evans, David T. *Sexual Citizenship: The Material Construction of Sexualities*. London: Routledge, 1993.

Fahnestock-Thomas, Mary. *Georgette Heyer: A Critical Retrospective*. Saraland, AL: PrinnyWorld Press, 2001.

Faludi, Susan. "America's Guardian Myths." *The New York Times*, September 7, 2007: 29.

———. *Backlash: The Undeclared War Against American Women*. 1991. Reprint, New York: Three Rivers Press, 2006.

"FAQ." Passionate Ink. http://www.passionateink.org/faq.

Farrar, Janet, and Stewart. *A Witches' Bible: The Complete Witches' Handbook*. Custer, WA: Phoenix Publishing, 1996.

Filson, John. "Life and Adventures of Daniel Boon." *The Garland Library of Narratives of North American Indian Captivities*, Volume 14. Edited by Wilcomb Washburn. New York: Garland, 1978.

Firestone, Shulamith. *The Dialectic of Sex: The Case for Feminist Revolution*. New York: Bantam, 1971.

Fisher, Helen. "The Drive to Love: The Neural Mechanism for Mate Selection." In *The New Psychology of Love*, edited by Robert J. Sternberg and Karin Weis, 87–115. New Haven: Yale University Press, 2006.

Flesch, Juliet. *From Australia with Love: A History of Modern Australian Popular Romance Novels*. Fremantle, Australia: Curtin University Books, 2004.

Fletcher, Lisa. *Historical Romance Fiction: Heterosexuality and Performativity*. Aldershot: Ashgate, 2008.

Foley, Gaelen. *Lord of Ice*. New York: Ivy Books, 2002.

Foster, Guy Mark. "How Dare a Black Woman Make Love to a White Man! Black Women Romance

Novelists and the Taboo of Interracial Desire." In *Empowerment Versus Oppression: Twenty First Century Views of Popular Romance Novels*, edited by Sally Goade, 103–128. Newcastle: Cambridge Scholars, 2007.

Foster, Hannah Webster. *The Coquette, or The History of Eliza Wharton*. Boston: William P. Petridge and Company, 1855. http://digital.library.upenn.edu/women/foster/coquette/coquette.html.

Foucault, Michel. *The History of Sexuality. Volume I: An Introduction*, translated by Robert Hurley. New York: Vintage Books, 1990.

Fowler, Bridget. *The Alienated Reader: Women and Popular Romantic Literature in the Twentieth Century*. Brighton: Harvester Wheatsheaf, 1991.

Frantz, Sarah S.G. "Darcy's Vampiric Descendants: Austen's Perfect Romance Hero and J.R. Ward's Black Dagger Brotherhood." *Persuasions On-line* 30, no. 1 (2009). http://www.jasna.org/persuasions/on-line/vol30no1/frantz.html.

———. "'Expressing' Herself: The Romance Novel and the Feminine Will to Power." In *Scorned Literature: Essays on the History and Criticism of Popular Mass-Produced Fiction in America*, edited by Lydia Cushman Schurman and Deidre Johnson, 17–36. Westport, CT: Greenwood Press, 2002.

———. "'I've tried my entire life to be a good man': Suzanne Brockmann's Sam Starrett, Ideal Romance Hero." In *Women Constructing Men: Female Novelists and Their Male Characters, 1750–2000*, edited by Sarah S.G. Frantz and Katharina Rennhak, 227–247. Lanham, MD: Lexington, 2009.

Frenier, Mariam Darce. *Good-bye Heathcliff: Changing Heroes, Heroines, Roles, and Values in Women's Category Romances*. Contributions in Women's Studies, no. 94. New York: Greenwood Press, 1988.

Fuss, Diana. "Inside/Out." *Inside/Out: Lesbian Theories, Gay Theories*, edited by Diana Fuss, 1–10. New York: Routledge, 1991.

Gabaldon, Diana. *Outlander*. New York: Dell, 1991.

Garwood, Julie. *Honor's Splendour*. New York: Pocket Books, 1987.

Gauntlett, David. "Ten Things Wrong with the Media 'Effects' Model." www.theory.org.uk/david/effects.htm.

George, Catherine. *Devil Within*. London: Mills & Boon, 1984.

Gerhart, Mary. *Genre Choices Gender Questions*. Norman: University of Oklahoma Press, 1992.

Gill, Rosalind. "From Sexual Objectification to Sexual Subjectification: The Resexualisation of Women's Bodies in the Media." *Feminist Media Studies* 3, no. 1 (2003): 100–106.

Gilman, Laura Anne. *Staying Dead*. New York: Luna, 2006.

Girard, René. *Deceit, Desire and the Novel: Self and Other in Literary Structure*, translated by Yvonne Freccero. 1961. Reprint, Baltimore: Johns Hopkins University Press, 1976.

———. Preface to *The Secret Sharers: Studies in Contemporary Fictions*, by Bruce Bassoff, ix–xv. New York: AMS, 1983.

———. *Things Hidden Since the Foundation of the World*, translated by Stephen Bann and Michael Metteer. 1978. Reprint, London: Athlone, 1987.

———. *"To Double Business Bound": Essays on Literature, Mimesis, and Anthropology*. Baltimore: Johns Hopkins University Press, 1978.

"Godwin's Law." *Wikipedia*. http://en.wikipedia.org/wiki/Godwin%27s_law.

Goffman, Erving. *Interaction Ritual: Essays on Face-to-Face Behaviour*. New York: Penguin, 1972.

Goodman, Jo. *Only in My Arms*. New York: Zebra, 2004.

Gornick, Vivian. *The End of the Novel of Love*. Boston: Beacon Press, 1997.

Graham, Dorie. *So Many Men ...* Don Mills, Ontario: Harlequin, 2005.

Greenblatt, Stephen. *Marvelous Possessions: The Wonder of the New World*. Chicago: University of Chicago Press, 1991.

Greer, Germaine. *The Female Eunuch*. London: Paladin, 1971.

Grescoe, Paul. *The Merchants of Venus: Inside Harlequin and the Empire of Romance*. Vancouver: Raincoast, 1996.

Grose, Francis. "Bitch." *1811 Dictionary of the Vulgar Tongue: A Dictionary of Buckish Slang, University Wit, and Pickpocket Eloquence*. Gutenberg Project. http://www.gutenberg.org/catalog/world/readfile?pageno=20&fk_files=9510.

"Guest Opinion: The Power of the Male Submissive by Joey Hill." Dear Author. http://dearauthor.com/wordpress/2008/10/21/guest-opinion-the-power-of-the-male-submissive-by-joey-hill/.

Guillory, John. *Cultural Capital: The Problem of Literary Canon Formation*. Chicago: University of Chicago Press, 1993.

Haddad, Emily A. "Bound to Love: Captivity in Harlequin Sheikh Novels." In *Empowerment Versus*

Oppression: Twenty First Century Views of Popular Romance Novels, edited by Sally Goade, 42–64. Newcastle: Cambridge Scholars, 2007.

Hall, Bradford "J." "Ritual as Part of Everyday Life." In *Readings in Cultural Contexts*, edited by Judith N. Martin, Thomas K. Nakayam and Lisa A. Flores, 172–9. Mountain View, CA: Mayfield, 1998.

Hampson, Rick. "Fear 'as bad as after 9/11'; In Michigan and elsewhere, Muslims worry about hostile neighbors and surveillance." *USA Today*, December 13, 2006: 1A.

Hart, Jessica. *Mistletoe Marriage*. Richmond, Surrey: Harlequin Mills & Boon, 2005.

Hartley, John. "Creative Identities." In *Creative Industries*, edited by John Hartley, 106–16. Malden, MA: Blackwell, 2005.

———. "Creative Industries." In *Creative Industries*, edited by John Hartley, 1–40. Malden, MA: Blackwell, 2005.

Hawkins, Harriett. *Classics and Trash: Traditions and Taboos in High Literature and Popular Modern Genres*. New York: Harvester Wheatsheaf, 1990.

Hazen, Helen. *Endless Rapture; Rape, Romance, and the Female Imagination*. New York: Scribner's, 1983.

Heinecken, Dawn. "Changing Ideologies in Romance Fiction." In *Romantic Conventions*, edited by Anne K. Kaler and Rosemary E. Johnson-Kurek, 149–172. Bowling Green, OH: Bowling Green State University Popular Press, 1999.

Henry, Astrid. *Not My Mother's Sister: Generational Conflict and Third-Wave Feminism*. Bloomington: Indiana University Press, 2004.

Heyer, Georgette. *Bath Tangle*. London: Heinemann, 1955.

———. *The Black Moth*. 1921. London: Heinemann, 1929.

———. *The Corinthian*. London: Heinemann, 1940.

———. *Devil's Cub*. 1932. Reprint, London: Heinemann, 1966.

———. *Frederica*. London: Heinemann, 1965.

———. *Friday's Child*. London: Heinemann, 1944.

———. *The Grand Sophy*. London: Heinemann, 1950.

———. *Lady of Quality*. London: Heinemann, 1972.

———. *The Reluctant Widow*. London: Heinemann, 1946.

———. *The Talisman Ring*. 1936. London: Heinemann, 1970.

———. *The Transformation of Philip Jettan*. London: Mills and Boon, 1923.

———. *Venetia*. London: Heinemann, 1958.

Hill, Joey W. *Holding the Cards*. Hudson, OH: Ellora's Cave, 2002.

———. *Rough Canvas*. Akron: Ellora's Cave, 2007.

Hill, Thomas D. "Androgyny and Conversion in the Middle English Lyric, 'In the Vaile of Restles Mynd.'" *ELH* 53, no. 3 (1986): 459–470.

Hirsch, Edward. *How to Read a Poem (and Fall in Love with Poetry)*. San Diego, CA: Harcourt, 1999.

"Historical Romance Authors of Sheiks and the Exotic." Romance Reader at Heart: Your Romance Novel Resource … From A to Z. http://romancereaderatheart.com/sheik/Authors.html.

Hodge, Jane Aiken. *The Private World of Georgette Heyer*. 1984. London: Arrow Books, 2006.

Holcomb, Roslyn Hardy. *Rock Star*. Columbus, MS: Genesis Press, 2006.

Holland, Isabelle. *Darcourt*. London: Collins, 1977.

Hollows, Joanne. *Feminism, Femininity, and Popular Culture*. Manchester: Manchester University Press, 2000.

Holly, Emma. *Beyond Innocence*. New York: Jove, 2001.

———. *Beyond Seduction*. New York: Jove, 2002.

———. *Ménage*. London: Black Lace, 1998.

———. *The Top of Her Game*. London: Black Lace, 1999.

———. *Velvet Glove*. London: Black Lace, 1999.

Holmes, Diana. *Romance and Readership in Twentieth-Century France; Love Stories*. Oxford: Oxford University Press, 2006.

Houel, Annik. *Le roman d'amour et sa letrice: une si longue passion, l'example Harlequin*. Paris: L'Harmattan, 1997.

"How to Write the Perfect Romance!" Harlequin Enterprises Limited. http://www.eharlequin.com/articlepage.html?articleId=1425&chapter=0.

Howard, Linda. *Diamond Bay*. New York: Silhouette, 1987.

———. *Duncan's Bride*. 1990. Reprint, Waterville, ME: Thorndike, 2004.

———. *Loving Evangeline*. New York: Silhouette, 1994.

_____. *Midnight Rainbow*. Toronto: Harlequin, 1986.

Howe, Jemima. "A Genuine and Correct Account of the Captivity, Sufferings and Deliverance of Mrs. Jemima Howe." Edited by the Rev. Bunker Gray, 1792. Reprint, *The Garland Library of Narratives of North American Indian Captivities*, Volume 19. Edited by Wilcomb Washburn. New York: Garland, 1977.

Hubbard, Rita C. "The Changing-Unchanging Heroines and Heroes of Harlequin Romances, 1950–1979." In *The Hero in Transition*, edited by Ray B. Browne and Marshall W. Fishwick, 171–179. Bowling Green, OH: Popular Press, 1983.

Hughes, Helen. *The Historical Romance*. London and New York: Routledge, 1993.

Hughes, Kalen. *Lord Sin*. New York: Zebra Books, 2007.

Hull, Edith M. *The Sheik*. 1921. http://www.gutenberg.org/dirs/etext04/sheik10.txt.

Humphreys, David. "An Essay on the Life of the Honorable Major-General Israel Putnam." *The Garland Library of Narratives of North American Indian Captivities*, Volume 19. Edited by Wilcomb Washburn. New York: Garland, 1977.

Hurley, Frances Kay. "In the Words of Girls: The Reading of Adolescent Romance Fiction." PhD diss., Harvard University, 1999.

Huyssen, Andreas. *After the Great Divide: Modernism, Mass Culture, Postmodernism*. Bloomington: Indiana University Press, 1986.

Hymes, Dell. "The Ethnography of Speaking." In *Anthropology and Human Behavior*, edited by Thomas Gladwin and William C. Sturtevant, 13–53. Washington, D.C.: The Anthropological Society of Washington, 1962.

_____. "Models of Interaction of Language and Social Life." In *Directions in Sociolinguistics: The Ethnography of Communication*, edited by John Gumperz and Dell Hymes, 35–71. New York: Holt, Rinehart & Winston, 1972.

Jagose, Annamarie. *Queer Theory: An Introduction*. New York: New York University Press, 1996.

James, Eloisa. "Biography." Eloisa James: About the Author: HarperCollins Publishers: Avon Books. HarperCollins Publishers. http://www.harpercollins.com/author/microsite/About.aspx?authorid=24747.

_____. *Desperate Duchesses*. New York: Avon, 2007.

_____. *Duchess in Love*. New York: Avon, 2002.

_____. *The Taming of the Duke*. New York: Avon, 2006.

Jameson, Fredric. "Ideology, Narrative Analysis and Popular Culture." *Theory and Society* 4, no. 4 (1977): 543–559.

_____. *The Political Unconscious: Narrative as a Socially Symbolic Act*. Ithaca: Cornell University Press, 1981.

JaneDavitt. "Pov Shifts? Bring Them On!" 28 April 2006. http://janedavitt.livejournal.com/.

Janet. "Review of Claiming the Courtesan." Dear Author. March 30, 2007. http://dearauthor.com/wordpress/2007/03/30/claiming-the-courtesan-by-anna-campbell/.

Jeffries, Sabrina. *A Dangerous Love*. New York: Avon, 2000.

Jenkins, Henry. *Fans, Bloggers, and Gamers : Exploring Participatory Culture*. New York: New York University Press, 2006.

_____. *Textual Poachers: Television Fans & Participatory Culture*. New York: Routledge, 1992.

Jensen, Margaret Ann. *Love's $weet Return: The Harlequin Story*. Toronto: Women's Educational Press, 1984.

"Joey W. Hill Interview." Author Island. http://www.authorisland.com/index.php?option=com_content&task=view&id=4340&Itemid=602.

Jones, Ann Rosalind. "Mills & Boon Meets Feminism." In *The Progress of Romance: The Politics of Popular Fiction*, edited by Jean Radford, 195–218. London: Routledge & Kegan Paul, 1986.

Jordan, Nicole. *The Heart Breaker*. New York: Avon, 1998.

Joyce, Lydia. "Behind the Scenes." Lydia Joyce. http://www.lydiajoyce.com.

Julad. "Anyone Who Had a Heart…" 10 May 2005. http://julad.livejournal.com/71396.html.

Kadaba, Lini S. "Anti-terror Programs Training Neighbors to Spy on Each Other." *Philadelphia Inquirer*, December 13, 2002: n.p.

Kael, Pauline. *For Keeps*. New York: Dutton, 1994.

Kaler, Anne K. "Introduction: Conventions of the Romance Genre." In *Romantic Conventions*, edited by Anne K. Kaler and Rosemary E. Johnson-Kurek, 1–9. Bowling Green, OH: Bowling Green State University Popular Press, 1999.

Kaler, Anne K. and Rosemary E. Johnson-Kurek, eds. *Romantic Conventions.* Bowling Green, OH: Bowling Green State University Popular Press, 1999.

Kamble, Jayashree. "Female Enfranchisement and the Popular Romance: Employing an Indian Perspective." In *Empowerment Versus Oppression: Twenty First Century Views of Popular Romance Novels,* edited by Sally Goade, 148–173. Newcastle: Cambridge Scholars, 2007.

Kane, Samantha. *At Love's Command.* Akron: Ellora's Cave, 2007.

Katriel, Tamar. "Griping as a Verbal Ritual in Some Israeli Discourse." In *Cultural Communication and Intercultural Contact,* edited by Donal Carbaugh, 99–113. Hillsdale, NJ: Lawrence Earlbaum, 1990.

Kearns, Cleo McNelly. "Dubious Pleasures: Dorothy Dunnett and the Historical Novel." *Critical Quarterly* 32, no. 1 (1990): 36–48.

Kelley, Joyce. "Increasingly 'Imaginative Geographies': Excursions into Otherness, Fantasy, and Modernism in Early Twentieth-Century Women's Travel Writing," *JNT: Journal of Narrative Theory,* 35, no. 3 (Fall 2005): 357–372.

Kennard, Jean E. *Victims of Convention.* Hamden, CT: Archon, 1978.

Kenyon, Sherrilyn. *Kiss of the Night.* New York: St. Martin's Press, 2004.

Khoury, Philip S. "Lessons from the Eastern Shore." *MESA Bulletin* 33, no. 1 (Summer 1999): 2–9.

Kinard, Amanda Marette. "Forbidden Pleasures: The Romance and Its Readers." PhD diss., Vanderbilt University, 1999.

King, Kathleen J. "Do You Use the B-Word?" DivineCaroline.com. http://www.divinecaroline.com/article/22362/27498.

King, Susan. *Taming the Heiress.* New York: Signet, 2003.

Kinsale, Laura. "The Androgynous Reader: Point of View in the Romance." In *Dangerous Men & Adventurous Women: Romance Writers on the Appeal of the Romance,* edited by Jayne Ann Krentz, 37–54. 1992. Reprint, New York: HarperPaperbacks, 1996.

_____. *Flowers from the Storm.* New York: Avon, 1992.

Kleypas, Lisa. *Sugar Daddy.* London: Piatkus, 2007.

_____. *Worth Any Price.* New York: Avon, 2003.

Kolodny, Annette. *The Land Before Her: Fantasy and Experience of the American Frontiers, 1630–1860.* Chapel Hill: University of North Carolina Press, 1984.

Komito, Lee. "The Net as a Foraging Society: Flexible Communities." *Information Society* 14, no. 2 (1998): 97–106.

Kramer, Daniela, and Michael Moore. "Gender Roles, Romantic Fiction and Family Therapy." *Psycoloquy* 12, no. 24 (2001).

Krentz, Jayne Ann, ed. *Dangerous Men and Adventurous Women: Romance Writers on the Appeal of the Romance.* 1992. Reprint, New York: HarperPaperbacks, 1996.

Kuhn, Annette. "Women's Genres: Melodrama, Soap Opera, and Theory." In *Feminist Television Criticism: A Reader,* edited by Charlotte Brunsdon, Julie D'Acci and Lynn Spigel, 145–154. 1984. Reprint, Oxford: Clarendon Press, 1997.

Kustritz, Anne. "Slashing the Romance Narrative." *The Journal of American Culture* 26, no. 3 (2003): 14.

Lamb, Patricia Frazier, and Diane L. Veith. "Romantic Myth, Transcendence, and Star Trek Zines." In *Erotic Universe: Sexuality and Fantastic Literature,* edited by Donald Palumbo, 235–55. New York: Greenwood Press, 1986.

Lazarsfeld, Paul F., Bernard Berelson, and Hazel Gaudet. "The People's Choice: How the Voter Makes Up His Mind in a Presidential Campaign." In *The Audience Studies Reader,* edited by Will Brooker and Deborah Jermyn, 13–18. New York: Routledge, 2003. Originally published in Paul F. Lazarsfeld, Bernard Berelson and Hazel Gaudet, *The People's Choice: How the Voter Makes Up His Mind in a Presidential Campaign* (New York: Columbia University Press, 1944).

Leavis, Q.D. *Fiction and the Reading Public.* 1932. Reprint, London: Chatto and Windus, 1939.

Lee, Amy. "Forming a Local Identity: Romance Novels in Hong Kong." In *Empowerment Versus Oppression: Twenty First Century Views of Popular Romance Novels,* edited by Sally Goade, 174–197. Newcastle: Cambridge Scholars, 2007.

Lee, Linda J. "Guilty Pleasures: Reading Romance Novels as Reworked Fairy Tales." *Marvels & Tales: Journal of Fairy-Tale Studies* 22, no. 1 (2008): 52–66.

Lensky, Lois. *Indian Captive: The Story of Mary Jemison.* 1942. Reprint, New York: Harper Collins, 1995.

Levine, Lawrence W. *Highbrow/Lowbrow: The Emergence of Cultural Hierarchy in America.* Cambridge, MA: Harvard University Press, 1988.

Lewis, Reina. *Gendering Orientalism: Race, Femininity, and Representation.* New York: Routledge, 1996.

Light, Alison. "'Returning to Manderley': Romance Fiction, Female Sexuality, and Class." *Feminist Review* 16, no. 2 (1984): 7–25.

_____. "'Young Bess': Historical Novels and Growing Up." *Feminist Review* 33 (Autumn 1989): 57–71.

Little, Denise. "The Mind of An Agent." In *The Official Nora Roberts Companion,* edited by Denise Little and Laura Hayden, 52–60. New York: Berkley, 2003.

_____, and Laura Hayden, eds. *The Official Nora Roberts Companion.* New York: Berkley, 2003.

Long, Elizabeth. *Book Clubs: Women and the Uses of Reading in Everyday Life.* Chicago: University of Chicago Press, 2003.

Lorber, Judith. "Heroes, Warriors, and Burqas: A Feminist Sociologist's Reflections on September 11." *Sociological Forum* 17, no. 3 (2002): 377–396.

Lukács, Georg. *The Theory of the Novel: A Historico-Philosophical Essay on the Forms of Great Epic Literature.* Cambridge: MIT Press, 1971.

Luttwak, Edward. "More harm than good." *The Globe and Mail* (Toronto), January 16, 2004: A17.

Lutz, Deborah. *The Dangerous Lover: Gothic Villains, Byronism, and the Nineteenth-Century Seduction Narrative.* Columbus: Ohio State University Press, 2006.

Macgregor, Kinley. *Taming the Scotsman.* New York: Avon, 2003.

Madigan, Molly. *The Taming of Lord Astor.* New York: Five Star, 2007.

Malone, Andrew. "Dark Heart of this Cult." *Daily Mail* (London), August 14, 2007: 11.

Mann, Peter H. *From Author to Reader: A Social Study of Books.* London: Routledge, 1982.

_____. *The Romance Novel: A Survey of Reading Habits.* London: Mills & Boon, 1969.

_____. "The Romantic Novel and Its Readers." *Journal of Popular Culture* 15, no. 1 (1981): 9–18.

Manning, Jackie. *Taming of the Duke.* New York: Harlequin, 2001.

Marcuse, Herbert. *The Aesthetic Dimension: Toward a Critique of Marxist Aesthetics.* Boston: Beacon Press, 1979.

Mather, Cotton. *Decennium Luctosum. The Garland Library of North American Indian Captivities,* Volume 3. Edited by Wilcomb Washburn. New York: Garland, 1976.

Mather, Increase. *An Earnest Exhortation to the Inhabitants of New-England (1676).* Edited with an Introduction by Reiner Smolinski. Lincoln: University of Nebraska Electronic Texts in American Studies. http://digitalcommons.unl.edu/etas/31/.

Matsuda, Paul Kei, and Christine M. Tardy. "Voice in academic writing: The rhetorical construction of author identity in blind manuscript review." *English for Specific Purposes* 26, no. 2 (2007): 235–49.

McAleer, Joseph. *Passion's Fortune: The Story of Mills & Boon.* Oxford: Oxford University Press, 1999.

McClone, Melissa. *If the Ring Fits....* 2000. Reprint, Richmond, Surrey: Harlequin Mills & Boon, 2001.

McGurl, Mark. *The Novel Art: Elevations of American Fiction after Henry James.* Princeton, NJ: Princeton University Press, 2001.

McLaren, Angus. *Impotence: A Cultural History.* Chicago: University of Chicago Press, 2007.

Merish, Lori. *Sentimental Materialism: Gender, Commodity Culture, and Nineteenth Century American Literature.* Durham: Duke University Press, 2000.

Michaels, Kasey. *The Return of the Prodigal.* New York: Harlequin, 2007.

Micheletti, Ellen. "Interview with J.R. Ward." *All About Romance.* March 1, 2007. http://www.likes books.com/jrward2007.html.

Milton, John. *The Complete Poetry and Essential Prose of John Milton,* edited by William Kerrigan and John Peter Rumrich. New York: Modern Library, 2007.

Mittermeyer, Helen. "Romance — A Woman's Intricate Journey." In *Writing Romances,* edited by Rita Gallagher and Rita Clay Estrada, 54–57. Cincinnati: Writer's Digest Books, 1997.

Modleski, Tania. "Introduction to the Second Edition." *Loving with a Vengeance: Mass-Produced Fantasies for Women.* New York: Routledge, 2008.

_____. *Loving with a Vengeance: Mass-Produced Fantasies for Women.* 1982. Reprint, New York: Routledge, 1988.

_____. "My Life as a Romance Reader." *Paradoxa: Studies in World Literary Genres* 3, nos. 1–2 (1997): 15–28.

_____. "My Life as a Romance Writer." *Paradoxa: Studies in World Literary Genres* 4, no. 9 (1998): 134–144.

_____. *Old Wives' Tales and Other Women's Stories.* New York: NYU Press, 1998.

Moffitt, Mary Anne. "Leisure Fiction and the Audience: Meaning and Communication Strategies." *Women's Studies in Communication* 16, no. 2 (1993): 27–61.

Moore, Margaret. *Kiss Me Quick*. New York: Avon, 2003.

Moore, Meredith. "Meet Author Laura Kinsale." The Romance Reader. http://www.theromancereader. com/kinsale.html.

Muscio, Inga. *Cunt*. Seattle: Seal Press, Avalon Publishing Group, Inc., 2002.

Mussell, Kay. *Fantasy and Reconciliation: Contemporary Formulas of Women's Romance Fiction*. Westport, CT: Greenwood Press, 1984.

_____. "*Paradoxa* Interview with Janet Daily." *Paradoxa: Studies in World Literary Genres* 3, nos. 1–2 (1997): 214–218.

_____. "*Paradoxa* Interview with Nora Roberts." *Paradoxa: Studies in World Literary Genres* 3, nos. 1–2 (1997): 155–163.

_____. "Where's Love Gone? Transformations in Romance Fiction and Scholarship." *Paradoxa* 3, nos. 1–2 (1997): 3–14.

Neal, Lynn S. *Romancing God: Evangelical Women and Inspirational Fiction*. Chapel Hill: University of North Carolina Press, 2006.

Nixon, Cheryl L. *Novel Definitions: An Anthology of Commentary on the Novel, 1688–1815*. Peterborough, Ontario: Broadview Press, 2008.

"Nora Roberts." Penguin.com. http://us.penguingroup.com/static/packages/us/noraroberts/books/books. htm.

Norton, Mary Beth. *Liberty's Daughters: The Revolutionary Experience of American Women, 1750–1800*. Boston: Little, Brown and Company, 1980.

Novak, Mary. "The Multi-Pervert Gay Villain Cliché." At the Back Fence Issue 106. All About Romance. 15 November 2000. http://www.likesbooks.com/106.html.

O'Dair, Sharon. *Class, Critics, and Shakespeare: Bottom Lines on the Culture Wars*. Ann Arbor: University of Michigan Press, 2000.

Olsen, Kristen. *Chronology of Women's History*. Westport, CT: Greenwood Press, 1994.

Opas, Lisa Lena, and Fiona Tweedie. "The Magic Carpet Ride: Reader Involvement in Romantic Fiction." *Literary and Linguistic Computing* 14, no. 1 (1999): 89–101.

Osborne, Laurie E. "Harlequin Presents: That '70s Shakespeare and Beyond." In *Shakespeare After Mass Media*, edited by Richard Burt, 127–149. New York: Palgrave, 2002.

_____. "Romancing the Bard." In *Shakespeare and Appropriation*, edited by Christy Desmet and Robert Sawyer. New York: Routledge, 1999.

_____. "Sweet, Savage, Shakespeare." In *Shakespeare Without Class: Misappropriations of Cultural Capital*, edited by Donald Hedrick and Bryan Reynolds. New York: Palgrave, 2000.

Osborne, Maggie. *A Stranger's Wife*. New York: Warner, 1999.

Owen, Mairead. "Re-inventing Romance: Reading Popular Romantic Fiction." *Women's Studies International Forum* 20, no. 4 (1997): 537–46.

Paizis, George. "Category Romance in the Era of Globalization: The Story of Harlequin." In *The Global Literary Field*, edited by Anna Guttman, Michel Hockx, and George Paizis, 126–151. Newcastle upon Tyne: Cambridge Scholars, 2006.

_____. "Category Romances: Translation, Realism, and Myth." *Translator* 4, no. 1 (1988): 1–24.

Palmer, Diana. "Let Me Tell You About My Readers." In *Dangerous Men & Adventurous Women: Romance Writers on the Appeal of the Romance*, edited by Jayne Ann Krentz, 155–58. Philadelphia: University of Pennsylvania Press, 1992.

Parameswaran Radhika. "Public Images, Private Pleasures: Romance Reading at the Intersection of Gender, Class, and National Identities in Urban India." PhD diss., University of Iowa, 1998.

_____. "Reading Fictions of Romance: Gender, Sexuality, and Nationalism in Postcolonial India." *Journal of Communication* 52, no. 4 (2002): 832–851.

_____. "Western Romance Fiction as English-Language Media in Postcolonial India." *Journal of Communication* 49, no. 3 (1999): 84–105.

Parrish, Rick. "The Changing Nature of Community." *Strategies* 15, no. 2 (2002): 259–284.

Parv, Valerie. *The Art of Romance Writing*. St. Leonards, Australia: Allen & Unwin, 1997.

Peacock, Molly. *How to Read a Poem ... and Start a Poetry Circle*. New York: Riverhead Books, 1999.

Pearce, Lynne, and Jackie Stacey, eds. *Romance Revisited*. New York: New York University Press, 1995.

Peirce, Leslie P. *The Imperial Harem: Women and Sovereignty in the Ottoman Empire*. New York: Oxford University Press, 1993.

Perrine, Laurence. *Sound and Sense*. New York: Harcourt Brace Jovanovich College Publishers, 1992.

Phillips, Susan Elizabeth. *Fancy Pants*. London: Futura, 1989.

_____. "The Romance and the Empowerment of Women." In *Dangerous Men & Adventurous Women: Romance Writers on the Appeal of the Romance*, edited by Jayne Ann Krentz, 53–59. Philadelphia: University of Pennsylvania Press, 1992.

Pickens, Andrea. *The Spy Wore Silk.* New York: Warner Forever, 2007.

pinkolaeses. Posting to "Word Etymology." SurLaLune Fairy Tales Discussion Board. September 28, 2008. http://surlalunefairytales.com/boardarchives/2002/oct2002/wordetymology.html.

"The Politics of Fear." Editorial. *The New York Times.* July 18, 2007.

"Post-Traumatic Stress Disorder." Wikipedia. http://en.wikipedia.org/wiki/PTSD.

"President Commemorates 60th Anniversary of V-J Day." The White House. http://www.whitehouse.gov/news/releases/2005/08/200508301.html.

Puri, Jyoti. "Reading Romance Novels in Postcolonial India." *Gender & Society* 11, no. 4 (1997): 434–452.

"Queer Studies." *Smith College.* http://www.smith.edu/swg/queerstudies.html.

Quick, Amanda. *Deception.* New York: Bantam, 1993.

_____. *Seduction.* New York: Bantam, 1990.

_____. *With This Ring.* 1998. Reprint, New York: Bantam, 1999.

Quimby, Karin. "*Will & Grace*: Negotiating (Gay) Marriage on Prime-Time Television." *The Journal of Popular Culture* 38, no. 4 (2005): 713–31.

Quinn, Julia. *The Secret Diaries of Miss Miranda Cheever.* New York: Avon, 2007.

Radway, Janice. "Introduction: *Writing* Reading the Romance." In *Reading the Romance: Women, Patriarchy, and Popular Literature.* 1984. Reprint with a new Introduction, Chapel Hill: University of North Carolina Press, 1991.

_____. *Reading the Romance: Women, Patriarchy, and Popular Literature.* 1984. Reprint with a new Introduction, Chapel Hill: University of North Carolina Press, 1991.

Rahill, Frank. *The World of Melodrama.* University Park: Pennsylvania State University Press, 1967.

Ranney, Karen. *Heaven Forbids.* New York: Zebra, 1998.

Raub, Patricia. "Issues of Passion and Power in E.M. Hull's *The Sheik*." *Women's Studies*, 21 (1992): 119–128.

"The Real Deal." Lucy Monroe.com. http://www.lucymonroe.com/AbouttheBooksTRD.htm.

"Reclaiming." *Wikipedia.* http://en.wikipedia.org/wiki/Reclaiming.

Reed, Ellen Cannon. *The Heart of Wicca: Wise Words from a Crone on the Path.* York Beach, ME: Samuel Weiser, 2000.

Regis, Pamela. *A Natural History of the Romance Novel.* Philadelphia: University of Pennsylvania Press, 2003.

Reid, Michelle. *The Sheikh's Chosen Wife.* Toronto: Harlequin, 2002.

Reviews of *The Kadin.* http://www.amazon.com/Kadin-Bertrice-Small/dp/0727817434/ref=sr_1_1?ie=UTF8&s=books&qid=1213856041&sr=1-1.

Richardson, Samuel. *Pamela.* Edited by Sheridan W. Baker, Jr. Los Angeles: William Andrews Clark Memorial Library, University of California, 1954. http://www.gutenberg.org/files/24860/24860-8.txt.

Ricker-Wilson, Carol. "Busting Textual Bodices: Gender, Reading, and the Popular Romance." *English Journal* 88, no. 3 (1999): 57–64.

Riley, A.M. *The Elegant Corpse.* San Francisco: Loose Id, 2008.

Roberts, Nora. *Black Rose.* New York: Jove, 2005.

_____. *Blue Dahlia.* New York: Jove, 2004.

_____. *Born in Fire.* New York: Jove, 1994.

_____. *Born in Ice.* New York: Jove, 1995.

_____. *Born in Shame.* New York: Jove, 1996.

_____. *The Calhoun Women.* New York: Harlequin, 1996.

_____. *Captive Star.* New York: Silhouette, 1997.

_____. *Chesapeake Blue.* New York: Jove, 2004.

_____. *Dance of the Gods.* New York: Jove, 2006.

_____. *Dance Upon the Air.* New York: Jove, 2001.

_____. *Daring to Dream.* New York: Jove, 1996.

_____. *The Donovan Legacy.* New York: Silhouette, 1999.

_____. *Face the Fire.* New York: Jove, 2002.

_____. *Finding the Dream.* New York: Jove, 1997.

_____. *Heart of the Sea*. New York: Jove, 2000.

_____. *Heaven and Earth*. New York: Jove, 2001.

_____. *Hidden Star*. New York: Silhouette, 1997.

_____. *Holding the Dream*. New York: Jove, 1997.

_____. *Inner Harbor*. New York: Jove, 1999.

_____. *Jewels of the Sun*. New York: Jove, 1999.

_____. *Key of Knowledge*. New York: Jove, 2003.

_____. *Key of Light*. New York: Jove, 2003.

_____. *Key of Valor*. New York: Jove, 2004.

_____. *Megan's Mate*. New York: Silhouette, 1996.

_____. *Morrigan's Cross*. New York: Jove, 2006.

_____. *Red Lily*. New York: Jove, 2005.

_____. *Rising Tides*. New York: Jove, 1998.

_____. *Sea Swept*. New York: Jove, 1998.

_____. *Secret Star*. New York: Silhouette, 1998.

_____. *Tears of the Moon*. New York: Jove, 2000.

_____. *Valley of Silence*. New York: Jove, 2006.

Roberts, Thomas J. *An Aesthetics of Junk Fiction*. Athens: University of Georgia Press, 1990.

Rogers, Edith. "Clothing as a Multifarious Ballad Symbol." *Western Folklore* 34, no. 4 (1975): 261–297.

"Romance Writers of America's 2005 Market Research Study on Romance Readers." Saralee Etter. http://www.saraleeetter.com/files/05MarketResearch_1_.pdf.

Romancing the Desert — Sheikh Books. http://romancing-the-desert —-sheikh-books.blogspot.com.

Rose, Mary Beth. *Gender and Heroism in Early Modern Literature*. Chicago: University of Chicago Press, 2001.

Rowlandson, Mary. *Narrative of the Captivity and Restoration of Mrs. Mary Rowlandson (1682)*. http://dig ital.library.upenn.edu/webbin/gutbook/lookup?num=851.

Rubin, Gayle S. "Thinking Sex: Notes for a Radical Theory of the Politics of Sexuality." In *The Lesbian and Gay Studies Reader*, edited by Henry Abelove, Michèle Aina Barale, and David M. Halperin, 3–44. New York: Routledge, 1992.

Rubin, Joan Shelley. *Songs of Ourselves: The Uses of Poetry in America*. Cambridge, MA: Belknap Press of Harvard University Press, 2007.

Rush Hour, directed by Brett Ratner. 1999; Burbank, CA: New Line Cinema, 2009. DVD.

Russ, Joanna. *Mommas, Trembling Sisters, Puritans & Perverts*. New York: The Crossing Press, 1985.

Said, Edward W. *Orientalism*. New York: Pantheon, 1978.

Salmon, Catherine, and Donald Symons. "Slash Fiction and Human Mating Psychology." *Journal of Sex Research* 41, no. 1 (2004): 7.

_____, and _____. *Warrior Lovers : Erotic Fiction, Evolution and Female Sexuality*. New Haven: Yale University Press, 2003.

Schneiders, Greg. "PR shares in blame for climate of fear that is gripping America." *PR Week*, August 25, 2008.

Scott, Amanda. *Lord of the Isles*. New York: Warner, 2005.

Seaver, James Everett. *A Narrative of the Life of Mary Jemison*. 1824. Reprint, New York: Garland, 1977.

Sedgwick, Eve Kosofsky. *Between Men: English Literature and Male Homosocial Desire*. New York: Columbia University Press, 1985.

Seidel, Kathleen Gilles. "Judge Me By the Joy I Bring." In *Dangerous Men and Adventurous Women: Romance Writers on the Appeal of the Romance*, edited by Jayne Ann Krentz, 199–226. 1992. Reprint, New York: HarperPaperbacks, 1996.

Shabby Sheikh: Romance Novels & Oriental Others. http://shabbysheikh.blogspot.com.

Shakespeare, William. *The Winter's Tale*. In *The Riverside Shakespeare*, edited by G. Blakemore Evans. Boston: Houghton Mifflin, 1997.

Shapcott, Tessa. "Harlequin Presents Writing Competition: Official Rules at I (Heart) Presents." http://www.iheartpresents.com/?p=146.

Sheikhs and Desert Love. http://sheikhs-and-desert-love.com.

Shufelt, Tim. "Police Finally Infiltrate Hells Angels." *National Post* (Canada), March 22, 2008: A15.

Shumway, David R. *Modern Love: Romance, Intimacy, and the Marriage Crisis*. New York: New York University Press, 2003.

Shusterman, Richard. "Don't Believe the Hype: Animadversions of the Critique of Popular Art." *Poetics Today* 14, no. 1 (1993): 101–122.

Slotkin, Richard. *Regeneration Through Violence: The Mythology of the American Frontier, 1600–1860.* Middletown, CT: Wesleyan University Press, 1973.

_____. *So Dreadfull a Judgment: Puritan Responses to King Philip's War 1676–1677.* Edited by Richard Slotkin and James K. Folsom. Middletown, CT: Wesleyan University Press, 1978.

Small, Bertrice. *The Kadin.* New York: Avon, 1978.

Small, Helen. *Love's Madness: Medicine, the Novel and Female Insanity.* Oxford: Clarendon, 1996.

Smith-Rosenberg, Carroll. "The Female World of Love and Ritual: Relations between Women in Nineteenth-Century America." *Signs* 1 (Autumn, 1975): 1–29.

Smolinski, Reiner. Introduction to *An Earnest Exhortation to the Inhabitants of New England (1676)* by Increase Mather. Edited by Reiner Smolinski. Lincoln: University of Nebraska Electronic Texts in American Studies. http://digitalcommons.unl.edu/etas/31/.

Snitow, Ann. "Mass Market Romance: Pornography for Women Is Different." *Radical History Review* 20 (Spring/Summer 1979): 141–61. Republished in *Women and Romance: A Reader*, edited by Susan Ostrov Weisser, 307–22. New York: New York University Press, 2001.

Sonnet, Esther. "'Erotic Fiction by Women for Women': The Pleasures of Post-Feminist Heterosexuality." *Sexualities* 2, no. 2 (1999): 167–187.

Spencer, LaVyrle. *Twice Loved.* New York: Jove, 1984.

Speranza. "Last Will and Testament." http://www.trickster.org/speranza/cesper/Testament.html.

Spongberg, Mary. *Writing Women's History Since the Renaissance.* Houndsmill, Basingstoke: Palgrave Macmillan 2002.

Stoller, Debbie. "Sex and the Thinking Girl." In *The BUST Guide to the New Girl Order*, edited by Marcelle Karp and Debbie Stoller, 75–84. London: Penguin, 1999.

Stone, Susan C. "An Interview with Tommy Dreiling." In *The Official Nora Roberts Companion*, edited by Denise Little and Laura Hayden, 359–365. New York: Berkley, 2003.

Storey, John. *An Introduction to Cultural Theory and Popular Culture.* 2d ed. Athens: University of Georgia Press, 1998.

Sturma, Michael. "Aliens and Indians: A Comparison of Abduction and Captivity Narratives." *Journal of Popular Culture* 36, no. 2 (2002): 318–334.

Sullivan, Andrew. "Dialogues: Gay Marriage." *Slate Magazine.* 4 April 1997. http://www.slate.com/id/3642.

Talbot, Mary M. "'An explosion deep inside her': Women's Desire and Popular Romance Fiction." In *Language and Desire: Encoding Sex, Romance and Intimacy*, edited by Keith Harvey and Celia Shalom, 106–22. London: Routledge, 1997.

"Talking to the Author Katherine Cross." Seren's Scribblings. 28 July 2007. http://serensscribblings.blogspot.com/2007/07/talking-to-author-katherine-cross.html.

Tan, Candy. "Blog Drama Drinking Game." Smart Bitches, Trashy Books. May 18, 2007. http://www.smartbitchestrashybooks.com/index.php/weblog/comments/the_blog_drama_drinking_game_special_sb_edition/.

_____. "The Completely Despicable Gay Über-Villain." At the Back Fence Issue 106. All About Romance. 15 November 2000. http://www.likesbooks.com/106.html.

_____. "A Cover So Bad, It's, Well, Bad." Smart Bitches, Trashy Books. February 5, 2005. http://www.smartbitchestrashybooks.com/index.php/weblog/comments/a_cover_so_bad_its_well_bad/.

_____. "Love Hurts." Smart Bitches, Trashy Books. March 13, 2005. http://www.smartbitchestrashybooks.com/index.php/weblog/comments/love_hurts/.

_____. "On the Presence of Bloggers and Costumes at the RWA Nationals." Smart Bitches, Trashy Books. July 17, 2007. http://www.smartbitchestrashybooks.com/index.php/weblog/comments/on_the_presence_of_bloggers_and_costumes_at_the_rwa_nationals/.

_____. "Quitcher Bitchin!" Smart Bitches, Trashy Books. July 24, 2005. http://www.smartbitchestrashybooks.com/index.php/weblog/quitcher_bitchin/.

_____. "*The Real Deal.*" Smart Bitches, Trashy Books. February 7, 2005. http://www.smartbitchestrashybooks.com/index.php/weblog/comments/monroe_therealdeal/.

_____. "This Week's Covers Gone Wild: Two Snarks for the Price of One." Smart Bitches, Trashy Books. February 20, 2005. http://www.smartbitchestrashybooks.com/index.php/weblog/comments/this_weeks_covers_gone_wild_two_snarks_for_the_price_of_one.

Tegan, Mary Beth. "Becoming Both Poet and Poem: Feminists Repossess the Romance." In *Empowerment Vs. Oppression: Twenty-First Century Views of Popular Romance Novels*, edited by Sally Goade, 244–278. Newcastle: Cambridge Scholars, 2007.

Teo, Hsu-Ming. "Orientalism and Mass Market Romance Novels in the Twentieth Century." In *Edward Said: The Legacy of a Public Intellectual*, edited by Ned Curthoys and Debjani Ganguly, 241–262. Melbourne: Melbourne University Press, 2007.

_____. "The Romance of White Nations: Imperialism, Popular Culture and National Histories." In *After the Imperial Turn: Thinking with and through the Nation*, edited by Antoinette Burton, 279–292. Durham: Duke University Press, 2003.

_____. "Romancing the Raj: Interracial Relations in Anglo-Indian Romance Novels," *History of Intellectual Culture* 4, no. 1 (2004). http://www.ucalgary.ca/hic/issues/vol4/3.

"Third Wave Feminism: Reclaiming Derogatory Terms." *Wikipedia*. http://en.wikipedia.org/wiki/Third_wave_feminism#Reclaiming_derogatory_terms.

Thomas, Calvin. "Straight with a Twist: Queer Theory and the Subject of Heterosexuality." In *Straight with a Twist: Queer Theory and the Subject of Heterosexuality*, edited by Calvin Thomas, Joseph O. Almone, and Catherine A.F. MacGillvray, 11–43. Urbana: University of Illinois Press, 2000.

Thomas, Glen. "Romance: The Perfect Creative Industry? A Case Study of Harlequin-Mills & Boon Australia." In *Empowerment Versus Oppression: Twenty First Century Views of Popular Romance Novels*, edited by Sally Goade, 20–29. Newcastle: Cambridge Scholars, 2007.

Thurston, Carol. *The Romance Revolution: Erotic Novels for Women and the Quest for a New Sexual Identity*. Urbana: University of Illinois Press, 1987.

Timpane, Jack. *It Could Be Verse: Anybody's Guide to Poetry*. Albany, CA: BOAZ, 1995.

Todorov, Tzvetan. *The Conquest of America*, translated by Richard Howard. New York: Harper Torchbooks, 1987.

_____. *Genres in Discourse*. 1976. Reprint, Cambridge: Cambridge University Press, 1990.

Trilling, Lionel. "The Fate of Pleasure." In *The Moral Obligation to Be Intelligent: Selected Essays by Lionel Trilling*, edited and with an Introduction by Leon Wieseltier, 427–449. New York: Farrar, Straus and Giroux, 2000.

Tual, Jacques. "Sexual Equality and Conjugal Harmony: The Way to Celestial Bliss. A View of Early Quaker Matrimony." *The Journal of the Friends' Historical Society* 55, no. 6 (1988): 161–174.

Uddin-Khan, Evelyn Angelina. "Gender, Ethnicity and the Romance Novel." PhD diss., Columbia University, 1995.

Vaughan, Elizabeth. *Warprize*. New York: Tor, 2005.

Vendler, Helen. *Poems, Poets, Poetry: An Introduction and Anthology*. 3d ed. New York: Bedford/St. Martin's, 2009.

Vinyard, Rebecca. *The Romance Writer's Handbook*. Waukesha, Canada: The Writer Books, 2004.

Von Drehle, David. "Uncertain is Sea Where All Swim: Vague, Looming Threat Calls Citizens to Brace for the Worst — Whatever That Is." *Washington Post*, February 16, 2003: A15.

Wainger, Leslie. *Writing a Romance Novel for Dummies*. Indianapolis: Wiley, 2004.

Walker, Kate. *Kate Walker's 12-Point Guide to Writing Romance*. Somerset: Studymates Limited, 2004.

Wallace, Anthony F.C. *The Death and Rebirth of the Seneca*. New York: Vintage Books, 1969.

Wallace, Diana. *The Woman's Historical Novel: British Women Writers, 1900–2000*. Houndsmill, Basingstoke: Palgrave Macmillan, 2005.

Ward, J.R. *The Black Dagger Brotherhood: An Insider's Guide*. New York: New American Library, 2008.

_____. *Dark Lover*. New York: New American Library, 2005.

_____. *Lover Awakened*. New York: New American Library, 2006.

_____. *Lover Enshrined*. New York: New American Library, 2008.

_____. *Lover Revealed*. New York: New American Library, 2007.

_____. *Lover Unbound*. New York: New American Library, 2007.

Wardrop, Stephanie. "The Heroine Is Being Beaten: Freud, Sadomasochism, and Reading the Romance." *Style* 29 (1995): 459–73.

Waters, Melanie. "Sexing It Up? Women, Pornography and Third Wave Feminism." In *Third Wave Feminism: A Critical Exploration Expanded Second Edition*, edited by Stacy Gillis, Gillian Howie and Rebecca Munford, 250–65. Basingstoke, Hampshire: Palgrave Macmillan, 2007.

Webster, Sarah Goodwin. "Romance and Change: Teaching the Romance to Undergraduates." *Paradoxa: Studies in World Literary Genres* 3, nos. 1–2 (1997): 233–241.

Weisser, Susan Ostrov. "The Wonderful-Terrible Bitch Figure in Harlequin Novels." In *Feminist Night-*

mares: Women at Odds: Feminism and the Problem of Sisterhood, edited by Susan Ostrov Weisser and Jennifer Fleischner, 269–282. New York: New York University Press, 1994.

Wells, Christine. *Scandal's Daughter*. New York: Berkley Sensation, 2007.

Wendell, Sarah. "Can This Cover Be Saved?" Smart Bitches, Trashy Books. January 22, 2007. http://www.smartbitchestrashybooks.com/index.php/weblog/comments/can_this_cover_be_saved/#22643.

_____. "*The Jewel of Medina* Is Now on Sale—No, Wait. Nevermind," Smart Bitches Trashy Books, http://www.smartbitchestrashybooks.com/index.php/weblog/comments/the_jewel_of_medina_is_on_sale_no_wait_nevermind/.

_____. "More Good News—More Cover Snark!" Smart Bitches, Trashy Books. March 9, 2007. http://www.smartbitchestrashybooks.com/index.php/weblog/comments/more_good_news_more_cover_snark/.

_____. "Sarah Spreads the Luuurve™." Smart Bitches, Trashy Books. August 1, 2005. http://www.smartbitchestrashybooks.com/index.php/weblog/comments/sarah_spreads_the_luuurve/.

_____. "Smart Bitch Secret Baby: the Cover Snark." Smart Bitches, Trashy Books. March 9, 2007. http://www.smartbitchestrashybooks.com/index.php/weblog/comments/smart_bitch_secret_baby_the_cover_snark/.

_____, and Candy Tan. *Beyond Heaving Bosoms: The Smart Bitches' Guide to Romance Novels*. New York: Fireside, 2009.

"We're Not Gay; We Just Love Each Other." fanlore. http://fanlore.org/wiki/WNGWJLEO.

Westman, Karin E. "A Story of Her Weaving: The Self-Authoring Heroines of Georgette Heyer's Regency Romance." In *Doubled Plots: Romance and History*, edited by Susan Strehle and Mary Paniccia Carden, 165–184. Jackson: University Press of Mississippi, 2003.

Wethington, Elaine. "Are Academic Opinions About Romance Novels All Negative?" All About Romance. www.likesbooks.com/elaine.html.

"What Is Romantic Fiction?" Romantic Novelists' Association. http://www.romanticnovelistsassociation.org/index.php/about/what_is_romantic_fiction.

"What Is Romantica©?" Ellora's Cave. http://www.jasminejade.com/t-romantica.aspx.

"Who Are We." Smart Bitches, Trashy Books. http://www.smartbitchestrashybooks.com.

Wiggins, Martin. *Shakespeare and the Drama of his Time*. Oxford: Oxford University Press, 2000.

Wiggs, Susan. *The Horsemaster's Daughter*. Don Mills, Ontario: Mira, 2008.

_____. *Lord of the Night*. New York: HarperPaperbacks, 1993.

Williams, Bonnie. "Readers of Romance Have Better Sex Lives." Articlecity, www.articlecity.com/articles/relationships/article_717.shtml.

Williams, Clover, and Jean R. Freedman. "Shakespeare's Step-Sisters: Romance Novels and the Community of Women." In *Folklore, Literature and Cultural Theory: Collected Essays*, edited by Cathy Lynn Preston, 135–168. London: Garland, 1995.

Williams, Raymond. "Base and Superstructure in Marxist Cultural Theory." In *Rethinking Popular Culture: Contemporary Perspectives in Cultural Studies*, edited by Chandra Mukerji and Michael Schudson, 407–23. Berkeley: University of California Press, 1991.

Williamson, Penelope. *Heart of the West*. 1995. Reprint, London: Signet, 1997.

_____. *The Passions of Emma*. New York: Warner, 1997.

Winspear, Violet. *Blue Jasmine*. Toronto: Harlequin, 1969.

Wirtén, Eva Hemmungs. "Global Infatuation: Explorations in Transnational Publishing and Texts: The case of Harlequin Enterprises and Sweden." PhD diss., Uppsala University, 1998.

_____. "Harlequin Romances in Swedish: A Case Study in Globalized Publishing." *Logos* 11, no. 4 (2000): 203–7.

Woodiwiss, Kathleen. *The Flame and the Flower*. New York: Avon, 1972.

Wu, Huei-Hsia. "Gender, Romance Novels and Plastic Sexuality in the United States: A Focus on Female College Students." *Journal of International Women's Studies* 8, no. 1 (2006): 125–34.

Yeazell, Ruth Bernard. *Harems of the Mind: Passages of Western Art and Literature*. New Haven: Yale University Press, 2000.

Young, Beth Rapp. "'But are they any good?' Women Readers, Formula Fiction, and the Sacralization of the Literary Canon." PhD diss., University of Southern California, 1995.

Young, Robert J.C. *Colonial Desire: Hybridity in Theory, Culture, and Race*. New York: Routledge, 1995.

Zakaria, Fareed. "A Rhetoric of Danger." *The Washington Post*, June 4, 2007: A15.

About the Contributors

Mary Bly is a professor of English literature at Fordham University in New York City and author of *Queer Virgins and Virgin Queans on the Early Modern Stage* (Oxford University Press, 2000). She is completing a manuscript with the working title "The Geography of Puns," parts of which have appeared in the *PMLA* and *Shakespeare Survey*. She also writes historical romances as Eloisa James, sixteen of which have been *New York Times* bestsellers.

Sarah S.G. Frantz is an associate professor of English at Fayetteville State University in North Carolina and president of the International Association for the Study of Popular Romance. She has published academic articles on Jane Austen, J.R. Ward, Suzanne Brockmann, and contemporary popular romance fiction. She is the co-editor (with Katharina Rennhak) of *Women Constructing Men: Female Novelists and Their Male Characters, 1750–2000* (Lexington Books, 2010).

An Goris received her PhD from the Katholieke Universiteit Leuven in Belgium, where she wrote her dissertation on Nora Roberts and the contemporary popular romance genre. Her research interests include critical theory (particularly about genre and authorship), popular culture, narratology, and translation studies. In 2009–2010 Goris was a Fulbright visiting scholar at DePaul University in Chicago.

Miriam Greenfeld-Benovitz is a doctoral student in communications at Rutgers University in New Brunswick, New Jersey. The topic of her dissertation is a new communicative technique that draws on both popular culture and natural understandings of argument in order to shift the ensuing discourse. Her research focuses on the impact of popular culture on Internet interaction.

Robin Harders, PhD, JD, has worked as a speech writer, spin doctor, and teacher; she currently serves as a policy advisor for California public higher education. Her scholarly interests focus on the intersections of literature, nation-building, and the construction of race, gender, and culture in America. She has written numerous papers and articles on diversity in higher education, speech rights and academic freedom, captivity narratives and Native American literature.

Jayashree Kamble was awarded the first Romance Writers of America academic research grant in 2004–05. Her PhD dissertation, completed at the University of Minnesota, was entitled "Uncovering and Recovering the Popular Romance Novel." In her other work, she examines the ways in which thematic and material elements in romantic narratives (novels and film) retract political and economic dilemmas.

257

Deborah Kaplan teaches fantasy and science fiction at the Simmons College Center for the Study of Children's Literature in Boston, and is an archivist at Tufts University in Medford, Massachusetts. Her research interests cover a wide range of fictions in the traditionally female spheres: romance, children's literature, and fan fiction. She studies fiction which crosses multiple genres, particularly the ways in which such works manifest and engage with expected narrative patterns.

Eric Murphy Selinger is an associate professor of English at DePaul University in Chicago and executive editor of the *Journal of Popular Romance Studies*. He is the author of *What Is It Then Between Us? Traditions of Love in American Poetry* (Cornell University Press, 1998). He has also published on poetry and Jewish American literature.

K. Elizabeth Spillman studies folklore and literature and is especially interested in the intersection of oral and literary traditions: the transmission, recycling, and retelling of tales in genres of prose narrative and contemporary genre fiction. She devotes particular attention to literary fairy tales and the role of the princess figure in popular and material culture.

Hsu-Ming Teo is a novelist and historian living in Sydney, Australia. She is the author of *Loving the Orient: Orientalism and the Mass-Market Romance Novel* (University of Texas Press, forthcoming) and the co-editor (with Richard White) of *Cultural History in Australia* (University of New South Wales Press, 2003). Her academic essays and book chapters have considered the history of romantic love in Australia, the history of travel and tourism, Orientalism, and popular fiction.

Kathleen Therrien is an associate professor of English at Middle Tennessee State University in Murfreesboro. Her teaching and research focus primarily on American women's and popular literature, particularly that of the late nineteenth and early twentieth centuries. She is also researching eugenics discourses in American popular literature and is generally interested in the relationships between discourses and representations of class, gender, labor, and ethnicity, and social policies and practices.

Glen Thomas is a senior lecturer in creative writing and literary studies at the Queensland University of Technology in Brisbane, Australia. His research interests include romantic fiction and publishing, popular culture, professional communication and American literature. With Eric Murphy Selinger and Toni Johnson-Woods, he organized the 2009 First International Conference on Popular Romance Studies.

Christina A. Valeo is an associate professor of English at Eastern Washington University in Cheney. She has previously published work on British Romanticism and children's literature. She is studying the con in the novels of Jennifer Crusie and the quest for an ideal father in J.K. Rowling's *Harry Potter* series.

Carole Veldman-Genz is the head of the scientific English department at the RWTH Aachen University, Germany. She specializes in contemporary cultural and gender theory. Her latest article has been published in *Bringing Light to* Twilight: *Perspectives on a Pop Culture Phenomenon* (Palgrave Macmillan, 2011).

Laura Vivanco is an independent scholar and regular contributor to Teach Me Tonight, an academic blog about the romance genre. She is the author of *For Love and Money: The Literary Art of the Harlequin Mills & Boon Romance* (Humanities Ebooks, 2011), that takes a literary-critical approach to Harlequin and Mills & Boon romances.

Sarah Wendell is the author of *Everything I Know About Love, I Learned from Romance Novels* (Sourcebooks Casablanca, 2011), and co-author (with Candy Tan) of *Beyond Heaving Bosoms: The Smart Bitches' Guide to Romance Novels* (Simon & Schuster, 2009). She is also co-founder of the romance novel review site Smart Bitches, Trashy Books, one of the most popular blogs examining romance fiction.

Tamara Whyte is a doctoral student in the Hudson Strode Program in Renaissance studies at the University of Alabama in Tuscaloosa. Her dissertation research focuses on adaptation and appropriation in Shakespeare's plays and in historical romance novels.

Index